"Anyone interested in South & South East Asian federations should start with Professor Bhattacharyya's survey; it addresses the established federations, the emergent Nepalese federation, and the more precarious case of Myanmar."
—**Brendan O'Leary**, *University of Pennsylvania, USA*

"Federalism as a political institution holds diverse societies together through an adroit conflation of self rule and shared rule, generating governance, political order, and legitimacy. Bhattacharyya applies this core idea critically to five federations of Asia. A hugely enjoyable book that enriches the classic wisdom and takes it forward."
—**Subrata K Mitra**, *Heidelberg University, Germany*

FEDERALISM IN ASIA

This comprehensive book critically analyzes the successes and failures of federalism in India, Pakistan, Malaysia, Nepal and Myanmar for the political accommodation of ethno-regional diversity and assesses their comparative democratic significance for other countries in Asia.

This revised new edition incorporates updated demographic, religious and linguistic data for the case study countries and examines some of the major changes that have taken place in formally federal states since 2010, including the 18th Amendment of the Constitution in Pakistan in 2010, which gave a major turn to decentralization by empowering the provinces; the new federal democratic Constitution that was introduced in Nepal in 2015; and the abolition of the Planning Commission and the National Development Council in India. The author thematically examines the growing tensions between nation and state-building in ethnically plural societies; modes of federation-building in Asia; persistent ethnic tensions in federations and the relationship between federalism and democracy; and federalism and decentralization.

The book will be of use to advanced undergraduate and postgraduate students of Asian politics, comparative federalism and modern Asian political history and institutions, as well as policy makers on ethnic conflict regulation and peace studies and stakeholders in ethnic power-sharing and political order.

Harihar Bhattacharyya is Professor of Political Science at Burdwan University, West Bengal, India. He has taught previously at Hull University, UK; Heidelberg University, Germany; and Delhi University, India. Known globally as an expert in Indian federalism and comparative federalism, he has published extensively on the subject. His book publications include *Federalism in Asia* (2010: Routledge); *India as a Multicultural Federation: Asian Values, Democracy and Decentralisation (In comparison with Swiss Federalism)* (2001); (co-authored) *Radical Politics and Governance in India's North East: The Case of Tripura* (2018: Routledge); and *Politics and Governance in Indian States: Bihar, West Bengal and Tripura* (2018: World Scientific). His journal articles include: 'Indian Federalism and Democracy: The Growing Salience of Diversity-claims over Equality-claims in Comparative and Indian Perspective' (*Regional and Federal Studies* 2015) and 'Pitfalls of India's Ethno-federal Model of Ethnic Conflict Management: Tension Between Tribal Ethnicity and Territory in India's North East' (*Ethnopolitics* 2019).

Routledge Studies in Federalism and Decentralization

Series Editors: Paolo Dardanelli, *Centre for Federal Studies, University of Kent, UK, and* John Kincaid, *Lafayette College, USA.*

Formerly Routledge Series in Federal Studies, edited by Michael Burgess and Paolo Dardanelli, Centre for Federal Studies, University of Kent, UK.

The series publishes outstanding scholarship on federalism and decentralization, defined broadly, and is open to theoretical, empirical, philosophical, and historical works. The series includes two types of work: first, it features research monographs that are substantially based on primary research and make a significant original contribution to their field. Second, it contains works that address key issues of policy-relevant interest or summarise the research literature and provide a broad comparative coverage.

Ethnic Conflict in Asymmetric Federations
Comparative Experience of the Former Soviet and Yugoslav Regions
Gorana Grgić

Emerging Practices in Intergovernmental Functional Assignment
Gabriele Ferrazzi and Rainer Rohdewohld

Swiss Federalism
The Transformation of a Federal Model
Adrian Vatter

Federalism in Asia
India, Pakistan, Malaysia, Nepal and Myanmar
Second edition
Harihar Bhattacharyya

For more information about this series, please visit: https://www.routledge.com/
Routledge-Studies-in-Federalism-and-Decentralization/book-series/RFS

FEDERALISM IN ASIA

India, Pakistan, Malaysia, Nepal and Myanmar

Second edition

Harihar Bhattacharyya

LONDON AND NEW YORK

Second edition published 2021
by Routledge
2 Park Square, Milton Park, Abingdon, Oxon, OX14 4RN

and by Routledge
52 Vanderbilt Avenue, New York, NY 10017

Routledge is an imprint of the Taylor & Francis Group, an informa business

© 2021 Harihar Bhattacharyya

The right of Harihar Bhattacharyya to be identified as author of this work has been asserted by him in accordance with sections 77 and 78 of the Copyright, Designs and Patents Act 1988.

All rights reserved. No part of this book may be reprinted or reproduced or utilised in any form or by any electronic, mechanical, or other means, now known or hereafter invented, including photocopying and recording, or in any information storage or retrieval system, without permission in writing from the publishers.

Trademark notice: Product or corporate names may be trademarks or registered trademarks, and are used only for identification and explanation without intent to infringe.

First edition published by Routledge 2010

British Library Cataloguing-in-Publication Data
A catalogue record for this book is available from the British Library

Library of Congress Cataloging-in-Publication Data
Names: Bhattacharyya, Harihar, author.
Title: Federalism in Asia : India, Pakistan, Malaysia, Nepal and Myanmar / Harihar Bhattacharyya.
Description: Second edition. | Abingdon, Oxon ; New York, NY : Routledge, 2020. | Series: Routledge studies in federalism and decentralization | Includes bibliographical references and index.
Identifiers: LCCN 2020002591 (print) | LCCN 2020002592 (ebook) | ISBN 9780367420819 (hardback) | ISBN 9780367418182 (paperback) | ISBN 9780367821630 (ebook)
Subjects: LCSH: Federal government—India. | Federal government—Pakistan. | Federal government—Malaysia. | Federal government—Nepal. | Federal government—Burma.
Classification: LCC JQ220.S8 B53 2020 (print) | LCC JQ220.S8 (ebook) | DDC 320.454/049—dc23
LC record available at https://lccn.loc.gov/2020002591
LC ebook record available at https://lccn.loc.gov/2020002592

ISBN: 978-0-367-42081-9 (hbk)
ISBN: 978-0-367-41818-2 (pbk)
ISBN: 978-0-367-82163-0 (ebk)

Typeset in Bembo
by Apex CoVantage, LLC

Dedicated to Prof. Amal K. Mukhopadhyay
my former teacher, who has always stood for
justice and humanity

CONTENTS

List of tables		*x*
Preface and acknowledgements		*xi*
List of abbreviations		*xiii*
	Introduction: federalism in Asia	1
1	The concept of federalism and its relevance	12
2	Ethno-national diversity and federalism	24
3	Origin and development of federalism in Asia: colonialism, nationalism, decolonization and revolution	55
4	Federalism and institutional innovations	85
5	Dynamics of federalism: political parties and ethnic movements	124
6	Centre–state relations: structure and processes	143
7	Federalism and forms of decentralization	169
8	Federalism and democracy: new questions asked	191
	Conclusion: beyond the diversity problematic	212
Bibliography		*226*
Index		*241*

TABLES

2.1	Demographic composition of the Indian states and Union territories (2011)	29
2.2	Religious composition of the Indian population (2011)	30
2.3	Official languages and speakers in India (2011)	31
2.4	Distribution of tribes and their percentage contribution to the total population in states and Union territories (2011)	33
2.5	Provincial distribution of population in Pakistan (2017); total population = 207,774,520	34
2.6	Multi-ethnic composition of provinces in Pakistan (2017)	35
2.7	Linguistic composition of Pakistan population (2017)	36
2.8	Ethnic composition of the population of Malaysia (1947–2017)	43
2.9	Ethnic composition of population in Nepal (2011)	48
2.10	Linguistic composition of the people of Nepal (2011)	49
2.11	Religion in Nepal (2011)	49
2.12	Ethnic/racial composition of the people in Myanmar (2014)	51
2.13	Religions affiliations in Myanmar (2014)	52
4.1	Party position in the second Constituent Assembly of Pakistan	91
5.1	Party position in the National Assembly in Pakistan (2018)	129
5.2	Party position in *Lok Sabha* (2009)	136
5.3	Constituent parties of *Barisan Nasional* (BN) (as of May 2008)	138
6.1	Latest criteria and their weightage in tax devolution in India (2015–20)	156

PREFACE AND ACKNOWLEDGEMENTS

Federalism is Asia's ascendant political currency. Asia today is more hospitable to federalism than ever before. While significant developments have taken place in postcolonial and formally declared federations in Asia – India, Pakistan and Malaysia were covered in the first edition (2010) – two new federations – Nepal and Myanmar – have emerged. The non-federal states have of late incorporated some federal features in their system of governance, particularly in respect of granting regional autonomy, such as in the Philippines and Indonesia. Sri Lanka has shown greater interest in considering a federal solution by converting its national parliament into a Constituent Assembly. Pakistan has embarked on a path of major provincial devolution by way of the 18th Constitutional Amendment Act (2010); major changes are taking place in India's federalism in the wake of the abolition of the Planning Commission and its replacement by the NITI Aayog, as well as the introduction of the Goods and Services Tax (GST). Neo-liberal reforms since the early 1990s have impacted upon major state restructuring in Asia's postcolonial federations in favour of decentralization and regional/provincial autonomy. This revised and enlarged new edition updates on the materials contained in the first edition of the book and brings the new cases of Nepal and Myanmar into the fold of comparative analysis. In the case of Nepal and Myanmar, the federal institutional designs backed up by the social, economic and political contexts have been discussed and compared rather than the performance aspects.

Argued from within a neo-institutional perspective that focuses on ideas, institutions, actors and contexts in making federalism work or fail, this new assessment brings to the fore a conceptual distinction I introduced in 2015 between the *diversity-claims* and the *equality-claims*. If a federation meets more easily, even with a lot of reluctance, the *diversity-claims* (ethno-religious, ethno-linguistic and ethno-regional identity claims) it produces a greater basis of political legitimacy. But the more difficult task of federalism is to meet the *equality-claims* – redistributive

xii Preface and acknowledgements

claims for land and resources; income; greater access to housing, education, health, sanitation and safe drinking water and so on for the vast majority. A post-globalized world has produced more inequality in Asia. In the long run, I argue that the failure to meet the *equality-claims* causes a crisis in political legitimacy. This study defends a case of federalism – at the national or subnational level – in which the issue of meeting the *equality-claims* is conjoined to meeting the *diversity-claims* for enduring political order and legitimacy.

In revising the book I have received help from Michael Breen (Australia), who is an expert on the new federations in Asia and Farzana Syed (Pakistan), who has obliged by sending many materials on recent developments in Pakistan. My sincere thanks go to Ganga Thapa (Nepal) for sending some materials on Nepal and clarifying some issues for me. I wish to record my sincere thanks to Brendan and Subrata K. Mitra for kindly reading the drafts and endorsement. Jessica Holmes of Routledge has been very encouraging and cooperative, for which my sincere thanks are due. My professional involvement in facilitating constitution making in Nepal and peace building for Sri Lanka and Myanmar offered me some useful insights. For Nepal and Myanmar, I wish to record my thanks to Nicole and Claudine. The three (anonymous) reviewers' comments and suggestions were very useful in revision.

This revision required many months of sustained and intensive involvement in writing. Without a leave from the university (there is none for such activities), but with regular teaching and research supervision at the department, this has meant tireless work on it. Family has of course suffered but stood by me. Saswati will see that the job has not after all been fruitless. My son, Sahon, has jumped in when so needed on technical problems and in indexing for which he deserves thanks.

Harihar Bhattacharyya
Burdwan
14 January 2020

ABBREVIATIONS

ADB	Asian Development Bank
ADC	Autonomous District Council
AGP	*Asom Gana Parishad*
AIADMK	All India *Anna Dravida Munnetra Kazhagam*
AIDMK	All India *Dravida Munnetra Kazhagam*
AL	Awami League
BJD	*Biju Janata Dal*
BJP	*Bharatiya Janata* Party
BN	*Barisan National* (National Front)
BNP (A)	Baluchistan National Party (Awami)
BPC	Basic Principles Committee
BPCR	Bengali–Punjabi Crisis Report
BSP	*Bahujan Samaj* Party
CA	Constituent Assembly
CPI	Communist Party of India
CPI-M	Communist Party of India (Marxist)
CPIN-M	Communist Party of Nepal-Maoist
DFID	Department for International Development
DGHC	Darjeeling Gorkha Hill Council
DMK	*Dravida Munnetra Kazhagam*
FATA	Federally Administered Tribal Area
FC	Finance Commission
FDI	Foreign Direct Investment
GNP	Gross National Product
GST	Goods and Services Tax
IMP	Independence Malayan Party
INC	Indian National Congress
JD (S)	*Janata Dal (Sanjukta)*

xiv Abbreviations

JD (U)	*Janata Dal* (United)
JMM	*Jharkhand Mukti Morcha*
KPP	Krishak Proja Party
LFG	Left Front Government
LTTE	Liberation Tigers of Tamil Eelam
MAMPU	Malayan Administrative Modernization and Management Planning Unit
MCA	Malaysian Chinese Association
MIC	Malaysian Indian Congress
ML	Muslim League
MLA	Member of Legislative Assembly
MMA	*Mutthida Majlis-e-Amal*
MPU	Modernization and Planning Unit
MQM	Muhajir Quami Movement
MU	Malayan Union
NAP	National Awami Party
NC	National Conference
NCA	National Cease-fire Agreement
NCLG	National Council for Local Government
NCP	National Congress Party
NDP	National Development Policy
NEP	New Economic Policy
NFC	National Finance Commission
NLD	National League for Democracy
NOC	National Operation Council
NITI Aayog	National Instittute for Transforming India
NLD	National League for Democracy
NPC	National Planning Commission
NPP	National People's Party
NWFP	North–West Frontier Province
PBRS	*Parti Bersatu Rakyat Sabah*
PBS	*Parti Bersatu Sabah*
PCI	Planning Commission of India
PEPSU	Patiala and East Punjab States
PKP	Khyber Pakhtunkhwa
PML (N)	Pakistan Muslim League (N)
PML (O)	Pakistan Muslim League (O)
PPBB	*Parti Pesaka Bhumiputera Bersatu*
PPP	Pakistan's People's Party
PRS	*Parti Rakyat Sarawak* (Sarawak People's Party)
RJD	*Rastriya Janata Dal*
SAD	*Shiromani Akalid Dal*
SAP	Structural Adjustment Programme
SAPP	Sabah Progressive Party

SP	Samajvadi Party
SPDP	Sarawak Progressive Democratic Party
SS	*Shiv Sena*
SUPP	Sarawak United People's Party
TC	*Trinamul* Congress
TDP	*Telegu Desam* Party
TFP	Tamil Federal Party
TMC	Trina Mul Congress
TRS	*Telenga Rashtraraksha Samity*
TTADC	Tripura Tribal Autonomous District Council
TULF	Tamil United Liberation Front
UAE	United Arab Emirates
UF	United Front
UMNO	United Malay National Organization
UNDP	United Nations Development Programme
UNP	United National Party
UP	Uttar Pradesh
UPA	United Progressive Alliance
USA	United States of America
USSR	Union of Soviet Socialist Republics
WB	World Bank

INTRODUCTION

Federalism in Asia

Federalism is now Asia's ascendant political currency. It is taken up seriously by the ethnically diverse yet unitary states such as Indonesia and Philippines not so much at the national level but in offering regional autonomy to Aech and the Moros respectively. Federalism has been adopted by what are usually considered unfamiliar actors, such as the Maoists, and in an unfavourable context in Nepal. Pakistan embarked on a near revolutionary devolution for the provinces with the 18th Amendment of the Constitution (1973) in 2010. Sri Lanka has converted its Parliament into a Constituent Assembly for seriously considering the case for federalism. In Myanmar the twenty-first-century Panglong conference – the second one after 1947 – was held in 2018 for better accommodation of ethnic minorities. India has made a major reform in fiscal federalism by the introduction of GST in 2016, and a GST Council as a federal body has been constituted. It is, as it were, Asia's federal century.

As a study in comparative federalism, this book critically examines the various institutional modes of political accommodation of ethnic and ethno-national diversity in India, Pakistan, Malaysia, Nepal and Myanmar, constitutionally declared as federations with reference to social and cultural diversity, the historical contexts within which such concerns took shape and the political actors responsible either positively considering the issue of accommodating diversity – or negatively suppressing them – and assesses the democratic effects of federalism. Recent research (e.g. Breen 2018; Kincaid 2019; Anderson and Chaudhry 2019) has shown that federal measures for regional autonomy have been adopted in unitary states in Asia and elsewhere in the world too. Asia is ethnically the most diverse continent in the world. Many countries in Asia are characterized by some very ancient social and cultural diversity, whether based on language, religion, tribal (aboriginal) communities, regional or other ethnic markers. But the relative absence of adequate institutional mechanisms for the political accommodation of such diversity in the political systems of Asia has meant that ethnic tensions and the resultant

2 Introduction

conflicts have remained as ever-growing challenge to political unity and governance. Located within the overall Asian context, this comparative study of federalism in India, Pakistan, Malaysia, Nepal and Myanmar seeks to analyze and examine the reasons for successes and failures of various federal measures adopted for the political accommodation of identity and to assess their comparative significance for other ethnically diverse countries in Asia, if not elsewhere. Of the five, the first three are postcolonial federations with their common problems of nation-building via the route of national integration; the last two are of a different genre called 'third generation' (Breen 2017: 1–25) in the existing literature on the subject. However, the case of Nepal is in a class by itself. Nepal, following a Maoist revolution in 2006, adopted the constitution of a federal democratic republic with a three-tiered federal structure with a pronounced inclusive orientation. Myanmar's case is old and new: it was held by the British (1825–42), and for a very period, Japan (1942–47), and then again under the British (1947–48) (Taylor 1987) which was recaptured by the British after the Second World War, but only to make the transfer of power to the nationalists. Myanmar was a parliamentary democracy from 1948–62; in 1962 it fell to the military, which adopted a socialist model with heavy centralization of power. After many decades of military dictatorship, it adopted a new constitution in 2008 committed to a 'union' type and heavily centralized federation which is yet to be put into practice.

The federation, as a compound polity that entails both shared rule for some general purposes and self-rule (region-based) for some other specific purposes in ethnically diverse societies, is increasingly taken to be the modular political association in this post-Cold War, post-Soviet and globalizing era. With growing awareness of the manifold weaknesses of the nation-state as a centralized political institution monopolizing all loyalties and seeking to engulf all identities, the idea of the federation has been attracting renewed attention from scholars, opinion-makers and political élites, the policy community and concerned scholars. Today, many leaders of ethnic movements demand federalization of the existing political structure as an important political step towards identity, recognition and autonomy, and political unity. Paradoxically enough, the failure of the so-called socialist federations in the former Soviet Union (USSR) and Eastern Europe has strengthened rather than weakened the case for federalism in the post-Soviet states.

Given this renewed global emphasis on federalism, the various surviving post-Second World War and postcolonial federal experiments in India, Pakistan and Malaysia and the 'third generation' (Breen 2017) federations of Nepal and Myanmar (postcolonial too) assume added significance. These five countries contain manifold ethno-regional and ethno-national identity groups. These countries, except Nepal, received federalism as an idea and institution in the wake of British colonialism, when, paradoxically, the British political tradition remained unitary, (Burgess 1995)[1] as a method of effective political control and governance in the midst of social and cultural diversity. India is predominantly Hindu, with a large and significant number of Muslims and other faiths in her population; Nepal is predominantly Hindu; Pakistan and Malaysia are predominantly Muslim countries;

and Myanmar is Buddhist. But all of them are marked by a high degree of ethno-regional and national diversity and conflict, often verging on secessionism. In 1965, Malaysia lost Singapore (by expulsion); and Pakistan lost its eastern wing, East Pakistan, which became Bangladesh in 1971. Unlike them, India so far has not experienced any territorial disintegration, although such threats were real for a long time since the 1960s, but with successive reorganization of its territory by creating newer federal units, most of such problems have been resolved (Bhattacharyya 2019a). It is still a problem in Pakistan and Myanmar but not so much in Nepal. Breen (2018) has argued that secessionism in Myanmar is not a real threat given the very small size of population of ethnic minorities compared to the Bamar majority.

What generates greater legitimacy in multi-ethnic countries in conditions of mass democracy remains central to the critical understanding of the role of institutions that genuinely seek to mitigate conflicts. This has perplexed politicians as well as policy communities. Watts's later work (2008) forewarned us that adoption of federalism in multi-ethnic countries is not enough; what is of critical strategic significance is the appropriateness of such institutional engineering relative to contexts. Added to that is the manifest and or latent intention of institutional designers. Often institutions are adopted with a motive to disempower the minorities and empower the majority. Often the federal institutions are adopted with the best of intention but have produced disasters leading to the break-up of the federations themselves. This has gone into suspecting federalism itself as a recipe for disaster. I argue here that federalism *per se* is not to be considered as the suspect but the inappropriateness of its design and application. Both do not always go together. As a component of this argument I emphasize that federal institutions are never perfect because the ethnic distributions of population and the demands for power-sharing are not. Federalism is not a ready-made design; neither does it offer a neat template. Federal institutional measures are and have to be varied relative to specific contexts and are never absolute. A unitary and centralized country's journey into a federation is tortuous and multiphased. As Watts (2008) said, federations are difficult to govern, but then there is no other way to govern a multi-ethnic country. I would add that since federalism requires power-sharing at many levels it is inherently democratic, for autocratic regimes do not believe in power-sharing, and decentralization is considered a recipe for disintegration and balkanization. But, as I have argued recently, (Bhattacharyya 2015, 2017, 2019a), we need to raise newer questions about democracy in order to gauze the democratic effects of federalism, that is, to assess if federalism via democracy has produced more equality or not.

Conceived within the broad parameters of historical sociology and a neo-institutional perspective, this study enquires into the efficacy of institutional measures adopted in the accommodation of ethnic and ethno-national identity; the role of the political élites in making and or unmaking federations; the specific contexts and historical compulsions; the political forces within the contexts that largely served to shape the contours, scope and limits of such institutional innovations; and the democratic effects of such measures critically viewed in the larger canvas

4 Introduction

of nation-building efforts in such countries. Thematically, this study is concerned with the following:

- Growing tensions between nation- and state-building in ethnically plural societies in Asia;
- Methods of federation building in India, Pakistan, Malaysia, Nepal and Myanmar;
- Types of institutional-political accommodation of ethno-national identities;
- Federalism, democracy and decentralization; and
- Democratic effects of federalism in Asia in terms of production of more equality.

It is argued here that the appropriate federal institutions that successfully combine shared rule with self-rule (regional and subregional) within a single polity has been the most important key to why India has avoided disintegration, and also why Pakistan and Malaysia, despite all the ethnic domination and communalism, etc., have not experienced further disintegration. It is further argued that rather than an abandonment of federalism in favour of a unitary state for more political control, a better federalism with democracy (that ensures power-sharing among the identity groups and generates more equality) provides the best option for such countries to stay together politically with a greater degree of legitimacy.

Daniel Elazar (Elazar 1987: 247) argued that Asia as a continent is more hospitable to federalism than Africa. No wonder, then, a variety of federal arrangements were introduced in many countries of Asia in the period after the Second World War and in the process of decolonization, although the success rates of the same have varied widely across the states. But the very fact that such arrangements were adopted by the political systems of Asia reflected the obvious need for accommodation of ethnic, religious or linguistic diversity in order to maintain national sovereignty and foster national economic development. A long time back, Ronald L. Watts forewarned us regarding the difficulties that many new federations in the developing countries were facing:

> Federal systems are not a panacea but in many developing countries they may be necessary as the only way of combining, through representative institutions, the benefits of both unity and diversity. Experience has shown that federations, both old and new, have been difficult to govern. But then, that is why they are federations.
>
> *(Watts 1966: 353)*

Elazar strongly advocates that if the new nation-states in Asia and Africa seek to come to grips with multi-ethnic issues, the only way open to them to peacefully accommodate the ethnic issues is 'through the application of federal principles that will combine kinship (the basis of ethnicity) and consent (the basis of democratic government) into politically viable, constitutionally protected arrangements

Introduction **5**

involving territorial and non-territorial polities' (Elazar 1987: 9). It must, however, be admitted here that kinship does not cover the entirety of the basis of ethnicity in these societies. While kinship is important here, the more challenging bases of ethnicity are language, religion, region, (aboriginal) tribal affiliations and so on. Again, not all the bases of ethnicity mentioned here are candidates for federal solutions. Religion, for example, is not usually considered as being entitled to constitute a basis of political arrangements in a federation. As any student of democracy must know, freedom of religion (to practice and propagate, and also to change one's religion), including the maintenance of religious institutions, can well be ensured in a democratic state, federal or not. But consent as an important federal principle (Elazar) is immensely significant, and strongly suggests that federal government is to be democratic and secular. Watts emphasized this point, including the basic objective of adopting federal solutions in such countries:

> Difficult as federal institutions are to operate, they may provide the only way in a diverse society of achieving or maintaining a political union which is based on consent.
>
> *(Watts 1966: vi)*[2]

Existing knowledge

Except for Watts's (1966, 2008) study, until very recently (Breen 2018; He 2007; Adeney 2007a; Bhattacharyya 2010, 2019a, 2019b; Singh and Kukreja 2014), federalism in Asia has remained neglected in the literature on comparative federalism as well as Third World politics. Watts's (1966) study was the first-ever comprehensive and comparative study of federalism, but it covered too broad a field: that is, all the postcolonial countries that adopted formally federal constitutions as well as those which had introduced some federal arrangements in their constitutions. It was thus limited in its focus as far as the three formally declared federations (namely, India, Pakistan and Malaysia) were concerned. Conceived broadly within a framework of a state–society interface (which is of immense value), Watts (1966) examined 'the reasons why federal political institutions were established in these countries, and also the subsequent working of these federal systems' (Watts 1966: vii) by focusing on both federal government and the society surrounding it.

Although there are country studies of federalism in Asia, particularly of India, comparative studies of federalism in Asia began to receive renewed attention from scholars as late as 2007. Adeney's research (Adeney 2007a) is a comparative study of India and Pakistan from the perspective of 'ethnic conflict regulation' by viewing federalism as a type of 'ethnic conflict regulation'. She follows a historical approach and focuses on 'one specific element of comparison; federal development and structures' (2007a: 5) in which the issue of federal units has received particular attention. She also apparently follows an institutional approach (Adeney 2007a: 9) and supposes that 'political institutions are autonomously important in the regulation of ethnic conflict, and that ethnic conflicts are situational' (Adeney 2007a: 9).

6 Introduction

One major methodological limitation of her study is her stress on the 'uniqueness of all states', which seems to undercut the very basis of comparison.

Baogang He (2007) study is the other, more comparative and comprehensive account of federalism in Asia written by different scholars from different perspectives, dealing with varied issues such as democracy, autonomy, ethnic identities, regionalism and so on. The country studies constitutionally cover federal states; those that have adopted some federal, decentralizing arrangements; and those which are averse to federalism (e.g. Indonesia and Myanmar). This study also contains some theoretical discussion on 'multi-nation federation' and 'regionalist federation'. He (chapter 1) and Galligan (chapter 13) provide useful summaries and contextualization of federalization in Asia and some of the common yet persistent problems faced in this region while introducing federalism. The special merit of the book is that it brings to the fore the cases of renewed interest exhibited since 2005 in federal solutions to ethno-nationalist problems in many states in Asia, those that were reluctant until now to consider federalism as a way out of their persistent ethnic conflicts. But at the same time, the consideration of the success stories of federalism in Asia, that is more particularly in India and Malaysia, as a 'huge exception' seems contrary to the essentials of comparison. As we will see later in this book, even as a federation, India has been difficult to govern, and her federation has passed through phases of crisis too. But her relative successes are not be considered as exception. India's experiment with power-sharing (territorial), accommodation of identity (both territorial and non-territorial), democracy and differentiation of structures of power-sharing holds immense lessons for comparison.

Breen's study (2018) of Nepal, Myanmar and Sri Lanka offers a critical roadmap of federalism for the countries ensconced in a neo-institutional approach, and much of it detailed and path-breaking. His study covers two 'second generation' and one 'third generation' federations. His central concern is accommodation of ethnic minorities and ethnic equality. He argues that the cases of federalism in Nepal, Myanmar and Sri Lanka are hybrid ones that take a middle ground. According to Breen (2018: 48), there are three generations in Asia: the first generation (India, Pakistan and Malaysia and Pakistan); the second generation (China, Indonesia and the Philippines); and the third generation (Nepal, Sri Lanka and Myanmar). For him, the first generation federations arose out of decolonization; the second generation incorporated federal features in unitary states; and the third generation federations are 'inspirational'. Breen's categorizations are useful, but there are areas of overlap over the issues of nation-building and the negative approach to ethnicity.

This revised volume is the first-ever research monograph on a comparative study of federalism in Asia covering India, Pakistan, Malaysia, Nepal and Myanmar. The first edition of the book (Bhattacharyya 2010) covered only three federations, when Nepal was still drafting its federal constitution and the case of Myanmar was not taken seriously as a federation. Since 2005, Asia has, as it were, turned federal: Indonesia's hybrid federalism for accommodating the case of Aceh; the Philippines' federalization for accommodating Muslim separatism (Anderson and Chaudhry 2019), the Dalai Lama's proposal for federalism in China to accommodate the case of Tibet, and China's move towards a de facto federation; Japan's moves to loosen its centralized authority in the already decentralized nation-state; and so on (He 2007). Added to the list is the case of Nepal, which has formally declared itself, after a Maoist revolution, to be a federation, in order to accommodate the varied and complex sociocultural and economic diversity. Viewed in this context, the detailed comparative study of the successes and failures of federal institutional measures in India, Pakistan and Malaysia, and new federations of Nepal and Myanmar (formally federal) in Asia assumes special significance for other countries in Asia faced with the similar problems of ethnicity and the demands for federal restructuring.

Diversity-claims and Equality-claims

Is identity recognition based on some ethnic markers enough for the ethnic people as a whole? Can ethnic self-rule ensure good results for the common ethnic brethren in a federation? Is ethnic self-rule by itself enough shared rule? While ethnic boundaries, territorially speaking, are not always clear cut, and the cross-cutting of ethnic people at the ground level is the rule rather than the exception, this raises also the question of adequacy of such a rule so far as the general ethnic masses are concerned. In the existing knowledge on the subject, the question of the extent of shared rule in a regional/ethnic self-rule is not examined. In the context of India's North East, this issue has been raised very recently for the first time in Bhattacharyya 2015, 2017, 2019b; Bhattacharyya and Mukherjee 2018). In the conceptual distinction between the *diversity-claims* and *equality-claims* that I introduced in 2015 (Bhattacharyya 2015, 2017, 2019a) I argued that the federal discourse in Asia has been preoccupied with meeting the various demands of identity, territory linked with ethnic identity, territorial power-sharing based on ethnic markers and so on. The creation of newer states; the provisions for substate regional and tribal district councils, or regional political autonomy to the ethnic Muslims in the Philippines and Indonesia, etc., are examples of what I have termed *diversity-claims*. The *diversity-claims* include recognition and accommodation of identity (language, tribal ethnicity, regional identity and so on) is unavoidable in countries in the postcolonial countries, transitional states in Asia and also post-Soviet/communist states, globally speaking. These have remained the key to the formation and establishment of federalism in the same. Conceding to such claims may include both territorial and non-territorial forms. I have also argued that not all forms of diversity are amenable to federal solutions; neither are they so needed. Non-territorial solutions *per se* do not constitute a federal solution unless it is linked to territorial power-sharing, such as in Belgium. In India, for example, recognition of language and its listing in the 8th Schedule of the Indian Constitution is only a symbolic recognition but not federal by nature. However, when a demand for a territory is formulated around linguistic–ethnic identity, this takes on the character needing a federal solution. I have pointed out that the solution to the *diversity-claims* in federations have attracted more official attention and more easily been met because such claims address themselves to emotions and sentiments of the ethnic people

8 Introduction

and have had the potential for disturbing law and order more quickly. To be sure, meeting the *diversity-claims* means meeting some democratic needs too insofar as the dignity of identity is concerned. The *equality-claims* for me refer to the realm of redistribution: land and other resources; access to health care, education, sanitation and better environment; jobs for the unemployed and social security measures and so on. When these are available to the vast majority of underprivileged sections, this would mean more equality has been generated in a society. An authority on the study of democracy and self-government, Adam Przeworski (2010), has pointed our attention to this by arguing that self-government may be limited in producing more equality. In this study we will seek to assess the effectiveness of federalism not simply by the accommodation of ethnic identity and the better management of ethnic conflicts that produces better political order and legitimacy but also by the extent of generation of equality as a result of this. As I have shown, the *diversity-claims* and *equality-claims* are not necessarily connected to each other. There are instances when the former has been achieved without the latter. But then, political order and legitimacy may not last longer if some *equality-claims* are not met. In other words, the so-called federal success may be short on the democratic success, as understood here.

This study is centrally concerned with the relation between federalism and ethnicity, that is, the dialectic between federal institutional opportunities (and constraints for some at the same time) in terms of powers and resources, on the one hand, and struggle of the ethno-national group (or groups) for recognition and protection of its identity and interests, on the other hand. The subject ultimately relates to the broader issue of federalism and nation-building. It shows how in both Pakistan and Malaysia federalism, albeit following different trajectories, has resulted in the emergence of what may be called ethnic suzerainty, of the Punjabis and the Malays respectively, as ethnic effects of federalism. In Myanmar, federalism has been designed in such a way so as to ensure permanent suzerainty of the majority Bamars. In Nepal, the secular federal designs are not geared to empower the Hindu majority. In other words, these two ethno-national groups have benefited most from the particular designs of federalism adopted in Pakistan and Malaysia. In the case of India, however, the same cannot be said to be true, because of the absence of a single majority ethno-national community; the deeply plural character of the federal system; democracy; and numerous safeguards for the minorities of many sorts. Had it been otherwise, most of India's Hindi-speaking states would not have remained backward, economically speaking. In fact, most of India's most developed states are inhabited by the country's linguistic minorities (Punjab, Gujarat, Maharashtra, Tamil Nadu, Andhra Pradesh, Karnataka etc.). The implications of these cases for nation-building are assessed in the Conclusion of this book.

Finally, this study emphasizes democratic federalism – involving not only a whole complex of institutional arrangements for recognition, autonomy and protection of identity and power-sharing at many levels of the federal polity – but also the democratic effects of federalization, that is, production of more equality, that together offer a better guarantee for the resolution of ethnic conflicts in favour of durable political order and legitimacy in diverse societies in Asia, if not elsewhere.

As regards comparison, each chapter begins with a comparative introduction, to be followed by the presentation of detailed country materials on the subject concerned, because the latter is important for a comprehensive understanding of the issues discussed. The country materials are presented thematically for comparative purposes.

Chapter 1 ('The Concept of Federalism and Its Relevance') is conceptual and deals with the origin, definition and meaning of federalism; the evolution of the concept; and its very recent resurgence in the wake of globalization. The underlying linkages of federalism with diversity and democracy are also highlighted in this chapter.

Chapter 2 ('Ethno-national Diversity and Federalism in India, Pakistan, Malaysia, Nepal and Myanmar') describes and examines the manifold social and cultural diversity in these federations within the broad context of Asia in order to gain a sense of the context of the operation of federalism in these countries and to assess the scope and limits of federalism in the same.

Federalism in our case studies has remained path dependent, intermeshed with colonialism, nationalism and decolonization, and oddly, Maoist revolution in Nepal. Chapter 3 ('Origin and Development of Federalism in India, Pakistan, Malaysia, Nepal and Myanmar: Colonialism, Nationalism and Decolonization, and Revolution') deals precisely with this subject. It shows how the conceptual and institutional development of federalism here has been profoundly affected by various political forces during colonial and postcolonial, post-transition and post-revolution periods

It has been widely accepted in the literature on federalism that designing the appropriate federal institutions has remained the most difficult of all tasks in federation-building. Federations have failed, or succeeded, mostly because of this. This is the most important key to ensure the dynamic political equilibrium that federalism implies. This is also the subject matter of Chapter 4 ('Federalism and Institutional Innovations') in which institutional innovations in our case studies are dealt with in the context of historical movements for conflicting claims of identity and nationhood and state-building.

Chapter 5 ('Dynamics of Federal Systems: Political Parties and Ethnic Movements') examines the role played by political parties and ethnic movements in maintaining, strengthening and fighting for federalism in Asian federations. Their role in fighting against a certain type of federation and ultimately carving up a separate nation-state (e.g. the Awami League in the creation of Bangladesh in 1971) is also considered. The role of political parties and movements in determining the contours of the future federation after decolonization is specifically examined too. It is argued, on the basis of current theoretical literature on the subject, that an 'integrated political party' offers a better guarantee for federal integration and stability. The major political parties of our case countries are specifically focused for substantiation of our argument. The role of regional parties as alternative agents in

10 Introduction

playing a critical role in the formation of alliances and coalitions at the federal level is also brought under the purview of analysis in this chapter.

Chapter 6 ('Centre–State Relations: Structure and Processes') examines the constitutional and political relations between the centre and the constituent units in the light of these issues. Centre–state/centre–provincial, or intergovernmental relations constitute the very important operational aspect of a federation, linked to the issue of identity, values of diversity, and the states' rights in the federations. The evolving relations, of cooperation and/or conflict or a combination thereof, between the centre and the constituent units most often define the reality of federations rather than what is enshrined in the constitutions. Since the constituent units are distinct sociocultural and often political entities, because there are distinct people behind the formal institutions, ethnic identity comes into the picture and serves to influence, via political parties and other groups, the course of centre–state relations.

Chapter 7 ('Federalism and Forms of Decentralization') discusses the relations between federalism and decentralization, examines the various forms of decentralization (identity-based as well as population-based) and assesses their significance for national identity and federalism. This chapter makes a distinction between decentralization in a federation and in a non-federal system and argues that the constitutional recognition and guarantee of self-governing representative bodies is what makes it federally significant. Decentralization in India and Pakistan has remained inextricably linked to federalization (although more successfully in India than in Pakistan!). In Pakistan, democratic decentralization has been a casualty under successive military regimes, although it was reintroduced since 2000 under a military regime with a different purpose specific to the regime and with anti-federal motives. However, in 2010 by way of the 18th Amendment to the Constitution of Pakistan (1973), a major, near-revolutionary devolution of powers to the provinces was made in Pakistan, although it is still mired in institutional complexities and yet to be put into practice. In Malaysia, democratic decentralization, suspended in 1976, is yet to be revived, although nominated local-government bodies of many types operate under centralized control as an adjunct to the federal government's drives for rapid urbanization and globalization. The Indian experiment in democratic decentralization, starting in 1957 and then on a major federal scale since 1993, has been long drawn out and successful, though not without limitations, as the lowest tier of government in rural and urban India is responsible for a wide variety of responsibilities. It is India's various forms of decentralization that have served to create an increasingly differentiated, multi-tiered federal structure. It is further argued that since decentralization in India is to be necessarily democratic, it has led to some resource redistribution among the disadvantaged sections of society, apart from the protection of their identity. In Nepal, after the inauguration of the Constitution in 2015, wide-ranging provisions have been made for different tiers of substate-level decentralization and local government. In Myanmar since 2008 there are different types of local self-government bodies such as the Self-Administered Zones, but there are heavy doses of control over them by the Union government.

Chapter 8 ('Federalism and Democracy: New Questions Asked') discusses the relationship between federalism and democracy, which has not yet been adequately problematized in the existing literature on the subject. And yet, without democracy, federal institutional space is meaningless, at least for the ethnic minorities. This chapter argues that federalization accompanied by democracy has served to bring about durable political stability and, conversely, shows that democracy in divided societies may not always be a factor of destabilization but a condition for order and stability. The mutually reinforcing relationship between federalism and democracy is also highlighted in this chapter. Further, the democratic effects of federalism are also examined.

In the Conclusion, an attempt, in brief, is made to sum up the findings; to assess their implications for nation-and state-building and political stability in multi-ethnic diverse countries as well as the limits of meeting the *diversity-claims*; and to highlight the comparative lessons that can be drawn. It is stressed that in any comparative study of federalism in Asia, if not elsewhere too, federalism's success is to be conjoined to its democratic success.

Notes

1 Burgess (1995) has provided an answer to this question. He argued that the use of the concept 'state' to the UK is problematic, and to describe it as a 'unitary state' is a misnomer, strictly speaking (pp. 10–11).
2 This is part of a new debate in Asian federalism where the covenantal intellectual tradition was missing (see He *et al.* 2017).

1

THE CONCEPT OF FEDERALISM AND ITS RELEVANCE

Introduction

Federalism appears to be the political principle of the current era, a time that is marked simultaneously by globalization and localization, 'diminished state sovereignty', the urge to live with differences, and decentralization. This principle seems to inform many institutional arrangements that the states nowadays are adopting for accommodating various ethno-regional differences and identities both within their 'boundaries' and outside of them in transnational modes. The deep-seated Anglo-French preoccupation with the unitary nation-state and the idea of its sovereignty and the resultant suspicion of federalism and decentralization are *passé* (John Pinder 2007: 1). Pinder has convincingly argued how the British and the French since the twentieth century have slowly worked towards the institutions and processes that have prepared a basis for considering federal arrangements as desirable for the sake of unity and cohesion in the same countries (Pinder 2007: 1–3).

This post-Cold War globalizing era, in other words, has, as it were, turned increasingly federal. A kind of federal revolution has been sweeping the world over the past few decades. From one estimate, some 40 per cent (about 2billion) people globally live under some kind of federation. The post-Soviet renaissance in federalism may not be as surprising, since the Soviet model of the so-called socialist federations in the former USSR and Eastern Europe was emptied of the real content of federalism, being highly centralist and undemocratic and mostly rhetorical: lacking in any real motive for power-sharing and hence real autonomy. The Soviet model ultimately failed to offer any durable space for accommodation of ethno-national diversity. The nineteenth century, as Walter Bagehot famously said (Hobsbawm 1992), was an era of nation-building when nations were born by nation-uniting, that is, disparate elements were united for building national unity in a manner which came to be eulogized the world over as 'unity-in-diversity'. Federations, or quasi-federations, wherever so adopted, provided one very important mode of nation-building by nation-uniting. The rebirth of many (post-Soviet) nations by splitting from the former Soviet Union, and the fragmentation of Yugoslavia and Czechoslovakia, apparently legitimized a negative principle of nationhood and were a pointer to the grotesque failure of socialist federations. But the failure of the so-called socialist federations did not signify the failure of federalism as such but the particular design adopted in a fundamentally different, and somewhat inhospitable, political environment. Marxism's unease with the issues of federalism, identity and difference is well-known (Bhattacharyya 2001a: 41–61). Paradoxical though it may seem, the 'socialist' failure in federalism and the resultant state crisis has offered a lesson or two for the rest of the world for rethinking the modes of accommodation of ethno-national identities for state unity.

Globalization and the resurgence of federalism

Globalization has added to the current relevance of the federal idea. The failure of socialism apart, it is globalization and its attendant effects on the nation-state that have cleared the space for the resurgence of federalism today. As I have indicated, a world marked by centralized nation-states and national sovereignty is not hospitable for federalism. The French Jacobins considered federalism to be counter-revolutionary. Paradoxical though it may seem, in the heyday of the unitary nation-states, Switzerland was the only country in Europe in the whole of the nineteenth century to adopt a federation in 1848! Federalism as a European dream was realized outside of Europe. Globalization has weakened the basis of these unitary centralized nation-states so much that the sovereignty of the nation-state is much diminished today. Globalization has encouraged an awareness of ethnic identity and conflicts whose resolution has called for a federal solution. Samuel Huntington has drawn our attention to the 'global identity crisis'. 'Debates over national identity,' he says, 'are a pervasive characteristic of our times'. In his own words:

> Modernization, economic development, urbanization, and globalization have led people to rethink their identities and to redefine them in narrower, more intimate, communal terms. Subnational cultural and regional identities are taking precedence over broader national identities. People identify with those who are most like themselves and with whom they share a perceived common ethnicity, religion, traditions, and myths of common descent and common history.
>
> *(Huntington 2004: 12–13)*

This has resulted, argues Huntington, in fragmentation of national identity worldwide, most vividly in the United States itself, where multiculturalism, racial, ethnic and gender consciousness are challengers to national identity (Huntington 2004: 13). The same has equally been a challenge to the authority of the nation-state so far taken to be the sole repository of people's loyalty and embodiment of people's

14 The concept of federalism and its relevance

identity. In the age of fragmentation of both national identity and the nation-state, the role of federalism, however, becomes critical. Rebuilding 'national identity' amidst weakening of the nation state in multi-ethnic societies is difficult indeed and intertwined with appropriate federation-building. This is particularly significant when the state gradually withdraws itself from social welfare and intervention, giving way to the full play of the market. Global scholarship on federalism tends to re-search for genuine federalist solutions to problems facing the ethnic-conflict-ridden world. The global concern with federalism has been well summed up:

> A major factor in the surge of interest in federalism . . . is that the world is paradoxically exhibiting simultaneously increasing pressures for integration and for disintegration. Because federalism combines a shared government (for specific purposes) with autonomous action by the constituent units of government that maintain their identity and distinctiveness, more and more peoples have come to see some form of federalism as the closest institutional approximation to the multinational reality of the contemporary world.
>
> *(Watts 1998: 118)*

Federalist solutions were also contemplated for long-drawn-out ethno-national conflicts in various parts of the world, for postcolonial, post-Communist as well as post-conquest; Sri Lanka; Burundi; Myanmar (Burma); Nepal; the countries of the former USSR and Yugoslavia; Afghanistan; and even Iraq. Nepal has adopted a democratic and inclusive federal structure after the Revolution; Myanmar has adopted a very centralized Union structure of federalism in 2008. Two historical factors that have propelled the federal idea to a central place today, according to Graham Smith, are thus the resurgence of ethno-nationalist tensions and the search for how best to organize national and ethno-national communities so that they can live with differences (Smith 1995: 1).

The most significant area of impact of globalization has, however, been the nation-state, so much so that scholars have already expressed concern about the prospects of the nation-state. The 'end of the nation-state', the 'decline of the nation-state', the 'crisis of the nation-state' etc. are already quite familiar titles in the growing literature on the nation-state. The extent of the impact of globalization on the nation-state is a subject of some debates among scholars, but both the skeptical and the transformation hypotheses, despite some differences, have concurred on the continuing relevance of the nation-state in the vastly changed context. Anthony Giddens, taking the side of the transformation hypothesis, argues that the nation-state still remains the principal actor within the global political order, although its power, functions and authority are being recast by globalization (Guibernau and Hutchinson 2001). David Held has located the impact of globalization on the nation-state in the emergence of a 'new sovereignty regime' that displaces the traditional ideas of 'statehood as an absolute, indivisible, territorially exclusive and zero-sum form of public power' (Held 1989: 11–56; 214–43). As a result, a post-classical nation-state,

The concept of federalism and its relevance **15**

it is being argued, has been taking shape with considerably limited state sovereignty; with less concern for homogeneity (over-emphasized in the heyday of the classical nation-state!) and greater concern for diversity and difference; and more prone 'to devolve power and provide legitimacy to regional institutions created within its territory'. This post-classical nation-state with 'diminished state sovereignty' provides the congenial context for the more adequate operation of federalism in which the constituent units of the federation enjoy more autonomy of action. Not the end of the nation-state but rather the gradual emergence of a post-classical, post-traditional nation-state (Guibernau and Hutchinson 2001: 242–69) has provided for the congenial atmosphere for federalism to take shape.

Origin and development of the concept

Federalism is an ancient idea. The Israelite tribes, some 3,200 years ago, were thought to have established the first 'federal' (to be exact, confederal) system in the world. Such ancient confederacies were also found among the many tribes in Africa, North America, Greece, and Asia too. The Roman Republic was also a kind of confederal arrangement.[1] In medieval Europe, self-governing cities were linked to each other by some kind of loose confederations for trade and commerce and defence purposes. The Swiss confederation of 1291 was a powerful illustration of this. Even as late as 1781, the newly independent states, after the American Revolution, established a confederation, although very soon its deficiencies led to its transformation into the first modern federation in 1787 (Watts 1996: 3).

Etymologically, the term 'federal' is derived from the Latin *foedus*, which means a covenant. The federal idea originates from the Bible, and the original usage of the idea was theological, referring to partnership between humans and God (Elazar 1987: 5). The federal idea, in its original form, was theo-political. With the biblical covenantal root, the federal idea came to mean – politically and subsequently – partnership relationships between individuals and families leading to the formation of a body politic, and between bodies politic, leading to the formation of a compound polity (Elazar 1987: 5). It was not until the seventeenth and eighteenth centuries that the federal idea became secularized through such compact thinkers as Hobbes, Locke and Rousseau, and finally by Montesquieu and Madison, who transformed the federal idea into a 'fully secular political principle and technique' (Elazar 1987: 115; Karmis and Norman (eds.) 2005). Elazar defines the federal arrangement that follows the federal idea:

> In essence, a federal arrangement is one of partnership, established and regulated by a covenant, whose internal relationships reflect the special kind of sharing that must prevail among the partners, based on a mutual recognition of the integrity of each partner and the attempt to foster a special unity among them.
>
> *(Elazar 1987: 5)*

16 The concept of federalism and its relevance

Two intertwined principles are involved in the federal idea: self-rule and shared-rule. Federalism, on the basis of the combination of those two principles, is able to link 'individuals, groups and polities in lasting but limited union in such a way as to provide for the energetic pursuit of common ends while maintaining the respective integrities of all parties' (Elazar 1987: 115). Federalism then, as a political principle, refers to constitutional diffusion of powers among the constituent elements in a way that fulfils the desire for unity for some common purposes and autonomy for some other purposes. For Elazar, then, federalism, politically speaking, has served as one of the three forms (the other two are conquest, and organic) in which polities have been historically organized. In the sense that federalism is covenantal, it is thought to involve choice on the part of the covenanting parties.

Although the idea of federalism gained popularity particularly among the countries in Latin America, Asia and Africa after the Second World War, in Europe, due to the heavy impact of the French Revolution and the idea of the nation-state (which turned out to be the predominant form of political organization), federalism did not have much sway. Bereciartu (1994) sees federalism as a European dream but realized outside of Europe (Bereciartu 1994: 166). Riker rightly says that federations were rare before the nineteenth century.

The real proliferation of federations took place in the post-Second World War period, mostly in the former colonies in Asia and Africa, but also in Europe, with the overriding need to unite multicultural societies. But such experiments were fraught with a host of problems, and as Ronald L. Watts, the world-famous authority on federalism, has shown, many of such experiments were cancelled or suspended (Watts 1966: 9). Again, of the three federations in Asia (India, Pakistan and Malaysia), India has achieved greater successes in uniting a vast and ethno-linguistically diverse country, although Malaysia and Pakistan have not experienced further disintegration after 1965 and 1971 respectively. By the 1980s, the limitations of such experiments were clear. Watts wrote: 'These experiences suggested that, even when undertaken with the best of motives, there are limits to the appropriateness of federal solutions or particular federal forms in certain circumstances' (Watts 1966: 9).

In the wake of the end of the Cold War, the disintegration of the Soviet Union and Eastern Europe and the reorganization of Europe under the leadership of the European Union, the federal idea gained considerable momentum in the 1990s. The federal idea is taken up once again for political solutions to problems and as a 'liberating and positive form of political organization' (Elazar 1987: 2). Belgium and South Africa became federations in 1993 and 1996 respectively. Spain has been moving towards such an idea since 1978, and in Italy there are strong pressures for establishing a federation. The federal idea is also mooted at the level of the European Union. We are truly in the period of the resurgence of federalism. Daniel Elazar believes that the federal idea is resurfacing as a significant political force in humanity's transition from the modern to the postmodern epoch (Elazar 1987: 2).

The concept of federalism and its relevance **17**

Since federalism has taken many forms in diverse contexts, defining federalism has not been found to be easy. The scholarly debate about the definition of federalism is too big to be taken up here even in a cursory form. The issues involved in defining federalism are varied and often complex: normative vs. descriptive aspects; the distinction between federalism, federation and federal political systems; a whole array of such federal arrangements as a 'union' and 'quasi-federations'; and also the complex application of some of the federal principles in political systems which are not formally federal. Finally, there is also the issue of federalism as a structure and a process(es), as well as a cluster of institutions.

According to Riker (1996), federalism is a 'constitutionally determined tier-structure', a form of government which implies arrangement of tiers of government 'in a permanent agreement' that ensures that governments at the constituent and central tiers always exist and retain their assigned duties. For him, the agreement or covenant in federalism is of a special character, since the Latin word *foedus* from which the term 'federalism' has been derived also means *fides* or trust. From this, he has concluded that even though federation is a bargain about government, this bargain is not based on an enforcement procedure but 'on simple trust itself' (Elazar 1987: 5).

Noticing the wide array of closely related terms such as 'federalism', 'federation' and 'federal political system', their often interchangeable uses and the ambiguous meanings attributed to them in the scholarly discourse, since the time of *The Federalist* (1788), Ronald L. Watts (Watts 1996, 1998) has distinguished between the three terms for more clarity in the use of those terms. According to Watts, normatively, federalism may involve one of two general approaches. First, it may advocate a 'pragmatic balancing of citizen preferences for (a) joint action for certain purposes, and (b) self-government of the constituent units for other purposes' (Watts 2008: 8–9). Second, ideologically and philosophically, it often refers to a utopian system espoused by thinkers and movements. In recent times, it has been conceptualized in the European tradition of federalism, in terms of the principle of subsidiary (Watts 2008: 6).

Federal political system is a descriptive term which refers to the genus of political organization marked by the combination of shared-rule and self-rule (Watts 2008: 8). But this may mean a whole lot of complex political arrangements. Watts says that this may include 'hybrids because the statesmen are often more interested in pragmatic political solutions than in theoretical purity' (Watts 2008: 8).

'Federation', according to Watts, is a species within the genus of federal political systems. He defines it as

> a compound polity combining constituent units and a general government, each possessing powers delegated to it by the people through a constitution, each empowered to deal directly with the citizens in the exercise of a significant portion of its legislative, administrative, and taxing powers, and each directly elected by its citizens.
>
> *(Watts 1998: 121)*

18 The concept of federalism and its relevance

The common structural characteristics of federations as a specific form of federal political system, as identified by Watts (1996), are worth mentioning here:

1 two orders of government, each of them acting directly on its citizens;
2 a formal constitutional distribution of legislative and executive authority and allocation of revenue resources between the two orders of government, ensuring some areas of genuine autonomy for each order;
3 some provision for representation of distinct regional views within the federal policy-making institutions, usually in the shape of a federal second chamber of parliament;
4 a supreme written constitution not unilaterally amendable and requiring the consent of a significant proportion of the constituent units;
5 an umpire in the form of courts or a referendum in order to rule on the disputes between governments; and
6 processes and institutions to facilitate intergovernmental collaboration in the areas of overlapping jurisdiction.

(Watts 1996: 7)

He has also mentioned the common objective of combining unity and diversity and other institutional structures and processes as common and varying features of federations (Watts 1996: 14–15). What is missing in the epithet of 'shared rule' and 'self-rule' is the question about the extent of shared rule in self-rule because regional/ethnic self-rule often results in rule by the dominant ethnic group at the cost of other ethnic (small) groups and the general ethnic people. There is thus the need for further reflections on how to make self-rule genuinely 'self-rule', politically as well as redistributively.

Federalism, diversity and democracy

We are perhaps living in an era of heightened awareness of diversity and difference. This awareness has both positive and negative aspects. While positively it encourages defending very many identities, and hence the habitat and people, their language and other cultural markers against the onslaught of the overarching 'nationalizing' nation-state and other global forces, negatively, it can serve to defend obnoxious traditions and customs, anti-humanist mores and beliefs. Which appropriate political institutional arrangement can best maintain and accommodate diversity in respect of society, culture and government has perplexed social and political thinkers for ages. Liberal individualism and the liberal political system, paradoxically speaking, have been thought to be less accommodative of diversity. The notion of the abstract individual at the very heart of liberalism is universalizing, standardizing and pro-uniformity. At a profoundly philosophical level, of which liberalism is an offshoot, the Western modernity has been accused of being Eurocentric and pro-uniformity, and hence the array of instruments that this modernity has given birth to have served to suppress diversity for the sake of uniformity and

The concept of federalism and its relevance **19**

unity. As the postmodernists have tended to argue, modernity's attempts at 'normalization' and standardization have wreaked havoc on the diversity of cultures and traditions and the voices of dissent and differences. The leading terms of debates in today's liberalism such as communitarianism, multiculturalism and group rights are symptomatic of the unease felt within liberalism with reference to diversity (Smith 2002; Bhargava 1999; Parekh 2000). The unitary political systems, although based on democratic liberalism, have created institutions which are not accommodative of diversity. That often gives the wrong impression that perhaps liberalism and federalism are incompatible, philosophically speaking.

The federalists do not agree, however, and in fact argue that 'liberal democracy is a fundamental requirement for the government of federations and their states' (Pinder 2007: 9).

The Concise Oxford Dictionary defines the term 'federal' as meaning 'a system of government in which several states form a unity but remain independent in internal affairs'. The latter part of this sentence ('remain independent in internal affairs') indicates the presence of the concern for diversity in federalism. Although etymologically the term 'federal' had nothing explicitly to do with diversity, its modern usage, based perhaps on practices, has acquired its association with diversity. That federalism seeks simultaneously to promote unity and diversity has been recognized by many scholars. Elazar argues that it is a 'mistake to present unity and diversity as opposites':

> Federalizing involves both the creation and maintenance of unity and the diffusion of power in the name of diversity. Indeed, that is why federalism is not to be located on the centralization-decentralization continuum but on a different continuum altogether, one that is predicated on non-centralization, or the effective combination of unity and diversity.
>
> *(Elazar 1987: 64)*

In any federation worth the name, the political institutions are to be found designed in ways that reflect diversity. Diversity then becomes the basis on which the federal political edifice is erected. If there is a divergence between a society's diversity and the institutional arrangements of federalism, then federalism falters and finally collapses. Diversity then is the most sensitive issue in federations, since it is related to people's identity, whether based on language, culture, region or a combination of these. Democratic political culture is often a part of people's culture/identity which they are not ready to sacrifice for unity. Federal unity is a process achieved also through processes from below. Federal history is of course replete with examples of the complete mismatch between what may be called a social or cultural federation at the base and the so-called political federation often imposed from above by the rulers for the sake of a so-called unity which in any case remains elusive.

It is better for the federation when the basic impulse for a federation has come from below, that is, diversity. Take the case of the formation of the world's first modern federation. With an apparently homogeneous population, the US

20 The concept of federalism and its relevance

federation (1787) was nonetheless formed to maintain diversity: 'regional variations in political culture and a considerable emphasis upon the value of state and local government' (Watts 1999: 21). Today's US federation comprises 50 states plus two federacies, three local home-rule territories, three unincorporated territories and over 130 Native American domestic dependent nations (Watts 1999: 21). The immense sociopolitical diversity in this institutional arrangement is not to be underestimated. The Swiss Confederation changed to a federation in 1848 has remained a paradigm case of the successful accommodation of diversity. The concern for diversity, that is to say, to maintain diversity, was the most powerful impulse, historically speaking, behind the formation of the classic federations, beginning with the United States. The constituent units, whether the states (in the United States) or the cantons (in Switzerland) while joining the federation or the union, for common security overall, were most concerned about the protection of their distinct identity. This has been well-reflected in the formulation of the so-called federal principle by K. C. Wheare, the doyen of modern federal studies: 'By the federal principle I mean the method of dividing powers so that the general and regional governments are each, within a sphere, co-ordinate and independent' (Wheare 1953: 11). In his discussion of the prerequisites of federal government too, his pre-eminent concern for the independent character of the regional units has been reiterated. He reminds us that the American states, the Swiss cantons, the Canadian provinces and the Australian states, 'although associated together prior to union in some way, enjoyed each a distinct history and a distinct government' (Wheare 1953: 40). He further says: 'Thus although they came to desire union in some things, they still desired to remain separate in others' (Wheare 1953: 40).

The pressing concern for uniting diverse, often vast peoples, intertwined with nationalism, was the compulsion for nationalist élites and state- and nation-builders in the colonies in Asia and also Africa to opt for some kind of federalism. Harold Laski declared the obsolescence of federalism in the wake of the Second World War, but in the post-war period it was in the colonies in Asia and Africa that the federal idea became popular and was widely received as a recipe not for disintegration but for unity and national integrity. As Ronald Watts has stated: 'The second half of the twentieth century has seen a proliferation of federations as well as other federal forms to unite multi-ethnic communities in former colonial areas and in Europe'.

The concern, even a genuine one, for diversity and its protection is one thing, but finding the appropriate institutions for doing so is a different story. Montesquieu, under the influence of Aristotle, was deeply concerned about the diversity of customs and forms of government and attempted to classify the latter in order to show which best protected liberty. His famous doctrine of 'separation of powers' was intended to limit despotic powers so that diversity was maintained (Aron 1965, Vol. 1: 17–73). In Montesquieu, 'representation' was an essential means of ensuring liberty of diverse ways of life, of customs and traditions. However, this eighteenth-century European Enlightenment thinker was quite sanguine about the role of 'representation' in protecting diversity; democracy's relation to social and

The concept of federalism and its relevance **21**

cultural diversity and hence its role in ensuring political order and stability has been a subject of considerable debate among scholars of later days. A long line of thinking since J. S. Mill has tended to believe that democracy is 'inherently difficult in societies with deep ethnic cleavages'. Mill asserted democracy's incompatibility with diversity a long time ago: 'free institutions are next to impossible in a country made of different nationalities' (Reilly 2001: 1). The other kind of questions raised in this connection today in the democracy debates is whether democracy can survive conflicts arising out of diversity (ethnic or otherwise) (O'Neill and Austin 2000). Democracy's positive role in resolving ethnic conflicts is also highlighted in another kind of analysis (Shapiro and Hacker-Gordon 1990).

Daniel Elazar stresses the republican dimension of federal polity to bring home the democratic essence of federalism (Elazar 1987: 107–9). He states:

> Federalism by its very nature must be republican in the original sense of *res publica* – a public thing; a federal polity must belong to its public and not be the private possession of any person or segment of that public, and its governance therefore requires public participation.
>
> *(Elazar 1987: 107)*

Drawing on the experience of the world's first (i.e. the US) federation, he argues that federal government must be republican in form and based on a popular base. He also directed our attention to the words of the Federalists: 'republican remedies for republican diseases' (Elazar 1987: 108). Following from this, a true federal legitimacy, for Elazar, is a democratic legitimacy. The strong federal system is one which, argues Elazar, combines a high degree of unity with a high degree of diversity (Elazar 1987: 66). (Switzerland is a case in point.)

The federalists thus look at democracy differently. Since federalism requires shared- and self-rule, which again entail power-sharing, democracy and true federalism are inseparable. How is diversity accommodated and thus maintained if there is no sharing of powers? It is not federalism proper if there is no self-rule at the regional, local level. Pinder has strongly emphasized this relationship too: 'Democratic political institutions in the governments of both the constituent states and the federations are also essential, because authoritarian regimes are not able to share their power'. According to him, if either of them is authoritarian, federalism does not work at the level of shared rule or the self-rule (Pinder 2007: 8). Africa, Asia and Central America as well as the former socialist states such as those of the former USSR and Yugoslavia lay in the authoritarian and dictatorial regimes which had stood in the way of power-sharing across the system (Pinder 2007: 8; Watts 1966). John Pinder has highlighted an additional factor in this respect. He says that even within democratic federations, a hegemon in the shape of a state may defeat the federal purpose if it is big and powerful enough to dominate the other states and eventually the whole federation (Pinder 2007: 8). This question takes us down to the issue of dominant nationality or a dominant ethnic group (majority or not) within a federation, an issue which could be the most decisive factor in the

22 The concept of federalism and its relevance

functioning of the system. The failure of federalism in Pakistan had much to do with this factor, as we shall see later in this book.

Democracy thus is in some ways intertwined with federalism, and hence it can be proposed that democratic federalism is a better, if not the best, institutional guarantee for the protection of diversity. Although formally democracy is not essential to define federalism, federalism without accompanying democracy has been doomed to failure, because it is democracy which guarantees the reflection of values of the people in the polity, one of the conditions for both unity and diversity in a multicultural society.

This has been recognized by Watts (1996) in his three broad conclusions, which also are suggestive of the conditions for the success of federations. First, federations are a 'practical way of combining the benefits of unity and diversity through representative institutions'. Second, the success of a federation depends on the appropriate political culture of a people who are prone to respecting constitutional norms and structures and is also marked by a spirit of compromise and tolerance. Third, there can be various applications of the federal idea, but the effectiveness of the application depends on whether it expresses the demands of the society in which it takes place (Watts 1996: 115).

The operational reality of a federation, itself caused by the social, historical, cultural and political context of the country concerned, is a very important determining factor, since each federal experiment bears the imprint of this reality and each federation comes up with its own meaning of federalism and thus adds to the conceptual vocabulary of federalism. Each federal arrangement is subject to the specific constellation of social, cultural and political forces and factors and hence has its own (Watts 1998: 133) federal debate, which is also, however, instructive for others, since it shows how certain common problems have been handled in certain ways, often in the face of severe setbacks, and a political equilibrium, if at all, has been achieved. A successful federal experiment is also the one which is successfully relativized to the context. In empirical terms, a relatively successful federation is also an experiment involving some principles of federalism. The normative dimension of federalism is then mixed up with the empirical dimension. As Watts (1996) has very rightly emphasized, there is no single pure model of federation applicable everywhere. Empirically, various federations variously combine elements of shared-rule with self-rule, for the purpose of unity and diversity at the same time. Federations, as Watts (1996) says, are 'essentially a pragmatically evolving rather than static form of government' (Watts 1996: 115). Only a pragmatically oriented federation can effectively respond to changing conditions and needs, more pertinent in the fast-changing postcolonial countries of Asia than perhaps in the West (although this is equally true in the West today) through 'incremental political adaptation' (Watts 1996: 115).

Concluding remarks

Federalism remains most relevant to Asia, the world's most diverse and complex region. Many formally non-federal states such as China, the Philippines and

The concept of federalism and its relevance **23**

Indonesia have adopted many federal measures to accommodate regional ethnic identity for autonomy (Breen 2018; Anderson and Chaudhry 2019). It has been seen that not all the federations introduced in the new Commonwealth after the Second World War have succeeded. In fact, many failed. In Asia itself, India and Malaysia are two success stories; Pakistan has so far remained a federation on paper only. However, since 2010, with the passage of the 18th Constitutional Amendment, things there have been changing, although slowly. The United Arab Emirates (UAE) is an effective federation of a different order, something based not on democracy but on power-sharing among the emirates. Federalism is more relevant to Asia today than ever before as the route to accommodation of diversity for political unity. The recent moves of many advanced Western liberal democratic states, most notably Italy, Spain, Belgium and even the United Kingdom, towards federalist and true decentralist directions are a testimony to the inability of unitary states, however liberal they might be, to accommodate diversity (Burgess and Pinder 2007). The disintegration of the former USSR, the Federal Republic of Yugoslavia and Czechoslovakia has also proved that the so-called socialist model of the accommodation of diversity may not work. Democratic federalism then remains the most valid option for true accommodation of diversity in Asia. It is true that the results of the introduction of federalism in Asia after decolonization were mixed, and experiments were far from satisfactory. But it must also not be forgotten that federalism in its various forms had been attractive to many countries in this part of world. The broad reasons why federalism remains so relevant to Asia are: first, this region contains 'greater undiluted ethnic heterogeneity'; second, there is still an obvious need here to devise institutional arrangements for accommodating ethnic, religious or linguistic diversity, or a combination thereof. This calls for paying particular attention to the nature of cultural diversity in Asia, more particularly in India, Pakistan, Malaysia, Nepal and Myanmar, for exploring the basis for introducing federal measures – a subject which is taken up in the next chapter.

Note

1 See, Elazar (1987), chapter 4, for a detailed account of the evolution of the federal idea.

2

ETHNO-NATIONAL DIVERSITY AND FEDERALISM

Introduction

Cultural diversity and its recognition and appropriate accommodation have remained a central concern in nation-building and state formation in Asian federations. Although the simple dictionary meaning of the term 'diversity' refers to 'unlikeness' or variety, the term has assumed a special meaning in the discourse on federalism. On the face of it, in federalism, not all variety or diversity is directly relevant and significant. That some group of people have different dietary habits or wear a different dress, as such, may not be important for federalism. That in some countries, there are linguistic problems where some groups of people suffer discrimination because of their language may not, as such, call for a federal solution; or that some countries have acute social discrimination, such as caste in India and Nepal; or there is discrimination on grounds of religion. Often a simple democratic solution that provides for the protection of the language rights of minorities may resolve the problem. It is true that nowadays the term 'personal federalism' is used to refer to non-territorial provisions for the solution of such problems. But one wonders whether such resolutions, bereft of any territorial arrangements existing side by side, should be called truly 'federal'. In Belgium, for example, the provisions for the three communities (the Dutch-, the German- and the French-speaking ones) with their own councils represent the non-territorial 'personal jurisdiction' of the 'Revolutionary federalization' that is under way (Watts 1999: 29), but the institutional arrangements for the community councils are to be understood in relation to the regions (three) and the territorial distribution of powers. People's food habits, culture, religion, language and other identity markers make sense for federalism when they imply some territorial significance, in the sense that the people having those traits reside in a particular territory where they may constitute a minority or a majority and where their culture, or habitat, broadly speaking, requires special protection. In the classic federations such as the United States and Switzerland, the political identity (including local government) and political culture of the constituting units constituted the *sine qua non* of the diversity that the resulting federation was supposed to protect. K. C. Wheare said that before the Swiss Confederation converted itself into a federation in 1848, there was 'great divergence of political institutions in the cantons' (Watts 1999: 46). K. C. Wheare (1953) further said that federalism was a way of reconciling the pressures for diversity and for unity, so that diversities are maintained as values in themselves (Wheare 1953: 244–5).

In recent times, the term 'federalism' has quite frequently been used, instrumentally speaking, as a tool for the accommodation and management of diversity and thus to achieve unity and integrity in multicultural societies. But this instrumentalist understanding, most often by international peace experts, does not specify the relation between diversity and federalism *per se*. Which diversity is sensitive to federalism? Which diversity is sensitive to what kind of federalism? Is federalism the solution to diversity? Is diversity always a problem that warrants a federalist solution? What is the optimal diversity condition for federalism? Such questions and many more are more easily raised than answered. Such questions equally puzzled K. C. Wheare when he said: 'Federal governments are rare because its prerequisites are many. It requires the co-existence of many national characteristics' (Wheare 1953: 35). Also, 'the most difficult question' for Wheare was to determine: 'In what conditions is it appropriate to adopt a federal form of government?' (Wheare 1953: 35).

Seen from the side of federalism, diversity may often be encouraged by the presence of federal democratic space available, or once available but now withdrawn. Elazar said that federalism aspires to generate and maintain diversity (Elazar 1987: 64). The relation between diversity and federalism then, is indeterminate and changing. For a variety of reasons, diversity may not be recognized at all; also, some parts of diversity may be recognized to the exclusion of the others. Once again, diversity may be recognized, but not adequately, in the sense that the institutional prescriptions are far short of what is required to truly reflect diversity in the polity and public policies. Unitary states are generally afraid and weary of diversity. Much of the ethno–national conflict in the world that tends often to disturb world peace is rooted in the mismatch between diversity and the political institutional arrangements. Federalism *per se* may not be the answer to diversity, as such, but what is of prime consideration are the most appropriate institutions that represent diversity within a given polity.

Asia's diversity and conflicts

Asia is the world's most diverse continent, socially and culturally speaking, and yet it remain mostly unfederal. In terms of language, religion, tribal affiliations, regions and other ethnic markers, Asia's diversity is proverbial. Jawaharlal Nehru's (India's top nationalist leader and the country's first prime minister) famously stated:

> The diversity of India is tremendous; it is obvious; it lies on the surface and anybody can see it. It concerns itself with physical appearances as well as

> certain mental habits and traits. There is little in common, to outward seeing, between the Pathans in the Northwest and the Tamils in the far south. Their racial stocks are not the same, though there may be common strands running through them; . . . yet with all these differences there is no mistaking the impress of India on the Pathans, as this is obvious on the Tamils.[1]

The Pathans and the Tamils are two extreme examples; the others lie somewhere in between. All of them have their distinctive features, all of them still have the distinguishing mark of India (quoted in Bhattacharyya 2007a: 57). In Nehru's passage here, there was, to be sure, a nationalist-ideological bias in finding a 'distinctive mark of India' on every cultural difference. But what baffled him was the country's immense diversity. What privileged India in this respect is that Indian's diversity was long recognized and acknowledged by the nationalist thinkers, and the nationalist movement against British colonial rule committed itself to accommodation of diversity politically once independence was achieved (Bhattacharyya 2011: 91–119).

After more than half a century since Nehru wrote, each and every country in Asia is found to be marked by some very ancient diversities of people and attendant ethno-nationalist conflicts in many of the countries. The record of accommodation of minorities and resolution of ethnic conflicts arising out of them is still unsatisfactory in most Asian political systems. However, of late, many countries, such as Indonesia, the Philippines and Sri Lanka, though not formally federal, have gone some ways to accommodate diversity through decentralization (Breen 2018). In Sri Lanka, the ethnic conflicts[2] are sharply divided between the Tamils (Sri Lankan Tamils at 11.2 per cent and Indian Tamils at 4.2 per cent, both mostly Hindus) and the Sinhalese,[3] who are a predominant majority (75 per cent) and are mostly Buddhists (70.2 per cent); the persistent and violent conflicts between them have defied any federal solution so far after many decades of negotiations, violence and international peace-making efforts (Wellikala 2019: 255–74). Since independence from British colonial rule in 1948, and with colonial democratic tradition, the minority Tamils who inhabit the north-east of the country have suffered extreme ethnic discrimination, deprivation and ethnic-outbidding by the majority Sinhalese (Oberst 1998; Phadnis and Ganguly 2001; Hettige 2000, 2012). The Tamils and the Sinhalese are two distinct nations, and the Tamils remained highly advanced with a language (Tamil) that is officially accepted as one of India's classical languages. But any claim of the latter for self-determination, even within the same polity, received only violent response from the Sinhalese. Since 1983 the conflicts have turned very violent, verging on civil war, but without any satisfactory solution. In 2009 (May) the then government of Sri Lanka resorted to ruthless military action against the Liberation Tigers of Tamil Eelam (LTTE), and since then, even a regional autonomy for the Tamils is not considered as an option (Wellikala 2019: 255).

While a federal prospect in Sri Lanka seems to be bleak and the ethno-national conflicts are stalemated, some other Asian countries have shown greater flexibility in constitutional transitions in favour of some kind of federal solutions to ethnic minority problems. In Indonesia, for example – marked by large numbers of territorial cleavages – since the country's democratization in 1998 and several constitutional amendments between 1998 and 2002, a political climate and space has been created in favour of regional autonomy. But paradoxically, it remains a classic example of 'highly asymmetric forms of federalism' co-existing with a highly centralized unitary state (Bertrand 2019: 119–39). Interestingly, a second chamber of Parliament (called DPD) has been created, not as a federal chamber but for regional representation (Bertrand 2019: 139).

In Iraq, another country with territorially rooted ethnic diversity, a transition to federalism via an Interim Constitution of 2003 has been mostly US-imposed and in collaboration with the majority Arabs (about 75 per cent) without popular consent (which was never taken into account) and (without) involvement of the minority Kurds; it has been fraught with many hurdles, and the so-called federalism proposed is 'hopelessly vague' (Zaidi 2019: 116). Of the absence of many institutions that can offer the federal back-up, Iraq does not have a tradition of strong judiciary that would be much needed to act as the final arbiter and guardian of the Constitution (Zaidi 2019: 115).

In the Philippines, an otherwise unusual case for a 'federal transition', the autonomy claims (*diversity-claims*) of the Moros, 13 ethno-linguistic groups professing Islam in the south and constituting about 6 per cent of the population (6 million out of 100 million), have been conceded in 2018 after nearly five decades of ethnic rebellions, violence and mass killings followed by negotiations and constitutional transitions (Lau 2019: 203–18). In the referendum held on 25 January 2019 to say 'yes' or 'no' to Bangsaro (Muslim) self-rule in the south replacing the existing status of an autonomous region with very little real powers, there was a landslide victory in favour of 'yes' to self-rule[4]. This is a remarkable constitutional change for a form of federal solutions through regional ethnic self-rule for the Muslims in a unitary state with a predominantly Roman Catholic people.

Ethnic diversity and federalism: India, Pakistan, Malaysia, Nepal and Myanmar

The four cases already discussed, briefly, have deeply territorially rooted sociocultural diversity but have not adopted federalism at the macro level as a method of accommodating the same and hence have suffered from a lack of governance and political stability. But there is a caveat here. In Iraq and Sri Lanka, the old problems of minority ethnic communities remains as a major challenge of governance; but in the Philippines and Indonesia, with regional ethnic self-rule having been conceded, the roots of regional and ethnic tensions are much dissipated. The five cases of India, Pakistan, Malaysia, Nepal and Myanmar are different, however. Of the five, the first three (India, Pakistan and Malaysia) had had a common historical trajectory determined by long-drawn colonialism and anti-colonial nationalist movements and the overriding goal of nation-building amidst diversity. The case of

28 Ethno-national diversity and federalism

Nepal did not have to experience such a trajectory but instead was more dictated by the concerns for unity and nation-building following periods of armed struggle by the communists against a feudal autocracy, with a federal democratic republic that is to be oriented to socialism. Myanmar's trajectory is different in some respects and similar in some other respects. It had had some kind of federal experience before it fell to the military, but the federal spirit has not apparently died down, especially with regard to the ethnic minority nationalities which are historically rooted in their respective territory such as the Shan, the Mon and the Chin. In all cases, the appropriate political expression of diversity has remained the most powerful challenge in that a dominant majority (Sri Lanka, Myanmar. Pakistan and Malaysia) – or a dominant ethnic group (s) in Nepal – limit the appropriate political expression of diversity and thus protection of minority ethnic identity. India, given the fact that there is no one all-India majority of any ethnic group (the Hindus are an overwhelming majority in population, but it had little to do with federalism per se), has facilitated better ethnic accommodation in the state level where the ethnic diversity was marked and needed reorganization of territory for right-sizing the federal structure in India. The federal unity that is often spoken of is supposed to be based on the mutual co-existence of such political expressions of diversity at different levels of the polity. Accordingly, not all forms of diversity are capable of political expression (Bhattacharyya 2015).

India

India, demographically speaking the second-largest country after China, with a population which has already exceeded 1billion, is, arguably the most diverse, socioculturally speaking, country in the world. It is bounded on the north-west and west by Pakistan; to the north by China, Nepal and Bhutan; to the east by Bangladesh and Myanmar; to the south-east by the Palk Strait and Sri Lanka and the Bay of Bengal; and to the south-west by the Arabian Sea and the Indian Ocean. Territorially, it is very vast, with an area of some 3,287,263 sq. km. Its 1-billion-plus population lives in 28 states (constituent units of the federation and themselves the result of federalization since Independence in phases) and nine union territories (directly governed by the Union government) (Table 2.1) and is distributed among many languages, religions, castes, tribes, races, regions, subregions, communities, subnationalist groups and of course classes. India's diversity is truly continental. Many of the constituent units of the Indian federation today are bigger in size and population than many countries of the world.

At a rough estimate, 12 states of India are bigger than 100 countries of the world! On the face of it, not all forms of diversity mentioned are capable of federal political expression, but most of them have played (and continue to play) an important role in eking out political units by 'disintegrating' the existing territory of the states but remaining within the federation, by the method officially known and acknowledged in India as 'States Reorganization' (Bhattacharyya 2019a: 81–99).

Ethno-national diversity and federalism **29**

TABLE 2.1 Demographic composition of the Indian states and Union territories (2011)

States	Population
Andhra Pradesh★★	84,665,533
Arunachal Pradesh	1,382,611
Assam	27,704,236
Bihar	103,804,632
Chhattisgarh	25,540,196
Delhi (NCT)★	13,850,507
Goa	1,457,723
Gujarat	60,383,628
Haryana	21,144,564
Himachal Pradesh	6,856,509
Jammu and Kashmir★★★	12,548,926
Jharkhand	32,966,238
Karnataka	61,130,704
Kerala	33,387,671
Madhya Pradesh	72,597,565
Manipur	2,964,007
Meghalaya	2,318,822
Maharashtra	112,372,972
Mizoram	1,091,014
Nagaland	1,980,602
Orissa	41,947,358
Punjab	27,104,235
Rajasthan	68,621,012
Sikkim	606,688
Tamil Nadu	72,138,958
Tripura	3,671,032
Uttarakhand	10,116,752
Uttar Pradesh	199,581,477
West Bengal	91,347,736
Union territories	
Andaman and Nicobar Islands	379,941
Chandigarh	1,054,685
Dadra and Nagar Haveli	342,953
Daman and Diu	242,911
Lakshadweep	64,429
Pondicherry	1,244,462

Source: Census Reports of India (2011).

Notes: ★Delhi is a National Capital Territory and a state with a Legislative Assembly but with limited powers. ★★ Bifurcated on 2 June 2014 into Andhra Pradesh and Telangana –the latter's population is 35 million now. ★★★On 6 August 2019 Jammu and Kashmir were bifurcated into two Union territories – Ladakh and J &K. This is the first time a state in the Indian federation has been demoted to a Union territory.

30 Ethno-national diversity and federalism

Formed over many thousand years as a country of immigrants who brought their own cultures and traditions, India's diversity is proverbial. Although predominantly inhabited by the 'Hindus' (about 80 per cent of the population) – who are, however, regionally rooted and specific; plural in beliefs and practices; and divided by castes and languages – India contains large proportions of Muslims (14.23 per cent, some 170 million in 2011) spread all over the country, with more than a million Muslims in as many as 13 states (out of 29), as well as Sikhs, Buddhists, Christian, Jains and so on (Table 2.2).

Three features stand out from Table 2.2 regarding the regional concentrations of religious groups in India. First, there are local concentrations of Muslims, very often the majority in the population too, in districts, towns and cities throughout the country. But there was only one Muslim-majority state in India, namely, Jammu and Kashmir (J and K), in which the Muslims form a majority in Kashmir. This was due not to the federalization of the Indian Territory, that is, the so-called reorganization of states, but to the fact that the Kashmiri Muslims had been living in Kashmir for centuries. The state had long been a kingdom. Nonetheless, J and K, as a state of the Indian federation, was not and could not be based on religion. Although it was the only state in the Indian federation to have had a Constitution of its own, because its Constitution was governed by Article 370 of the Indian Constitution, (considered as 'temporary provisions'), it was not allowed to establish a theocracy. Like other states of the Union, Jerstwhile and K also has had a parliamentary democratic political system.

Second, there are three Christian-majority states in India, all in the NorthEast, namely, Nagaland, Meghalaya and Mizoram. These states, again, were created since the 1960s by the carving up of Assam, not on the basis of religion but of tribal ethnicity. Third, Sikhs are concentrated in Punjab, where they form a majority. Punjab was created in 1966 as a result of the reorganization of Indian territories on an ethno-religious basis.

The relation between Indian federalism and religion has to be stated here clearly. First, the federation does not recognize any official religion, despite the

TABLE 2.2 Religious composition of the Indian population (2011)

Religions	Population (in million plus)	% of total population
Hindus	960	79.80
Muslims	170	14.23
Christians	27	2.3
Sikhs	20	1.72
Buddhists	844	0.7
Jains	44	0.37
Other religions	79	0.66
Religion not stated	28	0.24
Total		100

Source: Census Reports of India (2101) (www.census2011.co.im/religions.php, accessed 1 August 2019).

overwhelming numbers of 'Hindus' in the country. India is declared as a secular state. Second, religion here is not considered as an accepted basis for claiming statehood or political autonomy within the federation. In other words, religion is an illegitimate category for use in demanding further federalization of the Indian polity, and therefore, so far no political units have been created and recognized on the basis of religion. However, every citizen has the fundamental right to religion guaranteed by the Constitution of India.

India's linguistic diversity is as proverbial. By one estimate, there were some 1,632 languages spoken in India.[5] So far, 22 languages have been 'officially recognized' and placed under the Eighth Schedule of the Constitution (Table 2.3). Today, the speakers of these 22 languages constitute about 91 per cent of the population. Many of India's languages are very ancient, with strong literary traditions. Some of the so-called regional languages, most notably Tamil and Bengali, are, in fact, older than Hindi, the language that is spoken by the largest number of Indians (but not the majority). Hindi is the official language of the Union government. English is used as second official language of the Union government. During the period of British colonial rule, languages and administrative units (or provinces) did not always coincide. Thus, the provinces created by the British in

TABLE 2.3 Official languages and speakers in India (2011)

Languages	Speakers	Percentage of total population
Hindi	528,347,193	43.63
Bengali	97,237,669	8.03
Marathi	83,026,680	6.86
Telegu	81,127,740	6.88
Tamil	69,026,881	6.70
Gujarati	55,492,554	5.70
Urdu	50,772,632	4.58
Kannada	43,706,512	3.61
Odia**	37,521,324	3.10
Malayalam	34,838,819	3.10
Punjabi	33,124,726	4.79
Assamese	15,311,351	1.28
Maithili	13,583,464	1.26
Santali	7,368,192	0.61
Kashmiri	6,797,587	0.56
Nepali	2,926,168	0.24
Sindhi	2,772,264	0.23
Dogri	2,596,787	0.21
Konkani	2,256,502	0.19
Manipuri	1,761,079	0.15
Bodo	1,482,929	0.12
Sanskrit	24,821	N*

Source: Census Reports of India (2011).* Negligible.** formerly Orissa

32 Ethno-national diversity and federalism

India were not linguistically homogeneous. Many of the provinces as well as the princely autocracies (numbering 561!) were bilingual or even trilingual, and ethnically rather heterogeneous. In the wake of India's national liberation movements, many of the region-based linguistic groups became self-conscious and demanded self-determination.[6] The Linguistic Provinces Commission (popularly known as the Dar Commission) formed on 17 June 1948 to advise the Constituent Assembly (1946–49) correctly sensed the situation: Indian nationalism is deeply wedded to its regional languages; Indian patriotism is aggressively attached to its provincial frontiers.[7] In the post-Independence period, it is *language*, not religion, which, when coupled with regional identity, has provided the most powerful instrument for political recognition as an ethnic identity.

Language in India, as everywhere else, is a very important identity marker for people, particularly when the speakers of the language concerned are attached to a territory for a considerable period of time. Table 2.3 provides us with the speakers of 22 official recognized languages in India. The languages in India have in most cases a territorial attachment, and thus, 29 states and seven Union territories in India each contain one majority or dominant language, although, because of the movement of people from one part of Indian to the other since 1950, all states and Union territories have speakers of many languages. Although Hindi is considered spoken by the largest number of Indians (43.63 per cent), the linguists, however, point out that Hindi is actually a cluster of more than 45 mother tongues in India, which include Bhasha, Bundelkhani, Chambeali, Chhattisgarhi, Garwali, Haryanvi, Marwari, Pahari and so on (Mallikarjun 2004: 10). These mother tongues once again are spoken by people territorially located in regions of India.

The relation between India's linguistic diversity and federalism thus requires some explanation. To begin with, there are no states or Union territories created for the following Eighth Schedule languages: Urdu, Sindhi, Sanskrit, Maithili, Dogra and Santali.[8] Second, there are states created on the basis of tribal affiliations, such as Meghalaya, Mizoram and Nagaland, where the languages spoken by the majority of the people (for the first two) do not have scripts and are not, as such, official languages in those states. Third, 'Hindi' is the majority and official language of as many as nine states (Bihar, Jharkhand, Madhya Pradesh, Uttar Pradesh, Uttarakhand, Chhattisgarh, Rajasthan, Himachal Pradesh and Haryana. However, there are within each many distinct (linguistically) ethno-territorial identities which have been demanding political recognition as states within the federation. Fourth, there are as many as 92 languages (enumerated in the Census of 2011) comprising some 31 million speakers which are yet to be recognized as 'official' and placed in the Eighth Schedule. Finally, Telangana was created as a state in 2014 when the people there mostly speak the same language, Telegu. In this case, linguistic criterion of creating new states was underplayed in favour of distinct regional and historical identity. Telangana, though, is mostly bilingual: Telegu and Urdu – the latter is the second official language of the state (Bhattacharyya *et al.* 2017).

Apart from language, the other very important category of diversity in India that has been directly active with regard to political recognition of identity and hence behind further federalization of the polity is India's aboriginal population, constitutionally known as the 'Scheduled Tribes', making up about 8.6 per cent of the total population of India and spread all over the country, with a large concentration in India's NorthEast (Table 2.4).

The percentage of India's tribal population has increased since 1961 (6.9 per cent); 1981 (7.8 per cent); 1991 (8.1 per cent); 2001 (8.2 per cent); and 2011 (8.6 per cent). Arguably, this has to do with creation of tribal states and the autonomous district council for tribal self-governance which had ensured better protection of tribal identity. As is seen in table 2.4, the population of tribal majority states and Union territories are rather small; in the large states where the tribals are in a minority, they comprise very large population.[9]

The basic point that is being made here is that territorially rooted tribal affiliations in India have remained a form of India's social-cultural diversity, and provided a basis for further federalization of the Indian polity in the North East. (Bhattacharyya 2019b).

TABLE 2.4 Distribution of tribes and their percentage contribution to the total population in states and Union territories (2011)

States & UTs	Total population	Per cent (%)
Lakshadweep (UT)	61,120	94.8
Mizoram	1,036,115	94.4
Nagaland	1,710,973	86.5
Meghalaya	12,555,861	86.5
Arunachal Pradesh	951,821	68.8
Dadra & Naga Haveli	178,564	52.0
Sikkim	206,260	33.8
Manipur#	902,740	35.1
Tripura	1,166,813	31.8
Chandigarh	7,822,902	30.6
Chhattisgarh	7,822,902	30.6
Jharkhand	8,645,042	26.2
Odisha	9,590,756	22.8
Madhya Pradesh	15,316,784	21.1
Gujarat	8,917,174	14.8
Rajasthan	9,238,534	13.5
Assam	3,884,371	12.4
Jammu & Kashmir	1,493,299	11.9
Maharashtra	10,510,213	9.4
Andaman and Nicobar Islands	28,530	7.5
Andhra Pradesh	5,918,073	5.9
West Bengal	529,695	5.5

Source: http://tribal.nic.in/ST/Tribal%20Profile.pdf, accessed 1 August 2019); # excluding 3 sub-divisions.

34 Ethno-national diversity and federalism

Pakistan

To a casual observer, Pakistan, created as it was on the basis of Islam by separating it out of an undivided India on 14 August 1947, would appear to be a homogeneous society of Muslims probably speaking Urdu, the state's national language. But any closer observation of the country would reveal that it is highly diverse by any terms –that is, in terms of language, territorially rooted ethno-national identity and even religion.[10] Pakistan seems to be, demographically and otherwise, a prototype of India, provided that the 'Hindus' and the 'Muslims' swap their position in the populations of each country. As India's 'Hindus' are divided along many lines – mother tongues, region, cultural beliefs and practices, and above all the caste systems – so are the 'Muslims' of Pakistan. Pakistan, in other words, is a diverse country, socioculturally speaking. However, politically it is not so, because the Pakistan federation has failed to politically express the society's diversity, something that lies at the heart of the country's persistent problem of political order and legitimacy. Ethno-territorial conflicts have remained persistent in Pakistan ever since the early 1950s. In the wake of the landmark 18thAmendment of the Constitution of Pakistan (1973) in 2010, there have been renewed mobilizations for new provinces on the basis of ethno-territorial identity across the federation.

Geographically, Pakistan's location is strategic, in the sense that it occupies the junction between the Middle East and Asia. Pakistan is surrounded to the east by India; to the north by the Central Asian republics and China; to the west by Afghanistan and Iran; and to the south by the Persian Gulf and the Indian Ocean. The country has an area of 879,902 sq. km (Ghaus-Pasha and Bengali 2002)[11] and a population estimated to be around 208 million in 2017. After the disintegration of its eastern wing, East Pakistan, giving birth to Bangladesh in 1971, Pakistan today is a four-unit federation. Its territorial arrangements with regard to the distribution of population (as per 2017 census data) are given in Table 2.5.

TABLE 2.5 Provincial distribution of population in Pakistan (2017); total population = 207,774,520

Provinces	Area in sq. km	Population (%)
Baluchistan	347,190	12,344,408 (5.94)
Punjab	205,344	110,012,442 (52.95)
Sindh	140,914	47,886,051 (23.05)
Khyber Pakhunkhwa (KPK)★★	74,521	30,523,371 (14.69)
FATA★	27,219	5,001,676 (2.4)
Federal Capital Territory (Islamabad)	907	2,006,572 (0.97)

Source: Pakistan Bureau of Statistics. www.pbs.gov.pk/sites/default/files/PAKISTAN%20TEHSIL%20 WISE%20FOR%20WEB%20CENSUS_2017.pdf (accessed 19 July 2019)

★Federally Administered Tribal Areas. Figures within brackets indicate percentages. ★★North-West Frontier Province, renamed in 2010.

The four federal provinces are the home of the principal ethno-national groups: the Pathans (Pasto) in the North-West Frontier Province (NWFP), which became the province of Khyber Pakhtunkhawa (KPK) in 2010 by way of the 18th Amendment of the Constitution of Pakistan (1973); the Baluchs in Baluchistan; the Punjabis in Punjab; and the Sindhis in Sindh (Elazar 1987: 189). But, as we will see soon in Table 2.6, those four provinces also contain significant ethno-linguistic minorities rooted in their particular regions. The provinces' contribution to population, percentage-wise, is as follows: Punjab (52.95 per cent); Sindh (23.05 per cent); KPK (1469 per cent); Baluchistan (5.94 per cent); (Federally Administered Tribal Areas (FATA) (2.4 per cent); and the Federal Capital Territory (0.97 per cent). Constitutionally, Pakistan is declared as the Islamic Republic. As per the Census reports of Pakistan (2017), Muslims are 96.28 per cent, followed by Christians (1.59 per cent), Hindus (1.60 per cent), Ahmedis (0.21 per cent), Scheduled Castes (.0.25 per cent) and others (0.07 per cent) (www.pbs.gov.pk/sites/default/files//tables/POPULATION%20BY%20RELIGION.pdf, accessed 20 July 2019). Of the Muslims, the majority are Sunnis (85 per cent, approximately) and the Shias are about 12 per cent.[12] But the ethno-linguistic (nationalist) identity markers in Pakistan have overwhelmed the Islamic identity.

Urdu is the national language of Pakistan, spoken by 7.57 per cent of the population in 2017. Urdu and English are the official languages of the federation. Of the other languages, only Sindhi is considered as the official language of Sindh. Linguistically, Pakistan is very diverse, though, because as many as 80 languages are spoken in Pakistan. Table 2.7 contains data on the main languages of Pakistan. As Table 2.6 shows, Urdu speakers are mostly concentrated in urban Sindh (21.05 per cent of its population). They were the refugees (Muhajirs)[13] from India at the time of Partition (1947) and have remained a potent source of social and political conflicts in Sindh and in Pakistan since its birth in 1947. To begin with, their migration and settlement in Sindh have upset Sindh's demographic balance by

TABLE 2.6 Multi-ethnic composition of provinces in Pakistan (2017) (figures in per cent)

Provinces	Urdu	Punjabi	Sindhi	Pusto	Baluchi	Saraiki	Others
Baluchistan	0.97	2.52	5.58	29.64	54.76	2.4	4.11
KPK★	0.78	0.97	0.04	73.9	0.01	3.86	20.43
Punjab	4.51	75.23	0.13	1.16	0.66	17.36	0.95
Sindh	21.05	6.99	59.73	4.19	2.11	1.00	4.93
FATA★★	0.18	0.23	0.01	99.1	0.04	–	0.45
Islamabad★★★	10.11	71.66	0.56	9.52	0.06	1.11	6.95

Source: www.pbs.gov.pk/sites/default/files//tables/POPULATION%20BY%20MOTHER%20TONGUE.pdf (accessed 20 July 2019)

★ Khyber Pakthunkhwa. ★★ Federally Administered Tribal Areas, (with some 5 million tribal peoples), which now ceases to exist but is decided to be merged with KP province (31/5/18) although this merger process is to take two years from 2018. ★★★ Pakistan's capital, which is dominated by the Punjabi (71.66 per cent).

36 Ethno-national diversity and federalism

TABLE 2.7 Linguistic composition of Pakistan population (2017)

Languages	Per cent	Population in millions
Punjabi	38.78	80.5
Pasto	18.24	37.9
Sindhi	14.57	30.3
Saraiki	12.19	25.3
Urdu	7.08	14.7
Baluch	3.02	6.32
Hindco	2.24	2.6
Brohi	1.24	0.4
Kashmiri	0.17	0.4
Others	2.47	5.1
Total	100	207,774,520

Source: Census reports of Pakistan 2017 (http://defence.pk/threads/census-2017-language-data.56077, accessed 22 July 2019).

reducing the Sindhis from 74 per cent of the total population in 1951 to 59.71 per cent (2017) today. Even today, although the Sindhis are in the majority, it cannot be said that they are dominant. Second, the same migration has also alienated the local Sindhis from the growing conurbations, meaning that they concentrated in rural areas (where they make up 92.02 per cent of the population) even today. For a long time, their very disproportionate dominance over the civil-bureaucratic and political decision making was a cause of further alienation among the other ethnic groups, most notably the people in rural Sindh, Baluchs and Pakhtuns. However, subsequently, this Muhajir domination over the government and civil service in Pakistan was replaced by the Punjabis.

The data presented in Table 2.6 show that most of the provinces are bilingual; Punjab is trilingual; and Punjabi is the largest ethno-linguistic group. The federal capital, Islamabad, is Punjabi dominated. Sindhi is multilingual.

Unresolved ethno-national federal issues in Pakistan

The account of the significance of Pakistan's ethno-national diversity for federalism would remain incomplete without reference to the growing ethno-national and other sectarian conflicts and violence persistent over several decades since the inception of Pakistan (Pant 2017: 319–28). Since 2010 with the major devolutionary constitutional amendment (18th Amendment 2010), a new surge of demands for political recognition in the shape of provinces out of the existing ones have come out, and debates among scholars of Pakistan on the issue have highlighted the pros and cons (e.g. Asghar 2012; Mustaq 2016; Javaid 2018). For one thing, such ethnic conflicts have sought to articulate the grievances for political recognition of diversity in Pakistan in the absence of a federal democratic political space for negotiation on power-sharing and participation. The ethnic diversity is yet to

Ethno-national diversity and federalism **37**

be constitutionally recognized with provisions for political autonomy. Ironically enough, the Muslim League, the party of Pakistan's 'Independence' – which had demanded Pakistan (as a state for the Muslims) from India after having failed to negotiate a power-sharing arrangement with the Indian National Congress (INC) – has been found to be wanting in Pakistan in power-sharing with different but historically strongly embedded ethno-national groups such as the Baluchs, Sindhis and Pakhtuns/Pasto. The self-assertions of those nationality groups themselves are a proof that religion was not enough, but much needs to be done to accommodate ethno-national diversity in Pakistan federation.

However, unlike India since 1950, where there are flexible provisions for recasting the political map of the country by way of Article 3 of the Indian Constitution (Bhattacharyya 2019a: 81–99), this is difficult in Pakistan. Article 239 (4) of the Constitution of Pakistan provides for a very rigid method of changing the provincial boundaries or creating new provinces:

> A Bill to amend the Constitution which would have the effect of altering the limits of a Province shall not be presented to the President unless it has been passed by the Provincial Assembly of that Province by the vote of not less than two-thirds of its total membership.[14]

The Saraiki nationality question

The Saraiki-speaking people are a distinct identity group consisting of 12.19 per cent of the population of Pakistan, with a population of 25.3 million (2017). They comprise about 15 per cent of the people in Punjab and are located in the areas between southern Punjab and northern Sindh. Dera Ismail Khan, an area belonging to KPK, is said to be Saraiki-speaking. The Saraiki-speakers are tribespeople who have moved, historically speaking, into northern Sindh, where they make up the majority of the population (Ahmed, I.1995: 182–3). The Saraiki élite and intelligentsia, educated mostly in Urdu, like the rest of the Punjabis, have recently been claiming the status of a nationality on the basis of language. There are various interpretations (Kukreja 2003; Khan, A. 2005; Khan, W. 1998; Talbot 2002; Jaffrelot 2002a), however, about the status of their language relative to Punjabi, and Sindhi too. The main thrust of their argument has been that they had indigenous roots and hence they are not part of either Punjab or Sindh. Their main demand was the creation of a separate Saraiki province, something which has been rejected by the Pakistan government (Ahmed, I. 1995: 184). The inhabitancy of 25.3 million Saraiki speakers – itself pretty large in number – makes up about 48.5 per cent of the territory in Southern Punjab. The available writings by Pakistan scholars (e.g., Mustaq 2016) on the subject suggest that their demand is well justified, although there are debates about the nomenclature of the province. The Saraiki nationalists have proposed the name of the province as Saraikistan, while those who do not defend a case of ethnic identity are in favour of the administrative nomenclature as 'South Punjab'.

38 Ethno-national diversity and federalism

The Pakhtu[15] nationality question

The Pakhtun nationality problem, one of the most long-lived of its type in Pakistan, remains unresolved. The Pakhtuns (commonly called Pasto) are the predominant nationality group in the Pakistani territories of the former NWFP, now renamed Khyber Pakhtunkhwa (PKP) and FATA, making up 18.24 per cent of the total population, with about 38 million people (2017). In neighbouring Afghanistan, incidentally speaking, they comprise the majority in population. The British colonial demarcation of the boundary between Afghanistan and India in 1893, which came to be known as the Durand Line, was done artificially and separated the Pathans of Afghanistan on the other side of the border from their brethren in India. The Pakhtun nationalism had its roots in the resentment born of this artificial division of a single ethno-national group.[16] Historically speaking, the Pathans in the NWFP did not overwhelmingly support the cause of Pakistan. In the 1946 elections, for instance, the Frontier Congress of Abdul Gaffar Khan, a legendary national leader belonging to the Congress movement in pre-Partition India, had won an overwhelming victory, securing 49 seats, including 19 Muslim seats, leaving only 17 to the Muslim League (Ahmed, I. 1995: 184). After the British departure in 1947, the Pathans wanted to join neither India nor Pakistan but sought an independent state of Pakhtunistan, something not considered favourably by the departing rulers. In the referendum that was held in 1947 to determine the future of the Pathans, only about 50 per cent cast their votes, of which the majority (289,244 votes) voted for Pakistan.

In the post-Partition period, the Pakhtunistan issue came to the fore again. In the 1950s the issue figured prominently in Pakistani politics but met with harsher state repression. Because of the Pathans' pre-Partition support for the Congress in India and their demand for an independent Pakhtunistan on the eve of the rise of Pakistan, the Punjabi-dominated Pakistani establishment treated the leadership of the Pakhtun movement with disdain and contempt and as traitors. Its top leaders, including Abdul Gaffar Khan, were kept under detention. The leadership of the Pakhtun movement had accepted Pakistan to be a settled fact, but they demanded the true federal reorganization of Pakistan so that all Pakhtun people could unit in a single province of their own to be known as Pakhtunistan. Neither independence nor autonomy within the federation, but some 'economic opportunities', were made available for the poor Pathans as a result of the conversion, in the 1960s, of the existing provinces in western Pakistan into one unit of the province of West Pakistan so that the Pathans from the poverty-stricken NWFP could relocate in other directions to find jobs and opportunities (Ahmed, I. 1995: 185). A good number did indeed move to Sindh, as is evident by the multi-ethnic composition of the population of the province, with 4.9 per cent Pakhtuns. This was an administrative design to wean away the separatists. There is evidence of the recruitment of the Pakhtuns into the top levels of the army and bureaucracy (about 15–20 per cent, which is high in proportion to their population share).[17] There are now industrialists among the Pakhtuns; they now own 0.03 percent of the top 30 industrial houses in Pakistan (Ahmed, I. 1995: 185).

Ethno-national diversity and federalism **39**

These measures were far from satisfying the ethno-national aspirations of the Pathans, whose movement for autonomy and recognition gained further momentum with further developments in the region. For one thing, some 3million Afghan refugees crossed the border in the wake of the Soviet occupation of Afghanistan in 1978, and the civil war there further strengthened the cause of Pakhtunistan, as the nerves of the NWFP were heavily strained. The successive governments in Pakistan always fell short of resolving the problem but added to it by further repression and harsher measures (Kukreja 2003: 129–32). This made the Pakhtuns reflect more seriously on their demands. The suggestions that came up from various groups of the Pakhtuns differed: either strengthening the province by remaining in a new Pakistan redesigned along confederal lines, joining in the creation of a greater Afghanistan or outright secession of the province to a fully autonomous Pakhtunistan (Kukreja 2003: 129). Needless to say, the Pakhtun ethno-national identity which has required a genuine federal solution remains unresolved in Pakistan, which was a federation on paper only! Renaming the NWFP as Pakhtunkhwa as a province in the Pakistan federation by the 18th Amendment of the Constitution of Pakistan in 2010 went some ways towards satiating the anger of the Pakhtuns but made the people inhabiting the Hazara region of the province, mostly speaking Hidco, much discontented (Mustaq 2016: 295). The statistical evidence on the linguistic composition of the Hazara region shows that the Hidco speakers are in great majority in four out of five districts in the region (Mustaq 2016: 295). On balance, if the Pakhtuns are recognized in Khyber Pakhtunkhwa, the much smaller number of Hidco speakers (2.6 million) deserve autonomy in the lower order, such as four autonomous district councils *a la* the Sixth Schedule of the Indian Constitution. But then that requires the appropriate constitutional arrangements and designs currently not available in the Constitution of Pakistan.

The Baluch nationality question

The Baluch nationality question in Pakistan remains another classic case of an ethno-national identity neither recognized politically as such nor integrated into Pakistan. Baluchistan and the Baluch identity of course predate Pakistan and the Pakistani 'national' identity. Baluchistan is Pakistan's biggest province in terms of area but is sparsely populated. The province's 6.32 million (2017) inhabitants live in an area of 347,190 sq. km. The province's population makes up 3.02 per cent (2017) of the total population of Pakistan. In Baluchistan, there are three linguistic groups such as Baluch, Brauhi and Pakhtun (about 30 per cent now), although the first two are considered to be one ethnic group.[18]

Historically, Baluch identity formation has assumed a complex character, for a variety of reasons, but religion never was a defining feature of its identity (in fact, religious bonds among the various tribes were rather weak), and there was very little support in Baluchistan for the Pakistan movement of the Muslim League led by M. A. Jinnah. On the contrary, there was evidence of anti-Pakistan movements spearheaded by the native rulers comprising today's Baluchistan.

40 Ethno-national diversity and federalism

Deprived of the fruits of development, funds and opportunities, which have been monopolized mostly by the Punjabis in Pakistan, the province remains extremely backward. The Baluchs rose in revolt in 1973–77 and engaged in a violent confrontation of about 40,000 Baluch guerrillas with 70,000 Pakistani troops, who brutally suppressed the uprising (Kukreja 2003: 130–7; Hewitt 1998: 43–67). One estimate suggests that some 5,300 Baluchs were killed or wounded in the confrontation. Z. A. Bhutto, then prime minister of Pakistan, received US$200 million in emergency military and financial aid from Iran to crush the rebellion (Ahmed, I. 1995: 186). In 1977–76, many Baluch leaders and prisoners were set free, and an amnesty was announced for those who fled Pakistan to take shelter in Afghanistan.

This outline of the Baluch discontent and conflicts is a testimony to the difficulties of getting a fair deal faced by an aggrieved nationality historically rooted in the territory of Baluchistan in a federation in which political recognition of identity and power-sharing seem an undesirable proposition. The Baluchs' difficulty in integrating with Pakistan lay in a number of factors including the near secular nature of its identity and the result of the dominance of Sufism as well as a commitment to a liberal-reformist rather than communal approach to self-determination of the Baluchs and the near absence of any bases of support for the Pakistan movement in the region (Hewitt 1998). Added to the list was the ethnic exclusiveness of the Pakistan state, which is dominated by the Punjabis and the Muhajirs (Hewitt 1998).

The Sindhi nationality question

The Sindhi nationality question is perhaps the most complex of all in Pakistan and remains unresolved too, like those of the Baluchs, the Pathans and others. The province of Sindh is the second largest in terms of population (approximately 48 million in 2017) and ethnically the most diverse of all the provinces of Pakistan (Table 2.6). The Sindhis today are 60 per cent (2017) of the total population of the province, mostly rural (81.5 per cent) compared with the Muhajirs. The latter, the descendants of Urdu-speaking migrants from India, make up 21 per cent of the population but 54.4 per cent of the urban population (compared with the Sindhis, who are only 20 per cent urban). Sindh also has 7 per cent Punjabis, 5 per cent Pakhtuns and 2 per cent Baluchs – all the result of migration from other provinces and mostly settled in the urban areas. The province is also multi-religious: over 1million Hindus live in Sindh, the only province where they can be found.

The identity of Sindh as an ethno-territorial unit predates that of Pakistan, and the Sindhi identity is truly deep-rooted in history. From around the seventh century, various dynasties alternated in Sindh: Hindus; Arabs; Sindhis; central Asian Arghuns and Tarkhans; Mughuls; the native Kalhoro; the Baluch tribes; the Talpur; and the British in 1843 (Ahmed, I. 1995: 187). The British ruled Sindh as a single province between 1843 and 1847 when it was amalgamated into the Bombay Presidency, something the Sindhis opposed vehemently. From the turn of the twentieth century, the Sindhis began to publicly oppose Sindh's union with Bombay. The platforms of the All India Sessions of the Congress since 1913 were also utilized to air their grievances. The INC and the Muslim League extended support to the movement for separation. The INC later on vacillated in its support for separation,[19] but the League remained steadfast. In 1936, Sindh was separated from the Bombay Presidency and made into a proper province. The distinctive identity of the province was thus restored.

The province of Sindh was also distinctive in being a solid support base for the Pakistan movement and for putting forward the demand for a federation of autonomous states on the basis of the principle of self-determination for the Muslim-majority provinces. The Sindh Muslim League is said to be the first in India to articulate those demands in October 1938, under the leadership of G. M. Sayeed, who propagated the idea of Pakistan throughout Sindh. Interestingly enough, the peasants and lower middle-class Muslims, who for ages had been heavily indebted to Hindu money-lenders, saw the demand for a Pakistani stake as a means of getting rid of the Hindu money-lenders (Ahmed, I. 1995: 199).

But Sindh's support for the Pakistan movement soon petered out after the creation of Pakistan, because it was Sindh which bore the brunt of the Partition by receiving the majority of the refugees from across the border. Sindh received the Muhajirs, the Punjabis and later on the Baluchs and the Pathans, who all settled in the urban areas of Karachi, Hyderabad and Sukkur. This upset the demographic balance in Sindh and marginalized the Sindhis. Hamza Alavi has pointed out that the Muhajirs constituted (as per the 1981 Census report of Pakistan) 50 per cent of the population of the major urban areas of Sindh (the figure remains the same in 2017), while in the overall population they constitute about 22 per cent (Kukreja 2003: 139). In 1981, in Karachi, the capital of Sindh, only 6.3 per cent of people were Sindhi speakers. Economically, Sindh contributes a lot to the country's GDP and industrial production by being the major financial and industrial centre but remains alienated all around (Kukreja 2003: 140–1). Ironically enough, it was the same G. M. Sayeed, once a leading proponent of the Pakistan movement in Sindh, who in the 1980s launched a new movement called the *Jeyee Sindh* Movement for a Sindhudesh (a Sindh country, literally rendered). The original home of the Bhuttos (Julfikar Ali Bhutto, Benazir Bhutto *et al.*) of Pakistan and the Pakistan People's Party (PPP), Sindh is host of the multifaceted ethnic conflicts involving Sindh vs. the centre; the Sindhis vs. the Muhajirs; the Sindhis vs. the Punjabis etc., which remain unabated in the absence of appropriate federal measures.

Malaysia

The Malaysian federation, another success story after India, is based on much more complex diversity than Pakistan, and perhaps India too, in some respects. While the accommodation of territorially based identities may be easier within a single political system of federation, giving relatively more autonomy to such identities, the accommodation of communities that are ethno-linguistically and religiously so different from each other, and dispersed throughout the country, may be difficult. Typically, the latter kind of diversity is not susceptible to federal solutions. The very

42 Ethno-national diversity and federalism

special success story of the Malaysian federation, particularly after 1969 – when the major inter-communal (Malay-Chinese) riots broke out and the political system faced a major crisis – lies precisely there. The Malaysian federation has innovative mechanisms to accommodate otherwise irreconcilable diversities within the single political system.[20] The other important point that should be mentioned here is that accommodation of ethno-national identities was almost ingrained in the very body of the post-Independence Malaysian federation because the post-Independence efforts at federation-building were in fact the continuation and expansion of the federalizing efforts made in the colonial days – the Federated Malay States (1895), the Malayan Union (1946), and the Federation of Malaya (1948). In 1957 it was the Federation of Malaya which became independent, since the states within that federation had declared independence.

Malaysia, with an area of approximately 329,758 sq. km, is an important country in South-East Asia, which comprises Myanmar, Thailand, Cambodia, Laos, Vietnam, Singapore, the Federation of Malaysia, Brunei, Indonesia and the Philippines. The region as a whole lies to the east of India and to the south of China. It contains a series of peninsulas and islands. Malaysia itself lies to the east of India's Andaman and Nicobar Islands in the Indian Ocean and to the south of Thailand and Vietnam. Apart from Thailand, all of the countries of South-East Asia have long been part of Western colonial rule – British, French, Dutch or American. That apart, there is very little geographical unity evident among them (Fisher 1964: 2).[21]

The Malaysian federation today comprises 13 states, 11 in Peninsular Malaysia and two (Sabah and Sarawak) in northern Borneo. The latter are separated, geographically, by some 400 miles from Peninsular Malaysia. The total population of the federation is some 3.17 million (2017), with 63 per cent on the peninsula and the rest in the Borneo states of Sabah and Sarawak (about 2million in each). The total population of the federation is small compared with India and Pakistan. It is actually less than one-third of the population of an Indian state such as West Bengal and less than half the population of Pakistan's largest province of Punjab. But the size of the population of Malaysia is not as important as its ethnic composition (Table 2.8). Interestingly enough, the so-called *bhumiputra*, or *bhumiputera* ('sons of the soil'), that is, the original inhabitants of the country, were not the majority in the population in 1957 when the Federation of Malaya (FM) became independent. It is only since 1980 that the official statistics show the *bhumiputera* to be a growing majority (55 per cent in 1980, rising to 65 per cent in 2000!), in contrast with the dwindling size of the minorities.

Two other features of the demographic profile of Malaysia need to be clarified. First, the Malays as *bhumiputra* constitute an overwhelming majority (approximately 98 per cent) of the population of the peninsula. Second, in Sabah and Sarawak, the indigenous *bhumiputera* and the Malays Bhumiputera are also an overwhelming majority (approximately 65 per cent). The Chinese remain an important element of the population in both, together accounting for 14.7 per cent in 2017.

Malaysia is multiracial, multi-religious and multilingual, and above all, multi-ethnic. The Malays, Chinese and Indians are three different distinct races, speak

Ethno-national diversity and federalism **43**

TABLE 2.8 Ethnic composition of the population of Malaysia (1947–2017)

Year	Total (in millions)	Bhumiputra[a] (%)	Chinese (%)	Indian (%)	Others (%)
1947	4.9	49.8	38.4	10.8	1.0
1957	6.2	49.8	37.2	11.3	1.7
1961	7.23	50.0	36.0	11.3	2.7
1970	8.8	50.0	37.0	11.0	2.0
1980[b]	11.47	55.1	33.9	10.3	0.7
1991	18.38	60.0	28.1	7.9	1.4
2000	23.27	65.1	26.0	7.7	1.2
2017	31.6	61.7	20.8	6.2	0.9

Source: Bakar (2007: 70) (slightly adapted); www.indexmundi.com/malaysia/demographics_profile.html (accessed 3 August 2019)

Notes

a *Bhumiputra* (also used as '*bhumiputera*'), literally 'sons of the soil', refers to Malays and the indigenous people of Sabah and Sarawak.

b The 1980 percentage distribution of population among the ethnic groups, as given by Daniel Elazar (1994: 154), is: 47 per cent Malay, 34 per cent Chinese, 9 per cent Indian and 9 per cent others.

different languages and follow different religions and cultural modes of life. But unlike India, Malaysia's ethnic differences are not cross-cutting. Thus, in most cases, the Malays profess Islam; Indians Hinduism; Chinese Taoism, Confucianism and Buddhism; and the aboriginals (particularly of Sabah and Sarawak) profess either Christianity or varieties of animism (Bakar 2007: 71). Although linguistically diverse, the official language is *Bhasa Malaysia*, the language of the majority Bhumiputera (61.7 per cent of the total population). There are significant speakers of other languages: Chinese, Tamil, Telegu, Malayalam, Panjabi and Thai. English is also used in official purposes. Beyond that, there are some 134 living languages in the country. The federation is multi-religious, but Islam remains the official religion of the state. Muslims are 61.3 per cent; Buddhists are 9.8 per cent; Christians are 9.2 per cent; Hindus are 6.3 per cent; and others are 3.4 per cent (2017). At the primary level of education, the federation allows only these three languages for instruction and learning: Malay, Tamil and Mandarin.

Since those three ethno-national communities, their historical location in the country and their mutual relations and antagonisms, coupled with preferential government policies for the majority Malays, are all that matter in the politics of Malaysia, a very brief socio-historical account of these communities are called for. Such an account would help us to understand better the special significance of ethno-national diversity in Malaysia.

The Malays

The Malays are considered to be the indigenous people of Malay, although their geographical origins are diverse. Historical evidence suggests that many of the Malays living in Malay are of recent migrations from insular South-East Asia

44 Ethno-national diversity and federalism

(Means 1976: 15). However, the Malays today have a 'strong sense of communal-cultural identity', and their precise origins are not the subject of any academic or political debate (Means 1976: 15). They have remained nonetheless rural and backward until very recently in comparison with other communities in Malaysia. This has been the cause of much annoyance and irritation for the educated and urban Malays (Means 1976: 15), first and foremost because they did not make up the majority of the population until 1980 – although the sudden upsurge in the increase in the percentage of the Malays in the total population is a little doubtful – and second because they have remained economically backward, despite being the so-called 'sons of the soil'.

The Malays have remained overwhelmingly rural, and, until very recently, economically backward relative to the Chinese and the Indians. Their very deep attachments to Islam and their provincial loyalties have determined the contours of life for the Malays. The close association, if not identification, between a Malay and a Muslim has been sanctified by the federal Constitution and the legal system. Means has described the situation as follows:

> To abandon Islam would mean the renunciation of his Malay way of life (for the two are intertwined) and the loss of all legal and political privileges afforded to the Malays on the basis of their claim of being the indigenous people. All Malays go through the outward observances demanded by the Islamic faith, and the special Muslim courts established in every state enforce Muslim law and the religious obligations of Islam.
>
> *(Means 1976: 17)*

Both race and religion have defined the Malays as an exclusive community relative to other communities and have also made the Malays unassimilable into any of the other communities, such as those of the Chinese and the Indians. Quite predict-ably, this strong sense of community among the Malays has also often made them easy prey for communal mobilization for political purposes (Means 1976: 17).

The role of the British in keeping the Malays in semi-backwardness should not be underestimated. The Malays' essentially rural life and their dependence on subsistence and on rice and fish cultivation were connected with certain policy preferences of the colonial rulers. Hing has informed us that 'Policies adopted by the British were designed to encourage the Malays to remain attached to the land to ensure the production of food and insulate them from the vagaries of a modern economy' (Hing 1981: 219). The Malays, as a result, continued to live in the vil-lages and remained loyal to their ruler and chief, the sultan, whose standing, para-doxically, was enhanced after the reduction of actual powers by the British!

After decades of preferential government policies for the Malays, the Malays, while maintaining their predominant position in government service, the army and police, have, over the last three decades or more, moved from the rural to the urban areas, and they can now be found in all sectors of the economy (Andaya and Andaya 2001: 3).

The Chinese

The Chinese contact with the Malay Peninsula had begun as early as the fifth century, but the real influx of the Chinese into the region did not begin until the late nineteenth century, and that too, with the growth of British influence in the region. In 1872, the Chinese were found to be around 40,000 in number, and, in 1901, they constituted as much as 65 per cent and 46 per cent of the population respectively of Selangor and Perak (Means 1976: 26). It was the growing rubber industry that absorbed most of the Chinese labourers. However, the Chinese migrants suffered when the tin industry was mechanized, and many returned to China. But the number of new arrivals always surpassed those who returned to China. The slumps in both the rubber and tin industries around the turn of the twentieth century, and once again during the First World War and the Depression, meant that there was growing number of unemployed and also that a more restrictive immigration policy was adopted (Means 1976: 26–7). The Chinese came to Malay not to settle down but to get rich quick and then return to China. Thus the legal status that they enjoyed was that of resident aliens, meaning that they did not have the same rights and privileges as those enjoyed by the indigenous nationals. After the 1920s, the Chinese community lost much of its transient character, and the Chinese increasingly began to consider Malaysia as their permanent home (Means 1976: 27). The number of Chinese in Malaysia has dwindled over the decades since the country's Independence (1957), from 36 per cent in 1957 to 26 per cent in 2000 (Bakar 2007: 70) and 20.8 per cent in 2017. In Peninsular Malaysia, they make up only 8 per cent of the total population, but in Sabah and Sarawak together, they are 14.7 per cent (2017).

Like the Malays, the Chinese are also a close community. Historically protected by the British colonial government to run their life as they pleased, their religious practices and social and cultural modes of lives set them apart from other communities in Malaysia. But the fact that they have control over the greatest proportions of the country's economy has made them a subject of jealousy and envy, for the Malays in particular. Starting as an immigrant labour force in the colonial period, the Chinese have moved into small-shop trading; shop keeping; opencast tinmining and transportation; and latterly into rubber growing and processing, banking and other manufacturing industries. Until about the 1970s, they had had a good grip over the economy, business and capital markets, but that has declined since.

While the other communities, particularly the Malays, will have resented the Chinese wealth in Malaysia, the Chinese themselves, being the economically dominant community, have resented the government's restrictive, anti-Chinese policy bias and unsympathetic attitude to Chinese demands. To the Chinese, the government, whether colonial or post-Independent, seems alien. This has prepared the basis for the growth of what is termed 'Chinese nationalism', centering on the issue of their culture and identity and the right to participate fully in the Malaysian political process as equal citizens. The Chinese sense of deprivation and alienation in a country which they have adopted as their permanent home and in which they

46 Ethno-national diversity and federalism

are the most affluent has not augured well for building a cohesive 'national' identity in a multicultural country when the constitutional guarantee of the protection of their identity leaves much to be desired. Consider the following constitutional provisions of Malaysia. Article 160 defines 'Malay' as 'a person who professes the religion of Islam, habitually speaks the Malay language, and conforms to Malay customs' (Bakar 2007: 70). Article 153 of the Constitution thus protects the Malays and the natives: 'It shall be the responsibility of the *Yang di-Pertuan Agong* to safeguard the special position of the Malays and natives of any of the Sabah and Sarawak and the legitimate interests of other communities in accordance with the provisions of this Article' (Bakar 2007: 70–1). *'Yang di-Pertuan Agong'* refers to the king as the Supreme Head of the State in Malaysia. Ismail Bakar, himself a Malay, has observed:

> However, today, many Malaysians have become disenchanted with the spirit of this provision for uniting Malaysia and [this] is regarded by non-Bhumiputera as a kind of discrimination.
>
> *(Bakar 2007: 70)*

The Indians

The position of the Indians, the third-largest group (8 per cent of the population, mostly to be found in Peninsular Malaysia) and mostly of immigrant origin, is more precarious than that of the Chinese. Although Indian contact with South-East Asia dates back to the sixth century BC and South-East Asia owes its cultural debt to India, the arrival of Indians in substantial numbers did not take place before the rise of European influence in the region. The British, for instance, founded the settlement at Penang in 1786 and brought with them the Indian Sepoys and labourers. The Indian traders followed suit. Indian migration swelled in the wake of the opening up of the rubber industry at the turn of the twentieth century and subsequently for the construction of railways and roads (Means 1976: 36). However, the Indians, mostly the Hindus of south India, lived in isolated communities in the so-called labour lines and hence hardly interacted with the Malays and the Chinese. The overall Hindu religious and cultural practices among the Indians have served to reinforce their exclusive communal identity. If there is any meaningful social interaction between the Indians and the Malays, it is with the Indian Muslims: marriage between them and the Malays is quite common nowadays.

Despite the Indians' subsequent involvement in business and trade, to some extent, and entry into the service sectors and their claims, after the Second World War, to be permanent residents of the country, the Indians' integration with the Malays and the Chinese remains problematic.

Much of the ethnic tensions have their roots in the particular mode of operation of British colonialism in this region. It was British colonialism which 'encouraged the migration of the Chinese and the Indians in the nineteenth century as cheap labour for the expanding tin and rubber industries' (Hing 1981: 216). British colonialism once again was responsible for further promoting differences between the two races: British policy had been to permit the different races to be educated in their own vernacular language while a minority gained access to English-language schools. Differences in educational background promoted separate political outlooks (Hing 1981: 216).

Malaysia is evidently a diverse society. Its diversity is no less complex than that of India and Pakistan. The three major communities – the so-called *bhumiputera* (sons/daughters of the soil) (the Malays and the natives of Sabah and Sarawak), the Chinese and the Indians – are not themselves homogeneous but rather differentiated. The natives or the indigenous people, particularly of Sabah and Sarawak, are heterogeneous, and not all profess to be Muslims. However, there has been little inter-mixing among the three major communities in Malaysia, since the Malays, the Chinese and the Indians are all exclusive communities. Added to all these are embedded ethnic tensions in a state in which equal citizenship rights are not available for all. In a multi-religious country such as Malaysia, Islam is the state religion.

On the face of it, Malaysia does not appear to be a good candidate for ethnic peace and harmony. The 13 May 1969 ethnic riots seemed to offer a major signal that political order and stability in Malaysia was a difficult option, if at all achievable. As Andaya and Andaya have put it:

> In general, however, Malaysia has successfully maintained co-operation if not harmony among its different communities at a time when the world has witnessed disturbing racial and ethnic violence.
>
> *(Andaya and Andaya 2001: 6)*

While the country's fast economic growth, backed by high technology, may provide part of the answer to this apparent miracle, scholarly pursuits need to look beyond economic growth, as this, when distributed unequally, could be dangerous and a bad omen for political anarchy and collapse in the absence of appropriate institutional mechanisms that alone can accommodate the 'competing demands of its ethnic groups for equitable sharing of resources and equal access to political power' (Andaya and Andaya 2001: 6).[22] This calls for paying attention to how federalism as an institutional device, and as adapted in Malaysia, has tackled the problems, for the sake of enduring political order, stability and integrity.

Nepal

As a new and fledgling federation, the case of federalism in Nepal is a case apart in Asia. Following decades-long communist armed struggles, movements for state restructuring and constitution-making, the country democratically adopted its Constitution on 20 September 2015, but given the highly discriminatory and exclusionary social structure and deeply rooted social, economic and cultural inequalities, the inclusive democratic institutional arrangements perhaps deserve more attention than would be needed for a typical federal solution. In other words, Nepal's ethno-linguistic diversities are not, in most cases, so territorialized as to produce federal units based on ethnic majorities. However, the issue of its ethnic diversity and need for their accommodation can hardly be neglected. In the very Preamble of the Constitution of Nepal, it has been declared that the federation shall promote a 'multi-caste, multi-lingual, multi-cultural; and diverse' society of Nepal. Accordingly, the nationhood to be created and promoted in Nepal is plural: multi-ethnic, multilingual, multi-religious and multicultural (*Preamble Section 3 Nation*). Although caste hierarchy is an important symbol of social discrimination, the Preamble does not entail any goal of doing away with this, for one of the goals of the federation is to promote a 'multi-caste' nation!

Second given the long-drawn experience of feudal autocracy marked by extreme concentration of power, and that too is a small *pahariya* Hindu élites (high caste Hindus such as Chhetri and Bahun), along with the overriding need for democratization and devolution in favour of a decentralized state system, the federal rationale for Nepal has had an additional point of strength. Nepal could not be federal without being sufficiently democratic nor democratic without being sufficiently federal. Therefore, federalism for Nepal needed self-rule, adequately guaranteed by the Constitution at many tiers down the scale. Territorial dispersal of powers and authority down the levels from Kathmandu was as much required as protection and accommodation of ethnic identity. But the issue of complex diversity in Nepal remains and will continue to remain as a problem for quite some time.

Nepal is Asia's most diverse country, socially and culturally speaking. Its 26.5 million people (Census of Nepal 2011) is divided into too many groups: ethnic, caste, linguistic, regional, religious, hill people and the Terai plains people. Breen (2018: 60) reported that there are some 118 groups based on ethnic affiliation. Although predominantly Hindu (81.3 per cent in 2011), the Constitution declares itself a secular state in the sense that the federation does not have any official religion and that the Constitution guarantees freedom of religion to all. However, the Hindus in Nepal are regionally specific and divided by castes, regions and languages. Although Nepal is a multilingual country, Nepali in *Devnagiri* script is considered

TABLE 2.9 Ethnic composition of population in Nepal (2011)

Ethnic/caste groups	Population	Per cent (%)
Chhetri	4,398,053	16.6
Brahman/Bahun-Hill	32,269,031	12.2
Magar	1,887,733	7.1
Tharu	1,737,470	6.6
Tamang	1,539,830	5.8
Newar	1,321,933	5.0
Kami	12,585,541	4.8
Musalman	1,164,255	4.4
Yadav	1,054,458	4.0
Rai	620,004	2.3

Source: Census Reports of Nepal 2011.

Ethno-national diversity and federalism **49**

TABLE 2.10 Linguistic composition of the people of Nepal (2011)

Language spoken	Per cent	Population
Nepali	44.6	11,826,953
Maithili	11.7	1,353,311
Bhojpuri	5.98	1,584,958
Tharu	5.77	1,529,875
Magar	2.98	787,530
Doteli	2.97	787,827
Urdu	2.6	6,915,461

Source: Constitution of Nepal, Preliminary Section 2.10.

TABLE 2.11 Religion in Nepal (2011)

Religion	Population	Per cent (%)
Hindu	21,551,492	81.3
Buddhist	2,396,099	9.0
Islam	1,162,370	4.4
Kirat	807,169	3.1
Christian	375,699	1.4
Prakiti	121,982	0.5
Bon	13,006	–
Jain	3,214	–
Bahai	1,283	–
Sikh	609	–

Source: Census Bureau of Statistics, Nepal 2012.

as the official language of the federation. But at the same time, all mother tongues spoken in the country have been recognized as the national languages, signifying non-territorial accommodation and inclusion.

So ethnically there is no majority group in Nepal. The largest ethnic group is Chhetri which is only 16.6 per cent of the population. But, as Breen (2018: 60) suggests, the Chhetries and the Bahuns with some Newars could be taken together for their most influential hold on state power in Nepal for long as the dominant but not majority community.

Beyond the above, there are many identity groups which claim recognition and some autonomy, what I have termed elsewhere as *diversity-claims* (Bhattacharyya 2015, 2017), in Nepal. According to Breen (2018: 60), there are as many 59 groups which claim themselves to be 'Janajatis' meaning 'indigenous peoples' of which some 20 per cent are Madheshis.

Beyond the above seven languages (totaling 76.6 per cent), there are as many as 116 other languages for which there are a small number of speakers. But then, unlike many other federations, Nepal has recognized all of them as the languages of the nation. Two interesting features stand out here for attention. First, Nepali is

50 Ethno-national diversity and federalism

spoken by 44.6 per cent of the people, but it is not the language of the majority, as there is not a majority ethnic group in the country. The use of Nepali language is widespread, but it is not universal. (Breen 2018: 60) Second, speakers of any one language are not territorially so concentrated as to claim a territorial autonomy on the basis of language; neither are other ethnic groups. In Nepal, language and ethnicity are overlapping and intermingled in many respects. This makes the possibility of multi-ethnic, multicultural and multilingual provincial units which may, arguably, be a better solution than territorial units based on a single ethnicity.

On the face of it, religion may not have anything to do with federalism when the federation declares itself as secular. Religion-based territory claims for creating federal units are also ruled out by the same logic. But religions play a determining role in shaping ethnic identity of the people, especially when faced with an overwhelming religious majority. In the specific context of Nepal, as Breen (2018: 61) has pointed out, the *Janajatis* (indigenous peoples) are mostly Buddhist or animist, or both, who have resisted any attempt to impose Hinduism on them (Breen 2018: 61). Article 26 of the Constitution of Nepal guarantees all citizens the fundamental right of freedom to 'profess, practice and preserve'; however, forceful conversion is prohibited. The Constitution of Nepal under Article 83 regarding the constitution of federal parliament (the House of Representatives) provides also for proportional representation party-wise for 110 out of 275 seats in such a way that includes women, Adibasi, Janajatis, Madhesis, Tharus and the 'backward regions'. In such institutional arrangements, a 'balance in geography and provinces' has been sought to be maintained.

Myanmar

Like other federations in Asia, Myanmar (formerly Burma) is also ethnically sharply diverse, but the state has ever since 1948 (Independence from British colonial rule) persistently denied recognition and autonomy to the distinct and most often territorially rooted ethnic minorities who were and still are in majorities in their traditional homelands but yet to be recognized with the appropriate federal constitutional guarantees. Like India, Pakistan, Malaysia and Nepal, national unity has also remained a primal concern in Myanmar, most vividly evident in its preference for a 'Union' to a federation. And yet, accommodation of ethnic diversity in the seven states named after their ethnic or nationality identity remains the key to the Union's transition to a federation and national unity. Since the inauguration of a 'federal' Constitution on 7 February 2008, followed by a referendum on the Constitution on 10 May 2010 (which also is to be considered as the first general election in the country after many decades), the NLD, led by Aung San Suu Kyi, won the election with a supermajority. The next general election under the Constitution was held on 8 November 2015 and was also won handsomely by the NLD led by Suu Kyi (www.reuters.com/article/us-myanmar-election/myanmar-by-election-results-a-lesson-for-suu-kyis-party-idUSKCN1N90D2, accessed 28 August 2019). This seems to show a democratic transition in Myanmar, although the country has to travel many miles before it becomes a moderate federal and democratic country. That ethnic accommodation in a federal spirit is yet to be a reality in Myanmar is proved among other things by the disastrous performance of the NLD in by-elections (held on 19 October 2018) in ethnic areas in which the NLD lost five out of six seats to the Upper House (House of Nationalities). In Northern Kachin, the NLD came third in an Upper House race – the seat was won by NLD in 2015, though. Given the fact that the Myanmarese military (Tatmadaw) has 25 per cent seats reserved for it in both houses of Parliament and holds strategic position in the government, with Suu Kyi holding the position of state counsellor, Myanmar's transitions are yet to receive global academic attention.[23] However, developments in Myanmar since the 1990s towards a federal democratic state rekindled some interests among the long-term observers of Myanmar politics (e.g. Smith 2007 as well as new interest on how Myanmar can become a federation. (Breen 2018). The implications of ethnic diversity in Myanmar's transition to federalism inevitably confront the following issues: recognition of ethnic nationalities in full; appropriate federal autonomy to be conceded to them; and the concern for special protection of rights of the minority (non-Burman) groups generally in the face of a strong Burman majority (68 per cent).

Myanmar's 55 million (2019) population is ethnically diverse (see Table 2.12).

The ethnic composition of the population of Myanmar is subject to doubt. Breen (2018: 61) said that there are some 135 ethnic groups in the country, but the government does not recognize all of them. The government has put all of them under eight major ethnic groups. There is also resentment among many ethnic groups for the label 'ethnic minority' because they consider themselves as nationalities. As per data in Table 2.12, the Bamars are the large majority in population

TABLE 2.12 Ethnic/racial composition of the people in Myanmar (2014)

(Total population = approximately 52 million)	
Ethnic/racial groups	*Per cent (%)*
Bamar	68
Shan	9
Kayin	7
Rakhaine	3.5
Han-Chinese	2.5
Mon	2
Kachin	1.55
Indian	1.25
Kayah	0.75
Others	2.5

Source: https://en.m.wikipedia.org/wiki/Demographics_of_Myanmar#Ethnic_groups (accessed 28 August 2019).

52 Ethno-national diversity and federalism

TABLE 2.13 Religions affiliations in Myanmar (2014)

Religion	Per cent (%)
Buddhists	87.9
Christians	6.2
Muslims	4.3
Hindus	0.5
Tribal religion	0.8
Others	0.2
Religion not stated	0.1

Source: https://en.m.wikipedia.org/wiki/Demographics_of_Myanmar#Ethnic_groups (accessed 28 August 2019).

and live in the central and southern parts of the country. The so-called ethnic minorities are mostly territorially located in their traditional homelands in the border areas – north-west, north-east, east, west and south. The Nagas, for example, are a distinct ethnic group in Myanmar and control a 'self-administered zone' consisting of three townships in Sagaing Region. Chin, Karen and Shan are also to be found in neighbouring countries such as India and China. Many such ethnic minority groups are in majority at the local level as well as the state level. The Constitution of 2008 recognized seven states and seven regions plus some Union territories as territory of the Union. The seven states are ethnically named and were pre-existing: Kachin State; Kayah State; Kayin State; Chin State; Mon State; Rakhine State; Wah State; and Shan State, but they are considered as one type of territory rather than the homelands of the distinct nationalities. The Constitution has considered them as national races.

Linguistically, Myanmar is diverse, although Burmese is spoken by 65 per cent of the population and the official language and medium of instruction. The other languages not officially recognized but spoken by the minorities are many: Shan (6.4 per cent), Karen (5.2 per cent), Kachin (1.6 per cent), Mon (1.5 per cent) and Rakhine (1.5 per cent). English is taught as a second language in government schools, and the educated middle classes speak the language. When language divides the people, religion unifies them. As many as 87.9 per cent of the people in Myanmar are Buddhist (of the Theravada school). This means most ethnic groups are Buddhist. When considered at the state/region levels, the Buddhists are in large majority in all but Chin State, where the Christians are in majority (85.4 per cent). Christians have a significant presence in Kachin State (32.9 per cent) and Kayah (45.8 per cent), Sagaing (6.6 per cent) and Shan states (9.8 per cent) (https:// myanmar.unfpa.org/sites/default/files/pub-pdf/MyanmarCensusAtlas_lowres.pdf, accessed 29 August 2019). Kachins, who live in a tribal inhabited territory in the north-east of Myanmar (population around 590,000), are also found in neighbouring China (120,000) as well as India (www.britannica.com/place/Myanmar/ Myanmar-since-1988, accessed 29 August 2019). The Kachins speak a variety of languages including Jingpaw, which is officially recognized in China as a minority language. Nonetheless Kachin or Jingpaw is understood to be the lingua franca in Kachin State.

Islam has significant presence in Rakhine State (35.1 per cent).[24] Animists are 6.6 per cent in Shan State. Religion as such may not have anything to do with federalism, but given the overwhelming majority of the Buddhists in Myanmar, it is a powerful component of minority ethnic/nationality identity, which when territorially so rooted calls for federal solutions. At the same time, the very large majority of the Buddhists in all but one state/region serve also to undercut the inner strength of minority ethnic identity.[25]

Notes

1 Quoted in Bhattacharyya, H. (2007a). The 'Pathans' (inhabitants of the North-West Frontier Province) mentioned in the passage now belong to Pakistan, after Partition in 1947.
2 The so-called Tamil problem in Sri Lanka has already generated a huge outpouring of writings. See for instance, De Silva (1989), Oberst (1998) and Gunasinghe (1989).
3 See Edrisinha and Welikala (2008) for a critical and perceptive examination of the federal issues in Sri Lanka.
4 www.aljazeera.com/news/2019/01/philippine-voters-muslim-rule-mindanao-190125140146200.html (accessed 4 September 2019).
5 See Amnesty International (1997) *Ethnicity and Nationality: Refugees in Asia*, London: Amnesty International, p. 11.
6 Amnesty International (1997), op. cit., p. 11.
7 Quoted in Basu (1997).
8 For a case study, see Bhattacharyya, H. (1989). The first systematic articulation of Indian nationalism in the writings of Bankim Chandra Chattapadhyay, the nineteenth-century Bengali administrator-novelist, expresses the tension between the Bengali and the Indian national identity. See, for instance, Chatterjee (1986,1993).
9 Quoted in H. Bhattacharyya (2001a) *India as a Multicultural Federation: Asian Values, Democracy and Decentralization (In Comparison with Swiss Federalism)*, Fribourg, Switzerland: Institute of Federalism, p. 100.
10 It is estimated that 33 more Indian languages are waiting to be included in the Eighth Schedule. For details, see B. Mallikarjun (2004) 'Indian Multilingualism, Language Policy and the State', *Language in India*, Vol. 4, April 4.
11 Cohen says that 'Pakistan is one of the world's most ethnically and linguistically complex states'. For details on the ethnic diversity of Pakistan, see S. Cohen (2005) *The Idea of Pakistan*, New Delhi: Oxford University Press, chap. 6, pp. 201–30.
12 See A. Ghaus-Pash and K. Bengali (2002) 'Pakistan', in Griffith, A. and Nerenberg, K. (ed) *A Handbook of Federal Countries*, Montreal and Kingston: McGill Queen's University Press.
13 The Shias feel themselves to be persecuted in the confessional state of Pakistan dominated by the Sunnis. The Shias are not, however, territorially concentrated in Pakistan, so they could not give birth to any strong secessionist movement. The Shia political party, the *Tahrik Nifas-e-Jafaria*, has not been able to make any impact in the elections. The fundamentalist edge of the Sunni *ulema* in Pakistan is to be seen from the Sunni claim that Pakistan be declared a Sunni State. (For more details, see Ahmed, I. 1995: 171.)
14 http://na.gov.pk/uploads/documents/1333523681_951.pdf (accessed 21 July 2019).
15 The Wikipedia Internet sources quoting the government sources, however, give slightly different percentage distribution of the listed language speakers in Pakistan: Punjabi (44 per cent), Pashto [Pakhtun] (15 per cent), Sindhi (14 per cent), Siraiki (11 per cent), Urdu (11 per cent), Balochi [Baluchi] (4 per cent) and others (4 per cent).

54 Ethno-national diversity and federalism

16 The other terms used with the same connotations are Paktun, Pakthun, Paktoon and Pashtun.
17 K. Bahadur (1994) 'Ethnic Problems in Pakistan', *World Focus*, Vol. XV, No. 4–5, April–May, 27.
18 Abdul Wali Khan, the son of Abdul Gaffar Khan, and founder of the National Awami Party, also settled for regional autonomy within Pakistan.
19 Kukreja (2003). The critics point out that the collective benefits of the Pakhtuns' share of national power did not percolate down to the masses, since most of the recruitments into the military and bureaucracy came from two settled districts of Kohat and Mardan (Kukreja 2003: 128).
20 Ahmed, I.(1995: 185), Linguistically, Baluchi is Indo-Iranian and Brauhi is Dravidian. Baluch tribes can also be found in Iran and Afghanistan.
21 Ahmed Yar Khan, the last ruler of Kalat, who had been mobilizing for an independent Baluchistan, declared independence on 15 August 1947. The movement was, however, crushed by the Pakistan Government and the province was annexed forcibly.
22 After the Larkana riots in northern Sindh between the Hindus and the Muslims, in which the British rulers sided with the Hindus, the INC gradually changed its position, and preferred the province's union with Bombay. The riots thus shattered the growing Hindu – Muslim bond in Sindh (Morris-Jones 1957: 37–40).
23 For further details on the main lines of ethnic conflict in Sindh, see Iftikhar, H. Malik (1998) 'The Politics of Ethnic Conflict in Sindh: Nation, Region and Community in Pakistan', in Mitra, S. K. and Lewis, R. A. (eds) *Subnational Movements in South Asia*, New Delhi: Segment Books, pp. 68–103.
24 Critics tend to point out that the government politics, particularly those of the NEP, have remained discriminatory towards the non-*bhumiputera* (Bakar 2007: 71).
25 For details, see C. A. Fisher (1961) *South-East Asia: A Social, Economic and Political Geography*, London: Methuen & Co., chap. 1 'The Personality of South-East Asia'.

3

ORIGIN AND DEVELOPMENT OF FEDERALISM IN ASIA

Colonialism, nationalism, decolonization and revolution

Introduction

Federalism in India, Pakistan, Malaysia and Myanmar (to a very limited extent) has its origins in the British colonial period, but it cannot be claimed that in all four countries it is only a colonial legacy. Colonial legacies that there were (with their inherent limitations) were intertwined with the imperatives of anti-colonial nationalist liberation movements in multi-ethnic, diverse countries and substantially modified after decolonization. Nepal in this respect is a case in point. Federalism in Nepal as a concept was foreign until 2008 (and still is, to a large extent), and the institution has its beginning very late in the wake of the Maoist armed revolution and a long period of Constitution making from 2008–2015. In other ethnically diverse countries in Asia, federalism is yet to be adopted at the macro level, but some kind of federal solution in the shape of decentralization and autonomy to the distinct and territorially rooted minorities has been considered (Breen 2018; Anderson and Choudhry 2019). Nepal adopted a federal democratic republic in 2015. As far as India was concerned, the nationalists, especially the Indian National Congress (INC), rejected many colonial institutional measures such as the Government of India Act, 1935, and the Cabinet Mission Plan (1946) in favour of a radical alterative which most suited the conditions of the country and which fulfilled the democratic wishes of the people of a multi-ethnic country. However, since the idea of federalism had its roots in the colonial period (institutionally speaking), the derivative character of federalism, especially its Western origin (conceptually speaking), could hardly be denied.[1] It must be accepted that, in these countries, there was little evidence of an indigenous precolonial tradition of political thought defending federalism, both as a political principle of governance simultaneously advocating a shared- and a self-rule within the same polity[2] and as a form of government that resulted from that combination. The anti-colonial nationalist

56 Origin and development of federalism in Asia

leaders of these countries, who very often thought of federal solutions of governance after independence, did so only as an improvisation of the Western colonial idea and as an improvement on it. At any rate, the development of federalism in these countries has remained enmeshed with colonialism, anti-colonial nationalist movements, postcolonial experiments with democracy and nation-building, and post-revolutionary restructuring (Nepal). This entanglement has called for greater attention to be paid to the recognition of ethno-regional/national identity in both the categorical and the distributional senses. The successes or failures in this respect have determined the overall effectiveness of the federal design in the countries concerned as well as the extent of nation-building.

A few preliminary remarks are in order before embarking on a detailed analysis of the issue. First, the discussion of the origin and development of federalism in the colonial period will be limited to Malaysia and India, because Pakistan's 'federalism' is a postcolonial phenomenon. For Myanmar, though it was a former British and, for a short period (1942–48) Japanese colony (independent since 1948), the issue of federalism, strictly speaking, was a postcolonial issue, too, relating to the unification of the border ethnic states – which the British ruled in a different, sort of indirect way – with the Union of Burma. Interestingly, though, M. A. Jinnah, widely considered to be the founding father of Pakistan, was one of the earliest nationalist leaders of India to demand a federation. And the movement for a separate sovereign nation-state of Pakistan outside India (which became a reality on 14 August 1947) had gravely affected the evolution of federalism in the postcolonial period. Second, the examination of the historical development of federalism in these countries is important, because the current discourse of federalism in these countries and its institutional development are inseparable from the colonial and nationalist legacy. Third, in the postcolonial period, federalism, much revised and adapted as a 'hybrid concept' (Bhattacharyya 2016), also became conjoined with democracy, at least regularly and practically in India and Malaysia and very haltingly and more formally, in Pakistan. Given the complex diversity under a feudal monarchy till 2006, Nepal also faces the typical problems of nation-building in the post-revolutionary period, although, as we saw in Chapter 2, federalism in Nepal does not and cannot resolve all its structural problems of manifold social and cultural discrimination. The new and fledgling federation needs radical democracy along with federalism to adequately address those issues. Myanmar adopted a constitution in 2008 in the wake of its very limited transition from a hardened military dictatorship to civilianization and democratization, but it remains a 'Union' (of Myanmar) and has a long way to go before it becomes a federation.

Malaysia

Federalism came to Malay, as it was known then, in the late nineteenth century when the British colonial authorities persuaded four central Malay states – Perak, Selangor, Pahang, and Negri-Sembilan – to form the Federated Malay States in terms of a treaty (1895). Watts (1966) argued that the term 'federation' in the treaty was a misnomer because there was no real federal principle involved in the so-called federation (Watts 1966: 24). The real goal in the colonial federal design was consolidation of the British grip over the Malayan states through the establishment of a (British) resident-general whose advice in all matters of administration was to be followed (Watts 1966: 24). Watts further argued that, in terms of the treaty, while the native rulers had all the formal powers in their states, in practice 'substantial powers came to be concentrated in the federal secretariat under the Resident-General' (Watts 1966: 24). Thus, as far as the British colonial authorities were concerned, federalism stood for centralization and concentration of powers and not decentralization. The relative autonomy of the 'federating units', that is, the Malay states, did not simply arise, since the latter sacrificed whatever autonomy they had as native rulers. The term 'federation' was thus (mis)used by the colonial authorities as a weapon of colonial expansion and consolidation. The insistence, at considerable pains, of the five other unfederated Malay states – Johore, Kelantan, Trengganu, Kedah and Perlis – which had come under British protection in 1909 and which had witnessed the loss of sovereignty of their colleagues following the federation agreement, on 'independence from joining any inter-Malayan federation' was evidence of the colonial design. The Malay rulers' legal sovereignty that they had so jealously guarded very importantly covered the special protection given to the indigenous Malay ethno-national identity.

The Malayan Union: colonial federalism (April 1946)

The Malayan Union (MU) was the next institutional step that the colonial authorities sought to introduce, comprising the nine Malay states and the two British settlements of Penang and Malaca. The colonial administration's rationale apparently was efficiency in administration (there were as many as ten legislatures in a country slightly larger than England in size!) by bringing the previously mentionedunits under one political unit. This proposal was mooted by the imperial government during the Second World War, and there was little consultation with the local people, who very much resented the MU proposal. The Malays in particular were vehemently opposed to it because the equal-citizenship provisions for all the communities, such as the Malays, the Chinese and the Indians, in the MU went against the privileged status of the Malays, and also because the MU proposal dealt a death-blow to the sovereign status of the native rulers, to whom the common Malays looked for ultimate protection. Many saw in it a step towards further administrative centralization[3] under imperial rule. The provision for equal-citizenship rights, including granting political rights to non-Malays in a country where the indigenous Malays were not yet even in a majority, was of course viewed with apprehension by the Malays.

The Malay anger against the MU proposal served to prepare the basis for a rather powerful Malayan nationalism, which eventually forced the imperial authorities to withdraw the MU proposals. There were large-scale demonstrations, and in March 1946 a Pan-Malayan Malay Congress was held in Kuala Lumpur under the

58 Origin and development of federalism in Asia

leadership of Dato Onn bin Jaafar. The idea of the formation of the United Malay National Organization (UMNO) was mooted at this Congress, and at the Second Congress, held in May 1946, the UMNO came into being under the leadership of Dato Onn bin Jaafar. Interestingly, the UMNO confined its activities largely to matters concerning the position of the rulers and the Malays (Hing 1981: 229–30). It should be particularly pointed out that the UMNO and its English-educated leadership, especially belonging to the civil service, was to begin with an exclusivist Malayan entity that was even prepared to cooperate with the British if that served its Malayan ethnic interests.

It was not very important that the MU proposal was withdrawn, although its equal–citizenship provisions for all communities were a pointer quite early on to a different secular solution to the identity question in a multiracial and ethnic state.[4] All that was revealed, however, by the reactions to the MU proposals was the force of Malay ethnic mobilization and the uncertain basis of intercommunal/racial unity in a future Malaysia.

Federation of Malaya Agreement (1948)

The Federation of Malaya Agreement (1 February 1948) between the British and the UMNO leadership, which provided for a federal constitution, was the last colonial measure of federation-building in Malay. This institutional effort, backed as it was by the Malay leadership, was quite successful, as it formed the basis of the country's transition to independence and further federalization. Ethnically speaking, this so-called federal agreement was in effect a constitutional guarantee for Malayan identity and interests, to the relative exclusion of the Chinese and the Indians. The Malays achieved a lot: recognition of the identity of the Malay states; safeguards for the special position of the Malays; and the highly restrictive citizenship laws, which excluded half the Chinese and Indians from permanent citizenship and restricted their access to certain public goods (Watts 1966: 25). Hing (1981) argues that this 'federal' agreement helped the UMNO to strongly establish itself among the Malay community (Hing 1981: 230).

The specific ethnic content apart, institutionally the constitutional framework was far from being federal. Watts said that it was as 'unitary as the Malayan Union'.[5] For one thing, the central authorities were given powers to legislate on all matters except Malayan religion and customs. The central government was given the power to control the state and settlement governments; there was central control of budgets and a centralized civil service. (Watts 1966: 25) The so-called federal government was centred on the high commissioner, 'who was given full executive authority for the Federal Government' (Means 1976: 57).

During the nine years of life of the federal government (1948–57), while the bulk of state administration was left to the states (that was how a modicum of decentralized state administration was practiced), there was, however, progressive centralization, nonetheless justified, among other reasons because it was able to contain the Communist insurgency (Watts 1966: 25–6).[6] Paradoxical though it may

Origin and development of federalism in Asia **59**

seem, democratization of the central institutions and the leadership of the multi-community Alliance over the federal governmental structures during 1955–57 added to further centralization of powers in the federation.

Post-Independence Federation of Malay (1957–63)

Two distinct phases can be identified in the post-Independence development of federalism in Malay/Malaysia: 1957–63 and the period since 1963. One could even argue that a further period was added to the evolution of federalism in the country when Singapore was attached to the federation from 16 September 1963 to August 1965. Interestingly enough, Singapore's accession to the federation and its eventual expulsion from it was done on political and ethnic grounds.[7]

The first phase of postcolonial federation was inaugurated as a result of the Federation of Malay Agreement, 1957. The federal system was overhauled to some extent, but the powers of the central government were increased rather than decreased. To begin with, the legislative and financial powers were vested in the central government, leaving land, agriculture, forestry, and local government as exclusive state subjects. Unlike the previous arrangement, while the states' legislative powers were increased to some extent, their executive powers were substantially reduced. The central government was, in addition, given powers of control over exclusive state subjects for the purpose of treaty obligations, uniformity of state laws, need for national economic development and of course emergencies. Further, the central government was also given the predominant power to amend the Constitution, which required only special majorities in the Central Legislature.[8] During 1957–63 the federal experiment was a success, which brought about political stability and consolidation of the system. The Alliance, as we have indicated previously (more on it later), was the dominant force in both the levels of government, which meant political stability and increased central authority.

Actually, much more than that, it meant increased Malay confidence in the political institutions, to be precise, the federal ones, which were their own and which the Chinese and the Indians only shared! The passage of the centralized federation was smooth when backed by ethnic peace among its dominant group (i.e. the Malays) in a multi-ethnic country. The brief second phase in the post-Independence development of federalism in Malay (1963–65) was about the accession of Singapore and the North Borneo states of Sarawak and Sabah, and the expulsion of Singapore in 1965. Two different sets of reasons acted upon this expansion of the federation. In the case of Singapore, it was the fear of Communism: Singapore, with its pronounced socialist orientations, was to be taken under protective custody in order to subvert a Communist revolution and to save the federation. Sarawak and Sabah (with a preponderance of Malays and the indigenous people) were taken in order to offset the Malay fears of being swamped by the Chinese in their own land. The same ethnic factor also played a major role in the expulsion of Singapore from the federation. The accession of the these three units led to some substantial changes in the federation by the passing of the Malaysia Act, 1963 (Malay became

60 Origin and development of federalism in Asia

Malaysia from then on). The federation introduced asymmetry in the status of the units in the sense that new states were given considerably more legislative, executive and financial autonomy, and their special interests were safeguarded.

Rise of the Alliance and the development of federalism

The rise of the inter-communal Alliance in Malay in 1951 prior to the local council elections in 1951 has remained till today the strategically most significant event in Malaysian federalism. Born originally as an electoral alliance between the UMNO (a Malayan organization) and the Malayan Chinese Association (MCA) in 1951 in order to defeat the Independence Malayan Party (IMP) of Dato Onn, the Alliance has subsequently expanded itself to include the other community, that is, the Indians, through the joining of their organization, the Malaysian Indian Congress (MIC), and remains the role model for a multiracial/community political platform for electoral and governance purposes even today. Born and developed in and through a situation of growing ethnic tensions and political polarizations often taking on complex ethnic-cum-class lines, the Alliance has defined for itself a centrist yet federal position in the country's political system. Ironically, the IMP of Dato Onn was founded on multiracialism and so was structured to reflect multiracial society – this he wanted to do after having failed to transform the UMNO (whose legendary leader he was until 1951) into a multiracial organization. But the electoral victory of the Alliance in the Kuala Lumpur Municipality and then elsewhere in the country and the concomitant almost total rout of the IMP meant that the inter-communal/racial cooperation of the Alliance was more acceptable to the people than the multi-community/racial cooperation of the IMP. Hing has noted: 'The victory underlined the fact that interracial cooperation was easier to comprehend when individual communal interests were maintained' (Hing 1981: 238).

Added to this was the Alliance's astounding electoral victory in the country's first federal elections to the Legislative Council, held on 27 July 1955, in which it won 51 out of 52 seats contested. The supreme leader of the UMNO and of the Alliance, Tunku Abdul Rahman, became the chief minister. The Alliance's political strength was proved once again, and that too at the national level. The sultans, that is, the native rulers, who had so far been reluctant to accept the reforms and self-government, gradually came round at the instance of the Tunku Rahman to join the forces of independence and to work with the Alliance (Hing 1981: 243). The Alliance's hegemonic position was now assured. The electoral successes of the Alliance and its hegemonic position in the Malayan politics made it the party to negotiate the terms of *merdeka* (Independence) and also enabled it to produce a greater impact on the course of developments up until Independence. The British government was prepared, quite predictably, to hand over the responsibility for internal government to the Alliance, and full Independence came on 31 August 1957.

Before concluding this section, it should be pointed out that the transition from colonial rule to Independence in Malay was federal, democratic, constitutional and peaceful under the hegemonic leadership of the Alliance, something which compares unfavourably with that of India, whose Independence was marked by large-scale communal violence and the partition of the country between India and Pakistan on 14 August 1947. First, remarkably enough, in the case of the Malays, the predominance of the Malayan identity and its special position in the growing state structure was much assured. The institution of Paramount Ruler (although to be elected from among the sultans for a term) was designed to be a symbol of unity, but actually it would symbolize the Malayan character of the new state![9] Second, a federal system had taken shape in Malay since the late nineteenth century under British colonial rule, but there was no or very little question of states' rights or autonomy to defend in the endeavour. It was, on the contrary, an institutional innovation designed from the top to be imposed on the people for the purpose of uniformity in laws, policy and administration, something that is most dear to all administrators, particularly the colonial ones. In fact, the near revolt of the so-called Unfederated Malay States against joining the internal-Malayan union was one powerful indicator that the states were hardly, if at all, interested in the federation. Third, most interestingly, federalism took shape because it was accepted by people belonging to very different communities, more particularly the Malays, who are the indigenous and dominant community. The Malayan leadership saw in the evolving federalism a near-permanent means of safeguarding their privileged identity, special interests and preferential treatment thus far enjoyed under colonialism vis-à-vis other communities such as the Chinese and the Indians. In other words, a symbiosis developed between federalism and ethnic interests, cutting across territorial divisions in an inter-ethnic federation in which the junior partners acquiesced to unequal power-sharing and identity protection! Finally, the crucially strategic role of the Alliance, an inter-communal political platform, at a very critical moment of the country's transition and transformation was not to be underestimated. The Alliance appeared to be operating a prototype of the Malayan federation in securing, on the one hand, the dominant and majority position of the Malays, in demographic and political terms, and on the other hand, in defining the terms of collaboration of the junior partners in the Alliance and the federation. The Alliance's hegemonic leadership, which effectively meant the dominance of the UMNO, which incidentally had to grapple continuously with communal tensions within the Alliance, eventually became the *sine qua non* of the further development of federalism in Malay/Malaysia.

India

Compared with Malay/Malaysia, India's initial encounters with federalism were much more complex. While in Malaysia the development of federalism has facilitated the construction of Malayan hegemony in politics, the economy and society, the same cannot be said to be true for any specific community in India. In India, on the contrary, various ethno-national groups have, in fact, benefited, at least since Independence, from federalism. Federalism's ethno-national orientations in India have been and still remain, however, the most complex. Although federalism, institutionally

62 Origin and development of federalism in Asia

speaking, began to take shape in India in the early 1920s – in and through the demands for decentralization and the colonial authorities' doses of devolution for the same purpose – the origin, meaning and the development of the federal idea in India had had a complex trajectory. For one thing, the country's intellectual tradition and the ongoing nationalist movements (including nationalist thought) were favourable for federalism. Its varied and often inchoate articulations notwithstanding, the Indian nationalists were quite resistant to the British colonial method of federalism and most often rejected the latter. But the federal idea itself was taken on differently, and often incorrectly. Sumit Sarkar shows that Bipin Chandra Pal, a leading militant nationalist leader of Bengal, argued way back in 1905 (long before the British federal schemes were floated!) that India's autonomy 'presupposes the autonomy of every race and community in India itself', a federation comprising different religious communities. Earlier in the late nineteenth century, Bhudev Mukhopadhyay, a nationalist thinker who pioneered, so to say, a distinct trajectory of nationalist thought in defence of unity-in-diversity, recognized India's complex diversity:

> India is a sub-continent. It has seas and mountains, fertile lands and hills, plateau and valley, watery provinces and land-locked ones, all possible naturally given regions – it is like a world unto itself. As result, this has given India its distinctive identity, and her inhabitants bear the imprint of the same. Her inhabitants are not narrow-minded, but very tolerant *(udar)* by nature. Despite all the differences existing among peoples of different provinces, all are wonderfully tolerant *(udar)*. The Indians are more capable of accepting others as their kind than any other nation on earth. Her famous poets of different regions have condemned discrimination and exclusion and praised tolerance. Indians are hospitable so much so that the foreign travellers without a penny can travel around the country.[10]

This passage composed by an otherwise known 'conservative' social thinker was also symptomatic of the culture of tolerance that existed in India, which could 'accept others as their kind' rather than further 'othering' them, as was the practice in standard Orientalist thought. This pre-existing culture of recognition of diversity in India that Bhudev was concerned about was quintessentially a federal culture. While many other thinkers of modern India recognized the country's manifold diversity and emphasized unity simultaneously, Jawaharlal Nehru was representative of the most articulate sections in this regard.[11] Consider the two following significant passages written by Nehru:

> A kind of multicommunity state was built up, in which within certain limits and subject to some general rules, freedom was given to each group to follow its avocation and live its own life in accordance with its own custom or desires.
>
> *(Nehru 1980/1946: 247)*

That was how Nehru understood the rise of the state in ancient India after the arrival of the Aryans in India. Explaining further the traits of this state, Nehru mentioned that the entire social fabric was based on the notion of the group and not the individual, and that aim was social security, stability and continuance of the group (Nehru 1980/1946: 247).

The following passage dealt directly with India's manifold diversity, its recognition, and unity:

> The diversity of India is tremendous; it is obvious. It lies on the surface and anybody can see it. It concerns itself with physical appearances as well as with certain mental habits and traits. Yet, with all these differences, there is no mistaking the impress of India on the Pathans, as this is obvious on the Tamils. The Pathans and the Tamils are two extreme examples; others lie somewhere in between. All of them have their distinctive features; all of them have still more the distinguishing mark of India. It is fascinating to find how the Bengalis, the Marathas, the Gujeratis, the Tamils, the Andhras, the Oriyas, the Assamese, the Sindhis, the Punjabis . . . have retained their peculiar characteristics for hundreds of years, have still more or less the same virtues and failures of which old tradition or record tells us, yet have been throughout these ages distinctively Indian, with the same national heritage and the same set of moral and mental qualities.
>
> *(Nehru 1980/1946: 255)*

This passage in particular is a remarkable example of a tolerant approach to socio-cultural diversity and its recognition, and it has served to prepare the basis of a much required federal culture. Nowhere in the passage was any hint of any majoritarian bias, whether of religious or linguistic character. On the contrary, there is a sense of equality in Nehru's treatment of various ethno-national groups such as the Bengalis, the Gujaratis and the Tamils. The basic argument that is being made here is that in India there grew prior to Independence a distinct body of social and political thought that seemed to advocate federal solutions to India's problem of national unity out of diversity. In the case of Jawaharlal Nehru, India's first prime minister, it was more than mere thought: it was practical advice that he regularly gave to chief ministers in the art of governance of a multicultural mosaic. For instance, in his famous *Letters to Chief Ministers* he cautioned the Assam chief minister in the early 1950s with regard to aboriginal people in the state:

> It is difficult to treat them by some single formula because they differ greatly among themselves. It seems obviously undesirable to deny them some kind of self-government or autonomy[12]

Nehru was therefore vehemently opposed to any attempt at homogenization of different specific people. He wrote at length on the issue:

> There is a tendency in Assam for what is called integration of these tribes and for establishment of a homogenous state. This really means merging in a cultural and the like sense the tribal people into the Assamese. I think that

64 Origin and development of federalism in Asia

this is not a desirable movement and instead of achieving its objectives will lead to conflicts and difficulties.[13]

The above tolerant and federal approach to identity and differences was not merely the nationalist legacy. The post-Independence India does not seem to have deviated from her time-honoured accommodating approach to differences. Consider the following remarks of Mr R. K. Narayanan, former president of India, who wrote (1998) at length of the nature of India's nationhood:

> But, at the same time, we have come to realize that nationhood has different depths of meaning and varying levels. It contains both abstractions as well as particularisms. For every citizen, India means a country as well as a region; a region as well as a neighbourhood and a locality. It means a language as well as a dialect. . . . This bifocal perception of the distant and the near, the general and the specific, has made India's nation-building a unique and fascinating exercise. Given our continental proportions, diversity of race, languages, regions, our history and our past experience in nation-building during the five decades of independence, India could not but have acquired federal features. Unlike most other nations, we are not built around a single race, language or religion.[14]

The established scholars of federalism (e.g. Wheare 1953; Watts 1966, 1999, 2008; Elazar 1987; Livingstone 1956) have argued that federalism sustains itself in a cultural milieu marked by the 'explicit recognition of multiple identities and loyalties, and an overarching sense of shared purposes and objectives' among the public. Our very brief outline of India's 'federal' thought here is a proof that the required cultural milieu was not lacking in India.

Institutionalization of federalism in the colonial period

Institutional development of federalism in colonial India began to take shape in the early 1920s through doses of devolution, although hedged around with a lot of limitations within a highly centralized bureaucratized state structure. Morris-Jones (1987: 19) argued that the movements for self-government, not typically a federal theme, also contributed to the growth of federalism in India. As far as the British were concerned, the federal ideas were ambiguous, 'mixed with ideas about decentralization', and there were 'to-and-fro movements in the emergence of the federal themes' (Morris-Jones 1987: 19). Since the passage of the regulating Act of 1773, which created the three Presidencies of Calcutta, Bombay and Madras, independent of each other and separately related to the directors of the East India Company in London, the passage of colonial rule in India was through successive major legislation – the Acts of 1784, 1833 and finally 1858, when the Crown took over the Indian government from the East India Company – of increasing centralization of powers and authority. Morris-Jones commented that the colonial government was

Origin and development of federalism in Asia   **65**

'as centralized as it could be without being unworkable' (Morris-Jones 1987: 19). Quite naturally, the loud voices of reform, of decentralization and Indianization of the administration arose in the land, backed by a growing nationalist movement. The colonial governmental responses were lukewarm, serving up patchy and very inadequate reforms. For instance, the Commission on Decentralization (1909) only provided for administrative decentralization, to the exclusion of the financial and political, and whatever it provided for was more on paper than real. The Act of 1919 is said to have plugged many loopholes by carving out a range of 'transferred subjects' suitable for entrusting to ministers accountable to elected provincial legislatures and a balance of 'reserved' subjects left in the hands of officials under the governors. This scheme of 'dyarchy' required a preliminary relaxation of control by the central government (Morris-Jones 1987: 19). Morris-Jones cautioned us not to see this 'relaxation of control' as implying federalism in any sense but merely as a devolutionary measure. Be that as it may, the pre-1935 Constitutional reforms were far too short of any decentralization, let alone federalism, but they set in motion a process which was taken further by the Government of India Act, 1935 (itself based on the British North America Act, 1867). According to Morris-Jones, the Government of India Act 1935 'pointed firmly in the direction of federalism' (Morris-Jones 1987: 19). Watts says that from 1861, and more particularly after 1919 (Government of India Act, 1919), the history of British India was 'one of gradual devolution of power to the provinces, as administrators', the objectives being solution of the communal problems (mostly between the Hindus and the Muslims) and maintenance of contact with the subjects (Watts 1966: 17). But as we have seen already, the limited devolution took place within a unitary and centralized central state authority. However, the colonial authorities were coming round to the idea of a future federation for India being unavoidable. The Indian Statutory Commission (1929), for instance, admitted: 'The ultimate Constitution of India must be federal, for it is only in a federal constitution that units differing so widely in constitution as the provinces and the States can be brought together while retaining internal autonomy' (Ramasubramanium 1992: 116).[15]

Paradoxical though it may seem, the Government of India Act, 1935, which committed the government of India to a federation for the first time and which was also rejected by the Indian nationalists, was to become the foundation of the Constitution of India after Independence. The colonial motive behind this federation was 'unity'[16] of what was called two Indias, namely, British India, the directly ruled 11 provinces (which were experimenting with some degree of representative institutions), and about 560 princely autocracies (indirectly ruled) spread all over India under one political authority. The latter, greatly varied in size and complexion, comprised about two-thirds of the territory of India and about a quarter of the population of India. There were Hindu, Muslim and Sikh rulers. These rulers were without exception the most solid bases of support for British colonialism in India. Quite predictably, the anti-colonial democratic movements in the princedoms were not allowed in the states, and the Indian National Congress, the main party of India's independence, which was otherwise hostile to the princes' autocracy, did

66 Origin and development of federalism in Asia

not pay any important attention to the princely states for the purpose of mobilization before the Haripura Congress of 1938.

Main features[17] of the colonial federation (1935): institutionalization of communalism

The Government of India Act, 1935 (passed in the British Parliament) proposed for the first time a 'federation' for India; however, it was only partially implemented, and that too at the provincial level only since April 1937.

First, it prescribed a federation in which the provinces and the Indian states were taken as units. But then it was proposed too that it was optional for the states to join the federation and that the federation would only come into being after they had joined. The fact of the matter was that they did not join!

Second, there was provision for provincial autonomy, legislatively and administratively speaking. Powers were distributed between the provincial and central legislatures in terms of three lists, and the provinces were no longer considered as delegates of the central government, as before. The existing government of India assumed the role of the federal government vis-à-vis the provincial government. The provincial autonomy was put into effect in April 1937.

Third, the three Lists, namely, Federal, Provincial and Concurrent, distributed powers among two sets of governments, with the provision that the federal government would have exclusive jurisdiction over matters in the Federal List, the provincial government would have exclusive jurisdiction over matters in the Provincial List and that both the governments would have competence over the Concurrent List. However, legislatively speaking, the central government was given overriding powers over both the Provincial and the Concurrent Lists in exceptional circumstances such as the Emergency. In addition, the supremacy of the central legislation over provincial legislation was also assured in the case of any conflict over matters in the Concurrent List. On residual matters, the governor-general was empowered to authorize either the central or the provincial legislature to enact a law on such matters.

Fourth, at the provincial level, all executive authority was to be exercised by the governor, who would act on behalf of the Crown and on the advice of the ministers responsible to the legislature. But there was a provision of the governor to act on his or her discretion in certain matters not requiring the advice of the ministers, but under the control and direction of the governor-general.

Fifth, the executive authority of the central government was vested in the governor-general, who would act on behalf of the Crown and administer in reserved matters concerning defence, external affairs, tribal matters etc. 'in his discretion' with the help of counsellors appointed by him or her and who were not responsible to the central legislature. In other matters, he or she was to act on the advice of the Council of Ministers responsible to the legislature. But even here, he might act contrary to the advice of the Council of Ministers, in the role's 'special responsibilities'. The fact was that since the central part of the federation did not materialize, the old Executive Council as per the Act of 1919 continued until India's Independence!

It was beyond doubt that the proposed federation was highly centralized and inadequate. Envisaged in the growing communal discord between the Hindus and the Muslims and the so-called Ramsay MacDonald (the then British Prime Minister) Award ('Communal Award) of 4 August 1932 (that recognized the role of two religious communities in arriving at any future political settlement for India and provided for separate electoral representation for the Muslims, the Sikhs, the Europeans, Indian Christians and Anglo-Indians), the federal proposals were apparently meant to unify the various religious communities, particularly the Hindus and the Muslims, within a united India. But they failed on all accounts. The proposals were communally divisive because they provided for communal representation rather than universal suffrage. Also, it was a far cry from democracy, since the autocratic princes were considered to be partners in the federation. The idea of a federation consisting of units in half of which representative institutions were developing to a limited extent (the 11 provinces) and the other half in which a medieval autocracy was reigning supreme (the princely regimes) was simply ludicrous and suspect. The princes' refusal to join the federation added to its failure, nonetheless. Jawaharlal Nehru's trenchant critique of the Act was symptomatic of the standard Indian nationalist reaction:

> The Act provided for some kind of Provincial autonomy and a Federal Structure but there were so many reservations and checks that both political and economic power continued to be concentrated in the hands of the British Government. The Federal Structure was so envisaged as to make any real advance impossible. Thus, reactionary as this structure was, there were not even any seeds in it of self-government. The Act strengthened the alliance between the Government and the Princes, landlords and other reactionary elements in India . . . it retained in British hands complete control over Indian finances, military and foreign affairs, it made the Viceroy even more powerful than he had been.[18]

The democratic deficit apart, the federal scheme also lacked a real ethno-national content. The colonial authorities' idea of federalism was an institutional device to apparently solve the communal problems that were growing in the country, but the provision for separate communal representation in elections to the legislatures opened up institutional avenues for communalism, which would not augur well for the unity and integrity of the country in the following decade. The important point to consider here is that this so-called federal scheme was a colonial imposition from above rather than the result of agreement among the federating units for a union. The directly ruled 11 provinces, extremely heterogeneous in complexion and themselves the creations of the British colonial authorities for purely administrative purposes, did not have the kind of identity consciousness that one would have expected in desiring a union (as one witnessed in the case of the US states in

68 Origin and development of federalism in Asia

Philadelphia (1787) or the Swiss cantons). One major proof of this was the debate in the Constituent Assembly (CA) of India (1946–49) on state or provincial autonomy in the future Constitution of India. The CA debates, indeed, did not witness any deep-seated conflict of interests; on the contrary, there was a virtual absence of conflict between the centralists and the provincialists. Interestingly enough, the provincialists demanded increased revenues for the provinces but agreed that the (Union) central government should collect the money and then distribute it among the units. 'This', said Granville Austin, a famous expert on the Indian Constitution, 'could hardly be called a traditional defence of provincial autonomy' (Austin 1966: 187, 1999). That the states' rights issue in the CA was secondary and the provincial loyalties were muted was proof of the heterogeneous complexion of the provinces. However, a great deal of sentiment in favour of administrative decentralization was advocated by the provincial politicians present in the CA who had first tasted political power in the provinces in the late 1930s and who had resisted any tight centralization. But then they did not advocate for states' rights in the CA as a group (Morris-Jones 1957: 17). The right-sizing of the provinces – or the states, as they would be known after 1950 – ethno-nationally speaking, for the purpose of federalization of the highly centralized postcolonial state, would require, as we will see later, many reorganizations, the adjustment of boundaries, the creation of new states and so on.

The problems with the princes, the unwilling partners in the proposed federation, were of a different magnitude. The bulwarks of British colonialism in India, these medieval autocracies were not, by and large, willing to part with their autonomy and their so-called internal sovereignty for the sake of joining the federation. At the Round Table Conferences in London for the reforms of 1935, the Maharaja of Bikaner, broadly representing the princely views, stated on 1 December 1930 that:

> our willingness to consider Federation is subject to two essential and broad conditions, namely:
>
> 1 That India retains the British connection as an equal partner in the British Commonwealth of Nations; and
> 2 That an equitable agreement is reached between all the parties concerned to govern relations of the two India's – ensuring for the States their due position in the future constitution as co-equal partners with British India, guaranteeing their Treaties and internal sovereignty, and safeguarding their interests, including those of their subjects.[19]

However, had the princes joined the federation, as per the terms of the act, the INC and the Muslim League would not have accepted it. It should, of course, be pointed out here that Jinnah had no problems in accepting the 'Communal Award' (1932) that had provided for separate communal electorate and reservation of seats in the legislature and also the 'provincial autonomy' part of the 1935 Federation – a view which was at variance with the Congress's stand for rejection of the same *in toto*.[20]

The Cabinet Mission Plan (16 May 1946): the last colonial federalism

The Cabinet Mission Plan was the last British colonial institutional measure for the future Constitution of India, advanced at a critical juncture of post-war India's tumultuous route to Independence via the partition of the country between India and Pakistan. Like many previous colonial measures, the special safeguards for the 'minority' Muslim communities and the anxiety of the latter lest they be dominated by the 'Hindu majority' in a united India preoccupied the minds of the members. The Mission also took full cognizance of the demand of the Muslim League for a Pakistan consisting of the provinces of Punjab, Sindh, the North-West Frontier, British Baluchistan and the provinces of Bengal and Assam. The Mission noted carefully the main basis of the demand for a separate state of Pakistan:

> The argument for a separate state of Pakistan was based, first, upon, the right of the Muslim majority to decide their method of government according to their wishes, and, secondly, upon the necessity to include substantial areas in which Muslims are in a minority, in order to make Pakistan administratively and economically workable.[21]

But then the Mission also took note of the realities on the ground and found little to support the claim for Pakistan. Statistically, the Mission was overwhelmed by the 'very considerable' size of the non-Muslim population in all six provinces demanded by Pakistan: 37.93 per cent in the north-western area, and 48 per cent in the north-eastern area! The Mission thus came to the conclusion that:

> These figures show that setting up of a separate sovereign state of Pakistan on the lines claimed by the Muslim League would not solve the communal problem; nor can we see any justification for including within a sovereign Pakistan those districts of the Punjab and of Bengal and Assam in which the population is predominantly non-Muslims.
>
> *(Char 1983: 685–6)*

The Mission forcefully asserted:

> Every argument that can be used in favour of Pakistan can equally, in our view, be used in favour of the exclusion of the non-Muslim areas from Pakistan. . . . We have therefore been forced to the conclusion that neither a larger nor a smaller sovereign state of Pakistan would provide an acceptable solution for the communal problem.[22]

The Cabinet Mission finally could not recommend to the British government that the power should be handed over to two entirely separate sovereign states. Instead its concrete recommendations consisted, among others, of the following:

1   There should be a Union of India comprising both British India and the princely states, to deal with powers such as foreign affairs, defence and

70 Origin and development of federalism in Asia

communications and those powers to raise finances that are required for the above purposes;

2 All subjects other than the Union subjects and all residuary powers should be vested in the provinces;

3 The states will retain all subjects and powers other those not ceded to the Union;

4 There should be provisions for representation from British India, the states, and two major communities along with their veto powers, in the Union Legislature and the Executive, and so on (Char 1983: 687–9).

The Cabinet Mission Plans were hotly debated among the parties in India, each representing different communities singly or collectively. The Mission's proposal for a 'Union' with a 'weak Centre and strong provinces' did not find favour among many, most notably the INC. Eventually, the Mission proposals failed, since India was heading inevitably for Partition on 14 August 1947.

The Muslim League's position on federalism

The approach of the Muslim League (formed in 1906, which eventually demanded a separate state of Pakistan and successfully achieved one on 14 August 1947 after the Partition of India) to federalism in this connection requires some further discussion. Jinnah, the supreme leader of the League, was for quite some time after 1929 an advocate of federalism in India as a solution to the problems of the minorities. One of his famous 'Fourteen Points' (28 March 1929), declared that '[The] form of the future Constitution of India should be federal with residuary powers vested in the Provinces'; and '[A] uniform measure of autonomy shall be granted to all provinces', etc., so that there were adequate safeguards for the Muslims' interests in governing institutions of the state (Char 1983: 550–2). He did accept the need for 'territorial redistribution' of the provinces in future, but not at the cost of affecting the 'Muslim majority in the Punjab, Bengal and the North West Frontier Province' (Char 1983: 551). Reading between the lines of the rest of his 'Fourteen Points', one easily gets the sense that the interests of the Muslims kept him fully preoccupied in his federation plan. Consider Point 13: 'No Cabinet, either Central or Provincial, should be formed without there being a proportion of at least one-third Muslim Ministers' (Char 1983: 551). The League's partial acceptance of the federation proposal, as per the Government of India Act, 1935, as we have already seen, was also communally determined. However, the League would distance itself completely from federalism after its dismal electoral performance in the elections held in 1937 to constitute the provincial legislatures. The Muslim League could not secure a majority in any of the Muslim-majority provinces such as Bengal, the Punjab, Sindh and the North-West Frontier Province where the Muslims were at best in a dominant position although belonging to different groups and parties.[23] Banerjee commented: 'Politically speaking, the Muslims had no unity' (Banerjee 1978: 165).[24] At the famous Lahore Session of the Muslim League (24

March 1940), the League completely dissociated itself from the federation plan and demanded that Pakistan should exit from India. With a complete U-turn, this was resolved at the session:

> This session of the All-India Muslim League emphatically reiterates that the scheme of Federation embodied in the Government of India Act, 1935, is totally unsuited to and unworkable in the peculiar conditions of this country, and is altogether unacceptable to Muslim India.
>
> *(Philips 1963: 354)*

This was concealing one very significant political fact for the demand for a Pakistani state and also for federalism in Pakistan in future. The Muslim League's demands for Pakistan did not have much support in the Punjab and Bengal, where even the Muslim leaders remained, to quote Jaffrelot (2002a), 'hostile to the plans of the Muslim League' (Jaffrelot 2002a: 12).

Tariq Ali (1983) has reported that historically the Muslim League had weak bases even in West Pakistan (Ali 1983: 41–3). The Punjabi landlords were extremely hostile to the League; the Baluchs had hardly heard of the League and were never asked for their consent to be part of a new state; in the NWFP, the League was a novelty; and in Sindh, the League had grown into a 'house divided' between the landlords and their opponents (Ali 1983: 42). More than anybody else, Jinnah was painfully aware of the dilemmas and various inconsistencies of the foundation of the proposed state of Pakistan. He eventually relied heavily on the civil service of Pakistan, born of the Indian civil service, as his 'only political party' (Ali 1983: 42). The 'irrationality of the state of Pakistan' perhaps pushed him to look for a different, surprisingly and paradoxically, secular basis for state legitimacy. Consider his famous speech at the Constituent Assembly of Pakistan on 11 August 1947, which dealt, as it were, the death-blow to the Islamic foundation of Pakistan:

> You are free; you are free to go to your temples; you are free to go to your mosques or to any other place of worship in this State of Pakistan. You may belong to any religion or caste or creed – that has nothing to do with the business of the State. . . . We are starting with this fundamental principle that we are all citizens and equal citizens of one State. Now I think we should keep that in front of us as our ideal and you will find that in the course of time Hindus would cease to be Hindus and the Muslims would cease to be Muslims, not in the religious sense, because that is the personal faith of each individual, but in the political sense as citizens of the State.
>
> *(Ali 1983: 42)*

That apart, East Bengal, predominantly Muslim-inhabited, was not part of the original conception of Pakistan, either of Muhammad Iqbal or of Chaudhri Rehmat Ali. In Iqbal's famous Presidential Address at the Muslim League (1930), the regions envisioned are today's Pakistan. In the latter, the word Pakistan stood for an

72 Origin and development of federalism in Asia

abbreviation of a territorial reality: 'P' for Punjab; 'A' for Afghan (i.e. the Pathans in the NWFP); 'K' for Kashmir; 'S' for Sindh; and 'Tan' for Baluchistan (Jaffrelot 2002a: 12). In the famous Lahore Resolution of the Muslim League (March 1940), East Bengal's name also remained unacknowledged. East Bengali Muslims also did not really feel that they were in tune with the idea of a nation styled Pakistan. Jaffrelot believed that the so-called two-nation theory was superimposed on the strong regional feelings in East Bengal. Consider, for instance, the following Presidential Address of the Bengali Muslim League delivered by Abdul Mansur Ahmed in 1944:

> Religion and culture are not the same thing. Religion transgresses the geographical boundary, but *tamaddum* (culture) cannot go beyond the geographical boundary. . . . For this reason the people of Purba (East) Pakistan are a different nation from the people of the other provinces of India and from the 'religious brothers of Pakistan'.
>
> *(Jaffrelot 2002a: 14)*

That was enough early indication of the very weak cultural foundation of the proposed state of Pakistan, as well as the deep-seated ethno-regional concern for identity in East Bengal.

Federalism as an Indian nationalist legacy

The INC's rejection of the British colonial federal proposals in favour of its own alternative ones, the incorporation of the same in the agenda of the nationalist movements and the (somewhat) federal reorganization of the party itself in the same light deserve closer examination. The latter not only prepared the basis for subsequent constitutional arrangements for federalism but also democratically engulfed the people at large in the struggle for liberation and decolonization. Additionally, this had also ensured sound bases of support for the INC even a long time prior to Independence. Sumit Sarkar, a leading historian of India who dismissed outright any claims for colonial legacy in such areas as democracy, secularism and federalism in India, thus remarked:

> The connections between the imperatives of united mass anti-colonial struggles and the specific, federal, and secular form of democracy of Indian democracy in fact need to be explored much more than they have been so far. Indian federalism is often grounded, in over-formal ways, in late colonial British constitutional experiments.
>
> *(Sarkar 2001: 30)*

There are scholars who have failed, however, to perceive any long-term and genuine grounds for federalism in India beyond the immediate political situation. Consider the following statement on the study of the Constituent Assembly debates

Origin and development of federalism in Asia **73**

in India: 'Once the communal problem and the problem of integration of the Princely States had disappeared after partition, the "federal situation" had virtually evaporated with it' (Bhattacharyya, M. (1992).[25] Ironically, the colonial authorities and the Muslim League also tended to view federalism in that light! The fact of the matter was that the founding fathers nonetheless adopted a federal constitution for India, and so there were longstanding factors for the same beyond Partition and the integration of the princely states. Also, it needs to be clearly stated that, first, there was nothing federal about the demand for a Pakistani state (Jinnah himself was not sure about it!), and second, the integration of the princely states was not an example of federalization. In other words, the 'federal situation' had existed in India to a great extent and needed to be taken into consideration from early on.

From around the late nineteenth century, the Indian nationalists became aware that the ethno-linguistic diversity of India would need institutional solutions. This is around the time of the rise of the INC, if not before. The federalists among the Indians will remain indebted to Lokamanya Bal Gangahdhar Tilak, the Maharash-trian leader, for articulating a defence of federalism in India as early as 1891 on the basis of linguistic units. In the newspaper that he edited, titled *Kesari* (17 November 1981), he wrote:

> The present administrative division of India is the result of certain historic processes, and in some cases, purely the result of accident . . . if they are replaced by units formed on a linguistic basis, each of them will have some measure of homogeneity and will provide encouragement to the people and languages of the respective regions.[26]

That in effect set the tone of subsequent nationalist thinking on the issue. The INC actually grew out of many region-based political associations which were crucial for taking its views down to the people in the regions concerned (Das Gupta 2001: 51). As one recent researcher has argued, the INC 'initially served as an inter-regional coalition engaged in carefully generating a composite sense of national becoming' (Das Gupta 2001: 51).[27] Majumdar and Majumdar (1965), in their study of the Congress in the pre-Gandhian days, reported that after about a decade of the formation of the INC, some important leaders of the party visiting England to promote a nationalist demand for a greater share of the Indians in administration chose to identify themselves in a public statement as representatives of the regional associations based in different parts of India (Das Gupta 2001: 51). This regional orientation did not, however, make the party regionalist. On the contrary, this indicated the unavoidable objective compulsions under which a pan-Indian path to liberation and unity had to be worked out. The INC's resoluteness in going by the linguistic principle without compromising administrative efficiency was proven in its anti-Partition of Bengal movement post-1905 (the plan was revoked in 1911 under nationalist pressures by the British colonial authorities.) At its 21st Session in 1905 in Benares, the INC resolved: 'Congress recommends the adoption of some arrangement which would be consistent with administrative efficiency and would

74 Origin and development of federalism in Asia

place the entire Bengali community under one undivided administration'.[28] From the beginning of the twentieth century, the INC began to subject itself to a kind of federalization and thus reorganize itself along linguistic lines, defying the administrative boundaries created by the colonial masters. Beginning with a new Bihar Provincial Committee in 1908, its organizational overhaul went on, with as many as 21 vernacular units as 'Provincial Congress Committees'. A separate Andhra Circle and a separate Sindh Circle were created in 1917 and 1918 respectively.[29]

This major organizational shift in the INC was indicative of the major shift in Congress politics from an otherwise English-educated élite-led body to a mass organization under the leadership of Mahatma Gandhi. Gandhi would launch a major non-cooperation campaign in 1920, the same year in which the INC would also formally endorse its commitment to federal India based on the linguistically reorganized states at the Nagpur Session after Independence. As Partha Chatterjee (Chatterjee 2000: 74) has pointed out, the party's vernacular turn on the eve of the mass campaign of non-cooperation was not just an organizational affair but immensely significant, because the regional languages were to provide a much-needed means of communication below the provincial levels. Chatterjee has convincingly argued that this move was at once democratic and anti-colonial because it paved the way for the involvement of the linguistic groups in the arena of anti-colonial struggle (Chatterjee 2000: 74–5).

The INC's federal turn was gradually articulated within the discourse of the party from the beginning of the twentieth century. Dr Anne Besant's Presidential Address at the Calcutta Congress in 1917 was one instance:

> There is much work to do in helping the people to prepare themselves for the new powers, which will be placed in their hands. And for this, the work must be done in the vernacular of each Province, as only by their mother-tongue can the heart and brain of the masses be reached. Sooner or later, preferably sooner, Provinces will have to be delimited on a linguistic basis.
>
> *(quoted in Bhattacharyya 2008: 182)*

Since its formal endorsement at Nagpur in 1920, the issue of linguistic states for a reconstituted federal India after Independence remained very much alive as an agenda for the nationalist movement of the INC. The INC continuously emphasized the democratic basis of the linguistic identity of the people and asserted its commitment to linguistic provinces. Consider the following passage in the Nehru (Motilal) Committee Report of the INC (1928):

> Partly geographical and partly economic and financial, but the main considerations must necessarily be the wishes of the people and linguistic unity of the area concerned. It is well recognized that rapid progress in education as well as in general culture and in most departments of life depends on language. . . . No democracy can exist where a foreign language is used for the purposes. . . . So far as the provinces are concerned, this must be the

Origin and development of federalism in Asia **75**

provincial language. If a province has to educate itself and do its daily work through the medium of its own language, it must necessarily be a linguistic area. If it happens to be a polyglot area, difficulties will continually arise and the media of instruction and work will be two or even more languages. Hence it becomes most desirable for provinces be regrouped on a linguistic basis.

(Bhattacharyya 2008: 182)

The INC's commitment to an ethno-linguistic federalism for India entailed the following principles having larger implications. First, it was emphasized by the INC that the wishes of the people were to be the governing factor in determining linguistic redistribution. Second, in the party's understanding, the matter was not simply linguistic but involved 'a special variety of culture, of traditions and literature' – in other words, a distinct ethno-linguistic identity. Third, it was linked to self-determination of the people, to which the INC was committed for the whole of India, but not neglecting the same issue writ small. It was stated in the Nehru Committee Report (1928) that:

We who talk of self-determination on a larger scale cannot in reason deny it to smaller area, provided of course this does not conflict with any other important principle or vital question. The mere fact that the people living in a particular area feel that they are a unit and desire to develop their culture is an important consideration even if there may be no sufficient historical or cultural justification for their demand. Sentiment in such matters is often more important than fact. Finally, administrative convenience was also considered by the INC, but then such issues as geographical position, the economic resources and the financial stability of the area were thought to be a matter of arrangement, but 'must as a rule bow to the wishes to the people'.[30]

These were not merely the pious promises and sacred words on paper but were taken down to the people, and action was also taken. For example, as per the recommendations of the Nehru Committee Report, a separate Karnataka Provincial Committee comprising the Kannada-speaking areas of the Presidencies of Bombay and Madras and a Sindh Provincial Committee carved out of the Bombay Province were both created by the INC (Char 1983: 547).

In the end, the INC's approach to federalism was intertwined with nationhood in India at various levels. Its advocacy for the principle of self-determination, even of smaller linguistic groups, through federalism, was of course linked to democracy and thus also contained a civic dimension. The Congress's identification with ethno-linguistic federalism and self-determination, as briefly mentioned earlier, was actually a recognition accorded to already awakening nationality groups in various parts of India, who became, as Desai reported, 'politically aware' by the urge of self-determination: 'The movements of those nationalities were inspired by the urge for self-determination, by their will to live and develop their life as freely

76 Origin and development of federalism in Asia

as distinct nationality'.[31] Thus, the Indian federal situation was much more deeply rooted and inseparable from nationhood and democracy. The radical alternative nationalist legacy that was built for a true solution of the problem was far removed from the various colonial measures, which were short-sighted, communally divisive and anti-democratic.

Nepal

Federalism arrived very late in Nepal and is very young.[32] By the time Nepal adopted and inaugurated its Constitution on 20 September 2015 and declared itself as a 'federal democratic and secular republic', the federal idea had been part of the public and political debate for more than two decades. Despite Nepal's immense ethnic diversity, an oligarchy in the shape of various monarchies and others ruled over the country for two and a half centuries as a unitary and heavily centralized state and concentrated all powers in Kathmandu, the capital. Nonetheless, an idea of federalism and a federal future for Nepal gained some ground and momentum since the 1990s, and more particularly in the wake of the decade-long Maoist armed struggle (Jana Andolan 1 and 2, 1996–2006) and the growing demands (articulated by many ethnic groups and parties) for recognition of ethnic identity and autonomy. The interim Constitution of 1990 opened up some space for contestation around ethnic demands and autonomy by declaring Nepal as a multi-ethnic country (Lawoti 2012: 135). Historically speaking, the first and real credit must be given to the (Maoist) People's War for bringing federalism to the forefront of public discourse in Nepal (Malagodi 2019: 161). The Maoists took serious note of the special importance of ethnicity in Nepal, not because they were and still are ethnically oriented parties but because the ethnic minorities and lower caste people had borne the brunt of class and ethnic exploitation, exclusion and marginalization in Nepal. Such peoples were the victims of the worst feudal class exploitation as well as manifold social and cultural discrimination. This has been well examined in the existing writings about Nepal's transition in the context of its complex but discriminatory social structure.[33] Not untypically, the ethnic issues in Nepal appeared to be the issue of the 'oppressed nationalities' in the Leninist lexicon. The Maoists had already endorsed 'ethnic autonomy' in Nepal in July 1995 (Asia Report No. 1999, 2011: 6). The detailed empirical data collected in *Asia Report* (2011) on the issue show that the Maoists (Communist Party of Nepal-Maoist, or CPIN-M) from then on formulated a clear 'policy on the nationalities by endorsing national and regional autonomy within the right to self-determination' (Asia Report 1999: 6). It is further reported that the CPIN-M set up a central level ethnic department as a multi-ethnic front (Asia Report 1999: 6).

What in practice that would imply was territorial autonomy to such groups and democratic protection of their identity where they are not territorially rooted (Malagodi 2019). Interestingly, the federal debate in Nepal[34] was considered as an option for resolving many problems: ethnic provinces; language rights of ethnic minorities; citizenship rights to be granted to the Indians in the Terai region;

Origin and development of federalism in Asia **77**

regional and ethnic autonomy for smaller communities; and so on. To be sure, federalism was not and could not be the panacea for all ills; some other problems required a democratic solution.

In Nepal's subsequent constitutional developments with the 1st and 2nd Constituent Assemblies (2008–12 and 2013–15), the appropriate nature of federalism to be adopted remained a matter of debate between those who supported an ethnic federalism and those who opposed it (Malagodi 2019: 161–2). The real hurdle to any federal and democratic transition to Nepal was a hardened power structure: heavily unitary and centralized, dominated by the high caste *Pahariyas* (Chettris, Brahmins and Newars), which ensured the dominance of Hinduism, the Nepali language, and caste and ethnic discrimination; it was an oligarchy that Nepal lived with for many centuries despite changes in the monarchy. In Nepal, discrimination was manifold: linguistic, social and cultural as well as economic, so that the demands for social inclusion, equality, identity and participation became the rallying points for all parties, most notably the Maoist and other left parties in their opposition to the regime and for a constitutional restructuring agenda. Although the Interim Constitution 1990 declared Nepal as a multi-ethnic state, that was merely a declaration, as nothing changed on the ground, and the state continued to remain as it had been always: highly centralized, Hindu, discriminatory (along several lines) and so on. And yet the country housed many nationalities, indigenous and others, and district ethnic groups not on the basis of equality but inequality and discrimination. So the ethnic resentment was deep-seated. While many ethnic groups and parties took up the issues in protest, the Maoists' 'espousal of the right of self-determination and ethnic autonomy, and formed many ethnic fronts under their leadership (Lawoti 2012: 136; Breen 2018: 87).[35] There was evidently a strong impetus to push the country's constitutional developments towards a federal direction. But not only was the idea of federalism for Nepal not clear enough, given the immense diversity, territorial location of ethnic groups and relative lack of territorial boundaries corresponding with ethnic boundaries, but the rigid discriminatory and unequal social structure (Breen 2018: 61) and power structure inhibited the adoption of a federal solution. Beyond everything else, there was, and perhaps still remains, a linguistic problem of translating federalism terms into the Nepali language, which does not seem to have the appropriate synonyms.[36] Those who were opposed to federalism in Nepal were behind the media campaign to discredit the idea of federation as a solution to ethnic conflicts in Nepal (Lawoti 2012: 146–7). Quite typically, the media in Nepal is said to have negatively portrayed federalism as a recipe for division and disintegration (Lawoti 2012: 148–9).

Federalism remained, however, a very contentious issue since the 1990s and through to two Constituent Assemblies (2008–12; 2013–15), and its conceptual fate and designs were subject to the shifts and turns in Nepal's political transition and constitutional deadlock (Malagodi 2019: 168–80). Many agreements and negations that took place in between could not arrive at a consensus on the issues of the federalization of Nepal. The Madhesi's political pressure in favour of a Madhesi province in the Terai region (with about 51 per cent of Nepal's population) forced

78 Origin and development of federalism in Asia

constitutional amendments to the Interim Constitution 2007 and added force to the federal debate. Various political parties in Nepal offered their suggestions for a six-province or 11-province federation; on the factual level, however, it was not possible to demarcate and name provinces after ethnic markers because no province would have a clear ethnic majority. The debate was extended to the floor of the 2nd Constituent Assembly (CA 2) (2013). Significantly, in the CA 2, the Maoists' relative strength was reduced (the third position after the UML and the NC), and the Nepali Congress and UML together secured a majority of seats. The Maoists remained somewhat stuck, though, to ethnic federalism,[37] which found a strong supporter in the Madhesis for different reasons. The CA 2 finally arrived at a seven-province federation as a *hybrid solution*, which moved away from the ethnic model based on ethnicity and language to demarcate federal units based on ethnicity and geography. Nepal remains a classic case where a pure territorial solution to ethno-nationalist cleavages did not work. As we shall see later in Chapter 4, Nepal's complex diversity required multiple strategies to recognize and accommodate various identities accompanied by a concomitant policy of redistribution.

Myanmar

Federalism has remained central to the legitimate basis of unity in multi-ethnic Myanmar since the Panglong Conference on 12 February 1947 and Independence from the British in 1948 but is yet to be achieved. Unlike other federations in Asia, the federal issues in Myanmar were never very complex; they pertained to the terms of integration of the frontier hilly states with the 'Union' of Myanmar on a federal basis, that is, recognition, autonomy and protection of distinct ethnic nations or nationalities such as the Shan, Karen, Kachin, Chin and Mon. The ethnic peoples, such as those listed, have lived historically in their own 'homelands' for centuries with their respective identity markers and internal self-governance.[38] More importantly, the British colonial authorities ruled such frontier hilly states differently from those of the Burma Province (in lower/central Burma). Much like India's North East, except Assam, during the British rule, such ethnic regions enjoyed their autonomy and were 'self-governed'. The successive Constitutions of Myanmar – 1947, 1973 and 2008 – have declared the state as the 'Union', but in each, the 'Union' has been understood by the power that be to be a 'unitary' Union rather than a federal union, far removed from the three essential principles arrived at during the Panglong Conference,[39] namely, equality of opportunity; autonomy of the frontier areas; and the right to secede from the Union after Independence (Tun 2009: 447).

Any cursory look at the political developments in Myanmar since 1948 shows how the country has witnessed, under various constitutional guises, progressive concentration and centralization of political power and constitutional measures to further alienate rather than unite the minorities with the Union. The 1947 Constitution of the then Burma, although it provided for autonomy for the minorities, was in intent clearly unitary. The country's seven states and seven divisions enjoyed

Origin and development of federalism in Asia **79**

'some autonomy' during the first few years of its limited parliamentary democracy, which meant some powers for the minorities that are territorially rooted. But then, since the late 1950s, the country has been subjected to progressive centralization and concentration of powers. A long time ago, Watts (1966) warned us about the danger in such moves, for they ease a country's conversion to autocracy and are unlikely to allay minority fears (Watts 1996: 96). The so-called socialist constitution of 1973, which officially transformed a military government into a civilian one, granted limited autonomy to the states and divisions under the guise of the Socialist Republic of the Union of Burma, but it also abolished all political parties except the ruling one. This effectively sealed off minority political participation and paved the way for further alienation of minorities from the political system. No wonder various ethnic groups took up arms and got themselves engaged in long-drawn armed resistance against the Union government. The infamous Citizenship Law of 1982, if anything, completed this process of alienation by excluding all 'non-indigenous races' from holding governmental positions of any importance. This law denies most *Rohingyas* (a Burmese Muslim minority living in the northern Rakhine (Arakan state) full citizenship rights.[40] Ironically enough, various ethnic groups under various political organizations have united for a federal Union. Elazar reported that: 'In 1986 the groups (numbering about 10) relinquished their individual demands for autonomy and united behind the single demand for a federal system of government which would recognize each ethnic group' (Elazar 1991: 171). Nonetheless, within the heavy grip of a centralized militarized state, a federal democratic solution for the country and its minorities, although the only option left, seemed a difficult but not impossible task to perform. The absence of democracy (popular participation in the political process until the late 1990s) and the appropriate institutional measures for power-sharing for the minorities, in the environment of an ethnically prejudiced (with the Bamar dominating) state bent on assimilation, have stood in the way of accommodating minorities and ensuring governance and legitimacy in Myanmar. In reconstructing a federal democratic political structure in Myanmar, the important sociopolitical resources to build on are the tradition of the more than five-decade-long movements of various ethnic groups for democracy, federalism, autonomy and self-rule (Smith 2007: 188–212). Smith (2007) argues that in Myanmar, seven ethnic minority states and seven regions with the ethnic Bamar/Burman with 68 per cent of the population is now a consensus in the country, but there are many more ethnic sub-groups (numbering about 135) that are not recognized (Smith 2007: 188). From the military's point of view, those are a proof of fragmentation of the unity of the Union and hence are not to be recognized (Smith 2007: 188). The official recognition of seven ethnic minority states since 1947 has underlined the obvious need for their political recognition as equal to others in ethnic terms and the question of their true autonomy, including the right to secede.

But that has remained as yet unresolved. The complex history of nationalism and the concept of a Burman nationhood centred on Burman/Bamar ethnicity, Burmese language and culture and Buddhism offered powerful elements of such a

80 Origin and development of federalism in Asia

nationhood, but then that was a mono-ethnic/racial nationhood that excludes not only the non-Burman ethnic minorities such as the Shan, Kachin and others but also the Rohingya Muslims in the Rakhaine (Arakan) State from this nationhood concept. Taylor said:

> The importance of Buddhist religion in terms of both the state-centred and ethnically grounded notion of identity of the pre-colonial Burmese people provided an additional cultural tie for the majority with the notion of the Burmese nation. The colonial state further strengthened these sentiments in both negative and positive ways. . . . The growing assertiveness of Burmese nationhood, however, also enhanced fears and apprehensions of those people, foreign and indigenous, who did not share these terms of identity.
>
> *(Taylor 1987: 150)*

Donald Horowitz (1985) pointed out that there was an ethnic dimension in military dimensions of the nationalist movements in Burma. He says that the British forces in Burma were mostly composed of the Karens, Kachins, Chins and Shans, with practically no Burmese (Horowitz 1985: 515). While the Burmese Independence Army subsequently mobilized by the Japanese (Burma was occupied by Japan during 1942–47) was dominated by the Burmese, the bitter warfare that took place in 1942 was between the Karen troops and the pro-Japanese Burmans (Horowitz 1985: 515). Afterward, the Karen battalions 'disappeared from the government side' and the 'ethnic areas became centres of resistance to Burmese domination'. The Burmese military was purged of the Karen and other elements, and after the 1962 coup, the 'whole official corps' of the Burmese military became heavily dominated by the Burmans (Horowitz 1985: 515). Small wonder that this helped to complicate the process of future inter-ethnic accommodation, especially between the majority and dominant Burmans on the one hand and the minority ethnic groups on the other. This also served to instill prejudice among the ruling Burmans/Bamar towards the ethnic minorities. The long term observer of political developments in Myanmar has noted several hurdles to ethnic peace and 'genuine federalism' in the country: the Bamar-dominated and nationalist chauvinist military; the condescending approach to the aspirations of the ethnic identity as merely 'ethno-nationalism'; the so-called national leadership to be offered by the majority Bamars alone; and so on (Smith 2007: 203–6).

Thus, the federal momentum in Myanmar was lost in 1947 when the Panlong agreement could not be implemented. The failure to do so was of course conjoined with the regime changes in the country in directions not hospitable to federalism. Ethnic armed rebellion and insurgency in the hilly ethnic regions was to become the predictable fall out. The post-1990s development towards civilianization for democracy in Myanmar was mostly a military-propelled initiative with little progress toward democratic transformation (Smith 2010), but from 2008 onwards a slow process of democratization has taken place in Myanmar, which has witnessed the rise of the National League for Democracy (NLD), led by Aung San Suu Kyi,

Origin and development of federalism in Asia **81**

which won two successive general elections – 2008 and 2015 – and her election as state counselor. However, the military still retains considerable power in both parliament and the executive, constitutionally speaking. Following a nationally agreed ceasefire agreement (National Ceasefire Accord in 2015), another conference called 21st Century Union Peace Conference on 31 August 2017 at the new capital, Naypitow, was scheduled to agree upon the federal terms of the Union, that is, the ethnic regions' right to autonomy, self-determination and power-sharing. Nothing concrete as yet has come out, but many principles have been adopted for future dialogue. This has not found favour with the ethnic regions. In a by-election on 19 October 2018, for example, the NLD lost 5 out of 6 seats in the Upper House (House of Nationalities) in the ethnic areas. The recent military crackdown on the Muslim Rohingyas and the latter's displacement in millions, which has drawn considerable international attention, have raised questions about the real intention of the rulers of Myanmar in accommodating and recognizing the ethnic minorities in the country.[41] Peace and federalism in Myanmar are, as it were, two sides of the same coin, and bringing about both for a durable political solution to decades-long ethnic conflicts in the country are not in sight in the immediate future.

Notes

1 Sumit Sarkar, one of India's leading historians, has pointed out both the 'conjunctural' and 'long-term' dimensions of this 'historical inheritance' in respect of federalism in India. For details, see his (2001) 'Indian Democracy: The Historical Inheritance', in Kohli, A. (ed) *The Success of India's Democracy*, Cambridge: Cambridge University Press.
2 This was in contrast to a very rich tradition of federalist thought in the West. See, for instance, D. Karmis and W. Norman (eds) (2005) *Theories of Federalism: A Reader*, New York: Macmillan.
3 See Lee Kam Hing (1981) 'Malaya: New State and Old Elites', in Jeffrey, R. (ed) *Asia: The Winning of Independence*, London and Basingstoke: Macmillan, pp. 228–9 for further details on the events forcing the imperial authorities to withdraw the MU proposal. The imperial sensitivity to the interests of the non-Malays was not to be doubted, for in the White Paper on the proposed Malayan Union it was stated: 'all those who have made the country their homeland should have the opportunity of a due share in the country's political and cultural institutions' (Quoted in G. P. Means (1976) *Malaysian Politics*, London: Hodder & Stoughton, p. 52).
4 R. L. Watts (1966) *New Federations: Experiments in the Commonwealth*, Oxford: Clarendon Press, p. 25. See also Means (1976) op. cit., p. 57. Means said: 'The federal system created by the Agreement did little to guarantee the autonomous authority of the States', p. 57.
5 Watts (1966: 25).
6 For further details on the evolution of the Communist activities towards insurgency since 1948, see chap. 6 'The Malayan Communist Party' (pp. 68–80) in Means (1976), op. cit.
7 Singapore was taken in order to take the socialist government under protective custody, so that Singapore was not used as a base to subvert the Federation. The brewing racial tensions between the mainland Malays and the Chinese in Singapore, which erupted in August 1965, led to the expulsion of Singapore from the Federation (Watts 1967: 27).
8 See Watts (1967: 26), for a summary of the features of the 1957 federal arrangement.
9 Sarkar (2001), op. cit., p. 31. But Pal's concept of 'composite nationalism' certainly was not truly compatible with federalism. For details, see, his (1950) 'Composite Nationalism: A Nationalist View', *New India*, 27 May.

82 Origin and development of federalism in Asia

10 Bhudev Mukhopadhyay (1892) *Samajik Prabandha* (Essays on Society) (in Bengali) (edited with an Introduction by Jaknabi Kumar Chakrabarty), Calcutta: West Bengal Government Book Board, pp. 7–8 [my translation] Bhudev Mukhopadhyay's concept of '*jatiyabhav*' (sense of national identity, or sentiments) incorporates various indigenous elements such as the Hindus, the Muslims, tribes and other communities in the making of an Indian identity. Incidentally, Bankim Chattapadhyay, usually not included in the tradition of thought on unity-in-diversity, could just as well be included, for religious differences played little role in his considerations of the causes of India's loss of independence. (The pages of the literary magazine, now a classic, that he edited, *Bangadarshan*, are full of such elements of thought.)

11 This is yet to be woven together, and calls for serious scientific attention.

12 Nehru's *Letters to Chief Ministers*, Vol. 2, New Delhi: Oxford University Press, 1986, p. 364.

13 Nehru's *Letters to Chief Ministers*, Vol. 1, New Delhi: Oxford University Press, 1985, p. 150. For further details on Nehru's views on this aspect, see Bhattacharyya, H. (2001a).

14 Quoted in Bhattacharyya, H. (2001a: 249).

15 Ramasubramanium argues that the British interest in federalism was to protect their trading interests via the states, who were eager to collaborate provided that their autocracy was kept intact (op. cit., p. 106)!

16 See R. Jeffrey (ed) (1978) *People, Princes and Paramount Power: Society and Politics in the Indian Princely States*, New Delhi: Oxford University Press for the growth of political activities in the States. See also V. P. Menon (1956) *The Story of the Integration of the Indian States*, New York: Macmillan for the successful yet very complex story of the accession of the states to the Union of India.

17 This part of the discussion draws mainly on Basu (1997).

18 The Indian National Congress vehemently opposed the federation scheme devised in the Government of India Act, 1935, pertaining in particular to a federation of 11 provinces (with elected governments) with the autocratic princely states, and passed many resolutions condemning it. The matter was even taken down to the level of a political campaign. In the campaigns for elections to the Provincial Legislature scheduled on 27 December 1937, in which the Congress participated only conditionally, Jawaharlal Nehru explained the Congress perspective thus:

> The Government of India Act, 1935, the new Constitution, stares at us offensively, this charter of bondage which has been imposed upon us despite our utter rejection of it, and we are preparing to fight elections under it. . . . We go to the Legislatures not to cooperate with the apparatus of British imperialism, but to combat the Act and seek to end it, and to resist in every way British imperialism in its attempt to strengthen its hold on India and its exploitation of the Indian people. This is the basic policy of the Congress and no Congressman, no candidate for election, must forget this. . . . We are not going to the Legislatures to pursue the path of constitutionalism or barren reformism.
>
> (See S.V. Desika Char (1983) *Reading in the Constitutional History of India 1757–1947*, New Delhi: Oxford University Press, p. 601).

19 Charr (1983), p. 574.

20 See Char (1983: 599–602) for more details.

21 Char (1983: 574). There were different views also expressed on behalf of the princely States in the South of India. In the Round Table Conference, Mirza Ismail, representing the princely states of Mysore, Travancore, Cochin and Pudukota, was found to be very sensitive to India's diversity and amenable to a federal democratic solution for India's constitutional problems. He said:

> India is a land of many creeds and many communities and diverse interests; but I believe that it is this very diversity that will go far to ensure the requisite stability in the democratic institutions that are proposed to be established in our country.
>
> (Char 1983: 573)

22 See Jinnah's speech at the Legislative Assembly debate, dated 7 February 1935, published in A. C. Banerjee (1961) *Indian Constitutional Documents 1757–1947*, Calcutta: A. Mukherjee & Co., pp. 270–3.

23 Char (1983: 685). For details see 'The Cabinet Mission's Proposal for a Settlement, 16 May 1946', pp. 684–91. The Mission's incisive analysis, as mentioned earlier, was a pointer to Pakistan's latter-day acute problems of unity and disintegration.

24 A. C. Banerjee (1978) *The Constitutional History of India*, Vol. 3, 1919–1977, Meerut: Macmillan, p. 165.

25 M. Bhattacharyya (1992) 'The Mind of the Founding Fathers', in Mukerji, N. and Arora, B. (eds) *Federalism in India: Origin and Development*, New Delhi: Vikash Publishing House, p. 101. Alfred Stepan (1999) accepted this view rather uncritically, while branding the Indian case of federalism as 'holding-together' federalism, which appears to be quite uninformed. For details, see his (1999) 'Federalism and Democracy: Beyond the U.S. Model', *Journal of Democracy*, Vol. 10, No. 4, October.

26 Quoted in Q. Veritatem (n.d.) *Justice Shall Prevail: The Struggle for Samjukta Maharashtra*, Poona: Kesari Printing Press, p. 7.

27 J. Das Gupta (2001) 'India's Federal Design and National Construction', in Kohli, op. cit., p. 51. See also J. R. McLane (1977) *Indian Nationalism and the Early Congress*, Princeton, NJ: Princeton University Press.

28 Quoted in J. Mukherjee (2008) *Multicultural Decentralization in India*, The University of Burdwan, Unpubl. Ph.D. Thesis, p. 151.

29 Noted in H. Bhattacharyya (2008) 'Ethnic and Civic Nationhood in India: Concept, History, Institutional Innovations and Contemporary Challenges', in Saha, S. C. (ed) *Ethnicity and Sociopolitical Change in Africa and Other Developing Countries: A Constructive Discourse in State Building*, Lanham: Lexington Books, p. 182. At the institutional level of politics, however, the support for linguistic provinces was not as forthcoming even from towering nationalist leaders such as Surendranath Banerjee, Tej Bahadur Sapru and Sir Muhammad Shafi. From the proceedings of the Indian Legislative Council (Vol. LVI, 1917–18, p. 502), it is learnt that Rai Bahadur B. N. Sharma's motion for arrangement for linguistic provinces 'whenever and to the extent possible, especially where the people speaking a distinct language, large in number and desire such a change' received little support. (For further details, see Char (1983: 742).)

30 Nehru Report, in Char (1983: 547). For details, see, pp. 546–7. (Item 228: 'Nehru Committee on the Formation of Linguistic Provinces, 10 August 1928'.)

31 A. R. Desai (1946) *Social Background of Indian Nationalism*, Bombay: Popular Prakashan, pp. 387–8. The articulation of nationhood in the same script as the right of nations to self-determination took place even among many small groups, who resented not so much being part of Indian nationhood but against being dominated by another nationality group within India. For an illustration, see H. Bhattacharyya (1989).

32 The constitutional and political transition in Nepal has already attracted serious scholarly attention. See, for instance, S. V. Einsiedel, D. Malone and S. Pradhan (eds) (2012) *Nepal in Transition: From People's War to Fragile Peace*, New Delhi: Cambridge University Press. See also, M. Malagodi (2019) ' "Godot Has Arrived": Federal Structuring in Nepal', in Anderson, G. and Choudhry, S. (eds) *Territory and Power in Constitutional Transitions*, Oxford: Oxford University Press, pp. 161–81; 'Nepal: Identity Politics and Federalism', *Asia Report* no. 199 (International Crisis Group: Working to Prevent Conflict Worldwide); and D. Gellner and J. Hachhethu (eds) (2008) *Local Democracy in South Asia: Micro Processes of Democratization in Nepal and Its Neighbours*, New Delhi: Sage.

33 The Maoists invoked the Leninist doctrine of self-determination of nations in understanding the ethnic question in Nepal and in extending support to the ethnic cause but not the right to secede. In Leninist injunction, the right to secede is only a formal declaration whose application was hedged around its practical limitations. See, H. Bhattacharyya (2019) *Radical Politics and Governance in India's North-East: The Case of Tripura*, chap. 1 'Marxism and the National/Ethnic Question: Theory and Practice in India', Abingdon, Oxon: Routledge, pp. 1–17.

84 Origin and development of federalism in Asia

34 Lenin's' declaration of political equality and self-determination to nationalities in pre-1917 Russia had a different context, though, from that of Nepal, where, strictly speaking, there was no majority and dominant nationality as the oppressor and exploiter of other nationalities, although the smaller ethnic groups who were also both aboriginal (tribes) and lower castes had both ethnic and economic dimensions. The People's War in Nepal cannot simply be explained away as an instance of ethnic conflict.

35 For several experiments with democracy in Nepal prior to the formation of the CA in 2008, see Einsiedel, S. von et al. (2008).

36 The author was involved at some stage of constitution-making in Nepal in 2008 relating to federalism terms and facilitated as a researcher preparing an English-Nepali glossary. See *English-Nepali Glossary of Federalism Terms* (2009) (IDEA, Sweden and Forum of Federations, Ottawa, pp. 1–68). The task was not easy to translate federalism terms into Nepali.

37 Their position changed too in favour of a balance view (Breen 2018: 124).

38 See, S. A. Tun (2009) *History of the Shan State: From Origins to 1962*, Chiang Mai, Thailand: Silkworm Books. This is a well-documented account of the glorious antecedents of the Shan nation and establishes the claim of the Shan as a nation in its own right.

39 The Pang Long Conference dated 12 February 1947 and its proceedings remain a landmark event in the conceptual evolution of federalism in Myanmar. The Panglong Agreement was the first legitimate document that was purported to settle the terms of the hill (ethnic) peoples such as the Shan, Karen, Kachins and Chin joining the Union of Burma with the recognition of political equality and autonomy. However, the Agreement remained unimplemented till now. (See for details and the historical background, Hugh Tinker (1967) *The Union of Burma: A Study of the First Years of Independence*, London: Oxford University Press, chapter 1, pp. 1–34. See also, Tun (2008). Chapter 13, A Second Pang Long Conference and its Historic Agreement, 1947, pp. 281–303. Tun (2008) has reported with full details the background to and the proceeding of the First Multinational Political Conference at Pang Long on 26 March 1946. It was a conference among the hill peoples which sought to determine the terms of unity between the hill peoples and the mainland Bamars. (See, for details, chapter 11, pp. 207–15.) As per the terms of the National Ceasefire Accord (NCA) (October 2015) with the armed ethnic groups, a second Panglong Union Peace Conference was held on 31 August 2016 and concluded on 17 July 2018 at the National Convention Centre at the Union capital Naypyitaw. Many agreements were signed with some ethnic armed groups' representatives on several principles for a better and healthier discussion in future. It is apparent from the outcomes of the conference that more miles need to be travelled by the Myanmar government as well as the armed ethnic groups before a genuine federal 'Union' is established in Myanmar.

40 The Rohingya refugee crisis has been triggered by successive military crackdowns on the Muslim Majority Rohingya in the Rakhine State (Arakan State), who are not recognized as the citizens of Myanmar and have been stateless for decades. Decades-long armed ethnic conflict between the Rohingya Muslim Salvation Army and the Myanmar military establishment have taken place; the Rohingya Muslims have been displaced in millions who tried to take shelter in neighbouring Bangladesh. The Myanmar government is now under pressure from the international community, especially the UN itself, to bring them back and extend protection and security to the hapless people.

41 More knowledgeable sources expressed doubts about Aung San Suu Kyi's real sympathy for the Ethnic Armed Organizations and the latter's decades-long struggle for self-determination. Her limits are also pointed out: she is more keen on improving the relationship between the NLD government and the military. The overwhelmingly urban leadership of the NLD is composed of the Burmans/Bamars, which is not a favourable factor in developing a healthy approach to the ethnic minorities. See Asley South, 'Myanmar's stalled peace process' (https://theasiadialogue.com/2019/04/03/myanmars-stalled-peace-process/, accessed 23 October 2019). South wrote: 'Beyond paying lip service to the peace process, neither the government nor the military has much interest in listening to – let alone addressing – the concerns of long-suffering minority communities'.

4

FEDERALISM AND INSTITUTIONAL INNOVATIONS

Introduction

Federations are, as Ronald Watts says, difficult to govern because they are federations (Watts 1966: 353). But at the same time, for multi-ethnic countries, particularly when the distinct ethno-national groups in them are mostly territorially rooted, federations are also difficult to avoid. Under colonialism, appropriate – if not democratic – representation of various ethno-national groups in the 'polity', administration, resources and so on, was very limited – if not nearly absent. Ethnic favouritism was often indulged in if it served colonial interests. Apart from the large-scale deprivation and underdevelopment experienced by the large majority of people under colonialism, the unitary, centralized and repressive pattern of governance was the cause of manifold injustices done to ethnic groups, so that people had to face humiliation and suffer dishonour regarding their cultural and other identity markers. The age-old 'divide and rule' policy of the colonial rulers added insult to injuries. In India, for instance, 'the Hindu-Muslim divide' had much to do with the British policy of using one community against the other. Interestingly, many 'federal' solutions that the colonial authorities offered for solving the problems of unity in such countries were designed so as to arouse more suspicion than confidence. The term 'federation' became more often an 'F word', a synonym for disunity and disintegration, so to speak.

Therefore, designing the most appropriate institutions for federal governance in place of the colonial mode in India, Malaysia and Pakistan after independence so that the various, most often warring, ethno-national groups with ancient identity markers were satisfied was not easy, for a variety of reasons. For Pakistan, in particular, the task was Herculean, divided as it was, until its disintegration and the rise of Bangladesh in 1971, between its western and eastern wings by more than a thousand miles of an enemy territory, not to mention its many other internal

86 Federalism and institutional innovations

problems. Institutional innovation then entailed creating the Constitution itself; appropriate redrawing of the political map of the territory, if required for facilitating federal governance; appropriate constitutional and political recognition and protection of identity; decentralizing powers and resources in order to satisfy the ethno-national groups; distribution of powers between tiers of government so that national shared-rule and regional self-rule are possible within the same polity; and so on. Federalism requires a complex web of institutional arrangements for many tiers of governance, while federalism in complex multi-ethnic countries requires a more complex web of institutions for the same purpose. True, federations have failed in many ex-colonial countries in the non-Western world, but that is a proof that there was, and still is, is an obvious need to adopt federalism as an institutional method of accommodation of multi-ethnic reality and to maintain national sovereignty and identity, as well as fostering economic development. It was also a proof that many of the failures had to do with the failure to design the most appropriate federal institutions; federalism *per se* was not blame. Federal governance as a complex mode of governance refers to multi-level institutional governance within the same polity. It is thus sustained when it is backed by democracy, that is, when there is popular institutionalized consent in support of such governance. Federalism as a political form and union follows federal governance. But as we have already indicated, federal political form and union, itself the product of many factors and as a dynamic political equilibrium, is not easily achieved – if at all.

Above all, institutions, as the exponents of neo-institutionalism that Robert Putnam (Putnam *et al.* 1993) would have us believe, are path dependent. The appropriate, supportive and surrounding ideological environment articulated and expressed in the political ideas and beliefs of the country's élites is also of vital importance in designing political institutions and working them. Two considerations are of seminal importance. First, ethno-national identities are appropriately accommodated. Second, identity accommodation is democratically achieved. For many classical federations, a federalist tradition of political thought has come in handy in this regard. However, it is also true that an otherwise rich tradition of federalist thinking in a particular country has not been able to inform its political institutions (Karmis and Norman 2005).[1]

Pakistan

Unlike India, where federalism was a solid national legacy, as we have seen in Chapter 3 of this book, Pakistan was not as lucky. Ideologically, Pakistan as a federation was sought to be built on a somewhat doubtful legacy. Christopher Jaffrelot (2002a) has argued that Mohammad Ali Jinnah 'wanted to build a strong state relying on the threefold principle of one nation, one culture and one language'.[2] But Jaffrelot has also pointed out the foundational dilemma of Pakistan, as envisioned by Jinnah:

> Pakistan was intended to be a homeland of the Muslims of British India, and its language could be nothing else but Urdu. Jinnah had the ideology but he

missed the social and the geographical base. He represented the Muslims of the provinces of the Raj where they were in a minority and who, partly for this demographic reason, faced the threat of social decline. The Muslims of the United Provinces (today Uttar Pradesh) were a case in point.

(Jaffrelot 2002a: 8)

Ideologically, therefore, Jinnah's two-nation theory was based on Muslim minoritism, as the Muslim-majority provinces such as the Punjab and Bengal did not identify them with the Muslim separatism that the Muslim League and Jinnah espoused because the Muslims could govern such provinces in any way.[3] Jaffrelot's argument is that Jinnah's task was 'to convert these "majoritarian Muslims" to the two-nation theory' in the 1940s. Jinnah managed to do so only in the late 1940s, momentarily, as 'a brief moment of political unity'.

Paradoxical though it seem, Jinnah, considered as the founder of Pakistan, is also considered to be the founding father of Pakistan federalism. Pakistani scholars refer to his federalist ideas for ideological support. S. J. Ahmed (1990) believed that for Jinnah, federalism was the principle on which the Muslim state would be organized. He quoted Jinnah's statement dated 10 December 1945: 'Our Pakistan government will probably be a Federal Government modelled on the lines of autonomous provinces, with the key powers in matters of defence and foreign affairs, etc. at the Centre'. But Jinnah's views on federalism for India (not yet partitioned) and later for Pakistan should be examined in perspective. From the early 1920s to the late 1930s, Jinnah more or less consistently defended the case of federalism for India. At the All-India Muslim League's Lahore Session on 24–25 May 1924, for instance, Jinnah said of the future Constitution of India:

> The existing provinces of India shall be united under a Common Government on a federal basis so that each province shall have full and complete provincial autonomy, the functions of the Central Government being confined to such matters only as are of general and common concern.
>
> *(Ahmed, I. 1995: 25)*

At the All-Parties Conference that reviewed the Nehru Report (1928) on 22 December 1928, Jinnah continued to defend the cause of a 'greater quantum of autonomy for the provinces' including that 'residuary powers be vested in the provinces, as most suited for the federation of India' (Ahmed, I. 1995: 25). He reiterated the same in his 'Fourteen Points' (1929) as well as in the Round Table talks in London in the 1930s. The constitutional structure provided for in the Government of India Act, 1935, was not truly federal, but Jinnah had no problems in accepting the provincial autonomy part of the Government of India Act, 1935. For him, federalism, as he understood it, would solve the communal problems that so perturbed him. Also, he did not question the anomalous ethnic complexion of many of the provinces that the British had created; he was ready to work with the existing provinces. However, whatever federalist conviction that he had held so far began to dissipate after the dismal performance of the Muslim League in the 1937 provincial

88 Federalism and institutional innovations

level elections even in the predominantly Muslim-inhabited provinces such as the Punjab, Sindh and the North-West Frontier Province. As we have already discussed in Chapter 3, from the late 1930s, Jinnah distanced himself from the federal idea as a solution to 'communal problems'. From the early 1940s, after the formal demand for a state of Pakistan in 1940, he even castigated the idea of Pakistan including the notion of vesting residuary powers in the provinces. His verdict now was more in favour of a powerful central authority in which the units would be compelled to grant and delegate more and more powers to the central authority (Ahmed, I. 1995: 30). That was not any defence of federalism but rather its outright rejection in favour of a very powerful unitary state. Jinnah's speech as president of the Pakistan Constituent Assembly on 11 August 1947 expressed anxiety about the various forms of social and cultural diversity among people in Pakistan and was sensitive to equal rights among the citizens of the state but did not for once mention federalism in Pakistan. Paradoxically enough, since Jinnah (who died in 1948) wanted Pakistan to be a federation nonetheless, federalism apparently had a very limited audience in Pakistan. While the numerically and ethnically dominant Punjabis were opposed to it, even among the top leaders, military-cum-political, federalism was very often blamed for the country's growing separatism. For instance, President (formerly General) Muhammad Ayub Khan, who took power in a coup in October 1958, abrogated the Constitution of 1956; dissolved all elected bodies at the national and provincial levels; and introduced a highly centralized Constitution in 1962, who is also known for his so-called basic democracies and so on, blamed the federal principle for separatist tendencies in Pakistan (Watts 1966: 22–3). However, as we shall soon see, constitutionally, Pakistan has, since its birth on 14 August 1947, not given up federalism and is still committed to it.

In the existing literature of federalism, the case of Pakistan is considered as an illustration of the 'pathology of federations' (Watts 2008: 179–87). Unlike Sri Lanka, where all attempted federal measures have failed, Pakistan, constitutionally still declared a federation, has failed overall as a federation. A number of factors have militated against the innovation of appropriate institutions and their implementation that could sustain the federation. While Islam was taken to be the unifying ideological ground for claiming a separate sovereign state of Pakistan, the federal situation for Pakistan lay in the diversity of its regions (see Chapter 2).

But the primal fact that East Bengal (known as East Pakistan between 1955 and 1971 and Bangladesh since 1971), the most populous (about 55 per cent of the total population and inhabited by Bengali-speaking Muslims, plus some Hindus) part of the country, was geographically separated from its western counterpart, West Pakistan (itself very diverse and different from its eastern counterpart in many ways), by more than a thousand miles of enemy territory (India) – coupled with the region's very distinctive ethno-linguistic and regional identity – was not particularly favourable for running a federation born out of the Partition, large-scale communal violence, and population transfers. Watts said:

This geographical fact has dominated politics in Pakistan since its creation in 1947, and resulted in a unique federation with only two regional units balancing

Federalism and institutional innovations **89**

each other in a state of precarious equilibrium (Watts 1966: 20). Watts further argued that aside from the already-mentioned geographic remoteness, linguistic, cultural and economic disparity of the two regions presented to her leaders an 'insurmountable task of unification' (Watts 1966: 20). Ironically, while the birth of Pakistan was a success of minority secession (in the religious sense) in creating a nation-state, the birth of Pakistan resulted also in the minority domination (the western wing, itself dominated by the Urdu-speaking Punjab) over the majority (eastern wing) Bengali-speaking people so much so that the latter considered itself as a colony of the former. These social, economic and political facts, cited by many scholars, unmistakably have proved the widening disparity between the two regions, the eastern one being the victim. The growing sense of deprivation, culturally, economically and politically among the Bengalis in the eastern wing served to prepare a potent source of regionalism verging on secessionism, especially since the late 1950s, which, when coupled with the fragile sense of 'national' unity in the country as a whole, then and even now,[4] was reason enough to go for some kind of federalism to be conceded to, but centralization of powers took place time and again to counteract any tendency to disunity. The fear of disunity haunted the new republic deeply, and its characteristic response by centralizing more powers reinforced further regionalism and more fears of disunity in a cascading effect. The brewing ethno-regional tensions between the populous east wing and the west wing, the latter itself being very diverse, from the beginning of the republic, would only mature with the passage of time for the inevitable disaster resulting in state collapse and disintegration in 1971. The appropriate institutional innovation that could accommodate the ethno-regional identity, though attempted, was forestalled. The institution of democratic power-sharing among the ethno-regional identity groups within the single polity would not be allowed. The heavy pressures from West Pakistan – more exactly, the Punjabi dominated state structures – would stand in the way of developing the appropriate institutions of power-sharing among ethno-regional groups. Talbot has found in the growing centrist states structures in Pakistan the accompanying Punjabization of the state (Talbot 1998: 1). It was thus not surprising that, as Talbot commented, 'Successive bouts of authoritarian rule have reinforced centrifugal ethnic, linguistic and regional forces' in Pakistan (Talbot 1998: 1). Islam was (and still is) hardly able to unify people cutting across ethnic, linguistic and regional divides in Pakistan, before 1971 and after. Painfully enough, the growing sectarian conflicts between the Shias and Sunnis in Pakistan have further eroded the legitimacy basis of Pakistan as state by proving the Islam itself is divided and cannot offer the cementing ideological bond for the 'nation'(Jaffrelot 2002a: 34–5).

The net casualty of this was constitution-making for the new republic and any subsequent healthy institutional innovation. Since the provisions of the Government of India Act, 1935, were finally rejected by the Muslim League, after its dismal electoral performance in the 1937 elections in the Muslim-majority provinces, a new constitution was urgently needed for the new state. But that was not to be. For until 1956, the same Government of India Act, 1935, was to remain

90 Federalism and institutional innovations

the Interim Constitution for Pakistan, with certain adaptations,[5] which, however, reinforced the powers of the central government. Thus, the Pakistan federation exhibited, Watts believed, the usual features of a federal constitution: central and regional governments; the distribution of authority between them; and a federal court to interpret the written Constitution.[6] But the federation had a complex array of units: a single province of East Bengal (to be known as East Pakistan from 1955) with 55 per cent of the total population; three provinces in the west, the Punjab, Sindh, and the North-West Frontier Province; one Chief Commissioner's Province; ten acceded princely states; and a thin strip of Kashmir (Watts 1966: 21). To begin with, the various units did not possess symmetrical powers, but whatever powers they had were encroached upon by the central government as a matter of routine. Watts reported that from the beginning the central government had extensive legislative and executive authority, and during the period of the Interim Constitution (1947–56) there was persistent central intervention in provincial affairs by various means: employment of governors, control over the joint higher civil-services and the frequent use of emergency powers to suspend provincial governments (Watts 1966: 21).

Up to now, Pakistan has had five constitutions including the Interim Constitution (i.e. the Government of India Act, 1935) and those established in 1956, 1962, 1972 (Interim Constitution) and 1973. Sadly, because of the successive periods of martial law imposed and the introduction of military regimes post-1958, the constitutions, which came to be abrogated by successive military rulers, had had a trying time and were barely allowed to work. Nonetheless, a brief critical discussion on some constitutional issues, including actual creation of the constitution, is needed in order to make sense of the underlying socio-economic and political tensions that called for federal institutional solutions. To begin with, for the first Constitution of 1956 to be drafted and adopted, two Constituent Assemblies – the first (1947–55) and the second (1955–56) – were required. The first CA (a 79-member elected body on the basis of one seat represented a population of 1million) was dominated by the Muslim League, and the draft that was prepared was vehemently debated inside the CA and outside of it, with many simply opposing it on several grounds: the exact role of Islam in the state; centre–provinces relations (the centralization vs. autonomy issue); the national language chosen; and so on. Even the Objective Resolution of the CA, which incidentally took one and a half years to be passed (12 March 1949) following the formation of the CA, itself became the subject of considerable debate. The Resolution laid down the three broad principles on which the future Constitution would be based: the Constitution should be democratic, federal and Islamic. All three issues became the subject of heated debates. The relationship between democracy and Islam in the context of a modern representative state structure was a bone of contention among the Muslims. The second CA (1955–56) was an 80-member body in which no political party had a majority (Table 4.1).

The fact that the first CA was a Muslim League-dominated body was a colonial inheritance, because the CA was constituted of members elected by provincial

TABLE 4.1 Party position in the second Constituent Assembly of Pakistan

Political parties	Seats
Muslim League	26
United Front	16
Awami League	13
Congress	4
Scheduled Caste Federation	3
United Progressive Party	2
Others	16
Total	80

Source: B. P. Barua in Grover and Arora (1995: 162).

legislatures which had been elected in the colonial period on the basis of a very limited franchise. Also, the Muslim League, in the wake of the Pakistan movement in the 1940s, had had a considerable following not only in West Pakistan but also in the eastern wing, East Bengal. In the first ever elections held in the post-Independence period in East Bengal in 1954, a United Front (UF) of various political parties, from the right to the left, obtained 223 seats out of 237 Muslim seats, leaving the ruling Muslim League with only ten seats in a house of 309 seats. This meant the electoral rout of the ML in East Bengal. Many saw in this a vote against the central government which appeared to dominate East Bengal as if it were its colony. Sisir Gupta argued that the victory of the UF in the 1954 elections was a verdict on the deteriorating economic conditions of life of the people in the province in the last seven years after 1947, coupled with the failure of the Provincial League government to accord a state language status to Bengali along with Urdu.[7] Gupta reported that:

> The United Front's basic programme, however, could not be taken lightly as more than 90 per cent of East Pakistan's [Bengal] population voted in its favour, and their basic aim was among others, to get for East Pakistan *complete autonomy*. It was also pledged to the rejection of the Constitution and replacement of the Constituent Assembly by a newly elected body.
>
> *(Gupta 1995a: 28) [my emphasis]*

The federalist pressures here are to be noted: power-sharing, recognition of ethno-regional/linguistic identity in the evolving federal constitutional framework and resistance against central encroachment upon provincial governance. The results of the elections also undercut the basis for the legitimacy of many Muslim League members, who had so far been members of the CA but who lost the elections in 1954. Naturally, a demand for the reconstitution of the CA was voiced. But rather than heeding such a demand, while the first CA continued to function pathetically (the very poor attendance at the vital times when resolutions were passed, the lack of quorums for holding the sessions etc.), the central government

92 Federalism and institutional innovations

responded by dismissing the two-month-old democratically elected UF government in May 1954, and the governor's rule was imposed. The governor-general also dissolved the Constituent Assembly and the incumbent cabinet in June 1954. There followed a series of legal battles and a constitutional crisis.[8] Not only were no innovative institutions for federal governance worked out, but even the existing and emerging ones were thwarted by the fiats of centralizing authority.

After a year, in June 1955, the governor-General ordered the provincial legislatures to elect a new Constituent Assembly consisting of 80 members equally divided between the two wings of Pakistan, with 11 seats reserved for the non-Muslims.[9] The formation of the second CA, more representative in character than the first one, was a victory of democratic pressures from below – to be precise, the East Bengalis, who had already found the Draft Constitution prepared by the first CA, that is, its Basic Principles Committee (BPC), to be anti-Bengali and anti-federal and highly pro-West Pakistani (read pro-Punjabi) and centralizing.

The Report of the Basic Principles Committee of the first CA submitted to the latter on 22 December 1952, which became a kind of Draft Constitution for Pakistan, became a bone of serious contention. Its recommendation of a parity of representation between the two wings of Pakistan in both the houses of Parliament; its rejection of Bengali (spoken by the majority of the people) as a national language (since its Devnagri script smacked of Hindu religiosity); its acceptance of Urdu as the national language (though spoken by no more than 7 per cent of the people); the Islamic Constitution; and so on were criticized widely, especially by large sections of people from East Bengal. The Muslim members from the eastern wing are said to have proposed as many as 425 amendments to the Report, which contained only 125 clauses and three lists of subjects.[10] Many leaders in East Bengal could not accept the Report; many in East Bengal saw in the Report a move to subdue the Bengali numerical majority in the federation. The institutional design of the proposed ten-unit federation (nine in West Pakistan and East Bengal) was such that in the Lower House, East Bengal and West Pakistan would have an equal (200 each) number of seats. In the upper house too, there would be equality in the seats distributed: 60 each. In the Lower House, which had 347 Muslim members, ultimately West Pakistan would have 194 Muslim members and East Bengal would have 153 Muslim members.[11] This, coupled with the gross affront to Bengali language and identity, infuriated the Bengalis in East Bengal.[12] The leaders of West Pakistan, including those in the BPC, were also equally determined that West Pakistan would not become dominated by the Bengalis. Many therefore nicknamed the BPCR (1952) the 'Bengali–Punjabi Crisis Report' (Ahmed, S. J. 1990). Punjab was opposed to any federation where Bengalis could dominate. Interestingly, the Punjabi group in the first CA, always opposed to the Bengali group, floated various new federation proposals, all aimed at undercutting the Bengali domination. Incidentally, in the first CA, the Bengali speakers were also not allowed to speak in Bengali. One such proposal consisted of first constituting a 'Zonal Federation' of West Pakistan (if not a single unit) with the units in this area, and then that this sub-federation should be federated with East Bengal on the basis of parity.[13]

This provides one strong indication of the brewing ethno-regional tensions behind the constitution-making in Pakistan, which were symptomatic of the problematic of reconciling the extremely strong regional loyalties with the national, that is, Pakistani affiliations, which were yet to be identified and defined in Pakistan. The second CA was not at all free of conflicts and controversy: the role of Islam in the state, the strong vs. weak centre, joint vs. separate electorates, the national language and so on plagued the body in the same way as before. The Awami League–United Front combine in the CA appeared to be preparing for an ethno-nationalist rebellion, insisting on incorporating their '21-point' programme (their Election Manifesto) (1954). Abul Mansur Ahmed, a prominent Awami League leader, dwelt on more differences between the two wings of Pakistan (barring religion): language, culture, tradition, the customs, the calendar, standard time and even climate.[14] He even spoke of the two wings as 'two countries' and 'two peoples'.[15] The threat of secession was also openly aired by the leftwing of the Awami League, led by Maulana Bhasani, in a public meeting in Dacca (now Dhaka) on 15 January 1956.[16]

On 29 February 1956, the second Constituent Assembly adopted its first Constitution, entitled the 'Constitution of the Islamic republic of Pakistan'. Some of its salient features may be summarized here. First, its Preamble began with the words: 'In the name of Allah, the Beneficent, the Merciful' and enjoined the state to see that the 'principles of justice, freedom, equality, tolerance and social justice as enunciated by Islam, should be fully observed' and also that the 'Muslims of Pakistan should be enabled individually and collectively to order their life in accordance with the teachings and requirements of Islam, as set out in the Holy Quran and Sunnah', etc.[17] The Preamble also declares Pakistan 'a Federation, wherein the provinces would be autonomous *with such limitations on their powers and authority as might be prescribed'*[18] [my emphasis]. The Preamble also promises 'to safeguard the *legitimate interests* of minorities and backward classes'[19] [my emphasis]. Second, the Constitution (Article 214) recognizes both Urdu and Bengali as languages of the federation. A host of fundamental rights of the citizens are also recognized, and the constitutional provisions for their protection are also guaranteed. However, although declared to be a federation, only one chamber of Parliament, the National Assembly, was recognized, with parity of membership between East Pakistan and West Pakistan. The federation that was proposed was highly centralized, but the provinces were given the 'residuary power of legislation' (Article 109) on items not enumerated in any of the three lists (Fifth Schedule), including the corresponding executive authority.

Sadly, before the first Constitution of the Republic could take shape, Pakistan was placed under Emergency rule by the Presidential Proclamation dated 25 October 1958, which abrogated the Constitution; dismissed all governments and legislatures; and banned all political parties, and the whole country was placed under the command of General Muhammad Ayub Khan, Commander-in-Chief of the Pakistan Army, as the Chief Martial Law Administrator, an ominous practice which heralded the untimely death of all moves towards a constitutional democracy

94 Federalism and institutional innovations

for the nascent state. General-turned-President Ayub Khan introduced another Constitution in 1962 which abolished the federal system, creating a very centralized presidential system of government of two units on the basis of his so-called basic democracies. But such a Constitution could barely work under such a heavily authoritarian regime. The Bengalis in the eastern wing found it increasingly difficult to stay together and seceded in 1971 to form Bangladesh. In 1972, when Pakistan was under martial law under Mr Z. A. Bhutto as President and Chief Martial Law Administrator of Pakistan, an Interim Constitution was adopted by the National Assembly of Pakistan on 20 April 1972, the draft (modelled on the Government of India Act, 1935) for which was prepared by the Pakistan People's Party (PPP) of Mr Bhutto. The Constitution provided for a federal set-up with a presidential form of government. However, the need for a permanent constitution for Pakistan as a parliamentary federal form of government with 'maximum provincial autonomy' was highlighted by the president many times in 1972.

The basic federal traits of the Constitution of Pakistan (1973)[20] are:

1   Pakistan declared itself as an Islamic Republic, and the Preamble to the Constitution, decorated with lofty democratic values, all inspired by the great teachings of Islam, is no different from the 1962 Constitution.
2   The Constitution declares Pakistan to be a Federal Republic consisting of the following territorial units: (a) the four provinces of Baluchistan, the North-West Frontier, the Punjab and Sindh; (b) the Islamabad Capital Territory (as the federal capital); and (c) the Federally Administered Tribal Areas (FATA).
3   It provides for a bicameral federal parliament: the National Assembly (a 200-member popular chamber) and Senate (63-member upper chamber), with equal representation from the four provinces (14 members each) and five to be elected from the FATA and two from the federal capital to be chosen by the president.
4   It provides for a president to be elected by members of parliament in a joint sitting for a period of five years as the head of the state and as the symbol of unity of the republic.
5   The federal government shall comprise the prime minister (the Chief Executive of the Federation) and federal ministers which shall act in the name of the president.
6   There shall be a governor for each province who shall be appointed by the president and who shall act on and in accordance with the advice of the chief minister (and such advice shall be binding on him or her);
7   Additionally, seats shall be reserved for representation of the minorities, religious or otherwise, to provincial assemblies: one to Baluchistan; two to the NWFP; three to Punjab and two to Sindh.
8   The Constitution also provides for distribution of legislative powers between the federal and provincial governments in terms of two lists, namely, the Federal Legislative List with 67 enumerated legislative powers and the Concurrent Legislative List with 47 concurrent powers.

Federalism and institutional innovations **95**

9 Provinces have powers in residual matters not enumerated in any of the two lists.

10 There is the provision for a federal court known as the Supreme Court of Pakistan, with original jurisdiction in any dispute between any two or more governments. There is also provision for a high court for each province.

11 The constitutional procedures for amending the Constitution are rather complex.

12 The Constitution accepts Urdu as the national language of Pakistan, keeps English to be used for official purposes for quite some time, and allows the provincial assemblies to use a provincial language in addition to the national language.[21]

Given the extensive items in both the Federal and the Concurrent Lists on which the federal government has exclusive powers to legislate, very little of vital importance remains for the provinces to ensure their 'maximum provincial autonomy', as declared by the rules listed. Administratively, the federal government has the ability to intervene in the affairs of the provincial administration. The federal government has the power to appoint the governors who are to act as its agents, approve the dissolution of the provincial assembly, give directions to the provinces and so on. Because of this, Watts (2008) aptly remarked: 'When coupled with the provinces' relative dependence on the federal government for fiscal transfers, the autonomy of the provinces is severely limited' (Watts 2008: 40). Unfortunately, Pakistan had experienced 'democracy' for just about ten years in the 1990s in her history of more than 60 years. A military regime under martial law has reigned supreme in the country for most of her post-Independence political life. The extreme concentration of powers in a bureaucratic–military combine, defined as the state, and that too over-dominated by the Punjabis; the arbitrariness in the making and unmaking of Constitutions (three Constitutions plus two interim ones in the span of just about 60 years!) including their repeated abrogation and major amendments that emptied them of any real content; the extremely negative and rigid approach on the part of the rulers to accommodating, institutionally and otherwise, the ethno-national identity demands including even those of the majority (the Bengalis!), and thus complete unwillingness to share power; and so on have meant that appropriate institutions could not be innovated for federal governance. The institutions that have been attempted were not truly meant to provide for federal governance but to suppress it. The demands for a truly democratic federation that were voiced by the majority Bengalis (in the pre-1971 period) along with similar demands that have been voiced regularly by the Sindhis, Baluchs, Pathans/Pakhtuns and others in Pakistan in the post-1971 period[22] as usual have been met with extreme state repression, which ironically has further weakened the basis for the legitimacy of the state itself. Judged in this light, Pakistan is only 'nominally a federation' and in practice a 'dominantly centralized military regime'.[23] Pakistan as a federation has failed (or, perhaps, more truly, has been failed), but, ethnically speaking, the Punjabis, or to be more exact, the Punjabi ruling élites, have triumphed. However, with the

96 Federalism and institutional innovations

landmark constitutional reforms by way of the 18th Amendment to the Constitution of Pakistan (1973) calling for major devolution of powers to the provinces, federalism in Pakistan is said to have made significant innovation in institutional designs (discussed at length in Chapter 8).

Malaysia

Although the Malaysian federation represents a success story for federalism in Asia (the other and a major case being India), current research on the subject, however, seems to convey a somewhat negative meaning. In an important essay (2007), William Case has claimed, for instance, that 'In Malaysia, however, federalism has done less to promote democracy than to reinforce semi-democratic politics, a shifting amalgam of authoritarian controls and democratic space by which the Central Government has efficiently – and intermittently – extended its tenure'.[24] While this is not the place to engage in a long debate with such views, a couple or more comments are unavoidable. First, the term 'semi-democracy' is not a particularly desirable explanatory category in analytical scientific discourse. Ironically, the undesirable malpractices in the realm of democracy in Malaysia that William Case is found to be legitimately sensitive to would cancel out India's large claim as the 'world's largest democracy'! That, however, is not done. Second, the co-existence of mutually opposed features of the state, or principles – democracy/participation and authoritarianism – within the same polity, as Chain-Anan Samudavanija has argued in the case of the East Asian 'tiger economies' in his concept of the 'three-dimensional state',[25] is a hard fact of political life in non-Western countries as compared with Western political systems. Third, there is finally no instance of a maximal federalism that would allow us to speak of a minimalist one. It would be better to look upon federalism as a dynamic political equilibrium born of many factors, the most important of which appear to be the resolution of ethnic, ethno-regional, or ethno-nationalist conflicts within the same polity, so that both unity and diversity are maintained. There is no ideal situation for federalism; neither is there any ideal single model (as Watts would have us believe) of federalism to emulate or copy. In multi-ethnic countries opting for federalism, the space for federal bargains, whether at the stage of constitution-making or subsequently, is most often confronted with the need for accommodation of serious ethno-regional/national considerations. In the case of Pakistan, as we have just seen, the main failure in federation-building was due to the strong ethno-national pressures (in the beginning the Punjabis and the Muhajirs, and later only the Punjabis) against any institutional measure to accommodate the Bengalis, who, incidentally, were the majority yet were not politically and economically powerful in the newly carved out (of India) state of Pakistan. In the case of Malaysia, as we will see in Chapter 3 of this book, the federal bargain was achieved while keeping in mind the special protection to be accorded to the indigenous Malays and other *bhumiputera* ('sons of the soil'), so a kind of discrimination (albeit in favour of the largest, and later the majority, community) was built into the federal constitutional system itself. The UMNO,

Federalism and institutional innovations **97**

the Malay organization in the National Front (*Barisan Nasional*) which leads the central government, is the dominant and leading force. No realistic understanding of governmental institutions can ignore the fact that there are people behind the institutions, and people have identity!

Institutional innovation

Malaysia's federal institutional designs thus were path dependent. The country's transition to federalism, to independence and then finally to further federalization, as we will see in Chapter 3 of this book, was smooth and constitutionally peaceful but ethnically very calculative. For instance, the inclusion of the North Borneo states of Sabah and Sarawak in 1963, as well as the expulsion of Singapore from the federation in 1965, was designed to finally ensure the ethnic predominance of the Malays by often liberally defining them so as to also include the indigenous people of Sabah and Sarawak and by offsetting the Chinese dominance in the federation by expelling the Chinese-dominated and populous Singapore.

Second, the federation's constituent units were, since colonial times if not before, distinct territorial units. The units were, in most cases, governed by native rulers known as 'sultans' 'with whom the British concluded agreements ensuring peaceful condition of trade in and near the main ports'.[26] As Milne and Mauzy (1989) wrote:

> The rulers' powers were not removed; the British appointed a 'Resident' to their courts who conveyed appropriate 'advice'. In some ways, the rulers' powers were actually strengthened. The British regarded the influence of Islam as a force for promoting stability, and the sultans were reinforced by recognition of their religious status and by the introduction of more elaborate ceremonies.
>
> *(Milne and Mauzy 1989: 9)*

This historical fact prepared the basis for federalism in Malaysia, because the sultans were not ready to compromise their time-honoured territorial identity. The British had already united four peninsular states in the so-called Federated Malay States in the late nineteenth century. Today, the 13 states – 11 on the peninsula and two on Bornean islands such as Sabah and Sarawak – are all distinct territorial units; all except Penang (Chinese-dominated) are Malay/*bhumiputera*-dominated. In Sabah, the *bhumiputera* make up 80.5 per cent of the population, while in Sarawak they constitute 72.9 per cent of the population of the state (Bakar 2007: 71). The second-largest groups in these two states, however, are the Chinese: 13.2 per cent and 26.7 per cent respectively.[27] Malaysia therefore did not have to face the very complex problem of redrawing the political map of the country after Independence to right-size the territory so that the cultural identity matched with the political-territorial one, as India has, since 1950, been doing almost *ad infinitum*. More than ethno-national diversity, as in India and Pakistan, it was the territorial identity of

98 Federalism and institutional innovations

the states – which however, contained, diverse people, more particularly Penang (Chinese-dominated) and Sabah and Sarawak, with a preponderance of indigenous people (known as *orang asli*)– which mattered most for federal purposes. This historical-geographical factor forced the founding élites to go for a parliamentary federation in 1957 with 11 states with their distinctive ethno-regional identity, and with a combined population of 6.2 million. The federation was enlarged with the inclusion of Sabah and Sarawak in 1963, and Singapore (which was expelled in 1965).

Constitutional traits of the federation

First, as far as constitution-making was concerned, the Malaysian Constitution (1957) was the product of a conference (rather than of a constituent assembly, as in many other federations including India and Pakistan) held in London in 1956 in which a draft prepared by a Constitution Commission headed by a British judge and other members, representing one each from Britain, Australia, India and Pakistan, was presented. The commission of course considered memoranda from various sections of society. Quite predictably, the British parliamentary model of governance was basically accepted, combined with a federation in order to accommodate the local diversity.

Second, unlike India, Malaysia is named as a federation with 13 states which are mentioned in the Constitution (Articles 1 and 2). Art. 2 of the Malaysian Constitution gives powers to Parliament, by law, 'to admit other States to the federation; to alter the boundaries to any States' subject to the consent of the State Legislature of the affected State(s) and of the Conference of Rulers. This has similarities with Article 3 of the Indian Constitution, which empowers the Indian Parliament to almost unanimously change the names and boundaries of the states, create new states and so on. Comparatively speaking, this provision appears, constitutionally, to be anti-federal, but, in reality, it has been very functional for the growth of Indian federalism.[28] In the case of Malaysia, since the ethno-linguistic minorities, broadly speaking, are not so much territorially concentrated (such as the Chinese and the Indians who, in any case, were originally migrants; Penang is of course a Chinese-dominated state), the demands for the creation of new federal units that would involve changes to boundaries to existing states did not arise. However, this provision has facilitated the Parliament, by constitutional amendments, to declare Kuala Lumpur and Putrajaya federal territories carved out of Selangor in 1973 and 2001 respectively, and Labuan also a federal territory carved out of Sabah in 1984.

Third, Islam (Article 3) has been stated as 'the religion of the Federation', but this does not mean that Malaysia is a theocratic state, because other religions are allowed to practise in peace and harmony. Article 11 of the Constitution guarantees 'freedom of religion' to each individual without discrimination (Article 8) to profess and practise and not to pay any tax for religious purposes. This article (Article 11) also ensures the group right of religious believers 'to manage its own religious affairs'; to 'establish and maintain institutions for religious or charitable purposes';

Federalism and institutional innovations **99**

and 'to acquire and own property and to hold and maintain it' according to the law. What has religion to do with the Malaysian federation, especially when it is not established as a theocratic state? Unlike the Constitution of Pakistan, where the country declares itself an Islamic Republic and considers Islam and the Islamic laws, ways of life, culture, etc. as the source of the Constitution, in Malaysia, the fact that most of the Sultans are also the heads of religion of their respective states, along with the protection of the identity of the states by federalism, also implied the protection of their religious rights and privileges. Consider the provisions under Section 2 of Article 3 of the Constitution:

> In every State other than States not having a Ruler the position of the Ruler as the Head of the religion of Islam in his States in the manner and to the extent acknowledged and declared by the Constitution of that State, and subject to that Constitution, all rights, privileges, prerogatives and powers enjoyed by him as Head of that religion, are unaffected and unimpaired.[29]

Nonetheless, the supremacy of the Constitution, rather than of Islam, as the 'supreme law of the land' has been guaranteed (Article 4), along with the provision for a federal court (Article 122) with the 'federal jurisdiction' (Article 128) that includes its power to determine the constitutionality of laws, and to adjudicate disputes between the federal and state governments, if any. This provision of an independent judiciary with the powers of judicial review is taken from the British constitutional tradition. Also, the procedure for amending the Constitution is apparently not easy, requiring the support of two-thirds of the total members of each House of Parliament in both second and third readings of the bill before the assent of the *Agong*, the supreme royal head of the federation, is sought. In practice, however the Constitution has been amended many times (as many as 15 times in the first 14 years of the federation).[30]

Fourth, the Constitution establishes a parliamentary (cabinet)-federal political system in which all executive powers of the federation are vested formally in the *Yang di-Pertuan Agong*, 'the Supreme Head of the Federation', a royal who is elected to head the federation for five years by the Conference of Rulers. This provision was so devised because the native rulers were all states-based, and there was no national-level monarchy in Malay. As is the norm in parliamentary system, the *Agong* will act in accordance with the advice of the cabinet headed by the prime minister responsible to the Parliament. The Parliament consists of two houses: the House of Representatives *(Dewan Rakyat)* (a popular chamber elected for a period of five years) and the Senate *(Dewan Negara)* (second chamber) with an equal number of representatives (two) from each state plus those from the federal territories (four altogether). There is, however, a provision for 40 members to be appointed by the *Agong* to the Senate on the basis that those so appointed have provided distinguished service in various areas of the life of the country, as well as the need for representation of racial minorities and the aboriginal communities. The Senate is a permanent body in which members elected from each state are to be so

100 Federalism and institutional innovations

elected for a period of three years (two terms maximum) and by the direct vote of the electors of the state. The House of Representatives comprises 194 members distributed among the 13 states (182) and three federal territories (12). Both houses have almost equal powers of legislation, except for Money Bills, which can only originate in the popular chamber.

Fifth, the federation guarantees the relative sovereignty of the constitutions of the states (provided that they do not disregard the federal Constitution) (Article 71) and also protects the proceedings of the Legislative Assemblies (Article 72) from being questioned in any court of law. Article 71 states that:

> The Federation shall guarantee the right of a Ruler of a State to succeed and hold office, enjoy and exercise the constitutional rights and privileges of Ruler of that State in accordance with the Constitution of that State.[31]

Since the parliamentary (cabinet) form of government is also accepted at the state level, the position of a ruler of a state is that of a formal head of that state akin to that of a governor of a state in India. However, the federal Constitution recognizes him or her as the supreme person in that state.

Sixth, distribution of powers between the federal and state governments is perhaps the most vital part of the federal institutional design seeking to combine shared-rule and self-rule within a single polity in order to achieve, as Watts argues,[32] both unity and diversity. Watts (1999) has also pointed out that the pattern of distribution of powers between the two sets of governments varies a lot due to various factors concerning the mode of formation of the federation itself: geographical, historical, economic, linguistic, security-related, ecological and so on (Watts 1999: 35). Watts (1999) has further argued that the more homogeneous a society is, the greater the powers are allocated to the federal government; the opposite also holds true (Watts 1999: 35).

The formation of the Malaysian federation (1963) had followed the process of aggregation as opposed to devolution, so the residual powers of legislation were allocated to the states (Article 77). Watts (1999) argues that this measure was intended to underline the autonomy of the units and the limited nature of the powers given to the federal government (Watts 1999: 35). However, in the case of Malaysia, the picture is vastly different, because here the Federal List is not only too long but is also very exhaustive. The other two lists ('State' and 'Concurrent') are also exhaustive. Therefore, the scope of 'residual powers' vested with the states somewhat pales into insignificance. Second, although Malaysia is quite diverse and the Malay majority in the population was not achieved until 1980 (55 per cent) – and that too, with their categorization as 'bhumiputera ('sons of the soil') – greater powers have been assigned to the federal government (Federal and Concurrent Lists). The Chinese and the Indians are not only the second- and the third-largest ethno-national groups, but one state, namely Penang, is Chinese-dominated. In this respect too, Malaysia deviates from the existing patterns. This is due to the fact that except for Penang, the Malays/other *bhumiputera* were the largest ethno-national group in the states, so that at the founding of the federation the ethnic minorities could hardly advocate the territorial recognition of their identity. As we will see later, they had to live under a federal Constitution with a set of liberal rights, both individual and collective, but also with a pronounced bias towards the *bhumiputera*, then the single largest group, but now the majority, of the population. As we will see presently, 'reservation of Malays' and of the native communities/aborigines has specifically been mentioned as an item in the State List (Article 95B (1) (a), Item No. 2 (b)).

Distribution of powers

In the Malaysian federation, each tier of government has executive 'responsibilities in the same field for which it has legislative powers', a practice prevalent in some Anglo-Saxon federations.[33] Three lists (Federal, State and Concurrent) (Ninth Schedule) distribute the legislative powers between the federal and state governments in Malaysia. As we have already indicated, the Federal List (Arts 74, 77) is the longest one, with 26 broad items but over a hundred sub-items covering a wide range of subjects: external affairs, defence, internal security (police, public order, prisons, preventive detention etc.), civil and criminal law, citizenship, finance (currency, national savings and savings banks, public debt, taxes, fees, banking, moneylending, bills of exchange, capital issues etc.), trade, commerce and industry, shipping, navigation, transport, communication, education (elementary, secondary and university), labour and social security, welfare of the aborigines, newspapers, censorship, cooperation, tourism and so on. The State List has 12 broad items, which include Islamic law and personal and family laws; land tenure; land improvement; Malay reservations and reservation for the native communities in Sabah and Sarawak; compulsory acquisition of land; agriculture; forests; local government; public works for state purposes; boarding and lodging houses; markets and fairs; the Civil List and state pensions; state holidays; libraries and museums; and so on. The Supplement to the State List deals with the states of Sabah and Sarawak in such areas as native law and customs, their ports and harbours, Sabah Railways in Sabah etc. The Concurrent List is small, with only nine items plus the Supplement (another nine items) for the states of Sabah and Sarawak. It includes such items as social welfare; protection of women, children and young parents; scholarships; town and country planning; public health; fire safety; culture and sports; housing; etc. The supplementary items include personal law of marriage; divorce; family laws; adulteration of foodstuffs; theatres and cinemas; charities and charitable trusts; etc. The residual powers of legislation have been assigned to the states. As is quite obvious from the items already mentioned, the Malaysian federation is very centralized legislatively speaking if we take the Federal and the Concurrent Lists together, since the federal government has prevalence over the latter in the case of any controversy on legislation regarding items in that list. In addition, Parliament has powers to make laws on items in the State List under certain situations. It is, however, provided that the federal government by law may require the

102 Federalism and institutional innovations

administration of specified provisions of its laws by the state administration (Article 80 (4)).

Financially, the federal government is dominant in Malaysia: the majority of the major sources of revenues have been assigned to it (Watts 1999: 44). The federal government revenues before intergovernmental transfers as a percentage of total government revenue are very high in Malaysia: 86 per cent (for 2000–04), that is, higher than that of India (61.1 per cent in the same period).[34] Similarly, the federal government expenditures after intergovernmental transfers were the highest of some 15 federations: 84 per cent in 2000–04 (India's share was 44.6 per cent during the same period) (Watts 2008: 103). The percentage share of intergovernmental transfers as a share of provincial, or states revenues in Malaysia was 43.8 per cent, compared with India's 46 per cent during 2000–04 (Watts 2008: 103). This shows an improvement upon the figures in 1996 (17.9 per cent) (India: 39.41 per cent in 1994) (Watts 2008: 48). Conditional and unconditional transfers of money from the federal government to the states or provinces are a structural arrangement of federations and designed to provide protection to regional autonomy; they also testify to the latter's dependence on the former (this is known as the 'golden lead' in the German federation, Watts 2008: 48). In Malaysia, in 1996, conditional transfers as a percentage of federal transfers to the states were quite high, at 67.9 per cent (India: 38 per cent), which came down to 39.3 per cent in 2000–04 (India: 40.7 per cent) (Watts 2008: 107,1999: 49). However, the federal conditional grants as a percentage of states' revenues have not changed much over the years: 12.2 per cent in 1996 and 12 per cent in 2000–04 (India: 15 per cent in 1996; 18.7 per cent in 2000–04) (Watts 2008: 108,1999: 50). While all constituent unit governments would like to have more unconditional transfers than conditional ones, there are arguments both for and against 'conditional transfers' in the federations.[35] This dominant financial position of the federal government in Malaysia has not augured well for the functioning of the federation. Politically determined and discriminatory disbursement of revenues among the states by the federal government through the National Financial Council headed by the prime minister himself (who, incidentally, also selects the other members!) has been recorded and also resented by scholars of Malaysian federalism.[36]

The legislative, executive and financial dominance of the federal government of the National Front led by the UMNO has adversely affected the states' rights in various ways; as a result, the states have expressed much discontent and resentment. Their latest manifestation was evident in the last elections, in March 2008, in which Prime Minister Abdullah Badawi's National Front government was re-elected with a much reduced majority in Parliament (short of a two-thirds majority) (140 seats out of 220), and which saw opposition governments in five of 13 states[37] – the first time that this had happened in the federation since 1957. Apart from various urban issues, personality factors and the negative effects of globalization, there was a deep-rooted ethnic factor at work. The National Front, led by the UMNO (a Malay organization) government at the centre, has always been biased towards the Malays and against the ethnic minorities, who have fought against their marginalization (Loh 2008: 32). The Malaysian political observers believe that the federation needs to be strengthened, which requires, among other things, the curtailment of the anti-federal practice of the coalition government 'of encroaching on the powers of state governments' (Loh 2008: 32). The electoral outcomes therefore provide a warning that the federation should be reformed rather than further weakened.

Language and the Malaysian federation

Article 152 of the Constitution makes Malay the national and official language of the federation, despite the fact that the Chinese and the Indians constitute significant portions of the population, 28 per cent and 8 per cent respectively (2000). The Constitution does not, however, prohibit or prevent any person from using, teaching or learning any other language; neither does it prevent or prohibit the federal or state governments acting 'to preserve and sustain the use and study of the language of any other community in the federation'. The provision of Malay as the national and official language has significance far beyond language. It has to do with the promotion of Malay identity and dominance, especially when the same is inextricably linked to Islamic cultures, beliefs and practices in a society which is multiracial, multicultural and multi-religious. As Ismail Bakar (2007) has pointed out:

> Whenever the issue of language emerges, it is inevitably transformed into a racial issue because it tends to be viewed by other ethnic groups as a threat to their cultural and more importantly as an attempt at 'Malayanisation'.
>
> *(Bakar 2007: 72)*

Malay reservations

The suspicion of other non-Malay ethnic groups about the institutional framework for special protection of the Malays is not without grounds. Consider the following constitutional provisions under Article 153: 'It shall be the responsibility of the *Yang di-Pertuan Agong* to safeguard the special position of the Malays and natives of any of the States of Sabah and Sarawak'. The *Agong* is constitution-bound thus to safeguard their special interests and reserve positions in public services, scholarships exhibitions, grants of permits or licences and so on. The State List (Item 2, sect. b) specifically mentions the reservations for Malays and the natives of Sabah and Sarawak. The Malaysian federation is perhaps alone in providing for very discriminatory constitutional provision in favour of the majority community in respect of the distribution of public goods and business opportunities, including possession of land. The historical argument offered in favour of such a policy, as Bakar has mentioned, is that this was the only way that the economically backward position of the Malays (*bhumiputera*/sons of the soil) could be upgraded relative to the well-off position of the Chinese.[38] The federal constitution makes the Malays, or the so-called *bhumiputera*, permanently politically powerful, a position which has helped

104 Federalism and institutional innovations

to improve their economic position, particularly when the Constitution itself provides for their special protection. The major policy initiatives for development undertaken by the federal government have thus favoured the *bhumiputera* to the relative deprivation of the other ethnic groups such as the Chinese and the Indians. Andaya and Andaya (2001) have shown how the very strong Malay pressure put on the government grew into stronger state support in favour of the Malays. The first three five-year plans (1956–70) could not eliminate the long-held Chinese control over the corporate sectors. This created a lot of resentment among the educated and urbanized Malays who were the product of the affirmative policy pursued since the 1960s; they held important positions in the UMNO or were highly placed government officials. In 1965 the first *bhumiputera* Economic Congress was held to promote Malay capitalism; in a second meeting in 1968, resolutions were passed for greater state support for Malay commerce; and in 1968 the first *bhumiputera* commercial bank, known as the Bhumiputera Bank, was established for extending easier credit facilities for the Malays. In 1969 a Council of Trust for Indigenous People (Majlis Amnah Rakyat or MAR) was created for the same purpose.[39] Andaya and Andaya (2001) argue that, despite this, about half the population of Peninsular Malaysia remained below the poverty line (M\$33 per capita a month), and of these as many as 75 per cent were Malays! (Andaya and Andaya 2001: 302). The ethnic riots of 13 May 1969 added further fuel to the Malay situation. This was the background under which the new government of Tun Abdul Razak (Prime Minister during 1970–76) undertook a major economic policy initiative to be known as the New Economic Policy (NEP) to ensure economic growth while making sure that more resources and opportunities would be made available to the Malays (Andaya and Andaya 2001: 302–3). While the NEP changed the economic face of the country during 1971–90, with spectacular economic growth taking place in the country, critics point out that the policy was pro-Malay.[40] However, in its long journey, the NEP came to be combined with the promotion of the Malay Islamic identity and accommodation of both the *bhumiputera* and the Chinese capitalists, as well as since the late 1980s giving way to increasing privatization and so on. The National Development Policy (NDP) and 'Vision 2020' of Dr Mahathir Muhammad, the prime minister, which replaced the NEP in 1990 maintained the continuity in policy, with pronounced stress on the role of private capital in economic development in tune with the rising tides of globalization.

India

The institutional arrangements of Indian federalism have remained rather very complex, appropriately designed to respond to the world's most diverse country, socially and culturally speaking (see Chapter 2 of this book). But what has remained nonetheless central to India's innovation in federal institutions is a combination of shared- and self-rule at various levels of the polity so that identities have been accommodated and power-sharing has taken place. Backed by solid historical bases of support in favour of democratic federalism, India's federal Constitution was drafted by the Indian nationalists themselves sitting in the Constituent Assembly (1946–49), originally a central legislative body formed during the last days of British colonial rule in 1946 on the basis of a somewhat limited adult franchise and over-dominated by the members of the Indian National Congress (INC). Unlike Pakistan and Malaysia, India's federal Constitution (inaugurated on and from 26 January 1950) and modelled substantially on the Government of India Act, 1935 (which was based on the British North America Act, 1867) could not be seen as social contract or a compact heralding the victory of some dominant ethnonational group(s). The Indian Constitution has provided, on the contrary, the institutional space for the accommodation of ethno-national identities, whether based on language, region, tribal ethnicity or a combination thereof, and often religion within a broad secular liberal democratic framework based on the recognition of a set of rights for both the individuals and groups.

Although India is a federation and has functioned more or less successfully as such since 1950, withstanding all pressures for disintegration and defying many predictions of collapse, in the Constitution itself it is called not a federation but 'a Union of States' (Article 1 (1)). India's option for a federal 'Union of States' was linked to the specific modes of formation of the federation in the country. The process of federation-building in India (as yet incomplete) has followed the methods of both aggregation and devolution – both being interlinked in the case of India. Despite the appellation of 'Union of States', and given such a vast, populous country with such complex diversity coupled with the threat of insecurity and disintegration at Independence, the CA resolved almost unanimously that the constitutional framework of the country would be that of 'a federation with a strong Centre' (Watts 2008: 36).

Federal institutional arrangements for accommodation of manifold identity

Although it is a country with about 82 per cent of its population being made up of Hindus (even though the Hindus in India are regionally specific and plural in beliefs and practices and divided by language and castes – a form of social hierarchy), the Indian federation has not declared a religion for itself. This is in contrast to Pakistan and Malaysia; India has declared itself to be a secular state[41] in which religion is considered to be a matter of private belief. However, the right to religion has been guaranteed in the Constitution as a fundamental right. The Indian Constitution under Articles 25–28 guarantees the right to freedom of religion (of conscience, profession and propagation; administering of religious institutions; and management of religious affairs, and so on) subject to public order, morality and health and so on. Apart from the Jains (more than 3million in number) and the Buddhists (more than 6million), both of which are not specifically regionally concentrated, there are some regional concentrations of Muslims (more than 120 million in number), most notably in Jammu and Kashmir and some other districts and areas; the Sikhs in Punjab; and the Christians in India's NorthEast. The federal Constitution

106 Federalism and institutional innovations

of India prohibits the use of religion as a basis for political mobilization or, to be exact, for demanding a political identity (statehood within the federation). Except for Punjab, where a combination of linguistic and religious considerations (Sikhism does not apparently separate one's ethno-linguistic identity from the religious one) was conceded in the creation of the state in 1966, most of the states in India (federal units numbering 28 today) are the result of post-Independence federalization and are based on factors such as language, region and tribal ethnicity or a combination thereof. Jammu and Kashmir is India's only Muslim-majority state, which was a princely state (with a Hindu ruler ruling over the predominantly Muslim subjects) and the only state in India having its own Constitution, governed by Article 370 of the Indian Constitution, which guarantees extra autonomy to J and K compared with other states of India.[42]

In Pakistan and Malaysia (both Muslim-majority countries), adoption of Islam as the religion of the federations has had an extra-religious meaning linked to assertion of national identity (Pakistan) and formation and promotion of national identity (Malaysia). In the latter, the Malay national identity is sought to be Islamic.[43] In India, by contrast, despite the political forces advocating for a Hindu *Rashtra* (state) since the colonial days, the broad-based consensus arrived at was in favour of a secular state committed to a composite multi-tiered (and multicultural and multinational) national identity having both ethnic and civic elements.[44] In fact, Hinduism is not a single-book religion and is so diverse and amorphous in character, as competent authorities on the subject[45] have established, that it did not contain a coherent and total view of the state which could replace the state system that had evolved in India during the two centuries of British colonial rule up until 1947. On the contrary, Hinduism's better compatibility with secularism, as compared with Islam and Buddhism, has been highlighted by scholars.[46] Due to the consent of the citizens irrespective of religion, caste, colour or creed being the basis of democracy in the state, the constellation of a composite ethno-civic nationhood, despite many odds,[47] has been possible in India. Indian nationhood debates have also been inescapably linked to debates on Indian versions of secularism.[48] But secular solution of identity issues in India, as provided for in the Constitution and various legal enactments, and the widespread popular support for the same have meant that the federation's burden has been much lessened.

Ethno-national identity and the Indian federation

Unlike in Malaysia, the relative success of federalism in India has been contingent upon the appropriate institutional arrangements for differentiation and federalization of a once huge unitary state with units which were immensely complex containing warring ethno-national groups claiming recognition and power since the colonial days. During the colonial period, there were two types of territories in India: 11 directly ruled provinces and about 560 princely kingdoms of varied sizes and complexions which were indirectly governed by the British. While the kingdoms were themselves very diverse in sociocultural terms, the provinces were created for 'administrative convenience' of the colonial rulers rather than to create congruence between ethno-national identity and political boundary or identity. Apart from Orissa (in 1926), which was the only linguistically homogeneous state created during the period of British rule, the rest of the provinces and the kingdoms which fell under India (after the Partition in 1947) required a lot of adjustment and readjustment of boundaries and the creation, merger, splitting and so on of the units for the purpose of federal integration. The Herculean task was accomplished (it is still not complete, though) in many phases: 1950, 1956–66, 1972, 1987 and 2000 (Bhattacharyya, H. 2001a, 2001b, 2003, 2007a, 2008). India's federal units are therefore the result of federation-building in India rather than the other way round.

Territorial and non-territorial accommodation of ethno-national identity in Indian federalism

The powers of Parliament to create states

Indian federalism has provided three types of institutional measures for the accommodation of ethno-national identity, both territorially concentrated and dispersed. The Indian Constitution empowers the Union Parliament to reorganize the states to alter their boundaries or names (Article 3). Article 3 of the Constitution says:
    Parliament may by law:

1   form a new state by separation of territory from any state or by uniting two or more states or parts of states or uniting any territory to a part of any state;
2   increase the area of any state;
3   diminish the area of any state;
4   alter the boundaries of any state;
5   alter the name of any state.

(Basu 1997: 62)

The article provides that the Parliament by a simple majority and by the ordinary legislative process can form new states or alter the boundaries etc. of existing states and can thereby change the political map of India. The presidential recommendation is required for introducing such a bill, and the president is required, before he or she recommend the process, to refer the bill to the legislature of the state to be affected by the proposed changes for soliciting its views on the proposed changes within a specific period of time, although the president is not bound to accept the views as given. Thus, it is the Parliament of India which alone is empowered to disintegrate the states and territories of India, and the history of Indian federalism since 1950 is replete with examples of disintegration of existing states in order to create new states.

On the face of it, Article 3 (which is originally derived from the US Constitution via the Australian Constitution and the Government of Indian Act, 1935) appears to be most unfederal, if not anti-federal, since it infringes upon the

108 Federalism and institutional innovations

territorial integrity of the federal units. But given the specific Indian context, as we will see shortly, it has helped immensely in building a federal India by providing for flexible institutional mechanisms for territorial accommodation of identity by right-sizing the states.

When the Constitution was inaugurated on 26 January 1950, the first threefold process of accommodation was found to have been followed to simplify the very complex situation to some extent. First, 216 princely states were merged with the geographically contiguous provinces, and included in the category of Part B States (see the First Schedule of the Constitution). Second, 61 relatively small princely states were converted into Part C States (centrally ruled) (see the First Schedule of the constitution). Third, groups of states were consolidated into new units called the Union of States, and thus five Unions of States (including 275 states) emerged, such as the Madyha Bharat, Patiala and East Punjab States (PEPSU), Rajasthan, Saurashtra and Travancore-Cohin (these were included in the Part B category.). Some special kinds of states, such as Hyderabad, Mysore and Kashmir, were also included in the Part B states. There were above all the nine former provinces of British rule which were included in the category A States.

This account thus shows that reorganization of states within the Indian federation was undertaken at the early stage on pragmatic grounds, which involved a lot of adjustments and readjustments. But the most distinctive feature of this early attempt was that the newly emerging units of the federation were not accorded the same status. Three types of states emerged initially. First, there were nine Part A States (former provinces); second, there were eight Part B states (five Unions of States, and Hyderabad, Kashmir and Mysore); and third, there were ten Part C states (under central administration).

This remained more or less the picture until the next major and first linguistic reorganization of states in 1956, which abolished all the three categories of states and placed all the newly re-emerged states (numbering 15) on the same footing so far as their constitutional status was concerned. And yet the new further experiments with state formation within the Indian federation went on. The Union territories thus have been subsequently upgraded to statehood. The new categories of 'associate State' (Sikkim in 1974), and 'sub-State' (Meghalaya in 1969) were created as the first steps towards statehood (Sikkim in 1975 and Meghalaya in 1971). In the 1960s, some more states were created, including Nagaland (1963) and Punjab (1966). In the early 1970s, the NorthEast was reorganized and the states of Tripura, Manipur and Meghalaya were created. Arunachal Pradesh and Mizoram in the NorthEast became states in 1987, along with Goa. In 2000, three new states were carved out of existing ones: Chhattisgarh out of Madhya Pradesh; Jharkhand out of Bihar; and Uttarakhand out of Uttar Pradesh. While the linguistic considerations predominated in states' reorganization in the 1950s and 1960s and tribal ethnicity in the 1970s, in 2000 a combination of ethno-regional, tribal and ecological considerations played an important role in state creation.

The various types of tribal, district and regional councils formed in special areas inhabited by tribal people since the inception of the Constitution have also worked

Federalism and institutional innovations **109**

(and still do) as a kind of substate within the state, as a political institutional expression of the various minorities living in the areas concerned.

Achievement of statehood within the Indian federation thus remains the most effective institutional solution to India's minorities, the method through which minorities have sought to turn themselves into majorities in the operational dynamics of India's parliamentary federal democracy. Indian federal polity is based on the relative sovereignty of the states, despite the fact that 'Union' was not the result of an agreement by the units. The very first Article 1(1) of the Indian Constitution states: 'India, that is, *Bharat,*[49] shall be a Union of States'. The states are thus indispensable parts of the Indian federation, and their relative sovereignty is protected by provisions for federal distribution of powers and authority and the relatively autonomous political processes obtaining in each of the states. Dr B. R. Ambedkar, Chairman of the Drafting Committee of the CA, said in the Constituent Assembly that the 'States under our constitution are in no way dependent upon the centre for their legislative or executive authority'. The states in the Indian federation are distinct units, socioculturally, electorally and politically speaking, and the Constitution does take cognizance of that.

Substatehood

The Constitution of India contains special provisions under Schedules 5–6 for self-governance for certain areas and communities. The areas mentioned were 'Scheduled Areas' in states other than Assam, Meghalaya, Tripura and Mizoram (in India's NorthEast) and the tribal (aboriginal) inhabited areas in the states of Assam, Meghalaya, Tripura and Mizoram. Even though such areas fall within the states/ Union territories, these special provisions have been made in view of the backwardness of the people of these areas. The president of India has been empowered to declare an area 'scheduled' subject to legislation by Parliament, and the president has exercised such powers under the Fifth Schedule of the Constitution. The Fifth Schedule of the Constitution deals with the administration and governance of Scheduled Areas as well as of Scheduled Tribes in states other than Assam, Meghalaya, Tripura and Mizoram. This schedule provides for the formation of tribal advisory councils to give advice on such matters relating to welfare and advancement of the Scheduled Tribes in the states as may be referred to them by the governor. The governor (the formal head of a state government appointed by the president) is authorized to direct that any act of Parliament or of the state legislature shall not apply to a Scheduled Area or shall apply subject to modifications. While the Fifth Schedule makes the governor somewhat all-powerful in matters relating to governance of scheduled areas, the Sixth Schedule is more empowering for the district and regional councils that may be formed for the purpose. This constitutional provision is at once decentralizing and democratic: there shall be a district council for each autonomous district, consisting of not more than 30 members, of whom not more than four persons shall be nominated by the governor and the rest shall be elected on the basis of adult suffrage (Article 244 (2) and Article 275 (1)). After the

110 Federalism and institutional innovations

amendments made to the Sixth Schedule, the tribal areas mentioned in it today are nine. Such tribal areas are to be governed as autonomous districts. Although they are not outside the executive authority of the state concerned, provision has been made for the formation of the district and regional councils as representative bodies with certain legislative and judicial powers regarding forest management, inheritance of property, marriage and social customs, and other matters as may be conferred upon them by the governor. These councils have also the powers to assess and collect land revenues and to impose certain specified taxes. The laws made by the councils have, however, to secure the assent of the governor to become effective. The legislative autonomy of the councils has been protected by the Constitution, with the provision that the acts of the state legislature shall not extend to such areas unless the particular council so directs by public notification. The president of India and a state governor can restrict the application of the Union and state laws respectively to an autonomous area.

Before the inauguration of the Constitution, most of the tribal areas were under their respective traditional tribal councils or organizations, although in some areas, such as Tripura, the old order was breaking down due to the impact of a set of historical forces (Bhattacharyya, H. 1999). The Constitution leaves some scope for the accommodation of such traditional institutions. The consultative role of the tribal traditional organizations or councils was retained. It was said in the Sixth Schedule that the governor shall make rules for the first Constitution of the district councils and regional councils in consultation with the existing tribal councils or such other representative organizations. But in the governance of tribal life, the new democratically formed district councils were given so much primacy that the appointment and succession of tribal chiefs was made dependent on the power of the district councils. Quite predictably, the rise of such district councils signified the loss of power for the tribal chiefs, and they resented them. But the new emerging élites in such societies welcome them. Although the Constitution in some way sought to subordinate the traditional institutions of the tribespeople to the authority of the modern district councils, the tribal culture was respected and honoured, and not attacked in any way. For instance, Article 371 (A) (inserted as a result of constitutional amendments) says:

> Notwithstanding anything contained in the Constitution no act of Parliament in respect of religious or social practices of the Nagas, Naga customary laws and procedures, administration of civil and criminal justice involving decisions according to Naga customary laws, and ownership and transfer of land and its resources, shall apply to the state of Nagaland unless the Legislative Assembly of Nagaland by a resolution so decides.
>
> *(Mitra and Bhattacharyya 2000)*

Such constitutional provisions have proved to be very effective in managing the ethno-nationalist minority conflicts that characterized many of such areas and have simultaneously reflected the values of different communities in the Indian polity. They have also facilitated institutionalized power-sharing within the political system. Their legitimacy was never questioned; on the contrary, many subnationalist rebels in India's NorthEast fought for the introduction and implementation of the constitutional schedules, particularly the Sixth Schedule, in the areas concerned. The Indian Constitution has thus been a resource in federal nation- and state-building in India.

Non-territorial mode of accommodation of identity

Languages have (and still do) provided the main basis for the growth of subnationalist conflicts in India, often conjoined by religions – not only historically during the country's struggle for liberation against British colonialism but also ever since her Independence. Currently, there are no less than 1,652 languages spoken in India, of which 63 have non-Indian origins (Basu 1997: 387). Of them, 22 languages are so far recognized as 'official' and are listed in the Eighth Schedule of the Indian Constitution, and so could be taken as the major languages of the country, used by up to 91 per cent of the country's population. It has been stated in Article 343 of the Constitution that Hindi (in Devnagri script) shall be the national and official language of the Union and that English shall continue to be used for all the official purposes of the Union, originally for a period of 15 years, but in terms of the Official Languages Act (1963) English still continues to be used in addition to Hindi (Basu 1997: 390–1). The Constitution of India sought to afford relief to regional linguistic groups by allowing the respective state legislatures (Article 345) and the president (Article 347) to recognize some language or languages other than Hindi as the languages for intra-state official transactions. These provisions recognize the right of the majority of the state legislature or a substantial section of the population of a state to have the language spoken by them to be recognized for official purposes within the state. Article 344 provides for the appointment of a Language Commission (the first such commission was formed in 1956) to advise the president with regard to the official language, and the president shall constitute the commission with the representatives of the recognized languages, as specified in the Eighth Schedule. The Constitution also provides for the safeguards for linguistic minorities, and the appointment of a special officer to deal with such matters and to report to the president (Article 350B). The official recognition of a language and its placement in the Eighth Schedule of the Indian Constitution has meant more than a symbolic significance for the speakers of that language, particularly if they inhabit a particular region, or area within a state; very often this recognition has paved the way for mobilization towards substatehood or full statehood within the federation, with different degrees of success. Thus, today the Indian federation has 28 states (of highly asymmetrical sizes population-wise, and hence in representation in representative bodies) and seven Union territories (centrally ruled), including the National Capital Territory of Delhi, which has the special status of a state.

112 Federalism and institutional innovations

Institutions of a parliamentary-cabinet federal system

Being adapted to the decades-long British colonial system, and following it, the Indian federation has adopted a parliamentary-cabinet system of government at both the Union and state levels, in which the government originates in the Parliament (*Lok Sabha*) and state legislature respectively and remains responsible to it. While the prime minister at the Union level and the chief minister at the state level are the real executives of the governments respectively, there is provision for an indirectly elected president as the formal head of the government at the Union level and an appointed (by the president) governor for the state(s) as the formal head of the government at the state level. Members of the legislative assembly (MLAs) and members of Parliament – two houses, the *Lok Sabha* (popular chamber) and the *Rajya Sabha* (Council of States) – make up the Electoral College to elect the president. The president is part of the Parliament although he or she does not sit in it. His or her assent is essential for all bills to be passed as laws.

There is provision for bicameralism at the Union level and in many states too. At the Union level, while the *Lok Sabha* (currently 545 members) is directly elected by the citizens of India (of the age of 18 of older) after every five years, the *Rajya Sabha* is a permanent body of 250 members, of whom 12 are nominated by the president and the rest are elected by MLAs of the states that constitute the Electoral College and the Union territories for a period of six years. The states' representation to the *Rajya Sabha* is not, however, equal: it varies from only one member from Nagaland to 34 from Uttar Pradesh. Nonetheless, the federal character of the Council of States is accepted as it represents the units of the federation. The shared character of the rule at the federal level is further corroborated by the fact that the Constitution (Article 81 (1)) (1) provides that there shall be not more than 530 representatives of the states in the *Lok Sabha*. Both the houses have almost equal powers, except that Money Bills can only originate in the *Lok Sabha* and the *Rajya Sabha* can exercise its power of what Watts calls a 'suspensive veto' to the passage of such a bill for 14 days only, like in Malaysia.

The Indian federation is governed by a written Constitution (the lengthiest in the world) with the provision of a federal Supreme Court of India at the apex of an integrated judicial system as the guardian of the Constitution (with powers of judicial review) as well as the umpire in disputes between the two tiers of government. The Constitution of India, being the supreme law of the land, distributes the powers between the two tiers of government as well as governing the structures and powers and functions of the substate-level rural and urban decentralized representative bodies since 1993 (The 73rd and 74th Constitution Amendment Acts, 1993), which have been emerging as a form of a third tier of the federal system in India (more on this later). Watts (1999) has argued that 'constitutional supremacy' in theory and practice is an important prerequisite for the effective operation of the federation.[50] The amendment of the Constitution of India (Article 368), insofar as the federal aspects are concerned, is required to follow special procedures involving the states, too, although the subject itself has given birth to longstanding controversy in the Indian juridical community as well as the general public, particularly since the famous landmark judgement of the Supreme Court in the Keshavananda Bharati Case in 1973 in which the concept of a 'basic structure' theory (that includes federalism) was formulated by the Supreme Court, something which cannot be amended.[51] This has further strengthened the supremacy of the Constitution as a whole.

Distribution of powers

The recognition of a ethno-regional/national/linguistic identity amounts to nothing if such recognition is not accompanied by the appropriate powers and resources for the promotion, protection and celebration of such an identity. This is also linked to self-rule and the protection of diversity. The institution responsible for the distribution of powers between the tiers of government in a federation is designed precisely to respond to such needs. There is no ideal model of distribution of powers in this regard because it depends on various factors, the most important of which is the specific mode of formation of the federation. As is amply indicated already, the Indian federation was not a compact among sovereign states. The representatives of the provinces in the CA were hardly the traditional defenders of states' rights. The debates of the Constituent Assembly of India did not witness any deep-seated conflicts of interests or the conflict between the centralists and the provincialists, as was witnessed in Philadelphia in 1787. The provincialists who had tasted political power after 1937 resisted any tight centralization in favour of administrative decentralization, and even also demanded increased revenues for the provinces. But it was doubtful, argues Austin,[52] if that could be taken as either a traditional defence of state autonomy or advocacy for states' rights.[53] Although considered to be secondary – given the then grave situation – to the CA, the states' autonomy or rights were not sacrificed in the emerging political model. While introducing the Draft Constitution, Dr B. R. Ambedkar described the constitution 'federal inasmuch as it establishes what may be called a *dual polity* [which] will consist of the Union as the centre and the states at the periphery each endowed with *sovereign powers* to be exercised in the field assigned to them by the Constitution' [my emphasis] (Bhattacharyya 2001a: 126–7).

The Indian Constitution distributes powers and responsibilities between the two tiers of government in terms of three Lists – Union, State and Concurrent. The Constitution has made the federal government legislatively very powerful, with as many as 97 items in the Union List (on which the Union government will have exclusive powers to legislate) and 47 items in the Concurrent List (on which the Union will have prevalence in case of conflict), while the State List has 66 items. The Union List contains items such as income tax, corporate tax, excise duty, defence, atomic energy, diplomacy, citizenship, currency, foreign exchange, foreign trade and commerce, and so on. The Concurrent List contains items such as criminal law, forests, economic and social planning, trade unions, education, marriage, preventive detention and so on. The State List contains items such as

114 Federalism and institutional innovations

public order, local government, public health and sanitation, agriculture, fisheries, taxation, the police, the water supply, irrigation, canals, land rights, land tenure, taxes on agricultural income, tolls, capitation taxes and so on.[54]

Following the Anglo-Saxon tradition, each tier of government in India, like that of Malaysia, has executive powers over matters on which it can legislate. Like Malaysia again, the three lists are quite exhaustive, so that the scope of residual powers left to the Union government in India becomes limited and of less significance. The founders of the Indian Constitution wanted the provinces' powers to be specifically limited. Mathew has pointed out that over the years the lists have been subjected to constitutional amendments in favour of the Union government,[55] implying further centralization. Mathew (2002) has drawn our attention to various articles in the Constitution itself, including the emergency provisions (Articles 352, 356, 360, and 249 and 250), which infringe states' rights.[56] The issue itself has remained hugely controversial in the legal-constitutional debates on Indian federalism for many years, so it has taken many decades for the scholars, particularly Indian scholars, to recognize that the Indian federation was after all real.[57] Watts (1999) has, however, drawn our attention to a different and realistic understanding of the phenomenon. He argues that in Indian and Malaysia, 'state governments are constitutionally responsible for the implementation and administration of a wide range of federal legislation' (Watts 1999: 41). Watts' conclusion in this regard is worth quoting:

> Thus, while federations are relatively centralized legislatively, they are more decentralized administratively. These federations have shown that benefits can flow from the administrative decentralization of federal legislation particularly in adapting to the different circumstances and sensitivities of the various regions.

As far as the distribution of financial powers is concerned, most important revenue-raising powers have been assigned to the Union government in India (as in Malaysia too), although provisions have been made for redistribution of revenues among the states in various forms through an independent Union Finance Commission composed of a chairman and four other members appointed by the president of India every five years. The procedures of distribution of revenues between the Union and the states in India are quite complex, entailing such provisions as duties levied by the Union but collected and appropriated by the states; taxes levied and collected by the Union but assigned to the states; taxes levied and collected by the Union and distributed between the Union and the states; and so on.[58] Born in the heyday of the welfare state after the Second World War and the Keynesian theory of macroeconomic management and stability (Watts 1999: 44), the Indian federation has defined a major redistributive role for the states, something that is to be expected particularly in a country like India that has mass poverty, illiteracy and extremes of underdevelopment. Hence, the majority of resource revenue sources have been assigned to the Union. In 2000–04, Union government revenue as a percentage of total revenues before intergovernmental transfer in India was 61.1 per cent, which is higher than that of only the United States, Switzerland and Canada but is the lowest of that of many known federations (Watts 2008: 102). But since it is the states which have to implement most, if not all, welfare legislation (since the Union government is 'all staff and no line' according to Paul Appleby (1953)), various forms of intergovernmental transfer of resources take place for the purpose. One solid proof of the above is that after intergovernmental transfer, the Union government expenditure is only 44.6 per cent of the total expenditure (compared with Malaysia (84.3 per cent), which tops the list of many federations) (Watts 2008: 103). India's position in this respect is closer to Belgium, Germany, Canada and Switzerland. Beyond that, there are provisions for conditional, unconditional and equalization transfers to the states, in consideration of factors in the states such as population, per capita income, area, infrastructure, tax-collection efforts and the special needs of some states and, above all, the diversity needs of the regions.[59] While the issue of centralization has remained very emotive for those state-based politicians who tend to see only centralization in the federal system, the objective tendencies in the system have been such that that even the high degree of political centralization by the late Prime Minister Mrs Indira Gandhi could not throttle them. As Paul Brass has observed: 'Insofar as long-term tendencies or underlying persistent patterns can be discerned across institutions and policy areas in India, the directions or the underlying patterns are towards pluralism, regionalism and decentralization'.[60]

Nepal

The Constitution of Nepal (2015) has provided for a parliamentary-federal democratic republic – a liberal democratic structure of shorts – like India, but unlike India the local government (urban and rural) as a tier in the federal structure has received greater attention in Nepal. After a successful Maoist revolution, establishing a people's democracy was the natural course of action, but that was not to be. The very Preamble to the Constitution of Nepal has highlighted the importance of the 'sovereign right of the people and the right to autonomy and self-rule' and stressed the country's commitment to build the 'bases of socialism by democratic norms and values' within a multi-party open political system. In the *Preliminary* (Part 1) of the Constitution, the inclusiveness of the country has been stressed, and of the structure of a 'socialist-oriented federal democratic republic'[61] given as the characteristic of the proposed state. Although Nepal is predominantly a Hindu country, the state has been described as secular, unlike Pakistan and Malaysia, in which Islam has been adopted as the federation's religion. This goes better with democracy. However, Nepal's adoption of a liberal democratic federal republic is an innovative institutional step never witnessed before in the history of either democracy or federations.

Unlike India, Pakistan and Malaysia – all postcolonial federations – nation-building is not the central goal of the state, but the Constitution has officered a

116 Federalism and institutional innovations

clear-cut definition of the nation in Nepal: 'multi-ethnic, multi-lingual, multi-religious, multi-cultural, . . . all the Nepali people collectively constitute the nation'. To add further strength to this, all the mother tongues spoken in Nepal are declared as the national language. The Nepali in *Devnagiri* script is the official language of the federation, although it is spoken by only 44.6 per cent of the people, followed by Maithili (11.7 per cent), Bhojpuri (5.98 per cent) and Tharu (5.77 per cent). Provisions have been made for a province to use the language of majority in official business.[62] Article 32 provides for the fundamental right to language and culture: 'Each community living in Nepal shall have the right to preserve and promote its language, script, culture, cultural civilization and heritage'. This serves to add strength to the country's multicultural nationhood.

Given the large-scale social discrimination and deprivation suffered by the vast majority of the under-privileged sections under the monarchy for centuries, the issue of social inclusion has been figured prominently in the Constitution. Article 40 (under Fundamental Rights) provides for the right of *dalits* to participate in all aspects of the state on the principle of their proportion. In addition, there shall be special provisions for their education (free with scholarships) and employment including the public service. Furthermore, in Article 42 ('Right to social justice') it has been stated:

> Socially backward women, Dalits, Adivasi, Janajati, Janajati Adivasi, Madhesi, Tharu, minority groups, person with disability, marginalized groups, Muslims, backward classes, gender and sexually minority groups, youths, peasants, labourers, the oppressed and the citizens of the backward regions, and economically poor Khas Arya shall have the right to employment in state structures on the basis of principle of social inclusion.

This sounds a very ambitious approach to social inclusion of the underprivileged sections of society, but it raises at the same time the question of the size of the future state apparatuses and its effectiveness in making a more productive society, and that, too, towards socialism. At any rate, those provisions, if implemented, are democratic in nature and have little to do with federalism *per se*. But more democratic and inclusive a state is, it is always better for federalism, for it minimizes the extent of social and economic conflicts. In a way, such provisions serve at once the needs for meeting what I have termed elsewhere *diversity-claims* and *equality-claims*.[63]

The Constitution of Nepal has provided for a three-tier federal structure – federal, provinces and districts – with the corresponding legislative and executive organs and the lists of distribution of powers among the three tiers. For the local level, provisions have been made for village council, municipal council and district assembly as well as for the creation of autonomous regions for protection of special cultural and social needs of people at the local levels. Schedule 5 (Articles 57 (a) and 109) lists 35 items of national and international significance on which the bicameral federal Parliament (House of Representatives and National Assembly) can legislate. Schedule 6 lists the powers of the provinces (21 items), and Schedule 8 (22 items) lists the significant powers of the local governments. In the formation of the village assembly, special attention has been given to elect at least two women from each ward of the village. While the House of Representatives is the popular chamber, the National Assembly is the second federal chamber. In order to make the houses more representative, two systems of elections have been set, namely, first past the post (FPP) (165 members), and proportional representation (party-wise) (110) – the latter to be so done that women, *Dalits* and other underprivileged sections of society, and the backward regions are taken into consideration. In the case of the National Assembly, out of 59 members, 56 shall be elected by an Electoral College made up of members of the provincial assembly, chairpersons and vice-chairpersons of village councils, and mayors and deputy mayors of municipal councils with at least three women (with one *Dalit* women and one with a physical disability and or a minority). The composition of the federal Parliament in Nepal is thus made to be socially inclusive and the platform for representation of national, provincial and local perspectives and political inclusion from the underprivileged sections of society.

The Constitution of Nepal has also provided for a three-tiered integrated judiciary – Supreme Court, High Courts and district courts – with the Supreme Court at the guardian of the Constitution and final arbiter on interpretation of the Constitution and laws. Provisions have been made to ensure impartiality in the appointment of the judges. (Arts 129–30).

But the profoundly important issue in the institutional arrangements of federalism in Nepal remains largely unresolved: all the provinces are yet to be named, ethnically or otherwise! In the Constitution the seven provinces were named numerically. Each one contains many districts (from 8 to 14) (Schedule 4 of the Constitution, Article 56). As the number of districts within each province suggests, there will be many local level governments within the provinces. Since the inauguration of the Constitution in September 2015, three provinces have been named: Province 6 has been named Karnali (capital Surkhet); Province 4 has been named Gandaki (with Pokhara as its capital); Province 7 has been named Sundarpaschim (with Godabori of Kailali as its capital); and for the rest, debates and discussion have been going on regarding naming the provinces and their capitals. The available information suggests that these provinces are not only very complex, socially and culturally speaking, but there are questions about the weight of geography, regional and or party loyalty when different provinces are ruled by different political parties with a majority, or in coalition, in which case no party has a majority.[64] Since this power to name itself has been given to the provinces (Article 56 (3)) which by a two-thirds majority can decide the name and capital of the province, the process is not as complicated. Four or five years may not be seen as time enough to name a province in a country which saw only centralization and concentration of powers for centuries under the monarchies. But the method of creation of provinces in Nepal is more democratic and innovative, no doubt.

118 Federalism and institutional innovations

Myanmar

The institutional arrangements for federalism in Myanmar cannot be called 'innovative'. The Constitution of Myanmar (2008) ('Union of the Republic of Myanmar') provides for a 'Union', not a federation, and a parliamentary system of government with a very powerful president indirectly elected. Within a still fledgling democracy, political uncertainty on the borders where ethnic insurgents are very active and the very big stake the Myanmar military retains in the Constitution and overall power structure, the current Constitution has the trappings of a federation without much real content. As we have seen earlier (Chapter 3), the real key to federalize Myanmar lies in resolving the self-determination issues of various ethnic states – which the Panglong 1 (1947) promised but could not realize, and the so-called 21st century Panglong (2016–) has yet to settle down.

The Constitution of Myanmar provides for a three-tier 'Union' – the Union, state/region, and local (self-administered zones) levels of government, each level to be elected by direct vote in the system of first past the post. The Union is defined as comprising seven states and seven regions, all local level governments and the Union territories. The seven states are the ethnic states such as Shan, Mon, Rakhaine, Karen, Kachin and so on. There is provision for a second chamber at the Union level (*Amyiotha Hlutaw*) with representatives from the states/regions – 12 each from each state/region and 56 military personnel nominated by the commander-in-chief. In the lower house (*Pithu Hlutaw*) of 440 seats, 330 are elected directly by the people and 110 are nominated by the military. Each level has been assigned powers and responsibilities list in schedules,[65] although the Union government has been heavily empowered with many matters, including the police service, so that law and order does not belong to the states and the regions. The local level governments have also been assigned some powers and responsibilities.

However, the significant presence of the defence personnel in each tier of the legislature raises serious doubt about the democratic intention of the Constitution. Second, the overall institutional arrangements create the over-domination of the majority Bamars in all spheres of government, and there is no special provision for the protection of the rights of ethnic minorities – the latter being most important in a democracy and very important in federalism. In the upper house (the House of Nationalities) the principle of ethnic equality had always remained a source of grievances by the ethnic groups, which has now been somewhat redressed by the quality of representation from each state and region, but some ethnic groups find it still asymmetrical (Breen 2018: 92). The disenfranchisement of the Muslim Rohingyas (in the Arakan State in Myanmar) (in which the Buddhists are the majority) and the alleged ethnocide, and military onslaught very recently on them drove millions of Rohingyas out of the country to take shelter in refugee camps in Bangladesh; this has served to isolate the country internationally.[66]

The Constitution has been considered as the supreme law of the land, and a federal court called the Supreme Court of the Union is the guardian of the Constitution. There are also courts at each tier of the Union such as at the state, regional

Federalism and institutional innovations **119**

and other local levels. Citizens have been guaranteed some fundamental rights subject to certain conditions, and they can move the courts for redress.

There is also a provision (Article 46) for setting up a Constitutional Tribunal of the Union for settlement of disputes between different tiers of government as well as to adjudicate if the laws passed by any legislative bodies are in accordance with the Constitution or not.

Going by the six-point federal template advocated by Watts (2008: 9), Myanmar fulfills all of them: two or more tiers of government; a written Constitution as the supreme law of the land and not easily amendable; a formal constitutional distribution of powers between the tiers of government; an umpire in the shape of the Supreme Court of the Union; representation of regional views at the national level (second chamber); and a Constitutional tribunal for resolving disputes among governments. But Myanmar fulfills them on paper, not yet in practice.

With the military holding considerable power in the state structure, and the top democracy leader of the NLD, Suu Kyi, holding only the position of Adviser to the Government (State Counselor), Myanmar's democratic process is slow and tortuous. Federation building in the country will take a long time if the democratic process is sustained without interruptions. But the electoral verdict in 2015 has sent strong indications that the voters do not want the military's continued presence, and also that Suu Kyi has not yet achieved much in resolving long-drawn ethnic conflicts.

Notes

1 For details see D. Karmis and W. Norman (eds) (2005) *Theories of Federalism: A Reader*, New York: Macmillan. This excellent collection of some 26 chapters is a good testimony to a rich though varied tradition of political thought on federalism in the West.
2 Jaffrelot (2002b) 'Introduction' by Jaffrelot, p. 8. The term 'culture' in the three principles was probably used to refer to Islam.
3 Jaffrelot (2002a: 11). As proofs, Jaffrelot has said that at the All Parties Muslim Conference (1928), Jinnah was ready to exchange the advantages of separate electorates for a 33 per cent quota for the Muslims at the centre. Also, at the Round Table Conferences in the early 1930s, he stuck to this view when the Muslim representatives from Bengal and the Punjab were defending further decentralization (Jaffrelot 2002a: 11).
4 Ian Talbot, a keen observer of Pakistan's modern history and politics, ruefully remarked:

> Pakistan for much of its history has been a state searching for a national identity. The overlap of regional, Pakistani and religious identities was articulated most clearly by the Pushtun nationalist Wali Khan nearly a decade ago when he declared that 'he had been a Pushtun for 4000 years, a Muslim for 1400 years and a Pakistani for forty years'.
>
> (p. 1)

For further details, see his (1998) *Pakistan: A Modern History*, London: Hurst & Co.).
5 See V. Groverand R. Arora (eds) (1995a) *Political System in Pakistan, Vol. 2, Constitutional Developments in Pakistan*, New Delhi: Deep & Deep, pp. 313–54. The modified version of the Government of India Act, 1935, kept intact the autocratic powers of the Governor-General in matters of proclamation of emergency and in the issuance of ordinances for an indefinite period of time. At the provincial level of governance, a new Section 92A inserted in 1948 further empowered the governor to proclaim an emergency in the provinces at the behest of the governor-general whose agent he or she was. For

120 Federalism and institutional innovations

further details, see M. V. Lakhi (1995b) 'Constitutional Developments in Pakistan: The First Phase, 1947–56', in Groverand Arora (eds), Vol. 2, op. cit., pp. 122–36.

6 Watts (1966: 21).
7 S. Gupta (1995) 'The Political Crisis in Pakistan', in Groverand Arora (eds), op. cit., p. 28.
8 See B. P. Barua (1995) 'Constitution-Making in Pakistan, 1947–56', in Groverand Arora (eds), op. cit., pp. 161–2.
9 Barua (1995: 162).
10 S. Gupta (1995b) 'Constitution-Making in Pakistan', in Grover and Arora (eds), op. cit., pp. 100–1.
11 For further details, see Gupta (1995b: 105–7).
12 The founding leaders of Pakistan were found to be opposed to the very sensitive and legitimate demand of the majority Bengali-speakers of Pakistan to recognize their language as a state language along with Urdu. Liaquat Ali Khan, the first Prime Minister of Pakistan, for instance, stated in reply to Bengali protesters: 'Pakistan is a Muslim state and it must have its lingua franca the language of the Muslim nation. . . . It is necessary for a nation to have one language' (Quoted in Ali 1983: 45).
13 Gupta (1995a: 29). East Bengal considered this as a sinister move to form a country within a country with little prospect of developing a common national identity (Gupta 1995a: 29).
14 Barua (1995) in Grover and Arora (eds), p. 166.
15 Barua, in Grover and Arora (eds) (1995a), op. cit., p. 160.
16 Barua, in Grover and Arora (eds) (1995a), op. cit., p. 166. For further criticisms and suggestions, see Barua, pp. 166–70.
17 Grover and Arora (eds) (1995a) op. cit., Appendix IV, p. 369.
18 Grover and Arora (eds) (1995a), op. cit., p. 169.
19 Grover and Arora (eds) (1995a), op. cit., p. 169.
20 Passed by the National Assembly of Pakistan on 10 April 1973 and authenticated by the president on 12 April 1973 to come into force on 14 August 1973. The Draft of the Constitution was prepared by a Constitution Committee of the National Assembly of Pakistan as per the unanimous agreement of the leaders of parliamentary parties in Pakistan on the basic framework of the permanent Constitution of Pakistan. It envisaged a federal parliamentary system of government answerable to the National Assembly.
21 For the full text of the Constitution, see V. Grover and A. Arora (eds) (1995b) *Constitutional Developments in Pakistan*, Vol. 2, New Delhi: Deep & Deep, pp. 648–711 (appendix 13).
22 See Chapter 2 of this book. See also C. Jaffrelot (2002b) 'Introduction: Nationalism Without a Nation: Pakistan Searching for Its Identity', in Jaffrelot, C. (ed) *Pakistan: Nationalism Without a Nation*, New Delhi: Manohar, pp. 7–51, for a critical update on such movements against the Pakistani state.
23 Watts (2008: 41). In the 2008 elections, which also saw the gruesome assassination of Mrs Benazir Bhutto, the former prime minister of Pakistan during 1988–90 (for 18 months), took place to form the National Assembly, and a democratic government has just been set up.
24 W. Case (2007) 'Semi-Democracy and Minimalist Federalism in Malaysia', in He, B., Galligan, B. and Inoguchi, T. (eds) *Federalism in Asia*, Cheltenham: Edward Elgar, p. 124.
25 Chain-Anan Samudavanija (1991) 'The Three-Dimensional State', in Manor, J. (ed) *Rethinking Third World Politics*, Essex: Longman, pp. 15–23.
26 R. S. Milne and D. K. Mauzy (1989) *Malaysian Politics Under Mahathir*, London: Routledge, p. 9.
27 Bakar (2007: 71).
28 See H. Bhattacharyya (2001), chap. 6 'Institutional Arrangements for Minorities and the Formation of Federal Units', in *India as a Multicultural Federation: Asian Values, Democracy and Decentralization (In Comparison with Swiss Federalism)*, Fribourg, Switzerland: Helbing and Lichtenhahn, pp. 235–75 for details.
29 Anon. (2002) *Federal Constitution (of Malaysia) as at 10th April 2002*, Kuala Lumpur: International Law Book Services, p. 20.

Federalism and institutional innovations **121**

30 Milne and Mauzy (1989: 15–16). The opinion-makers in Malaysia believe that the supremacy of the Constitution has been impaired by frequent amendments, a view which is contentious because the number of amendments is not the sole index of the supremacy of the Constitution (see Sonia Randhawa (2008) 'Malaysian PM Faces Pressure from Ethnic and Pro-Democracy Forces', *Federations*, February–March, p. 27).

31 Anon., *Federal Constitution* (2002), p. 87.

32 Watts (1999: 35). See pp. 35–6 for further details.

33 Watts (1999: 36). Watts (1999) says that this 'reinforces the autonomy of legislative bodies', and also is in conformity with the principle of parliamentary executives responsible to their legislatures (pp. 36–7).

34 Watts (2008), op. cit., p. 102.

35 See Watts (1999: 48–50), for a neat summary of the arguments.

36 Case (2007: 133–5). Case has also pointed out that state governments run by opposition parties in Malaysia have been routinely deprived of their dues in grants received, while those run by the ruling National Front have gained special patronage. For further details, see, pp. 135–41.

37 Francis Loh (2008) 'Malaysia: Governing Coalition Weakened by Losses in Regions', *Federations*, June–July, p. 28.

38 I. Bakar (2007) 'Multinational Federations: The Case of Malaysia', in Burgess, M. and Pinder, J. (eds) *Multinational Federations*, London: Routledge, p. 73. Such one-sided pro-Malay national-identity protection and promotional measures in Malaysia have remained the basis of a precarious ethnic balance in the State, which is, however, disturbed almost routinely. Since the infamous 1969 ethnic riots between the Malays and the Chinese, the country has witnessed more ethnic clashes (Bakar 2007: 74). The banning of the Hindu Rights Action Force on 16 October 2008 by the Malaysian federal government, which has been demanding equal rights for the minorities in this Muslim-dominated state and which played an important role in the last March 2008 elections, on the grounds of 'public order and security', is a further sign that ethno-national accommodation on more egalitarian basis in a further federalized Malaysia may not be easy to obtain. (See *The Statesman*, Kolkata, dated 17 October 2008 for the report of the banning incident.)

39 B. W. Andaya and L. Y. Andaya (2001) *A History of Malaysia*, second edition, Hampshire: Macmillan, p. 302.

40 See Andaya and Andaya (2001: 303–36), for detailed discussion on various aspects of the policy and their implementation.

41 However, the term 'secular' does not occur anywhere in the Constitution but was inserted in the Preamble in 1976.

42 For detailed legal and constitutional provisions guaranteeing the special status of J and K, see Basu (1997: 249–58) (chapter 15 'The State of Jammu and Kashmir'). J and K's history since its accession to India (26 October 1947) has remained chequered for a variety of reasons (bilateral, political and so on), but for Jawaharlal Nehru, the first prime minister of India, J and K's remaining within India had some special meaning too. Granville Austin remarked in this connection: 'Beyond his affection of the place as a Kashmiri, the inclusion of the valley's Muslims in India constituted for him evidence both of the country's secularism and of Pakistan's malevolent challenge to it'. See G. Austin (1999) *Working a Democratic Constitution: The Indian Experience (1950–85)*, New Delhi: Oxford University Press, pp. 151–2.

43 Article 160 of the Malaysian Constitution defines 'Malay' as a 'person who professes the religion of Islam, habitually speaks the Malay language', [and] conforms to Malay custom' (Bakar 2007, p. 70).

44 I have explored this aspect of Indian national identity in various places. See, for instance, my 'Federalism and Competing Nations in India' (pp. 50–68) in Burgess and Pinder (eds) (2007) op. cit.; also my 'Ethnic and Civic Nationhood in India: Concept, History, Institutional Innovations and Contemporary Challenges', in Saha, S. C. (ed) (2008) *Ethnicity and Socio-Political Change in Africa and Other Developing Countries: A Constructive Discourse in State Building*, Lanham: Lexington Books, pp. 169–95.

122 Federalism and institutional innovations

45 See, for instance, A. L. Basam (1982) *The Wonder That Was India*, New Delhi: Rupa; Kshiti Mohan Sen (1961) *Hinduism*, Harmondsworth: Penguin Books; Nirod C. Choudhury (1996) *Hinduism: A Religion to Live by*, New Delhi: Oxford University Press, 1996/1979); D. E. Smith (1963) *India as a Secular State*, Princeton, NJ: Princeton University Press.

46 D. E. Smith (1999) 'India as a Secular State', in Bhargava, R. (ed) *Secularism and Its Critics*, New Delhi: Oxford University Press, pp. 177–234, esp. p. 187 for a comparative chart of Asian religions and their compatibility with secularism.

47 Communal clashes between communities, attacks by the majority on the religious minorities and tribal communities and so on, since Independence have remained a matter of much anxiety to all concerned in India.

48 See, for instance, Bhargava *et al.* (eds) (1999), op. cit.

49 That is the ancient indigenous name for the country. The term is used in various Indian languages. Ironically, the term 'Indian' is translated to refer to '*Bharatiya*', the adjective for '*Bharat*'.

50 Watts (1999: 101). For further details, see pp. 101–8.

51 The ambit of 'basic structure' has expanded over the years through various judgments to include: supremacy of the Constitution; rule of law; the principle of separation of powers; the Preamble Objectives; judicial review; federalism; secularism; the parliamentary system of government; and so on. (See Basu (1997) op. cit., pp. 154–5. See also G. Austin (1999), chapters 7–12; L. Rudolph and S. Rudolph (1987) *In Pursuit of Lakshmi: The Political Economy of the Indian State*, Chicago: University of Chicago Press, chap. 3, pp. 103–21 for the ongoing debates over the issue.)

52 G. Austin (1966) *The Indian Constitution: The Cornerstone of a Nation*, New Delhi: Oxford University Press, pp. 186–7. According to Austin, in India for quite sometime until the late 1940s, communal demands were manifest in federal forms, particularly in the case of the Muslims. In the CA, it was community rights rather than states' rights which became politically more emotive and significant. The Congress leadership in the CA was wary of it. The allegiance to provincial governments was thus muted. Consider Dr B. R. Ambedkar's remarks while introducing the Draft Constitution: 'The proposed Indian Constitution is a dual polity with a single citizenship. There is only one citizenship for the whole of India. There is no State citizenship' (p. 189).

53 W.H. Morris-Jones (1957) *Parliament in India*, London: Longman, p. 17.

54 See, for details, Anon. (2001) *The Constitution of India*, New Delhi: Delhi Law House, pp. 374–88.

55 G. Mathew (2002) 'India (Republic of India)', in Griffiths, Ann L. and Nerenberg, K. (eds) *Handbook of Federal Countries*, Montreal and Kingston: McGill Queen's University Press.

56 The Supreme Court of India has from the 1990s defended States' rights and federalism.

57 See H. Bhattacharyya, (2001a: 18–37); also H. Bhattacharyya (2005a) 'Changing Contours of India's Federal Debates', *West Bengal Political Science Review*, Vol. 3, No. 1–2, January–December, pp. 59–86.

58 For details, see Anon. (2001) *The Constitution of India*, New Delhi: Delhi Law House, pp. 156–69.

59 For a detailed discussion of fiscal federalism and diversity needs in India, see H. Bhattacharyya (2000) 'Federalism, Decentralization and State-Building in India: Aspects of Centre-State Fiscal Relations', in Bird, R. and Stauffer, T. (eds) *Intergovernmental Fiscal Relations in Fragmented Societies*, Fribourg, Switzerland: Helbing and Lichtenhahn, pp. 245–305.

60 P. R. Brass (1989) 'Pluralism, Regionalism and Decentralizing Tendencies in Contemporary Indian Politics', in Wilson, J. and Dalton, D. (eds) *The States of South Asia: Problems of National Integration*, London: Hurst & Co., p. 225. Brass (1989) also observed a 'high degree of interdependence of the Centre on the States and the States on the Centre' (p. 225).

Federalism and institutional innovations **123**

61 However, the fundamental right to property under Article 25 of the Constitution seems to undercut the socialist orientation of the Constitution.
62 See H. Bhattacharyya (2015) for the initial coinage of the conceptual distinctions between the two.
63 UNI Friday 6 December 2019. 'Nepal; Why Delay in Deciding Name, Capital of Four Provinces', www.uniindia.com/nepal-why-delay-in-deciding-names-capitals-of-4-provinces/world/news/1634557.html (accessed 6 December 2019).
64 Fundamental Rights and Duties (Part 3) apart, Part 4 of the Constitution on 'Directive Principles, Policies and Responsibilities of the State' pinpoints the State responsibilities in matters of social justice, inclusion, development and so on.
65 Schedule 1 (Union Legislative List with about 112 items); State/Region list with 45 items; Schedule 3 lists local government powers.
66 Aung San Su Kyi is fighting the legal battle in the International Court of Justice at the Hague against the charge of genocide brought by Gambia.

5

DYNAMICS OF FEDERALISM

Political parties and ethnic movements

Introduction

Federalism does not work on its own but is to be worked. Neither is it a natural process of a country's historical development. It has to be demanded and constructed. The constitutionally derived meaning of federalism suggests that it is a formal system of governance, mostly two-tier (today a substate tier is also more or less accepted), the national and the state/provincial/cantonal each enjoying its constitutionally demarcated powers and performing its responsibilities, and so on and so forth. A formalist-legalistic or, in political science literature, what is called the 'traditional approach' would have us believe that this is the basic nature of a federal system. The real fact of the matter, however, is that this view only suggests at best how such a system *ought* to function rather than how it functions in reality or how it is worked. Before proceeding any further, we need to clarify two related issues. First, however clearly demarcated the powers and responsibilities between different tiers of government in a federation, the evolving reality never neatly matches that, so that modifications, adjustments and adaptations are always needed in actual operation. Second, the newer needs and aspirations of the people are articulated and aggregated by political parties and other groups in order to create pressures upon the system, for recognition, autonomy and power. Very often political parties or ethnic movements make a federation difficult to govern. Thanks to these pressures, the federal system is compelled to respond – democratically, if it is a democratic system, or violently with the means of repression if it is an authoritarian/military regime, if it seeks, as it were, to further lose its legitimacy and collapse. As Ronald Watts notes (Watts 1999), the operational reality of federalism is more important than what is constitutionally designed if federalism as a political equilibrium is to be produced. The term 'operational reality' may consist of two components. First, it may refer to the institutional operation of the system.

Second, it may refer to the surrounding societal reality, comprising the values, identity and the interests of the individual, groups and regions. Livingstone (1956) highlighted the societal aspects of federalism a long time ago, although looking at federation from a functionalist standpoint. Be that as it may, a federation, being a compound polity, needs to reflect the values of diversity as well as the unity to be achieved institutionally as well as politically. Needless to say, federations, unavoidably, are difficult to govern.

The previous paragraph has already hinted at where the role of political parties and ethnic movements figures in a federation. To be more exact, they perform very important 'input' functions – to use a phrase from the systems approach to politics. While this is vitally important, the constitutive role of political parties and ethnic movements in federations are as important, if not more important, because the federations most often bear the imprint of the dominant political reality, comprising the political parties, political alliances, coalitions and ethnic movements.

In modern democracies, political parties are indispensable. Political parties are also indispensable in federations. Federations, like democracies, need to be operated, and they are better operated by the appropriate party systems than by a bureaucratic system. The relation between the federation on the one hand and the political parties and ethnic movements on the other hand is, however, two-way. While the federations determine and condition the nature and patterns of political parties, the latter also impact upon the former, structurally and functionally, and shape the real state of the federation. K. C. Wheare (Wheare 1953: 86–90) considered a 'good party system' to be of 'primary importance' in a federation, as a factor in the 'organization of federal government':

> And a good party system is one in which sectional differences of interest and opinion have their opportunity and their due weight but where also an integrated organization can be created capable of effective political action on a nationwide scale.
>
> *(Wheare 1953: 87)*[1]

And yet the subject of parties and party systems has remained, as pointed out in the current literature on the subject (Filippov *et al.* 2004), grossly neglected as 'critical components of federal system or federal design'. Wheare (1953) did not spend more than three pages dealing with political parties in the federations, and his analysis was self-critically sketchy and partial. However, political parties did not suffer the same fate in the earlier generation of scholarship (Key 1964; Riker 1964; Wechsler 1954; Truman 1955). Political parties also remain neglected in the studies of Asian federalism (He 2007). Filippov *et al.* have argued that the 'political parties are the primary organizational vehicle' in a democracy for the political élites to win and maintain office and hence play a 'pivotal role in any understanding, not only of democracy generally, but of the intergovernmental relations of federations in particular' (Filippov *et al.* 2004: 178).[2] Taking the cues from Riker and Wheare, Filippov *et al.* have advanced the argument in favour of 'integrated

126 Dynamics of federalism

parties' being conducive to federal stability. Their argument refers to a party system in which the 'politicians at one level of government bear an organizational relationship to politicians at other levels (as well as to politicians within their level)' (Filippov 2004: 190). Dyck (1991: 120) has been quoted for further definitional clarity of the concept: '[I]f a political party functions more or less successfully at both levels of government and if the relations between the two levels are generally close, it can be called an integrated political party' (Filippov *et al.* 2004: 190). The concept of integration in this regard is crucially important not only for political parties in a federation but also for any sustaining federation. Without a level of federal integration (institutional, values, interests and identity), no federation can hold itself together. Political parties, when integrated at both governmental and organizational levels, as Filippov *et al.* suggest, provide the most critical element in federal integration generally.

Pakistan

In the matter of the role of both the political party(ies) and ethno-nationalist movements, Pakistan's federation represents a case of grotesque failure. While the ethno-nationalist movements in Pakistan are numerous and there are strong forces demanding recognition, power and autonomy – as is to be expected in a complex multi-ethnic society, and that, too, lacking in democracy for most of the time since Independence (1947) – the federation has failed so far to accommodate them. On the contrary, the federation's privileged accommodation of the Punjabis, the dominant ethno-national group (who are in effective control of the state), to the exclusion of the minority ethnic groups has meant that ethno-regional/national tensions run high and offer a potent and almost perennial source of threat to the unity and integrity of the state itself. The federation has suffered most seriously from the failure of the founding party, that is, the Muslim League (ML), which, having its original bases in India (Uttar Pradesh) and incidentally not being federally based, had failed to put down any roots, let alone deep ones, in post-Independence Pakistan provinces. Thus, while Pakistan remains as a federal state for the Muslims, its founding organization almost disappeared after the formation of the state. The death of M. A. Jinnah immediately after the formation of Pakistan apart, the discontinuity in the ML, along with its very weak organizational presence in the provinces and among the various ethno-regional groups, meant that a great missing link confronted the fledgling federation which has produced crippling effects on the future prospects of the federation.

This is not the place to discuss the historical backdrop of Muslim separatism in colonial India,[3] which gave birth to the Muslim League in 1906 (in Dacca/now Dhaka, the capital of Bangladesh) that ultimately spearheaded the movement for the demand for Pakistan in the 1930s, formalized in the famous Lahore Resolution of the ML in 1940. Ironically enough, the terms of the Lahore Resolution, which incidentally had not mentioned 'Pakistan', were vague and seemed to go against the so-called two-nation theory of the ML and offer much encouragement to the latter-day ethno-nationalist movements in Pakistan.[4] Certain uncomfortable historical facts should be highlighted about the ML and its bases of support in pre- and post-Partition periods which had immense implications for Pakistan's federal prospects, including the policy of accommodation of ethno-nationalist identity demands. First, the ML, to begin with, was a party of what Jaffrelot called 'minoritarian Muslims' (Jaffrelot 2002b: 10), that is, the Muslims in the United Provinces (now Uttar Pradesh) and the Bombay Presidency (Jinnah's native region). With Partition and the birth of Pakistan in 1947, the ML lost its original bases of support and was indeed uprooted. Second, the Muslim-majority provinces such as Bengal and Punjab did not find Jinnah's separatist agenda attractive, because, being in the majority, they often ruled their own regions (Jaffrelot 2002b: 11). Also, unlike Jinnah, the political élite in the latter regions were keener on further decentralization of the colonial state, because that meant more powers and resources for them. Not surprisingly, the ML got only 5 per cent of the Muslim votes (Jaffrelot 2002b: 12) in the 1937 Provincial Legislative Assembly elections following the Government of India Act, 1935, from the Muslim-majority regions. Third, in the provinces now making up Pakistan, the ML was a weak force. For example, in Punjab, the major province, the ML could make some electoral headway as late as 1946, and that too, with the help of and on the back of the Unionist Party (founded in 1922), a peasants' party which had won all elections during 1923–37, leaving very little space for the ML (Jaffrelot 2002b: 13).[5] In Sindh, the ML also failed to become the party of the Sindhis until at least the mid-1940s. Even then, the Muslim League of Sindh, under the leadership of the legendary G. M. Syed, was more interested in promoting Sindhi nationalist culture and identity than an Islamic state (Jaffrelot 2002b: 13).[6] In the North-West Frontier Province (NWFP), the ML had greater hurdle to overcome. Here the ML had to compete with 'Frontier Gandhi' Abdul Gaffar Khan, a Gandhian Pathan leader who led a movement (known as *Khudai Khitmatgor*) centering on a strong Pakhtun identity since the late 1920s, which confined all influences of the ML to the non-Pakhtun, to be precise, the Hazara region (Jaffrelot 2002b: 14). In the 1946 elections to the Central Legislative Assembly, the ML had to be content with only 17 seats, leaving 30 to the Congress (Jaffrelot 2002b: 14).[7]

As indicated earlier, the ML did not have a clean and clear sweep in Bengal, another Muslim-majority province and most populous of all Pakistan's provinces (with 54 per cent of the total population of Pakistan), at least not until 1946. The ML here had confronted two powerful competitors in the Congress, on the one hand, and the *Krishak Proja* Party (KPP) (a peasants' party) (founded in 1936) of A. K. Fazlul Haq, on the other. In the 1937 elections, the KPP came first, securing 31 per cent of the valid votes, leaving the ML with only 27 per cent (Jaffrelot 2002b: 14). It was only in 1946 that the ML swept the poll with 113 seats out of 119 (and 87 per cent of Muslim votes)[8] on the basis of a campaign that highlighted the two-nation theory and need for the creation of Pakistan. But then the underground

128 Dynamics of federalism

regional Bengali nationalist moorings were not sacrificed in favour of the so-called two-nation theory.[9] However, in eight years' time, in 1954, the Awami League (AL) (formed in 1949 and representing Bengali nationalism) would almost erase the ML from East Bengal/East Pakistan. The AL in a United Front with the KPP of Fazlul Haq (the mover of the Lahore Resolution of 1940) captured as many as 223 out of 237 Muslim seats (with 57 per cent of the votes polled) in the 1954 elections to the National Assembly of Pakistan (Maniruzzaman 1973: 255). Interestingly, the AL also resurrected the spirit of the Lahore Resolution in support of its initial demand for regional autonomy (Maniruzzaman 1973: 254), which in the face of the most brutal repression from the Pakistani Army since the late 1960s culminated into the demand for independence, the liberation struggle, and the rise of Bangladesh in 1971.

The ML thus failed to become 'a national party for all Pakistanis, and even managed to alienate a majority of the Muslims in East Pakistan, the NWFP, and Baluchistan, in what was widely interpreted as an effort to impose rule by Muhajirs on the country' (Rose 1989: 112–13). Rose argues that by the time the Pakistan Constituent Assembly was reconstituted in 1954, the ML had already collapsed, giving birth to a party system that was highly factionalized (Rose 1989: 113). Pakistan was thus deprived of one major political resource early on for operating a federation in a highly complex ethno-nationalist context. Political parties that were formed subsequently in Pakistan were all province-based, ethnically oriented and lacking in true national orientation. Even the Pakistan People's Party (PPP) of the late Z. Bhutto, the father of the late Benazir Bhutto (of Sindh), which got a majority in the National Assembly in 1970 and ruled Pakistan during 1972–77, could not go above this, as evident in its anti-federal functioning by denying the units a participatory role in vital matters of constitutional amendments (Ali, M. 1995: 474–501).[10] In any case, it is also a Sindh-based party. Sadly, in Pakistan, in an environment of successive bouts of military dictatorship and the weak and fledgling democratic regimes in between, a party system failed to put down deep roots, so the political parties found to be contesting elections are only province-based (read also ethnicity-based) political groupings, factionalized and highly leader-centric. Although the PPP remains the largest party in terms of popular votes polled and the number of parliamentary seats secured, it obtained only 94 elected seats out of 266 in the last parliamentary elections, held in 2008 after eight years of military dictatorship (Table 5.1).

This brief account suggests that the ML was not representative of the diverse ethno-regional interests of the provinces comprising Pakistan, nor had it the required continuity to be rebuilt into a representative body in the post-Independence period. Tariq Ali remarked that the 'weakness of the League in West Pakistan meant that the only 'political party' that Jinnah could rely on was the civil service of Pakistan' (Ali, T. 1983: 42). Despite the provinces-based organizational structure of the ML, such as the East Bengal Muslim League and the Muslim League of Sindh, the ML failed to articulate a national identity above and beyond the ethno-regional ones,

Dynamics of federalism **129**

TABLE 5.1 Party position in the National Assembly in Pakistan (2018) (total seats = 342)

Parties	General	Women	Minorities	Total
PTI★	117	27	5	149
PML (N)	63	16	2	82
PPP	43	9	2	54
MMA	12	2	1	15
Ind	13			13
MQM-P	6	1		07
PML (Q)	3	2		05
BAP	4	3	1	05
BNP	3	1		04
GDA	3	2	1	03
JWP	1			1
TLP	1			1
ANP	1			1
Others	3			3
Total				342

Source: https://eeas.europa.eu/sites/eeas/files/final_report_pakistan_2018_english_0.pdf (accessed 22 December 2019).

★ See Abbreviations for the full name of the parties.
Note: (Voter turnout = 51.9%) (Direct election = 272; proportional representation party-wise 60 women and 10 non-Muslims)

which in fact were better nurtured, unavoidably, by the provincial units of the ML. Cohen has observed in this connection:

> The leaders of the new state assumed that Jinnah's leadership and a common faith would override any differences between the major ethno-linguistic groups. This was a real concern, since support for the Pakistan movement was tepid among Sindhis, Pakhtuns, and Baluch. North Indian Muslims had strongly supported the Pakistan movement, but it was mostly the leadership and the professional classes who had undertaken the harrowing migration after partition.
>
> *(Cohen 2005: 203)*

It was and still remains a great question in the discourse on nationhood and nationalism: whether a national identity could be defined independently of any common sociocultural, regional and historical content. A nation, to be sure, cannot be forged simply on the basis of a faith, however lofty that faith might be. As Cohen has rightly pointed out: 'Pakistan is one of the world's most ethnically and linguistically complex states' (Cohen 2005: 201–2). We have seen already in Chapter 2 of this book the solid bases of ethno-regional nationalist movements in various provinces of Pakistan. Cohen has also given a detailed description of the ethno-nationalist movements and the pattern of conflicts in Pakistan (Cohen 2005: 207) since the

130 Dynamics of federalism

1960s in various provinces of Pakistan and has pointed out that the country's 'ethnic and linguistic minorities often cite the founding document of Pakistan, the Lahore resolution, as legitimizing their claim to greater autonomy' (Cohen 2005: 206). While the narratives of the ethno-nationalist movements in Pakistan had a lot in common in terms of autonomy and identity, they 'vary widely' regarding their ties to the idea of Pakistan. Cohen says: 'The Muhajirs were in the forefront of the Pakistan movement; others were disinterested or marginal to it' (Cohen 2005: 208). Compare that with the remarkable continuity in the condescending approach of the rulers of Pakistan since 1947 to the demands for regional autonomy for ethnoregional/national groups. If Jinnah's approach had had a somewhat different tone underlining, ostensibly, a civic space of the nation, going by his famous speech as President of the Pakistan Constituent Assembly on 11 August 1947 as well as on other occasions,[11] then post-Jinnah leadership (whether civil or military) was blatantly intolerant of regionalism and refused to compromise with provincial autonomy (Cohen 2005: 205–6). Jinnah's one-sided approach to a civic nationhood that underplayed ethno-national identity (read provincialism) on the one hand and the hardened and intolerant approach of the post-Jinnah leadership to the issue of ethno-regional/national identity on the other meant that the appropriate space for accommodation of both the ethnic and civic through federalism, as I have argued elsewhere (Bhattacharyya, H. 2007a, 2007b, 2008) – as happened for instance in India and Switzerland – was foreclosed time and again in Pakistan. For the purpose of federalism *per se*, Pakistan has not witnessed the development of an 'integrated party system' that Wheare thought would be beneficial for a federation and that Filippov *et al.* consider as essential for federal stability.

The data in Table 5.1 show the fragmentary nature of the party system in Pakistan as well as, perhaps more importantly, the relatively weaker position of the erstwhile Muslim League, which was the political platform of the Pakistan movement and federalism. The most recent (2018) general elections in Pakistan suggest that there is as yet no national party in Pakistan and that all major political parties are regional.

India

The relative success of federalism in India has much to do with its party system, particularly the Indian National Congress (henceforth the INC),[12] one of the oldest in the world and the oldest in Asia, formed in 1885. Formed originally as a movement and broad political platform of different sections of Indian society for fighting against British colonialism, it gradually developed into a political party engaged in the struggle for political power and government. Since pre-Independence days, the Congress has remained an integrated party, having its organizational sweep from the national down to the village levels via the provinces and districts. The other political parties – those which are not specifically regional, of both left and right persuasions – are also integrated parties in the sense defined here. To take the example of the left-wing parties, the Communist Party of India (Marxist) (henceforth the CPI-M), the leading left-wing party in India today, has organizational set-ups at national, state, district, zonal, local and village levels throughout the country (Bhattacharyya, H. 2004b). The INC was the main party of India's Independence and a decisive factor in determining the nature of the polity that India would have after Independence too. Federalism, as we discussed in Chapter 3 of this book, was one of the main nationalist pledges of the INC since 1920 when, at the famous Nagpur session of the party, it resolved to reorganize India after Independence into a federation based on linguistic states. In fact, the INC, organizationally speaking, had already begun to federalize itself by creating linguistically based subnational units such as the Maharashtra and Gujarat Provincial Committees after 1917, when administratively such units were not there. The INC and the Indian federation thus developed somewhat symbiotically.

The INC was the dominant and most determining factor in the Constituent Assembly of India (1946–49), which drafted the federal Constitution of free India, and the ruling party of India for most of the time since Independence (about 49 years out of 62 years). The continuity in the party apart, India was also blessed with a heritage of nationalist leadership in the shape of such towering figures as Jawaharlal Nehru and Sardar Ballavbhai Patel, who were instrumental in making possible a relatively smooth transition to a liberal democratic regime. The Emergency interlude of 1975–77 (21 months), a clampdown by the late Mrs Indira Gandhi which cancelled India's democracy, was a mere aberration because the democratic system was restored in 1977, and the INC was defeated for the first time since 1952 (when the first general elections in post-Independence India took place). The Janata Party, a conglomeration of various parties and political formations – all anti-Congress – which ruled India during 1977–80, restored not only democracy but also federalism and decentralization (Rudolph and Rudolph 1987; Bhattacharyya, H. 2001a). The regimes of non-Congress governments at the federal level (during 1977–80, 1989–91, 1996–98 and 1998–2004) by various coalitions and alliances such as the National Front, the United Front and the National Democratic Alliance (led by the *Bharatiya Janata* Party, the BJP) (the party of the Hindu right in India), despite their ideological differences and regional catchment area, did not deviate from the federalist tradition of India. On the contrary, such coalitions and alliances, composed largely of region- and state-based parties[13] have meant better prospects for Indian federalism in terms of better deals for the states. Recent writings on Indian political parties recognize the growth in influence of state-based parties in national politics and federalism (Hardgrave and Kochanek 2000: 243; Arora 2004; Manor 1995; Manor 1988; Hasan 2004; Sridharan 2004: 475–504).

Various state- and region-based parties are merely the political expressions of ethno-regional/national identities. Ethno-regional/national identities in India are deeply rooted in history, and they became self-conscious in the wake of India's national liberation movements led by the INC and other political forces. For one thing, the INC itself became a major vehicle for them in articulating both their regional and the national aspirations – not, however, without contradictions or

132 Dynamics of federalism

problems. The basic point that is being stressed here is the INC's sensitivity to regional, local and ethno-national identities and its readiness to accommodate them. Various scholarly studies[14] of the INC contain enough material to show that the INC became a political expression of India's very complex social and cultural diversity and heterogeneity, as a catch-all party with all the attendant internal problems of continuous adjustments, compromise and accommodation of often mutually opposed interests and values, however. Chhiber and Petrocik (1989) argue that the 'social base of the Congress party conforms to the social cleavage theory of party systems':

> The Congress is a coalition of State and local parties which differ substantially among themselves in the groups and interests they represent. In terms of its supporters, the Congress is several parties, with a social base in some parts of the country that is at odds with its social foundations in other regions. Looked at from the national level. . ., Congress supporters represent a variety of social classes, occupational groups, religions and languages. But community by community (and to a lesser extent State by State), the electoral support of the Congress is quite homogeneous.
>
> *(Chhiber and Petrocik 1989: 195)*

This passage serves to explain both the heterogeneity and homogeneity in the social bases of Congress support, the latter more prominent the lower down the level we go. This serves also to show the integrated nature of the party.[15]

As several studies of the Congress have shown, as already indicated, the nature of Congress as a 'coalition of State parties' was built in the pre-Independence period, when it tried to offer the broad platform to all possible sectional, regional, religious and linguistic interests.[16] In the post-Independence period, given the compulsion of federalism and the electoral laws, the INC had 'to mobilize support on a state by state basis' (Chhiber 1999: 80). The INC being in power at a stretch from 1947 to 1977, ethno-regional/national accommodation of identity in the form of formation of states (federal units) in several surges since 1956, which federalized the once centralized colonial and postcolonial state, was possible in the aforementioned historical and political backdrop. The INC therefore was like a replica of the Indian nation-state and the Indian federation. The various ethnic movements for 'self-determination', recognition, autonomy and powers in India have had a better chance to be successful. As I have discussed in greater detail elsewhere (Mitra and Bhattacharyya 2000; Bhattacharyya, H. 2001a, 2001b, 2003, 2004a, 2004b, 2005a, 2005b, 2005e, 2007a), the different degrees of statehood within the federation accorded to these different ethnic movements have meant that the Indian federation has been increasingly differentiated; ethno-national identities have been accommodated; and the basis for the legitimacy of the nation and the state has been strengthened. I have further shown how autonomous tribal district council experiments in Tripura have served to protect the tribal identity from being further marginalized in Tripura, a state in India's NorthEast (Bhattacharyya, H. 1999, 2003).

It must be stressed here that India's tradition of accommodation of diversity and ethno-regional identity in the form of autonomy has been honoured even during the period of NDA government, when in 2000 the last three new states, namely, Chhattisgarh, Jharkhand and Uttarakhand, were created (Bhattacharyya 2001b).

The observers who have studied the evolution of the INC have identified many phases, shifts and turns, crises, restorations and so on, producing in turn their effects on the government (Hardgrave and Kochanek 2000: 244–86). For instance, 1947–67 is known as the period of 'one-party dominance' based on the Congress 'system' (Kothari 1967) when the INC was the 'single party of consensus' occupying a central position (Hardgrave and Kochanek 2000: 244–5). And yet the highly factionalized Congress was sensitive and responsive to pressures from the margins so that 'the opposition did not constitute an alternative to the ruling party but functioned from the periphery in the form of parties of pressure' (Hardgrave and Kochanek 2000:245). However, Kothari (1967) noted two prominent features of this 'system'. First, there was plurality within the dominant party, which made it representative, provided flexibility, and sustained internal competition (Hardgrave and Kochanek 2000: 245). Second, it was able to 'absorb groups and movements from outside the party preventing thereby other parties from gaining ground' (Hardgrave and Kochanek 2000: 245). There have been splits in the party; personalization of power by the late Mrs Indira Gandhi; induction of her sons into politics and the party; a quest in search of the exact nature of the organization and its leaders (post-1991); and the 'restoration of Nehru-Gandhi dynasty' after Mrs Sonia Gandhi's assumption of the presidency of the party since April 1998. A new genre of scholarship on the INC has developed which has termed the post-1967 developments in the party as an instance of 'deinstitutionalization' of the party, which eventually served to prepare the basis for deinstitutionalization of the governing institutions at the national as well as state levels (Bhattacharyya, M. 1992: 64–85).[17] The national Emergency under Article 352 of the Indian Constitution during June 1975–March 1977 (21 months), which cancelled the political process, was the culmination of this process. The post-1977 period has witnessed restoration of federalism, democracy, constitutionalism and other governing institutions and, with the renewed decentralization since the 1990s, democratization at the base of the system.

What then has been the relationship between federal governance and India's parties? Have the Indian political parties been functional for Indian federalism? During the first three decades after independence (1947–77), the INC, organizationally speaking, had had a major grip on the political system and greatly facilitated the process of federalism in India. Morris-Jones, one of the earlier observers of Indian politics, who saw 'hard competitive bargaining' as the 'character of Indian federalism throughout' (Morris-Jones 1987: 152), argued that the single-party dominance had served as a 'lubricant to the practical mechanism of federalism' (Morris-Jones 1987: 153) by settling much of the centre–state and interstate issues, first within the walls of the organization, to begin with in the Working Committee, and after 1951 increasingly in the Parliamentary wing of the party (Kochanek 1968: 307)

134 Dynamics of federalism

dominated by the prime minister (Jawaharlal Nehru). According to Kochanek, the Working Committee was like a 'sounding board by which the Prime Minister could test the acceptability of new policies as well as an important feedback mechanism by which to assess the reactions of party and state leaders' (Kochanek 1968: 307). But it was beyond doubt that during the period of 'one-party dominance' (1947–67), the federalism that was produced was tightly moulded, because the states' bargaining position was after all to be channelled through the disciplinary mechanisms of the party. Morris-Jones (1987) rightly called it 'hard competitive bargaining'! (my emphasis added). The post-1967 assertions of the states for more power, revision of centre–state relations and so on (Bhattacharyya, H. 2009) offered very important counter-factual evidence for this. However, it must be pointed out here that the quantum of central financial transfers to the states in various forms (Planning Commission, union Finance Commission and ministerial) overall were hardly if ever affected by the political centralization and personalization of powers at the national level.[18]

The 1967 fourth general elections, which reduced the Congress majority in Parliament and in which the party lost electoral majorities in 8out of the 19 states, appeared to reverse the balance of power from the centre to the states, 'leaving the centre at the mercy of the states' (Morris-Jones 1987: 153). But that might be an exaggeration, as Morris-Jones argued, because except for the CPI-M-led governments in West Bengal and Kerala, very few non-Congress governments were inclined to enter into conflict with the centre (Morris-Jones 1987: 153–4). However, the rise of political competition in the 1967 general elections and its disastrous effects on the organization of the Congress (Chhiber 1999: 80–5) has affected the course of Indian federalism. It is not the place here to engage ourselves in any detailed discussion of the issue. The basic point to be stressed here from the point of view of federalism in India is the increase in the importance of the states and the rise of state-based and regional parties that would significantly change the course of Indian politics generally and Indian federalism in particular. The regionalization of Indian politics that would be very prominent from the 1990s onwards had its roots in this post-1967 political backdrop. India's regional parties (officially called 'state parties') numbered 60 in the first general elections in 1952, but after that the numbers shrank to only 12 in 1957. By 1967, there were 21 (including the national parties), but numbers remained more or less stable through to the late 1980s. From 1991, the number of parties began to grow quite rapidly: to 27 in 1991, 42 in 1996, 40 in 1998 (Hardgrave and Kochanek 2000: 315–16) and 43 in 2009. There are lots of differences among different state parties in terms of their goals, organization, ideological basis, leadership and ethnic character, if any, and so on. The secessionist elements in them are not something inherent but have often come to the fore in specific circumstances. The most prominent and longer-lasting state parties are the DMK and the AIADMK (Tamil Nadu); *Akali Dal* (Punjab); *Asom Gana Parishad* (Assam); National Conference (Jammu and Kashmir); the *Bahujan Samaj* Party (mostly UP-based); and the (All India) *Trina Mul* Congress (West Bengal, formed in 1998). Given the very heterogeneous social and cultural mosaic of India, the proliferation of regional parties is not considered to be surprising in the studies of regional parties in India (Manor 1995: 105–35; Arora 2004: 532). Manor has argued that with the increased prominence of regional parties at the national level of politics since the late 1980s, better prospects have been created for Indian federalism than ever before because the Congress Party leaders are today 'more inclined towards bargaining and accommodation which characterized the Nehru period' (Manor 1995: 111).

Arora argues saying: 'The growth and increased prominence of state-based parties, or regional parties introduced a new element in the working of the federal system. It engendered new conventions which ought to enhance the participation of the states in national policy making' (Arora 2004: 505). He has further commented that the new political situation born since the late 1980s in India 'owes its existence primarily to the increased importance and expanding role of state-based political parties, and the necessity of building federal coalitions which reconcile regional aspirations with national cohesion' (Arora 2004: 507). For example, during 1996–99, the state parties and others together gained more or less the same per cent of seats in Parliament as national parties such as the INC and the BJP. In 1999, the state parties received 32.2 per cent of the seats, while Congress gained 21 per cent and the BJP's share was 33.5 per cent (Arora 2004: 510).[19]

Since the late 1980s no single party has been able to secure a majority position in the *Lok Sabha* (the popular chamber of the Indian Parliament), so that fronts, coalitions, alliances, etc. with various state-based parties have come to govern India at the national level. The Congress-led UPA (United Progressive Alliance) governments (2004–09 and 2009–) are the latest versions of the vastly changed political scenario in India. Although the Congress has improved its strength in this election, its partners are all region-based parties. The same is true for NDA and the Third Front and the Fourth Front (Table 7.2).

Two conclusions follow on from this. First, regional/state parties have become politically very important in national-level policy-making, despite the increase in the Congress tally and the decrease in strength in some state-based parties. Second, it has opened up better prospects for Indian federalism by bringing to the fore the states and their interests, a process which has been furthered by globalization in India since the 1990s (Bhattacharyya, 2009). However, with the rise to power at Delhi by the BJP-led NDA in 2014 with the BJP's own majority, reinforced by the outstanding victory of the NDA 2019 with the BJP's very good majority, the trend has been disturbed to some extent. Indian politics is now sandwiched between the pull of the Hindu nationalist move towards centralism on the one hand and the forces of regionalism on the other.

While the Congress-led UPA was returned in 2009 for another term with some changes in the partners, the BJP-led NDA took over the rein since 2014, in which the BJP itself got a majority, and in 2019 *Lok Sabha* elections, the party's majority was very substantial (303 out of 543), and with the allies, another 50. This repeated mandate to rule by the BJP has raised the question of its impact on federalism because federalism is something that the Hindutva politics does not, ideologically, defend.

136 Dynamics of federalism

TABLE 5.2 Party position in *Lok Sabha* (2009)

Parties/alliance	Seats obtained
United Progressive Alliance (Congress-led)	262 (Congress = 206+)
National Democratic Alliance (BJP-led)	157 (BJP = 116+)
Third Front (Left and others)	80 (Left = 22+)
Fourth Front (SP and RJD)	27
Others	17
Total seats	543

Source: *India Today*, 23 May 2009 (Internet edition as of 23 May 2009).

Notes:
UPA partners and seats obtained: DMK (18); NCP (9); TC (19); JMM (2); NC (2); and others (5).
NDA partners and seats obtained: JD (U) (20); SS (11); SAD (4); AGP (1); RLD (5).
Third Front: Left (20); BSP (21); JD (S) (3); AIADMK (9); TDP (6); TRS (2); BJD (14); and others (3).
Fourth Front: SP (23) and RJD (4).

Malaysia

The Malaysian federation (post-1963) represents another success story, post-India, for Asian federations in respect of the relationships between political parties on the one hand and the federation on the other. In a way, the Malaysian case appears to be better than the Indian, insofar as the institutionalization of political parties in relation to the federation is concerned. The ethno-national context of Malaysia (Chapter 2 of this book) is highly racially and communally charged, and the way the Malayan identity has been constructed over the years since Independence (*Merdeka*) for the sake of achieving a 'majority' (added to that are the special rights and privileges accorded to the Malays in the Constitution and the favouritism in favour of the Malays assured in the NEP) has remained contentious. The 13 May 1969 communal riots, which led to the cancellation of democracy and the political process for two years under the imposition of an Emergency rule and the governance of the country being handed over to the National Operation Council (NOC) (Ahmed, H. Z. 1989: 247–50), offered an important early signal to the delicate racial–communal balance among the three communities in the country – the Malays, the Chinese and the Indians – and the fragile health of the federation and democracy. But that aside, which appears in retrospect to be an exception, the federation has had an enviable record of political stability, social peace and development, and national integrity.

The key to the relative and dynamic political equilibrium – smooth transfer of power; regularity in elections; rule of law; independence of the judiciary; and more or less tension-free centre-state relations – is a grand coalition known as the National Front *(Barisan Nasional* in Malay) (henceforth BN, for short) of political parties representing various racial/communal and ethnic groups as a sort of 'consociational' power-sharing among the élites in the parties. The BN (the idea being mooted in 1972), as the successor to the Alliance (1951–74), was born in 1973 in the aftermath of the 13 May riots and the Emergency (1969–71) as a more participatory and corporatist political formula and leadership in order to avoid the pitfalls of the 1967–71 period and to ensure more enduring political order and stability. The underlying idea of the BN was a 'native-based system' (read Malay supremacy), which should imply 'cooperation with all the other races in the country' (Ahmed, H. Z. 1989: 365–8). The Alliance, as we saw in Chapter 2 of this book, was composed of three political parties (UMNO, MCA and MIC) representing the three major racial/communal groups, namely, the Malays, the Chinese and the Indians respectively. It proved its power and credibility in the country before Independence, first by winning as many as 51 out of 52 seats to the Legislative Council (held on 22 July 1955) and subsequently by fighting for Independence as the party of Independence. The UMNO-led Alliance established its hegemonic leadership over the federation, although it had to grapple with communal tensions within the Alliance (because power-sharing was not equitable) and beyond. The BN is, however, registered as a political party for electoral purposes, although membership of the BN is possible only through one of the constituent parties. However, the BN calls itself a 'confederation of political parties'. The BN as a grand coalition increasingly expanded its ambit by incorporating more parties (Table 7.3), so the potential opposition to it is blunted. It was also meant to allow more participation from the ethnic groups across the states, including the two Borneo states. The BN dominates the party system in Malaysia, and until March 2008[20] has maintained its overwhelming parliamentary majority, securing over two-thirds of seats in Parliament. The BN pro-federal role has been highlighted by Malaysian scholars:

> In Malaysia, the parties' coalition works hard in the cause of national unity, maintaining a parliamentary majority since 1957 and clearly contributes to maintain and preserve federalism and federation.
>
> *(Bakar 2007: 77)*

The differences between the Alliance (1951–71) and the BN (1973–) need special emphasis. The Alliance was merely a three-party organization, while the BN (now a 14-party organization) sought to include other parties representing both Malay and non-Malay interests. The most important non-Malay party was the DAP. The most important party to join the BN (1974) was the PAS, which was a real challenger to the BN in Kelantan but left in 1977 after a party split (Milne and Mauzy 1989: 24). After some initial hesitation, even *Parti Bersatu Sabah* (PBS), which had come to power in Sabah in mid-1985 and had had a pronounced non-Malay character, was admitted to the BN, although for strategic reasons (Ahmed, H. Z. 1989: 367).

The reasons why the smaller parties joined the BN were many, but the most important was patronage from the federal government (Milne and Mauzy 1989: 24). In return, the BN acquired support for the implementation of its policies and securing the required two-thirds majority in Parliament for amending the Constitution (Milne and Mauzy 1989: 24). Since its formation in 1973, the BN did

138 Dynamics of federalism

rather well in all subsequent parliamentary elections, losing its two-thirds majority status only in 2008. (However, it retained its majority status by winning 140 out of 220 parliamentary seats.) The other, strategically more significant, difference was in the operation of leadership: in the Alliance, the leader was 'less formal and more personal'; in the BN the leader was less accessible but could deal with the leaders of the constituent parties on a one-to-one basis (Milne and Mauzy 1989: 24–5). It is argued that this has offered an important opportunity to the prime ministers (including Dr Mahathir, the former prime minister, who changed the economic face of Malaysia) to appreciably increase their powers (Milne and Mauzy 1989: 25). In any case, the enlargement of the inter-ethnic alliance since the 1970s has been conducive to better political stability and unity, albeit, as before, under the aegis of a presumed Malay leadership, supremacy and control.

From the federal standpoint, the rise of the BN, on the foundation built by the Alliance, was to signify more accommodation of both ethnic and state demands, especially of the states of Sabah and Sarawak, although the feeling among the citizens in the latter that there was increasingly central encroachment remained persistent (Ahmed, H. Z. 1989: 374). Also, the BN-run central government has shared powers, with a chief minister belonging to the Chinese community of the state of Penang, in which the non-Malays are more numerous than the Malays (Ahmed, H. Z. 1989: 374). Conversely, it has also so happened that the Central Emergency Rule has been enforced on a non-BN government in Kelantan comprised overwhelmingly of Malays (Ahmed, H. Z. 1989: 374). The latter indicates the conflict between the BN and the opposition parties in the actual politics of the day. Many such cases have taken place in Kelantan (1959–78, and 1990 to the present); Terengganu (1999 to the present); and Sabah (1985–94) (Bakar 2007: 78). Case (Case 2007: 135–41) has shown that the BN-run federal government followed the

TABLE 5.3 Constituent parties of *Barisan Nasional* (BN) (as of May 2008)

1   United Malay National Organization (UMNO)
2   Malaysian Chinese Association (MCA)
3   Malaysian Indian Congress (MIC)
4   *Gerakan Rakyat* Malaysia (Malaysian People's Movement)
5   People's Progressive Party (PPP)
6   *Parti Pesaka Bhumiputera Bersatu* (PPBB)
7   Sarawak United People's Party (SUPP)
8   Sabah Progressive Party (SAPP, withdrew on 17 September 2008)
9   *Parti Bersatu Sabah* (PBS)
10   Liberal Democratic Party
11   *Parti Bersatu Rakyat Sabah* (PBRS)
12   United *Pasokmomogun Kadazandusun Murut* Organization
13   Sarawak Progressive Democratic Party (SPDP)
14   Sarawak People's Party *(Parti Rakyat Sarawak)* (PRS)

Source: Compiled from various Internet sources of the BN (www.2008bn.org.my/) (accessed 23 May 2009).

approach to non–BN-run state governments, as compared with those state governments run by the BN. In such cases, the state-level UMNO, in particular, has been handy (Case 2007: 136). Such measures do not smack of federalism *per se* but serve to show the instrumentalist gains that the UMNO through the BN has tried to garner, by limiting the political space to the opposition so that there is no serious challenge to its authority and to the entrenched Malay special rights and privileges built into the system.

But it is beyond doubt that the Alliance and then the BN in Malaysia have worked out an ingenious political formula and institutional device, grounded in concrete empirical reality, for inter-communal accommodation of identity and interests – something the opposition is yet to work out, by contrast – which has greatly facilitated the institutionalization of federalism in a country with a very delicate racial/communal balance rather than harmony. To be sure, inter-communal/racial power-sharing is not considered federalist *per se*, but with the Belgian case in mind (Watts 2008; Burgess and Pinder 2007), the Malaysian situation seems to have some credence. But in the Malaysian case again, it must be pointed out that the racial/communal interests are mediated through the states in the federations in which the communities are rooted, so that federalism operates in terms of a combination of community and territory. Given that only one state, namely Penang, has a Chinese majority, the Indians are not in a majority in any state, and Sabah and Sarawak (two East Borneo states) have populations which are considered as '*orang asli*' meaning part of the '*bhumiputera*' (sons of the soil) requiring special protection and privileges, the scope for the minorities to manoeuvre is limited.

The Alliance/BN is merely an institutional-political manifestation of Malaysian diversity, although not without problems. From the very beginning, the UMNO leadership over it has ensured privileged and inequitable Malay shares in development goods, to the relative deprivation of other communities (Fenton 2004: 144–57). Ironically enough, a substantial section of Malays – poor peasants, fishermen, hawkers, etc., remain economically poor and insecure (Zawawi 1989). The BN's model of inter-racial/inter-communal power-sharing among the communities' élites segregates society across racial lines, and hence its effectiveness in bringing about endurable social integration in such a fragmented society is in doubt, especially when social and economic goods are not equitably distributed. The BN's relative success so far has not been able to monopolize all political space in the political marketplace, because, beyond its 14 partners, there are as many 20 political parties, major and minor, including the influential DAP, PAS and PKR (comprising the opposition under the People's Alliance), which seek to organize peoples' support, although not always on ethnic lines. In the last general elections on 9 May 2018 for the 222-member of Parliament of Malaysia (*Dewan Rakiyat*, i.e., the lower house of parliament) the BN was ousted from power for the first time by an Alliance of Hope (People's Alliance) led by Mohammed Mahatir, whose party, HP, won 113 seats, and with its alliance partner WARISAN another 8, leaving only 79 seats to the BN. The election was won mostly on economic corruption charges against the incumbent Prime Minister Najib Rajak and a long-term incumbency

140 Dynamics of federalism

of the BN. This political change is unlikely to affect the federal politics as such in Malaysia, particularly because the prime minister Mahatir was once associated with the UMNO and BN for decades since 1957.

Notes

1 However, Wheare (1953) was well aware of the possible negative effects of 'sectional differences' on parties in a federal government, but content to note, with the experiences of the US and Canadian federations, how well the political parties had worked in bringing unity and strength into the working of the general governments (p. 87).

2 For further details, see chapter 6 'Political Parties in a Federal State' (pp. 177–225) in Filippov *et al.* 2004, which, incidentally, also contains an analytical discussion of the Indian case..

3 Much has been written on the subject. See, for instance, Robinson, F. (1974) *Separatism Among Indian Muslims: the Politics of the United Provinces' Muslims (1860–1923),* Cambridge: Cambridge University Press; and Jalal, A. (1994/1985) *The Sole Spokesman: Jinnah, The Muslim League and the Demand for Pakistan,* Cambridge: Cambridge University Press.

4 The Lahore Resolution did not mention 'Pakistan', but suggested that the independent state that the ML demanded should have 'constituent units' that would be 'autonomous and sovereign'. For further details, see Cohen, S. P. (2005) *The Idea of Pakistan,* New Delhi: Oxford University Press, p. 206. See also, Jaffrelot, C. (2002b) 'Introduction: Pakistan: Nationalism Without a Nation: Pakistan Searching for Its Identity' in Jaffrelot, C. (ed.) *Pakistan: Nationalism Without a Nation,* New Delhi: Manohar Publications, p. 12. For further details on the Lahore resolution (23 March 1940), see chapter 18 'The Lahore Resolution' (pp. 306–323) in Nagarkar, V. V. (1975) *The Genesis of Pakistan,* New Delhi: Allied Publishers Pvt. Ltd. The relevant portion of the Lahore Resolution is worth quoting here:

> . . . no constitutional plan would be workable in this country or acceptable to the Muslims unless it is designed on the following basic principles, namely, that geographically contiguous units are demarcated into regions which should be so constituted, with such territorial readjustments as may be necessary, that the areas in which the Muslims are numerically in a majority, as in the north-western and eastern zones of India, should be grouped to constitute independent states in which the constituent units shall be autonomous and sovereign.
>
> (p. 322)

5 The Congress was also a powerful force in the Punjab, particularly in the cities, and it is suspected that the main motive behind the Unionist Party (UP)'s decision to help the ML take roots in the province was to curtail the growing strength of the Congress.

6 Syed was so imbued with Sindhi nationalist concerns that he advocated the cause of regional self-determination in front of the Cabinet Mission in 1946, which was enough for him to be expelled from the Muslim League (Jaffrelot 2002b, p. 13).

7 The ML made little or no headway in Baluchistan, Pakistan's largest province, territorially speaking, in which a Baluch ethno-regional nationalism remains a potent force forced to the path of insurgency since the 1970s. For further details, see Chapter 2 of this book. Tariq Ali says that the 'Baluchs had hardly heard of the Muslim League, and had, in any event, never been asked whether or not they wished to be part of the new state' (see Ali, T. (1983) *Can Pakistan Survive: the Death of a State,* London: Penguin, p. 42).

8 Maniruzzaman, T. (1973) 'Radical Politics and the Emergence of Bangladesh' in Brass, P. R. and Franda, M. F. (eds) *Radical Politics in South Asia,* Cambridge, MA: MIT Press, p. 252.

9 The following Presidential Address of the Bengal Muslim League by Abdul Mansur Ahmed in 1944, offered enough indication:

> Religion and culture are not the same thing. Religion transgresses the geographical boundary but *tamadum* (culture) cannot go beyond the geographical boundary [. . .]. For this reason the people of *Purba* (Eastern) Pakistan are a different nation from the people of the other provinces of India and from the religious brothers of Pakistan.
>
> (quoted in Jaffrelot 2002b, p. 14)

10 Mehrunnisa Ali argued in her article on 'Federalism and Regionalism in Pakistan' that during the regime of PPP under Bhutto, the concessions that were made to accommodate the minority provincial concerns were all short-lived. For example, Bhutto dismissed the NAP-JUI government in Baluchistan and resorted to force to suppress the so-called irredentist move for separation in the province. For further details, see pp. 474–501, reprinted in Grover, V. and Arora, R. (eds) (1995) *Political System in Pakistan*, New Delhi: Deep & Deep.

11 In the Pakistan Constituent Assembly in Karachi, Jinnah addressed the Pakistanis:

> You are free; you are free to go to your temples, you are free to go to your mosques or to any other place of worship in this state of Pakistan. You may belong to any religion or caste or creed – that has nothing to do with the business of the state. We are starting with this fundamental principle that we are all citizens and equal citizens of one State. Now I think that in course of time Hindus would cease to be Hindus and Muslims would cease to be Muslims, not in the religious sense, because that is the personal faith of each individual, but in the political sense as citizens of the State.
>
> (Ali, T. 1982, p. 42)

On another occasion, Jinnah reiterated the same:

> You have carved out a territory, a vast territory. It is all yours; it does not belong to a Punjabi, a Sindhi or a Bengali. It is all yours. You have got your Central Government where several units are represented. Therefore, if you want to build yourself into a nation, for God's sake, give up this provincialism.
>
> (quoted in Cohen 2005, p. 205)

12 After many splits since 1969, INC (I) (for Indira Gandhi, the late Prime Minister of India) remains the main core of the parent body. Today it is led by her daughter-in-law Mrs Sonia Gandhi, the widow of the late Rajiv Gandhi, former Prime Minister of India. The INC (I)-led coalition called the UPA (United Progressive Alliance) has been in power at the Union level since 2004, and has just been returned in the general elections held in April-May 2009.

13 The number of regional, State-based parties has grown since the 1990s. For example, in 1998, the Election Commission of India recognized seven national parties and 40 State parties on the basis of certain criteria. In 2009, the Election Commission recognized four national parties and 43 State parties.

14 See, for instance, Weiner, M. (1967) *Party Building in a New Nation*, Chicago: University of Chicago Press; Brass, P. R. (1966) *Factional Politics in an Indian State: the Congress Party in Uttar Pradesh*, Berkeley: University of California Press; Brass, P. R. and Robinson, F. (eds) (1987) *The Indian National Congress and Indian Society, 1885–1985: Ideology, Social Structure, and Political Dominance*, New Delhi: Chanakya; Kochanek, S. A. (1968) *The Congress Party of India*, Princeton, NJ: Princeton University Press, NJ, USA; Sisson, R. and Wolpert, S. (eds) (1988) *Congress and Indian Nationalism: The Pre-Independence Phase*, Berkeley: University of California Press; Sisson, R. (1970) *The Congress Party in Rajasthan*, Berkeley: University of California Press; Chhiber, P. K. and Petrocik, J. R. (1989) 'The Puzzle of Indian Politics: Social Cleavages and the Indian Party System', *British Journal of Political Science*, Vol. 19, April, pp. 191–210; All India Congress

142 Dynamics of federalism

Committee (1985) *A Centenary History of the Indian National Congress,* 5 vols, New Delhi: Vikas; Chhiber, P. K. (1999) *Democracy Without Associations: Transformation of the Party System and Social Cleavage Theory,* New Delhi: Vistar Publications.

15 One important proviso that should be made here is that, despite the above status of Congress, the party was hardly ever able to secure even close to 50 per cent (except in 1984, which was an exceptional situation) of the popular votes polled in the parliamentary elections, which means that a political plurality in the electoral system in India exists in which people's divergent political allegiances are controlled by diverse political forces. This adds some important credence to federalism. (See Brass, P. R. (1989) 'Pluralism, Regionalism and Decentralizing Tendencies in Contemporary Indian Politics' in Wilson, A. J. and Dalton, D. (eds) *The States of South Asia: Problems of National Integration,* London: Hurst & Co., p. 242 for data up to 1980.) With further regionalization of the political system since the late 1980s, and the relative loss of power of Congress in the 1990s, the scenario is unlikely to have changed significantly. In the just-concluded *Lok Sabha* (parliamentary poll) elections, for instance, the Congress-led UPA, a multi-party alliance, got 48.23 per cent of popular votes.

16 It cannot be said, however, to be the case for the tribal people in India, whose movements, historically speaking, had enjoyed autonomy, and which the INC failed to represent equally forcefully within its fold. (See Bates, C. (1988) 'Congress and the Tribals' in Shepperdson, M. and Simmons, C. (eds) *The Indian National Congress and the Political Economy of India 1885–1985,* Aldershot, UK: Avebury, pp. 231–252.) However, this did not stand in the way of post-Independence accommodation of tribal interests at several levels of the polity, including, more importantly, tribal political autonomy in the form of autonomous district councils and tribal statehood in India's North-East. (See for further details, Mitra, S. K. and Bhattach-aryya, H. (2000) 'The Multicultural Challenge: the Post-Colonial State and SubNational Movements in India's North-East', pp. 91–135, in Basta-Fleiner, L., Bhattacharyya, H., Fleiner, T. and Mitra, S. K. (eds) *Rule of Law and Organization of the State in Asia: The Multicultural Challenge,* Fribourg, Switzerland: Helbing and Lichtenhahn; Bhattacharyya, H. (2001a) *India as a Multicultural Federation; Asian Values, Democracy and Decentralization (In Comparison with Swiss Federalism),* Fribourg, Switzerland: Institute of Federalisms, chap. 6, pp. 235–275; and Mukherjee, J. (2008) *Multicultural Decentralization in India,* Unpubl. Ph.D. Thesis, University of Burdwan, chap. 6, pp. 237–269, 'Tribal Statehood'.

17 Bhattacharyya, H. (1992) 'Deinstitutionalization of Indian Politics: a Micro Critique', *Journal of Socio-Political Studies* (Burdwan University), Vol. 1, No. 1, 64–85, for a summary of the different strands in the said thesis, and their implications.

18 See Brass, P. R. (1989), op. cit., pp. 232, 236 for statistical evidence.

19 Balveer Arora (2004) has pointed out with statistical evidence that with the State-parties' rise into national prominence since the late 1980s, there has also been a corresponding decline in the use of the President's Rule (Art. 356) (p. 520). For further details, see his 'Political Parties and the Party System: the Emergence of New Coalitions', in Hasan, Z. (ed.) *Parties and Party Politics in India,* New Delhi: Oxford University Press, pp. 504–532.

20 In this election, the BN gained 140 out of 220 seats in Parliament. Political analysts noted, however, a gradual erosion of support, and that too, among the Malays, for the BN since 1990s. In the 1999 parliamentary election, for instance, the seats held by the BN had decreased from 166 to 148; and in the State Assembly elections in the same year (they are held simultaneously in Malaysia), the BN's share of seats decreased from 338 to 281 (p. 70). For more details, see Mutalib, H. (2000) 'Malaysia's 1999 General Elections: Signposts to Future Politics', *Asian Journal of Political Science,* Vol. 8, No. 1, June, 65–87.

6

CENTRE–STATE RELATIONS

Structure and processes

Introduction

The study of centre–state relations, or intergovernmental relations, as known in federations like Canada, constitutes the operational aspect of federations. It refers to how federalism is worked, if worked at all: How does the federal government of the day deal with the federal units? It also covers the issues of how the federal units respond to issues, typically of national and international importance. Going beyond the bounds of legal–constitutionalism of federalism, the subject is linked also to issues of identity, values of diversity and interests that the federal units are supposed to uphold and represent in terms of states' rights, or autonomy in federations. Since a federation is a compound polity involving at least two levels of authority acting on the same citizens, and since the written constitutions cannot so neatly formally determine and demarcate the boundaries of jurisdiction of central and state/provincial or cantonal (as in Switzerland) authorities, some areas of overlap, interdependence, cooperation and also conflict in respect of powers and functions, operationally speaking, are unavoidable. Intergovernmental relations cover wider areas of study in federalism than centre–state relations because the former also cover the interstate, or interregional, interprovincial, relations. The latter aspect, quite important in its own right in the study of federalism, remains beyond the scope of the current study.[1] As we have seen in Chapter 5, the party system, in particular, is a great determinant of not only inter-unit relations but also centre-state relations in federations. The formal constitutionally determined distribution of powers and functions, as we have discussed already in Chapter 4, is of course one of the most important factors that in a way predetermines the shape relations are likely to take between the centre and the states. There is, in other words, a structurally in-built factor in this regard. All five federations (except perhaps Nepal) under study are structurally centralized – although the extent of this centralization varies – a fact that is itself the result of the circumstances leading to their formation, including the special weight of leading political factors and so on. Second, all federations except Malaysia seem to have an unfinished character and have yet to be fully consolidated. This is more true for India and Pakistan, to some extent, and for Malaysia until 1965 when it experienced disintegration by the secession/separation of Singapore (which had joined the federation only in 1963!) but which had also expanded by inclusion of two units (namely Sabah and Sarawak) in 1963;those units, however, stay with the federation with some additional special (unequal) rights. Third, the ethno-national identity issue is of crucial importance in examining the centre–state relations (as well as inter-unit ones), an issue which works through the political parties and which lies behind but acts as a very powerful influence shaping the centre–state relations in Asian federations. Since each of the units in such federations are so distinct, socioculturally speaking, being inhabited by distinct peoples, the relative deprivation of the resources and opportunities experienced by such units, in conditions of backwardness and lack of development, seems to exacerbate conflicts. Finally, democracy is another very important factor which performs its role in various ways in this respect. It allows, to begin with, any relationship worth the name between the centre and the states/provinces in the sense of active interaction that may entail dialogue, meeting, conferences, bargaining, contestation, opposition, conflict and cooperation. It is democracy, operationally speaking, which offers the most congenial atmosphere for centre–state relations in federations. It does not promise to solve all the problems in a federation but certainly allows all the questions in centre–state relations to be brought to the fore. Authoritarianism does not allow any relations, that is, dialogue, bargain, negotiation etc., so that conflict becomes the predominant form of relations, if there be any, between the central authority and the states or provinces. Pakistan until 2010 in our study will offer a glaring example of this. Since a federation inevitably implies at least two sets of government, the polity can only work through, as Watts argues, 'extensive consultation, co-operation and co-ordination between governments' (Watts 1999: 57). The failure to do so, due to excessive centralization, authoritarianism, absence of democracy and other anti-federal practices, results in the erosion of the principle of federalism itself, which cuts into the very basis of the federation.

Pakistan

Pakistan is considered a case of failure of federalism and democracy, or what Watts (Watts 1999, 2008) would term a 'pathology of federations', and nowhere is the failure so grotesque and glaring than in the failed, somewhat stalled, centre–provincial relations. The country's first experience of disintegration in 1971, in which its eastern wing (East Pakistan) broke away to form Bangladesh, was the inevitable result of such a failure to begin with. The eastern wing's initial demand was not secession but autonomy within the federation, which was rather typical in any federation, particularly in a highly centralized and militarized one. The military dictatorship's total insensitivity to the legitimate demands of the majority of the citizens in the federation stood in the way of accommodation of diversity and paved the way for eventual secession from the federation itself. Some have argued that behind the military-bureaucratic regime's opposition to accommodate the diversity demands of the federations' provinces, particularly the eastern wing inhabited by the Bengalis, lay the political élites' attempts to overcome the country's many forms of diversity in favour of a 'new national Pakistani identity based upon loyalty to the state and Islam'. For example, Urdu was adopted as the national language when it was not native to any of its four provinces! In the name of consolidating the nascent state, the central government concentrated more and more powers in its hands and showed the early signs (within a fortnight of the formation of the state) of more centralization by dismissing the provincial government in the NWFP, and that of Sindh seven months later. It is argued strongly that the provincial politicians had little choice but to submit to the command of the civil servants of the central administration in the early years. As any student of Pakistan knows, within less than a decade of its formation, the political power slipped from the civilian bureaucracy into military hands (post-1958), and the country has not looked back ever since in this process, except some short spells of democratic government, which, incidentally, had little leverage. One anonymous writer aptly argued that the successive military regimes in Pakistan have almost totally insinuated themselves into the country's government, foreign policy, nuclear programmes and economy, business and money-making.[2] In matters of centre–provincial relations, something has not changed, however: 'the drive for centralization and the suppression of provincial autonomy'.[3]

It goes without saying that behind the institutional arrangements are people who have their interests, values and aspirations, which are supposed to embody and to represent them, and hence the denial of state autonomy and centralization of powers (and resources) (which itself is not always bereft of ethnic content and bias, given the time and context) hit at the heart of the diversity, identity and values of the collectivities at stake. To take the example of Urdu being adopted as the national language, spoken by not more than 3 per cent of the population when it was adopted in 1947/1956, this state action had 'a final ethnic dimension' (Adeney 2007a: 109). Since the initial days of the Republic, the bureaucracy and the army had remained the strongest elements of government, and Urdu also happened to be the language of the Pakhtuns, Punjabis and Muhajirs, communities who also dominated the bureaucracy and the army, so it is not surprising that Urdu came out on top (Adeney 2007a: 109). It is reported that Urdu was the language of lower level administration during British rule in the NWFP, 'British' Baluchistan and Punjab.[4] But, in provinces such as Sindh and the most populous Bengal, that was not the case. And yet, like Urdu, Bengali and Sindhi were and still are quite developed literary languages. Thus, adopting Urdu as the national language was not as neutral a decision as it was presented to be. Second, the refusal of the rulers to recognize regional languages as languages of administration for a long time after Independence also showed the early signs of the shape that centre–provincial relations were going to take in the Pakistan federation. Who does not know of the

146 Centre–state relations

disastrous consequences of language-based political mobilization in East Pakistan, leading to the major secession in 1971 in the form of the creation of Bangladesh? Therefore, in understanding the nature of centre–provincial relations, the underlying ethnic-identity issues can hardly be ignored. In the post-Bangladesh years, with the ascendance of the Punjabis to power through the army's taking control over the realm of affairs, the ethnic content of centralization of powers and the suppression of provincial autonomy assumed added significance.

The other related consideration is the attitude and orientations of the rulers towards the need for accommodation of ethno-national identity(ies) in the form of appropriate political associations, which would require many territorial adjustments that respect the identity aspect rather than the typical narrow political considerations. The way that things were carried out in Pakistan in this respect, as we have seen in Chapter 2 of this book, has shown a lack of sensitivity to the ethnic identity of the people. As Adeney (2007a) has further shown, 'at independence, Baluchistan was split between 'British Baluchistan with a sizeable Pashtu [Pakhtu]-speaking community (41 per cent) and the Baluchi States Union, which was predominantly Baluchi and Brahvi speaking' (Adeney 2007a: 110). But the whole thing, itself flawed on ethnic grounds, was dissolved (in favour of a single province of Baluchistan) in the One Unit scheme introduced in 1970.[5] Subsequently, some, albeit limited, accommodation of languages has been allowed so that Sindh could change its provincial language from Urdu to Sindhi (Adeney 2007a: 110). Nonetheless, with bouts of successive authoritarian regimes punctuated by heavy doses of ethnic bias, the centre–provincial relations in Pakistan remained deeply conflictual. Note that one of the 'aims and objectives' of the ex-military General Musharraf (2000–8) on assumption of power was the need for better centre–provincial relations and 'to strengthen federation, remove inter-provincial disharmony and restore national cohesion' (Adeney 2007a: 110), which was sufficient indication of the deep malaise from which the federation had been suffering. There is no reason to believe that the situation has improved since; on the contrary, since the increasing ascendancy of military power over the entire state has most often meant the suzerainty of the Punjabis (who dominate the military), a 'strong sense of distrust towards the centre among the constituent units' is perceived by commentators on Pakistani politics.[6]

Politically speaking, centre–provincial relations in Pakistan have been very troubled. The historical factors apart (that is, the way that the state was created, which also entailed forcible annexation of some provinces which were unwilling to join Pakistan), the factors responsible were the lack of democracy for most of the time since Independence; bureaucratization and militarization of the political system; failure of the central leadership to accommodate the diversity demands of the groups and the provinces; intermeshing of the ethnic-identity issues with federal relations; and Punjabization of the state so that the Punjabis increasingly turn out to be the *staatsvolk* (the dominant ethno-national group claiming to own the state) of the federation.[7] While the military rulers have been habitual centralizers in Pakistan, there are no records to suggest that the elected national leaders such as Z. A. Bhutto or his daughter Benazir Bhutto, or for that matter Nawaz Sharif, were any less centralizing or respecters of provincial autonomy. Ironically enough, ex-General Musharraf's resolve to restore federalism and harmony in centre–provinces relations coincided with the increase in the Baluch insurgency, which, with an earlier history of insurgency, has intensified since early 2005.[8]

The argument that is being made here is that since the formation of the federation in Pakistan has followed a different trajectory from that of the conventional type; since the issue of nationhood in Pakistan has remained grossly unresolved, reflected, among other things, in internecine ethno-national conflicts; and since the federation has favoured centralization and the major ethno-national group, the Punjabis, the centre–provincial relations, very bitter and full of friction, are hardly intelligible within the formal terms of the constitutional provisions. Various historical, political and sociocultural factors, as indicated earlier, are very important considerations. Judged thus, inter-ethnic relations, as mediated through the political parties and the governmental apparatuses, then already decide upon the patterns of centre–provincial relations. One very recent observer of Pakistan politics aptly remarked: 'The federal politics of Pakistan are driven by friction among its six ethnic groups: the Punjabi, Sindhi, Pashtun [Pakhtun], Baloch [Baluch], Seraiki and Muhajir' (Ahmed, S. 2007: 5). Following the same source, it is possible to sum up some recent examples of the shape that the centre–provincial relations in Pakistan have taken. First, the province of Sindh has been experiencing bloody ethnic conflicts. Second, a 'low-level insurgency' has been enveloping Baluchistan, challenging the centre, the issue being the latter's exploitation of the natural resources not only of Baluchistan but also of Sindh and the NWFP. Third, there is opposition developed in the NWFP against the centre's big dam-centred development plans, which seem mostly to benefit the Punjabis. Such opposition to the centre's moves has cost the provinces inhabited by smaller ethnic communities their rights and self-government, in which the centre, especially that part dominated by the military administrators, has tampered with impunity. Fourth, under army rule, which has resulted in the reduction in the significance of the National Parliament in favour of the increased powers for the president (otherwise a mere titular head of state in a parliamentary system of government), a position also occupied by the army chief, the provinces' rights have further been curtailed, adding to the resentment of various smaller ethno-national groups (Ahmed, S. 2007: 5–6). As a result, the Pakistan federation, already very fragile and still fledgling, has failed to develop the 'national consensus on power sharing' without which no federation can survive, more particularly in conditions that are ethnically so charged.

As far as the financial relations are concerned, there is little to give the federation's units reasons to rejoice, particularly those units inhabited by the smaller ethno-national groups. As we have already discussed in Chapter 4 of this book, the Constitution (of 1973) makes the centre very powerful in almost all respects. The bulk of revenue is collected by the central government, while the bulk of work is to be done by the provinces, which have little or very limited taxing powers. There are then factors such as the differential capacity of the provinces to deliver services

148 Centre–state relations

and to promote development. All of these factors result, inevitably, in both vertical and horizontal imbalances.

Nonetheless, some amount of disbursement of resources between the central government and the provinces has taken place through the National Finance Commission (NFC) (Article 160 of the Constitution) and the National Planning Commission. The NFC (formed once every five years) decides the quantum of money to be retained by the central government, as well as the sum to be distributed among the provinces. It is found that, since 1974, population has remained the sole criterion of distribution of resources among the provinces. As per the last NFC award in 1997, 37.5 per cent of the Divisible Pool was distributed among the provinces, again on the basis of population alone.[9] The provinces were allowed to retain the revenues which had their origins in the provinces after paying a 2 per cent collection charge to the central government. The 1997 award also provided for special grants of Rs 3–4 billion each to Baluchistan and the NWFP, due to their relative backwardness. Provisions also were made for matching grants to the provinces. All in all, the provincial share of this award came to 43.6 per cent.[10] In the Interim Award in 2005, announced by the then President Musharraf, increased the Divisible Pool to 41.5 per cent for 2006–7 and to 46.25 per cent for 2010–11.[11] It was decided that a further sum of Rs 27.75 billion would be given to the provinces as grants to be distributed in the following manner: Punjab (11 per cent), Sindh (21 per cent), Baluchistan (33 per cent) and the NWFP (35 per cent).[12] The latter grant reflects the backwardness factor at play in some ascending order in grants disbursement for the provinces. However, the fact remains that the major source of revenue-sharing among the provinces is the Divisible Pool, in which case using population as the sole criterion disproportionately benefits the most populous state, that is, Punjab.

Needless to say, the provinces have demanded a greater share of resources, to the extent of 50 per cent, if not more, out of the Divisible Pool, since the existing dependence of the provinces, financially speaking, on the centre reduces their autonomy. The other considerations which have been brought to the fore by the provinces in fiscal transfers are based on a formula that takes into account such criteria as backwardness of the states, their fiscal health, fiscal efforts and population size. That is designed to ensure a more balanced fiscal federalism. Due to the many factors already indicated, federal–provincial relations in Pakistan are troubled, and a strong sense of distrust exists towards the centre among the provinces (except Punjab), who do not see the centre as an 'honest broker' in respect of protecting the interests of the smaller provinces.[13] Federal loyalty (defined as loyalty both to the Union and an overarching identity) is thus very much lacking in Pakistan. The major provincial devolution by the 18th Amendment of the Constitution (2010), if and when implemented, may usher in healthy centre-provincial relations hitherto not witnessed.

Malaysia

The centre–state relations in Malaysia are no less complex, enmeshed as they are in complex ethno-communal interests and identities. Structurally highly centralized as the federation is, observers have difficulties in extending full recognition to it, and hence such terms as a *'dejure* federation which is a *defacto* unitary state', 'a semi-democratic minimalist federation' and so on, are commonly used to describe the federation.[14] Within Malaysia, its federalism has until very recently not been able to generate genuine debates among scholars and opinion-makers because apparently a highly centralized structure accompanied by the rise of the Malay-dominated *Barisan Nasional* (National Front), which had ruled until March 2008 over the centre as well as 12 of 13 states, seemed to foreclose any discussion of the scope of state autonomy and the consequent challenge to the authority of the all-powerful central government. No wonder the opposition performance in the last general elections (March 2008), winning 5of the 13 states and depriving the BN of its long-held two-thirds majority in the national Parliament that was required to almost unilaterally amend the Constitution, has created a lot of enthusiasm for the right path towards federalism in the country. When the same party, or a coalition, rules in the centre and the overwhelming majority of the states, comparable with the Indian scenario until 1967 (we will discuss this later), genuine federal dialogue (bargain, contestation, conflict, opposition, and so on) between the centre and the constituent units is unlikely to take shape because issues at stake are then settled within the four walls of the party or the coalition. Nonetheless, the federation has survived and has not – since the departure of Singapore (1965) and the communal riots in 1969 – been confronted with any serious threat to its stability and integrity.

By constitutional design, the federation in Malay/Malaysia was meant to be highly centralized, and all of the constitutional and political developments since the inauguration of the federation in 1957 have served to further centralize the federation. Consider the following recommendation of the Reid (Constitutional) Commission (1956) that in effect prepared the Constitution, in which the Constitution of Malaya was to provide for:

> [T]he establishment of a strong central government with states and settlements enjoying a measure of autonomy . . . with the machinery for consultation between the Central Government and the states and settlements on certain financial matters to be specified in the constitution.[15]

In addition to various constitutional provisions including the emergency powers of the centre, Shafruddin (1988) has also documented a series of constitutional amendments and court cases, the former as instances of the centre's increasing encroachment on states' rights and the latter as instances of resistance of the states against the same (Shafruddin 1988: 12–21). Shafruddin has rightly pointed out that many such amendments to the Constitution have impacted adversely on centre–state relations and the 'agreed federal relationship'. To take one major instance, the centre has progressively altered the composition of the Senate, the house of the states, from the original proportion of state-appointed to centre-appointed senators, i.e. from 28:22 to 28:32 in 1964. In 1965, the states' proportion was further reduced to 26 without any change in the centre's proportion (the current position in 2009 is still 26:32). Shafruddin (1988) has further argued that the terms under

150 Centre–state relations

which the three federal units, namely, Singapore, Sarawak and Sabah, were admitted to the federation in 1963 were also at variance with the original terms under which the 11 states joined the federation (Shafruddin 1988: 13). This expansion of the federation violated the principle of equality among the federal units and introduced the principle of inequality between the original 11 states, on the one hand, and three new states (particularly the two North Borneo states, namely Sarawak and Sabah), on the other.[16] Singapore's secession from the federation in 1965 (not permitted, constitutionally) was also subject to much criticism. And yet the BN's more than two-thirds majority of seats in the national Parliament meant that the central government could pass amendment after amendment without much effective opposition.

This does not mean of course there was not conflict between the centre and the states. Conflicts were bound to arise when the centre was so powerful and encroaching. From as early as 1959 the opposition (PAS)-run Kelantan, for instance, became, involved in political conflict with the centre and came out as the defender of states' rights. It has also happened that at the height of the conflict, the Kelantanese identity became more marked than the Malaysian identity.[17] There were also occasions when the central rule was imposed in the states in order to stave off a political crisis. It happened in Sarawak in September 1966 and in Kelantan in November 1977. The tussle between the centre and Kelantan reached such an impasse that by the Emergency Powers (Kelantan) Act, 1977, the Kelantan State Constitution was suspended, without, however, suspending the prerogatives of the sultan. Court cases challenging the authority of the centre have also been initiated (Shafruddin 1988: 19–21). It must, however, be stressed here that the states joined together as a force to fight against the centre, as has also happened in India and, as we will see later, has not occurred in Malaysia due to the long-drawn dominance of the BN over the centre as well as its dominance in most states. We should not lose sight of the associated ethnic content of this political dominance.

Financially, the Malaysian federation is also very centralized, as we have seen in Chapter 4 of this book (see the section on 'Malaysia'). Its tax-raising powers place it in the fourth highest rank of 15 selected federal countries (Watts 2008: 102). Malaysian federal government revenues before intergovernmental transfers constitute 86.9 per cent, which compares unfavourably with India (61.1 per cent). Unlike India and perhaps most federations, the spending powers of the federal government in Malaysia are very high expenditure powers; it shares as much as 84.3 per cent of all public expenditure. This fact reflects the much wider-ranging legislative powers of the federal government (Ninth Schedule Articles 74, 77 of the Constitution) that includes even the police, the prisons, public order, internal social security, justice, education, health and welfare, and so on. In India, the comparable percentage is 44.6 per cent.[18] This is reflective of the wider-ranging activities that the state governments in India have to undertake, including implementation of many federal laws and programmes of development and empowerment. Watts (2008) has termed the Malaysian federation an 'executive' in which the federal government is dominant (Watts 2008: 113). The overall increase in the powers of the federal government has been well reflected in its growth in revenues by four times relative to that of all the states together, between 1985 and 1999. The National Petroleum Act of 1974 is an important means through which the federal government 'took control over the returns on petroleum and gas sales from the oil-producing states of Terengganu, Sarawak and Sabah', which subsequently received only a 5 per cent royalty, and that too, of a conditional nature (Adeney 2007a: 132). To conjoin fiscal federalism to federal politics while the federal funding to the states has never been withheld, there have been occasions when the flow of the funds to opposition-run states has been restricted and delayed. Also, partisanship in transfer of grants to state governments of the UMNO-led *Barisan* has been commonplace.

As a result, the states have felt deprived and discontented. After the secession of Singapore, the central rulers have persistently pursued the theme of unity of the federation around the notion of 'a united people through language, formal education and even arts'.[19] And yet regionalism symbolizing states' discontent, at least in some states, could not be avoided. Andaya and Andaya (2001) have pointed out that in the year 2000 regionalism remained 'a point of identity' in Sarawak and Sabah (Andaya and Andaya 2001: 340). Such regional discontent was not limited to the geographically separated and mostly aboriginal-inhabited Borneo states of Sarawak and Sabah. There were peninsular examples, too, which were strong enough to change the electoral verdict in 1999. Andaya and Andaya (2001) wrote:

> The northeastern peninsular states of Kelantan and Terengganu form another area with an intense regional pride. In defiance of the centre, the people of these two states rejected government parties in 1999 in favour of PAS, thus reaffirming their claims to be the heartland of both Islamic and Malay values.
>
> *(Andaya and Andaya 2001: 340)*

This passage is an indication that UMNO's claim to be the sole representative of Malay identity and values was not universally accepted in Malaysia. Andaya and Andaya (2001) have cautioned us that regionalism in Malaysia should not be seen simply as secessionism, because regionalism here appeared to be a cover for protesting against the centre's neglect and demanding more resources from the centre, more equitable distribution of resources and a greater stake in national-level decision-making (Andaya and Andaya 2001: 340).

The issue, finally, is related closely to the federation's national identity of being Malay, which has not been easy to achieve, if at all. For one thing, there is tension between the notion of 'Malay' and the *'bhumiputera'* ('sons of the soil'), the latter being a more recent construction which seems to cover more ground than a Malay identity would, ethnically speaking. For instance, the term *'bhumiputera'* was 'created to refer to the Peninsular Orang Asli, the indigenous peoples of Sabah and

152 Centre–state relations

Sarawak, and Malay' (Andaya and Andaya 2001: 342). Andaya and Andaya (2001) have argued that:

> In practical administrative calculations regarding employment, education and economic quota, the Bhumiputera category virtually replaced that of Malay. Yet, distinctions within the Bhumiputera category persist.
>
> *(Andaya and Andaya 2001: 342)*

Various kinds of discrimination in matters of public goods are practised among the segments in the same *bhumiputera* category. Andaya and Andaya (2001) have observed that Malaya *bhumiputera* are favoured over *orang asli* Bhumiputera and that in Sabah and Sarawak, Borneo *bhumiputera* are favoured over those from the Peninsula (Andaya and Andaya 2001: 342). There are also religious grounds for discrimination in these two Borneo states. For example, the *bhumiputera* groups have received preferential government treatment as compared with the Christian ones such as the Iban in Sarawak and the Kadazandusun in Sabah (Andaya and Andaya 2001: 342). Quite predictably, this has made the ethnic situation in Malaysia ever changing and more complex.

Finally, to take a longer-term view of the developments in Malaysian federation, since the Malay/Malaysian federation was not an ethnic compact but formed mainly on territorial grounds (the unity of nine Malay Sultanates with their indigenous political systems), the state-based non-Malay ethnic groups were sought to be accommodated within the federal arrangements. As Shafrud-din has argued (1988), the federal formula of 1957 did not address itself to the questions of non-Malay, non-Muslim and non-Chinese ethnic groups, who have since become politically assertive.[20] The 1963 federal formula was not professedly ethnic, but the inclusion of Sabah and Sarawak with significant proportions of *bhumiputera* people – Sabah (80.5 per cent, including 19.0 per cent Malays) and Sarawak (72.9 per cent, including 31.6 per cent Malays) – the federation took on, at least partially, an ethnic character vis-à-vis Sabah and Sarawak. Nonetheless, various ethnic groups in the states,[21] most notably in Sabah and Sarawak, have been mobilized in articulating the demands of the states against the centre. In the early 1970s Sabah even threatened to secede.[22] All of these factors suggest that the UMNO-led BN government at the centre is not to be seen as undiluted and undisputed Malay dominance; the challenges to it are many indeed. But the federation has survived and adapted itself to many changes: secessionism, contraction, expansion and so on. However, it must be noted that the original federal principle has suffered to a significant extent.

India

The centre–state relations in Indian federalism constitute a fascinating area of studies in federalism in their own right. To be sure, as the major inheritor of the Raj and the centralized colonial state apparatus built over two centuries, the post-Independence Indian federation remains highly centralized, constitutionally speaking. Although constitutionally declared a 'Union of States' in 1950, for quite a long time it remained mostly an unfinished federation, despite many phases of reorganization for 'right-sizing' the constituent units so that the political boundary corresponds with the cultural one. It remains incomplete as a federation even now because there are still demands to create more states by reorganizing the existing ones. Paradoxical though it may seem, the constituent units of the Indian federation are the result of federalization rather than the other way round. As I have discussed in many places (Bhattacharyya 2001a, 2001b, 2005a, 2005b, 2008), the process of right-sizing the federal units in many phases in India has been emblematic of the accommodation of ethno-national identity of many sorts – language, region and tribal affiliation or a combination thereof.

This is precisely where ethnic or ethno-national identity comes into the picture of centre–state relations. While the strong ethno-regional or ethno-national pressures from below have acted upon the centre in respect of redrawing the political map of the federation for recognition, autonomy and resources, the central dominance has never been synonymous with the dominance of any particular ethnic group, unlike in Pakistan and Malaysia. The reason is the absence of any dominant all-India nationality. Of course that did not mean the absence of any conflict between the centre and the states, the latter being representative of some ethno-national identity group(s). On the contrary, centre–state relations have been marked by cooperation, conflict, bargaining and even confrontation. One important result of the states' assertions, particularly since the late 1960s, against the centre's encroaching powers and for more state autonomy has been further decentralization in the federation. While the creation of newer, smaller states out of the existing larger and multi-ethnic ones has meant decentralization of the otherwise centralized federation, the states' struggle for more autonomy, when backed by an enfranchised and politically (and ethnically too) mobilized people, has also brought some resources down to the states.

Constitutionally, the Union government (the centre) has of course been highly empowered, legislatively as well as financially. Administratively too, the centre is very powerful, at least theoretically speaking, because, following the Anglo-Saxon tradition, in India's parliamentary federation each tier has administrative authority over the matters on which it has legislative authority. As we saw in Chapter 4 of this book (see the section on 'India'), the Constitution vests all very important powers in the Union government, plus all emergency powers and the special powers to encroach upon the State List and state administration (Articles mentioned in this context are: 356, 352, 360, 256, 257, 365 and 249). While many reasons are cited in favour of the centre's very powerful position vis-à-vis the states,[23] federally the more accurate constitutional explanation seems to be the specific mode of formation of the federation in India, which is more top-down than bottom-up in nature. It is common knowledge that the Constituent Assembly of India (1946–49) did not witness any heated debates *à la* Philadelphia in 1787 between the centralists and the provincialists. The province-based politicians in the CA, who incidentally had tasted political power following the 1937 elections, were content with the centre

154 Centre–state relations

collecting most of the taxes but distributing them later on between the centre and the states.

The structural position of the states in the Indian federation should be stated clearly, otherwise one will have an incorrect knowledge of the Indian federation. First, the Indian Constitution gives the states significant powers in areas such as the police, public order, public health, social security, land tenure, land revenues, local government, agriculture, fisheries, agricultural taxation, water supply, irrigation, canals, land rights, tolls, capitation fees, industrial infrastructure, power development, roads (other than national highways), urban development and so on (66 items as per the State List). Those are again the areas which most concern the citizens in their daily lives and are developmental. In the wake of India's globalization over the last two decades, the states' strategic significance thus has increased in matters of implementation of structural adjustment programmes. Second, the states have concurrent jurisdiction over the Concurrent List (47 items), which contains such items as criminal law, preventive detention, forests, economic and social planning, trade unions, education, marriage and so on. Although the centre has a paramount position in the case of disputes, the states' powers over the list should not simply be underestimated.

Third, there is an interesting administrative dimension here too. Beyond their own administration, the states also have what Hardgrave and Kochanek have termed a 'critical administrative role'[24] in the federation. The fact of the matter is that the centre 'depends heavily on the states to implement many of its policies'.[25] This has so happened because of the particular nature of the administrative system that had evolved in India. Paul Appleby, who prepared the first post-Independence survey of the administrative system in India, aptly described it as follows:

> No other large and important government . . . is so dependent as India on the theoretically subordinate but actually rather distinct units responsible to a different political control, for so much of the administration of what are recognized as national programmes of great importance to the nation.[26]

The Union government, as Appleby aptly remarked, is all staff and no line, so that the centre's dependence on the states for administering its policies and programmes is unavoidable. This gives the states a lot of room to manoeuvre in the implementation of policies, and in partisan dispensation of goods and services for building bases of political support as well as maintaining the ones already built. Sudipta Kaviraj[27] would go a step further and say that the policies created at the higher levels become diluted as they move lower down the bureaucratic hierarchy, as those at the lower levels have their own perception of reality. But that is a separate theoretical issue in understanding the state. One thing which is certain is that, politically and administratively, both the tiers of government are functionally interdependent, a fact which is so important for political stability and integrity.

Before we move into discussion of the 'politics' of centre–state relations – which would involve a lot of partisanship and misuse in the exercise of constitutional powers by the party in power, the resultant political instability in the states, the states' combined struggles against the centre and a major revision of the constitutional relations between the centre and the states – we should pay some attention to the fiscal relations between the centre and the states. As I have argued elsewhere in greater detail,[28] fiscal federalism is very much part of the political process in India. It operates within the broad contours of India's mode of federal governance, geared mostly, despite many odds, to meeting the diversity needs of the federation and decentralization. India's federalization since 1950 thus has witnessed the rise of a differentiated federal structure: the rise of new states, associate states, substates and regional, tribal and district councils with guaranteed relatively autonomous powers, all co-existing within the single federal polity (Bhattacharyya 2000: 258). This shows the sensitivity of the federation to diversity and to power-sharing at many levels of the polity and prepares the political culture, broadly speaking, of fiscal decentralization too.

Institutional arrangements for fiscal federalism are very complex, being conditioned more by historical, linguistic and political factors than by economic efficiency.[29] Hemming and others have argued that the complex nature of intergovernmental fiscal relations in India are rooted in the country's diversity as well as the long-standing vertical imbalance between the revenue-raising and expenditure powers of the states.[30] The Indian Constitution has specified the revenue-raising powers of the two orders of government in terms of the Union and State Lists. In India there is no concurrent sphere in the matter of tax legislation. So the powers to tax and raise money by each layer of government follow from their legislative powers as enumerated in their respective lists. Each layer of government has the legislative power to levy tax. However, the revenue-raising and expenditure powers vary greatly between the two tiers of government.

Constitutionally, the Union government has tax-raising powers on most important sources of revenue: income tax (other than agricultural tax); customs; corporate tax; taxes on capital values of assets of individuals and companies; surcharges on income tax, etc. The state governments have the powers to levy an estate duty in respect of agricultural land, to impose taxes on the sale or purchase of goods (other than newspapers) and on vehicles, goods and passengers, excise, stamp duty and registration, etc. Sales taxes constitute the major source of revenue of the state governments. In 1990–91, sales tax constituted as much as 56 per cent of the states' total tax revenues.[31]

Along with tax raising, the distribution of the proceeds among the layers of government in India is also very important to consider.[32] In India, the following five principles are followed in respect of both tax raising and the distribution of the proceeds:

1   Some duties are levied by the Union government but are collected and entirely appropriated by the states after collection.
2   Some taxes are both levied and collected by the Union government, but the proceeds are then assigned by the Union government to those states within which they have been levied.

3   There are taxes that are levied and collected by the Union government, but the proceeds are distributed between the Union government and the state government.
4   There is provision for a grant-in-aid in favour of states in need, such as for tribal welfare and other special needs.[33]

The Constitution (Articles 270, 273, 275 and 280) has provided for the formation of a Finance Commission, to be so formed after every five years as an important instrument or mechanism through which multiple channels of intergovernmental fiscal transfers take place. The union Finance Commission (FC) distributes the net proceeds of taxes between the Union and the states, determines the principles governing the grant-in-aid of the revenues of the states, decides upon the measures needed to augment the Consolidated Fund of the States to supplement their resources etc. and considers any other matter that the president may refer to it in the interests of sound public finance (Bhattacharyya 2000: 278).

Over the last five decades since 1951, FCs have been formed regularly, and they have also functioned regularly and made recommendations. It is found that the states' share in all sharable Union taxes has risen over the years, and the 14th Finance Commission has increased the share from 32 per cent to 42 per cent (Reddy and Reddy 2019: 75). The criteria in disbursement to the states have also changed in order to provide for a more rational, locality sensitive transfer. For example, for a long time up to 1978, the states' contribution in tax collection and their population were criteria for distribution. After 1978, an additional criterion of GDP was taken into consideration. Since 1989, a further criterion of a composite index of backwardness[34] was included. The criteria have undergone further changes in order to adapt to circumstances, given the vast and varied experiences of the states of the federation.

Rao and Singh (2005) have given us the latest criteria and their weight in tax devolution (Table 6.1). Rao and Singh (2005) have shown with a wealth of statistical data how over the years the transfers from the central government have contributed a significant part of the states' finances.[35] They have also pointed out that per-capita central transfer at constant prices (1981–82) had also steadily increased well into 1992–94 but had declined slightly afterwards due to the need for 'greater fiscal compression' (Rao and Singh 2005: 191).[36]

However, the role of the FCs in India has also been subjected to differential assessments. One extreme view suggests that the FCs have made the states utterly

TABLE 6.1 Latest criteria and their weightage in tax devolution in India (2015–20)

Criteria	Weight (%)
Population	27.5
Income (distance method)	50.0
Area	15.0
Forest cover	7.5

Source: Reddy and Reddy (2019: 98–9)

dependent upon the centre, which in turn has been accused of political wire-pulling. The more positive view suggests that the FCs have, by and large, maintained the balance between the Union and the states.[37] Rao and Singh (2005) have also not ruled out the 'political considerations' at play in the case of the FCs, although they are statutory bodies and expected to be non-political (Rao and Singh 2005: 212–13, 222). Austin (1999) mentioned that even the hypercritical Rajamannar Committee (Tamil Nadu Government) (more on this later) had complimented the FC's 'independence and impartiality and its ability to hold the scales even as between [sic] the competing claims' (Austin 1999: 616).

The Planning Commission of India (PCI) with the prime minister as its head was another major instrument for intergovernmental transfers in Indian federalism but was a hugely controversial subject among scholars, who tend to see its role largely as a destroyer of federalism. As already indicated, the PCI disbursed plan assistance and loans to the states as well as giving the resources for implementation of its various schemes, such as poverty alleviation, employment generation and so on. In 1985, as many as 262 centrally sponsored programmes of development (for specific purposes) were implemented in the states. Of late, the central schemes constitute the bulk of activities of the local self-government bodies throughout India.[38] It is also to be pointed out here that due consideration of the diversity needs of the states was taken when distributing plan assistance to the states. For instance, in 1991, a complex set of criteria was adopted: special-category states, non-special-category states, poor per-capita income states and fiscal performance, tax efforts, fulfilment of national objectives and some special problems, etc.[39] The PCI, being an extra-constitutional body, might not always have an easy relationship with federalism, and the grounds for suspicion may also be genuine. But the political bias of such bodies may not hold much truth. Had it been so, Uttar Pradesh, India's largest and one of the most backward states, should have been the most developed one, because it has supplied most of India's prime ministers and most members of Parliament. In any case, since federalism in India, as perhaps elsewhere too, also inevitably involves a political relationship between the centre and the states, the actual working of the federation also needs to be taken into account.

Before we move to the discussion of the political relationship between the centre and the states, a couple of final issues need to be sorted in respect of fiscal federalism in India. First, when considering the expenditure powers of the states, it is found that the states have broader constitutional expenditure responsibilities, since they have to undertake most of the development activities plus the additional task of implementing a number of centrally sponsored schemes. The expenditure powers are more popular than tax raising. During 2000–4, the federal government expenditures (after intergovernmental transfers) as a per cent of total government expenditure in India were 44.6 per cent (the rest being shouldered by the states!), which compared very unfavourably with that of Malaysia (84.3 per cent) (Watts 2008: 103). When read in conjunction with the proportion of central transfer as a per cent of state revenues (46.0 per cent; cf. Malaysia 30.4 per cent) (Watts 2008: 105), the relatively precarious position of the Indian states becomes clear. The

158 Centre–state relations

states' dependence upon the centre in carrying out increasing expenditure is thus obvious. Since 1976, the states' revenues have also registered some decline. Second, whereas the states' expenditures have increased, the central transfers as a per cent of state revenues have declined from 1998–99 onwards so that, in 2001–2, it was only 38 per cent, as compared with 44.91 per cent in 1997–98 (Rao and Singh 2005: 192). Today, central transfers finance only about a third of the states' expenditures, which means that the states seem to be confronted with deficits and shortages to make ends meet. Globalization, gradual withdrawal of state welfarism, fierce competition among the states (that is, those who can afford to compete!) and shrinkage of the centrally funded schemes have meant that Indian federalism is experiencing a crisis. In short, the whole paradigm of centre–state relations has changed radically, so that the authors[40] on the subject have yet to take full cognizance of it.

Centre-state relations: conflict and confrontation

It is almost a truism in constitutionalism that written constitutional provisions are one thing, but the operational reality is a somewhat different matter. In the Indian case of federalism, the federal practice has often overwhelmed formal constitutional arrangements. The current state of Indian federalism post-1991 (post-liberalization), in which the states enjoy more freedom of action in respect of wooing foreign investment and implementing SAP, is a case in point. During the Nehru era (1947–64) and also the period up to 1967, when the Indian National Congress (INC) was in power at the centre and in almost all the states, the federal bargaining took place most often within the four walls of the party. The states' anger and the grievances, if any, could also be dealt with within the party's organizational networks. Things, however, began to change after the fourth set of general elections in 1967, in which the INC lost its dominance for the first time in the majority of states, which came under the rule of the various region-based non-Congress parties. This, coupled with the way the late Mrs Indira Gandhi (president of the Congress) centralized and concentrated power in her own hands, a strong partisan attitude towards the states' interests and issues, and a host of other factors ultimately led to the declaration of Emergency rule in the country (June 1975–March 1977) that also cancelled the political process and federalism. The point that is being made here is that, from the late 1960s, the states began to mobilize themselves against the centre and began to demand a thorough revision of centre–state relations. Since I have discussed this elsewhere, in greater detail,[41] I will only sum up the most important aspects that should merit attention here.

There are basically two issues to which we should pay attention. First, the nature of the states' struggle against the centre, and the reasons for the same, should be considered. Second, the suddenly changed role of the states in the wake of India's globalization since the 1990s should also be examined.

First, it was through the states' struggle for more powers and autonomy that the conception of states' rights has taken shape in the Indian federation since the late

1960s. In a dialectical opposition to the growing centralization in the federal system at the hands of the central leader of the Congress Party, most notably the late Mrs Indira Gandhi, the political campaign by the states – on the back of intense articulation of regional and ethnic identities and moorings[42] – demanded more autonomy and powers to the states through a revision of centre–state relations and better mechanisms for the protection of the rights of the states as enshrined in the Constitution itself. Interestingly enough, this was also the period when the Indian economy began to liberalize itself (Hardgrave and Kochanek 2000: 367–91). Various anti-Congress regional parties and left-wing parties (to be exact, the CPI-M) in power in the states were active in the campaign for state autonomy. The relative defeat of the Congress Party in the fourth set of general elections in 1967, in which the ruling party lost for the first time since Independence in half the states (to the regional parties and region-based political formations), was the main impetus for such campaign. Since the 21-month-longnational Emergency rule (June 1975 to March 1977) was the first major blow to Indian democracy and federalism along with the very constitutional structure, the issue of the protection of states' rights became a major plank in the political mobilization by the anti-Congress opposition parties, most notably the left in the post-Emergency period. The rise of the anti-Congress Janata Government in Delhi (1978–80) was a further encouragement to the move. At any rate, the sociocultural and regional identity of the states provides the basis for political mobilization against the centre and for the assertion of states' rights. The existing research[43] on the subject has analyzed deep-seated regional or ethno-regional moorings, articulated in various brands of politics of the states' rights. It could hardly be forgotten that the Indian states are simply distinct ethno-cultural regions (whether based on language, religion or tribal affiliations or a combination thereof) and hence politically highly vulnerable to mobilization.

The demands for a major revision of centre–state relations to give more powers and autonomy to the states became the major vehicle for the assertions of states' rights. The political parties and groups made it the point of their campaign. Some state governments articulated the demands in the shape of memoranda to the Union government authorities. The Indian left showed the way in this regard. The United Left Government of Kerala (a state in India's south) in 1967 presented a *Memorandum to the National Development Council* for a major revision of the financial relations between the centre and the states. Articulated in the backdrop of the rise of many non-Congress governments in the states following the fourth set of general elections in 1967, this memorandum highlighted the need for the following:

- 'widening the tax bases for the states so that their autonomy may not be curtailed by their having to depend on the centre for their resources';
- 'the establishment of a permanent finance commission with a view to examining the tax potential of the various states, their resources and their needs', etc.;

160 Centre–state relations

- 'the establishment of a centre-state council' as a national forum for discussing major monetary and fiscal policies, and assessing their impact on the states', etc.; and
- 'reviewing the pattern of plan assistance to various states in favour of minimizing the "tied" assistance to the maximum extent possible', etc. (Kurian and Varughese 1981: 229–51).

The document critically examined how the concept of planning and the Planning Commission, an extra-constitutional body, had served to undermine federalism in the sense that while the planning had entailed a lot of social and economic responsibilities for the states, the states were made to depend on the centre and its discriminatory and often 'politically' motivated plan assistance along with discretionary grants or loans for meeting the budgetary needs of the states. It was also pointed out that the tax-sharing provisions of Articles 268–272 were 'totally inadequate to meet the new demands' and also that the substantial bulk of central assistance for the plans was in fact in the form of loans (Kurian and Varughese 1981: 232). All in all, the memorandum expressed grave concern for the loss of fiscal autonomy of the states and the latter's increasing subordination to the centre.[44]

Written in the immediate aftermath of the Emergency and the loss of power of the Congress Party in the general elections in 1977 for the first time since Independence, the CPI-M-led Left Front Government (LFG)'s *Memorandum on Centre-State Relations* (1 December 1977) (Kurian and Varughese 1981: 215–28) to the Union government has remained another landmark document in the history of federalism in India. Sharply highlighting the special significance of India's manifold diversity for India's unity and integrity on the one hand and the history of increasing centralization in India since Independence on the other, the document recorded:

> During the last two decades, while the demand has been growing for greater powers to the states so as to make the states' autonomy real and effective, there have been persistent efforts to erode even the limited powers of the states and reduce the democratic functioning of the government there. The right of the people to manage their affairs even within the limited sphere allotted in the state list of the constitution has sought to be reduced to a farce.
>
> *(Kurian and Varughese 1981: 209)*

Although specifically focused on the political aspects of the relation between the centre and the states, this document nonetheless recommended the deletion of Articles 249, which empowered the Union Parliament to legislate on items in the State List; 256 and 257, which empower the president to dissolve the State Assembly on the pretext of the breakdown of Constitutional machinery in the states; and 360, which provides for a financial emergency, and so on. The memorandum upheld the principle of equality of representation of the states in the Council of States, except those with a population of less than 3million. The document also

Centre–state relations **161**

pleaded for insertion of the word 'federal' to replace the word 'Union' in all places of the Constitution and advocated a federation of a strong centre with strong states:

> We are definitely for strong states, but on no account do we want a weak centre. The concept of strong states is not necessarily in contradiction to that of a strong centre, once their respective spheres of authority are clearly marked out.
>
> *(Kurian and Varughese 1981: 210)*

Those memoranda are landmark documents in the history of struggle for states' rights in India and of federalism generally. Despite the Sarkaria Commission on Centre-State Relations (1983) and subsequently the Constitution Review Commission in the 1990s, the constitutional structure regarding federalism has remained more or less the same. That has, however, not led to a greater loss of rights of the states ever since, because the Constitution is what it does, and hence the operational context is more important than the constitutional provisions. For example, Article 356 is still retained, although its application is more circumscribed than before, but there is little outcry nowadays about its use or misuse. The point is the national political scenario changed vastly after the demise of the one-party dominant system and the rise of multi-party coalition governments with a greater weight of region-based parties and groups at the centre since the 1990s.

The situation today, with the onset of globalization in India since the early 1990s, seems more favourable for the operation of a federal system with more autonomy of action for the states. Rudolph and Rudolph,[45] taking a little more optimistic view of things, argue that in the 1990s 'a multi-party system with strong regional parties displaced a dominant party system; and market forces and practices displaced the planning and the "license permit raj"'. The result, argue Rudolph and Rudolph, has been very congenial: the federal system gained a new lease of life, with the states gaining ground at the expense of the centre (Rudolph and Rudolph 2001: 129).

Where and how do the states in the Indian federation figure in the process of globalization? Is globalization beneficial or harmful to the Indian states? Does globalization signal the decline or the regeneration of Indian federalism? To be sure, a federation provides for a different space for (reform) policy interaction and implementation from that of a unitary state, and hence the constituent units of the federation become strategically important in this respect. In the Indian constitutional system, as S. Guhan has rightly pointed out, the most important key sectors which are central to India's globalization are states' competences: industrial infrastructure; power development; agriculture, and its allied sectors and irrigation; roads (other than highways), health, education, medical services, nutrition, water supply and urban development, and so on.[46] And yet until the mid-1990s, the states' involvement in the reform process was less than satisfactory. Guhan says that the centre was both 'unwilling and unable' to involve the states in the process, for a number of reasons: external agencies' preference for policy dialogue only with the national

162 Centre–state relations

government; the centre's sole competence in macro-economic stabilization; and the variegated nature of state governments, politically speaking (Guhan 1995: 229).

The growing literature on globalization and Indian federalism, although mostly written from the standpoint of political economy, suggests that Indian federalism has been drastically changed, so it needs to be redefined.[47] We have already referred to Rudolph and Rudolph (2001), who argued that as, a result of the impact, the interventionist state in India had given way to a 'regulatory state', which again was more suited to a growing multi-party system. Lawrence Saez (2002) does not of course subscribe to this view, because he believes that 'India's redefined federal system requires the Central Government to play a critical role' (Saez 2002: 2). He is also not sure that a regulatory state will be able to mitigate the growing competition among the Indian states in the era of globalization (Saez 2002: 4). However, he believes that Indian federalism has undergone some major transformations from intergovernmental cooperation to interjurisdictional competition (among the states) (Saez 2002: 4).

The various forms of the states' growing reassertions have also been noticed by acute observers of Indian politics and federalism since the 1990s (Arora and Verney 995; Rao and Singh 2005; Bhattacharyya 2001a; Saez 2002; Dua and Singh 2003). C. P. Bhambri said that: 'The state governments are very important players in the economic development of the country, more pronounced of course since the 1990s' (Bhambri 2003). This striking fact has become clear in the 1990s, because investors have to contact every state government before launching a project. Since the central state is gradually withdrawing itself from its social responsibilities, including welfare-oriented development, most clearly evident, among others, in the shrinkage of the number of centrally sponsored welfarist development schemes, as Bhambri (2003: 328) has shown, centre–state relations have often taken peculiar forms. Cajoling, persuasion and even bribery could often become tactics resorted to by the centre in order to involve the state governments in the process of economic reforms and restructuring.[48] Rao and Singh (2005: 9) have recognized that the states' role has expanded due to the market economy, which demands more decentralized levels of governance, but also that not all the states are equally equipped to access the opportunities afforded by the market.

The relation between globalization and the Indian states then is nonetheless complex. The Indian federal system, seen from one side, offers both opportunities and constraints for structural reforms. The constraints refer to the variegated political complexion of governments at the centre and in the states. This may facilitate (if the same party rules in the relevant states as in the centre) the reform process or stand in the way of implementation of any uniform reforms package if the rival party rules in the states. The coalition governments thus often become worse victims of such eventualities. When seen from the viewpoint of globalization, given that the states are today offered more freedom of action in respect of adopting and implementing structural adjustment programmes, the states have become more competitive with regard to inviting investment, industrialization, trade and commerce, and entrepreneurial governance for development. Globalization thus is

Centre–state relations **163**

encouraging more rights for the states, although it is hard to conclude that all the states will benefit equally from globalization and also that the people in each state will be able to reap the benefits of globalization, if any, equitably. Much depends on the policy preferences of the state governments concerned and the space for exercising such a preference.

In any case, the states' role is very crucial in India's reform process. Three considerations in this connection are of vital importance. First, globalization, as a predominantly economic and political process, is ultimately to be implemented in the states. Second, constitutionally, the states are responsible for a variety of development works, since the Union government simply does not have the bureaucratic machinery to implement its laws; it has to depend on the states for the job. Third, democratically mandated state governments are more politically vulnerable, because, being close to the people, it is they who suffer from the after-effects of the policies of globalization. In other words, implementation of some 'unpopular' structural adjustment policies may cut into the democratic basis of state governments. Since the states are distinct sociocultural units, the state governments' political vulnerability, especially in the face of rival mobilization of popular discontent, is of particular concern to the party in power. At the same time, globalization may create risks and uncertainties for the states' governing parties' legitimacy, since an uncritical approach to and implementation of the reform process inevitably adversely affects the socially and economically vulnerable sections of society, and paves the way for what is termed a 'democratic deficit'.

Finally, two other challenges are to be considered. First, this globalization-propelled current assertion of the states for autonomy of policy and action occurs in the age of what is fashioned as 'rolling the state back', i.e. the increasing withdrawal of the states from social welfare. Thus, the so-called states' rights may not mean people's rights. (Bhattacharyya 2012: 26–39) It must not be forgotten that this re-federalization of the Indian polity, or any true federalization ever taken place, is market oriented and globalization friendly! Second, given the growing interstate and interregional disparities in terms of investment, whether by FDI or otherwise, when placed in the context of the withdrawal of the central state, there are genuine grounds for fear that the situation will accentuate interregional tensions and encourage ethnic conflicts, which will adversely affect the sense of national identity. The researchers are already making the distinction between 'forward states' and 'backward states' (Tremblay 2003: 341–2) in development terms, which has immense ideological and political implications for India's unity and integrity. Reddy and Reddy (2019), in the most recent assessment of the relation between the centre and the states, are a little apprehensive of the new turn in Indian federalism since the NITI Aayog, which replaced the Planning Commission in 2015, does not have any active role in financial disbursement (p. 211); the perception of the states to see the centre as an encroacher on the states' responsibilities remains (p. 215).

In light of this discussion, one can perhaps safely conclude that globalization has expanded the scope of states' rights in India in terms of autonomy of action in the vital sectors of trade, commerce and development. More opportunities have been created for employment and investment. The states' GDPs have been growing. The new meaning of federalism that has been emerging in India is one that is market friendly and development oriented. The so-called forward states with higher and better indices of development and higher percentage of FDI inflows (Delhi, Haryana and parts of UP having 25.40 per cent; Maharashtra with 20 per cent; and Tamil Nadu with about 6 per cent during 2000–6) are after all the product of globalization. This is a welcome development. India's Marxist-ruled state governments, which otherwise should be strange bedfellows of capitalism, globalization and federalism, ideologically speaking, are also engaged in reaping the benefits of India's globalization! During 2000–6, for West Bengal, a late starter, the share of FDI inflows was 1.4 per cent (US $273.1 million) (as per the Reserve Bank of India sources). Kerala, in India's south, the only surviving state ruled by the Marxists (LDF), has also been growing fast, producing in its wake growing inequality too. Indian federalism has changed, thanks to globalization, into a developmental federalism with more freedom of action for the states in matters of trade, commerce and development. Since 2016 the federal government revenues (tax) remain at around 80 per cent of the total and non-tax revenues at 20.1 per cent in 2018 (www.treasury.gov.my/pdf/ekonomi/fiscal/FISCAL_UPDATES_2017.pdf, accessed 3 January 2020).

Notes

1 Inter-state relations, both formal and informal (in fact, the informal aspects tend to be more significant), take one to the world of federal dynamics, where the party systems, pressure groups, and social and economic forces seem to determine, to a great extent, the nature of the operation of federalism, and, in important respects, Centre-State relations too.

2 'Troubled History of Federal-Provincial Relations' (http://alaiwah.wordpress. com/2008/09/24Pakistan-constitution-national finance commission/).

3 'Troubled history', etc., op. cit.

4 Adeney (2007a), op. cit., p. 109. The Punjabis did not mind it, not because they were a great lovers of the language, but more because their own language was not as developed as a written and literary one.

5 However, the province of Baluchistan remains an inhomogeneous region, made more complicated by the influx of further Pakhtuns from across the Afghan border after the Soviet invasion of Afghanistan in 1978.

6 'Troubled History', etc., op. cit.

7 Many authors have written on the vexed issue of the Punjabi domination of the Pakistani state. See, for instance, Kukreja, V. (2003); and Talbot, I. (2002) 'The Punjabization of Pakistan: Myth or Reality? (pp. 51–63) in Jaffrelot, C. (ed.) *Pakistan: Nationalism Without a Nation?,* New Delhi: Manohar. See also Alavi, H. (1989) 'Politics of Ethnicity in India and Pakistan' in Alavi, H. and Harris (eds) *South Asia: Sociology of Developing Societies* London: Macmillan, pp. 222–246. Alavi has noted the implications of ethnic mobilization in Pakistan *vis-à-vis* Punjabi domination, as follows: the most striking difference is that ethnic movements in Pakistan take the form, primarily, of sub-national movements, directed against the central power, demanding regional autonomy. The autocratic power of the Central Government is identified by disadvantaged groups as Punjabi domination (p. 222).

8 Adeney (2007a), p. 117. Baluchistan has suffered from a sense of 'economic deprivation and political isolation', despite having good reserves of natural gas, minerals, fruit and numerous sheep. The province was reluctant to join Pakistan, which the latter took over by force in the face of rebellion by the Khan of Kalat, one of the rulers of Baluchistan, in 1948. The province's relations with the central authorities have remained very troubled ever since. Repeated political upheavals have therefore remained persistent, taking the forms of militant insurgency during 1973–77 (Bhutto's regime), and then again since the early 2000s. See, for further details, see Ataur Rahman (1989) 'Pakistan: Unity or Further Divisions' in Wilson, A. J. and Dalton, D. (eds) *The States of South Asia: Problems of National Integration (Essays in Honour of W. H. Morris-Jones),* London: Hurst & Co., pp. 200–201; and Hewitt, V. (1998) 'Ethnic Construction, Provincial Identity and Nationalism in Pakistan: the Case of Baluchistan' in Mitra, S. K. and Alison, L. (eds) *Subnational Movements in South Asia,* New Delhi: Segment Books, pp. 43–68. Hewitt argues that rather than the support for the so-called two-nation-theory (Hindus and Muslims) in favour of the creation of Pakistan, 'there existed by the mid-1940s a clear demand for a "Greater Baluchistan" which not only sought Independence from the British, but which actively sought to unite Baluchi tribes in Afghanistan and in Iran within one sovereign territory' (p. 43).

9 'Troubled History', etc., op. cit.

10 'Troubled History', etc., op. cit.

11 'Troubled History', etc., op. cit.

12 'Troubled History', op. cit.

13 'Troubled History', op. cit.

14 See, for instance, Case (2007); Wong, Chin Huat 'Weakened Federalism in the new Federation' (Internet sources accessed on 31 January 2009).

15 Quoted in Safruddin, B. H. (1988) 'Malaysian Centre-State Relations by Design and Process' in Safruddin, B. H. and Iftikhar, A. M. (eds.) Between Centre and States: Federalism in Perspective. Kuala Lampur Institute for Strategic and International Studies, p. 7 (for details, pp. 3–29).

16 This became the subject of much criticism in parliamentary debates. Opposition MPs voiced their protest against such an encroachment on the federal principle. (For details, see Shafruddin (1988) pp. 14–15.)

17 The particular point of contention in this connection was the Government of Malaysia (Amendment) Act, 1965 (No. 31/1965), which amended Article 95C (1) by virtue of which the States were to execute laws in respect of any matter in the federal list, an obligation, then restricted to the Borneo States, which is now applicable to all States. For more details, see Shafruddin (1988), p. 15.

18 Watts (2008), p. 103.

19 Andaya and Andaya (2001), p. 340.

20 Shafruddin (1988), p. 26. The unity of these groups at the State level, for the purpose of blocking the entry and intrusion of the UMNO, and to vote out of power the *Barisan Nasional* State Government, has been recorded in the Borneo States (Shafruddin 1988, p. 26).

21 These ethnic groups, quite distinct in their identity, are not small in number in Sabah and Sarawak, but then, first they are not so territorially concentrated in the states, and second, the Constitution does not provide for any local/regional-level territorial solution of their identity issues. (See Bakar, 2007, p. 71 for the exact figures on such groups in these two Borneo States.)

22 Shafruddin (1988), p. 27.

23 The factors cited are the emergent historical conjuncture of the rise of both Indian and Pakistan in 1947 after the bloody communal holocaust followed by the Partition of the sub-continent; the special problems of integration of the 500-odd medieval princely States; the overriding need for unity and integrity;, and development. If Charles Tilly, the famous political sociologist of state formation in the West, is any guide, then one

166 Centre–state relations

would also add that the underlying state formation in India itself undeniably entailed concentration and centralization of powers, in the process submerging all that were regional, local and antecedent. See Tilly, C. (ed.) (1975) *The Formation of National States in Western Europe,* Princeton, NJ, USA: Princeton University Press, and also his (1985) critique of the process in his 'War-Making and State-Making as Organized Crime' in Evans, P., Rueschemeyer, D. and Skocpol (eds) *Bringing the State Back In,* Cambridge: Cambridge University Press, pp. 169–192. The process came, however, to be resisted in cases where federations were formed, in which case the polity turned out to be more decentralized in character. The differences in historical trajectories in state formation in specific contexts have been examined in Doornbos, M. and Kaviraj, S. (eds) (1997) *Dynamics of State Formation: India and Europe Compared,* New Delhi: Sage.

24 Hardgrave, R. L. Jr and Kochanek, S. A. (2000) *India: Government and Politics in a Developing Nation,* sixth edition, Orlando, FL: Harcourt College Publishers, p. 137.

25 Hardgrave and Kochanek (2000), p. 137.

26 Appleby, P. (1953) *Public Administration in India: Report of a Survey,* New Delhi: Government of India, p. 21 (quoted in Hardgrave and Kochanek (2000), p. 138. The terms 'theoretically subordinate' in the above passage might not be the most accurate description of the constitutional position of the States in the Indian federation. The States' relative sovereignty in their respective jurisdictions has been recognized in the Constitution. Also, the very first Article of the Constitution describes India as a 'Union of States', which means that the States are indispensable parts of the Union. Practically too, the States have not performed as 'subordinate' bodies since, but rather as a 'co-ordinate authority' in the making of what turned out to be a case of cooperative federalism, which is administratively decentralized. (See Watts 1966, 1999, 2008.) Within just three years of the inauguration of the federal republic, the practical scenario indicated above was yet to evolve. The States in India have developed as important political forces to be reckoned with, subsequently as a result of many factors: their combined struggles; the decline of the one-party dominant system; the Supreme Court's defence of Indian federalism in a series of landmark judgements; increased ethno-national consciousness among groups within the States, and so on.

27 See Kaviraj's 'On State, Society and Discourse in India' in Manor, J. (ed.) (1991) *Rethinking Third World Politics,* London: Longman, pp. 72–99.

28 Bhattacharyya, H. (2000) 'Federalism, Decentralization and State-Building in India: Aspects of Centre-State Fiscal Relations' in Bird, R. and Stauffer, T. (eds) *Intergovernmental Fiscal Relations in Fragmented Societies,* Fribourg, Switzerland: Helbing and Lichtenhahn, pp. 247–305.

29 Bird, R. (1986) *Federal Finance in Comparative Perspective,* Toronto: Toronto Tax Foundation, p. 206.

30 Hemming, R. (1997) 'India' in Ter-Minassian, T. (ed.) *Fiscal Federalism in Theory and Practice,* Washington DC: IMF, p. 527.

31 Rao, G. and Vaillancourt, F. (1994) 'Interstate Tax Harmony in India: A Comparative Perspective', *Publius: The Journal of Federalism,* 24 (Fall), p. 105, quoted in Bhattacharyya (2000), p. 267

32 See Bhargava, P. K. (1984) 'Transfers from the Center to the States in India', *Asian Survey,* Vol. XXIV, No. 6, June, pp. 665–687, for a critical discussion of the economic aspects of Centre-State relations in India up until the mid-1980s.

33 See, Bhattacharyya, H. (2000), pp. 270–271 for more details.

34 Rao and Singh (2005) informed us that the variables used in the index of backwardness were the population of 'Scheduled Castes' and 'Scheduled Tribes', and the number of agricultural labourers, with equal weightage given to each (quoted in Bhattacharyya, H. 2000, p. 273).

35 Rao, G. and Singh, N. (2005) *The Political Economy of Federalism in India,* Delhi: Oxford University Press, pp. 191–195.

36 From the statistics given in table 9.2 (p. 194) in Rao and Singh (2005), it is clear that since the fourth plan period (1969–74) up until 2001–02, the proportion of multiple

Centre–state relations **167**

transfers (i.e. through the UFC, the Planning Commission, and other grants from Ministries) from the Centre to the States has remained more or less steady.

37 See Bhattacharyya, H. (2000), p. 274 for details.

38 Ironically, these are the central dynamics of sub-State-level decentralization in India over the last two decades or so, and offered the rival political parties a potent source to build political support by patronage dispensation and by the delivery of development goods locally. The Government of West Bengal, which has been run by the CPI-M-led Left Front continuously since 1977, offers a major illustration of the case.

39 For further details on the weight of each category in the Plan disbursement, see Rao and Singh (2005), p. 304, quoted in Bhattacharyya, H. (2000), p. 302.

40 See, for two very recent accounts on the subject, Manor, J. (2001) 'Center-State Relations' in Kohli, A. (ed.) *The Success of India's Democracy,* Cambridge: Cambridge University Press, pp. 78–102; also Das Gupta, J. (2001) 'India's Federal Design and Multicultural National Construction' in Kohli, A. (ed.) (2001), pp. 49–78.

41 Bhattacharyya, H. (2001a), chapters 2, 3 and 6; Bhattacharyya, H. (2000); and Bhattacharyya, H. (2009). 'Globalization and Indian Federalism: Re-Assertions of States' Rights' in Lofgren, H. and Sarangi, P. (eds) *Politics and Culture of Globalization: India and Australia,* New Delhi: Social Science Press. The following section draws mostly on Bhattacharyya, H. (2009).

42 See, Brass, Paul R. (1994) *The Politics of India Since Independence,* second edn, New Delhi: Foundation Books, pp. 65–66. Brass argues that while the States ruled by the same Congress Party followed the central party directives, the non-Congress-run States did not oblige, naturally. As a result, the political system seemed to polarize between the centralizing and regionalizing tendencies (p. 66).

43 See, for instance, such regional-level studies in Indian Communism as Franda, M. F. (1971); Nossiter, T. J. (1982); and also Nossiter (1988); Singh (1994); Bhattacharyya, H. (1999); and Bhattacharyya, H. (1998a).

44 The Rajamannar Committee's recommendations also drew our attention to various Articles and provisions of the Constitution that were inimical to state autonomy, and recommended their deletion, or revision. The Articles mentioned were 256, 257, 330 (2) and 344 (6), which provide for Central direction to the States. The recommendations also called for the deletion of all the emergency powers of the Union, and vesting residuary powers of legislation and taxation with the States, and for making the Planning Commission into an independent body having no political control. They also upheld the principle of equal representation of the States in the *Rajya Sabha* (Council of States). The unilateral powers of the Union Government to amend the Constitution in matters affecting the States were also criticized in favour of suggestions for the ratification by at least two-thirds of the States representing three-quarters of the population of all States, etc. Its other detailed suggestions for revision of various provisions of the Constitution were protective of States' rights, autonomy and powers.

45 Rudolph, L. and Rudolph, S. (2001) 'Redoing the Constitutional Design: From an Interventionist State to a Regulatory State' in Kohli, A. (ed.) *The Success of India's Democracy,* Cambridge: Cambridge University Press, p. 129.

46 Guhan, S. (1995) 'Federalism and the New Political Economy in India' in Arora, B. and Verney, D. V. (eds) *Multiple Identities in a Single State: Indian Federalism in Comparative Perspective,* New Delhi: Konark Publishers Pvt. Ltd., p. 241.

47 Hardgrave and Kochanek (2000) have captured the vastly changed scenario in the backdrop of the increasing regionalization of Indian politics; the relative loss of authority of the central institution; renewed political separatism in Punjab and Jammu and Kashmir; the erosion of cultural unity by the rise of religious and caste identities, and finally the breakdown of the socialist federations, on the one hand, and the onset of globalization, on the other hand: [which]

> enabled the provincial governments to emerge as powerful actors in the economy – competing with each other for federal funds and foreign direct investment – and

168 Centre–state relations

by the emergence of coalition governments at the Centre made up of essentially regional parties. The result has been the gradual devolution of India's centralized, parliamentary federal system and a new era of Indian federalism

(pp. 131–132)

48 Bhambri (2003) has drawn our attention in this connection to the energy sector reform in respect of the reform of the State Electricity Boards through FDI (for details, see p. 328).

7

FEDERALISM AND FORMS OF DECENTRALIZATION

Introduction

On the face of it, the relationship between federalism and decentralization appears to be contradictory in a double sense. First, the verbal form of the term 'federal', 'to federate', means 'to band together in league for some common object' (Oxford Concise Dictionary). This suggests that the federating units unite only for the common purpose and not for specific objectives for which they retain their distinctive identity. In this sense, decentralization is somewhat built in to the very idea of federation. So long as a federation has been the result of some bottom-up process such as that seen in the United States and Switzerland, traditionally such federations have remained bottom heavy, with the federating units having their own jurisdiction guaranteed. In the Swiss case, although municipalities (the Communes), the lowest tier in the federation, are governed under the cantonal constitutions, the 1999 Swiss Constitution added further protection to their identity.[1] The constitutional guarantee of the existence of the decentralized local self-governing bodies, plus autonomy, is what distinguishes a local self-governing body from those that are governed by the laws of the canton, local or central governments.[2]

Second, the literal meaning of the term 'decentralization' suggests a process 'to do away with centralization' or 'to distribute powers among local centres', etc. Both the meanings go against the conventional idea of a federation, which requires some unavoidable extent of centralization (for performing some general functions for the country as a whole). In a typical unitary state, perhaps, decentralization carries more meaning than in federations. Federation as a compound polity that combines, as Daniel Elazar reminds us, shared-rule (common purpose) with self-rule (specific regional purpose) entails, as it were, decentralization in respect of self-rule. Nowadays, however, scholars quite comfortably discuss federalism in conjunction with decentralization, for a variety of reasons.[3]

170 Federalism and forms of decentralization

While we will discuss those reasons, to some extent, shortly in the next section, we need to stress here that in the Asian federations, more particularly in India and Pakistan, decentralization has remained inextricably linked to the very process of federalization itself, because here it is through different forms of decentralization that federation has been built, rebuilt and resized in order to achieve the optimum sizes of federal unit for the sake of ethno-national homogeneity. Since the Indian and Pakistani federations were once the centralized 'unitary' state (under the British colonial rule) out of which the federations have emerged, and since the federal units here have been the result of federation-building, doses of decentralization at various levels congruent with the ethno-cultural boundaries of the people have informed the process of this federation-building. The other important reason why decentralization has received widespread support is the constitutionally guaranteed very powerful position of the central government in these postcolonial federations – which has been reinforced by the agenda of nation-building. The five Asian federations under study are but various illustrations in this regard. A distinction is, however, to be made here between India and Malaysia, on the one hand, and Pakistan, on the other. In the latter, under successive military regimes until 2008, excessive centralization and the near absence of the autonomy of the federal units have characterized the so-called federal system – so much so that many provinces have resorted to insurgency. In the cases of both India and Pakistan, given their complex diversity and the territorial rootedness of the communities with their distinct ethnic identity, localism and regionalism have remained quite powerful forces since the inception of the republic, if not before, demanding autonomy and power – that is to say, forms of decentralization – within the body politic. In the case of India, as we will see shortly, ethnic-identity-based yet democratic decentralization has helped immensely to territorialize the ethnic conflicts before they spilled over at various levels of the polity, as a condition for national unity and integrity. Since the early 1950s, Pakistan, by contrast, has failed to extend recognition to the very strong and self-conscious Bengali ethno-national identity for autonomy, power and decentralization, a failure which has paved the way for the disintegration of the province from the federation in 1971. The federation has yet to be sufficiently sensitive to respond to the ethno-nationalist demands of various self-conscious groups engaged in the struggle for recognition, decentralization, autonomy and power within Pakistan. In the discussion of decentralization, and that, too, in the context of federations, the implications of this ethnicity-based yet democratic decentralization do often evade adequate academic attention. The simple population-based and uniform administrative units-based decentralization have received comparatively more attention. And yet, where ethno-regional/national pressures from below are very strong and demand political recognition and power, as in India and Pakistan, and to some extent in Malaysia, we should not lose sight of the specific ethnic dimensions of decentralization. True, often localism and regionalism, when confronted with the no-solution situation, that is, when faced with state repression and violence rather than the prospects of negotiation, bargaining and compromise, turn secessionist. Conversely, when handled properly and accommodated within the realm of the possible, the local and the regional seem to serve in the making of the national and become indispensable parts of the nation.[4] The relationship between federalism and nationalism, the prospects of development of nationhood in conditions of federalism and so on are the subject-matter of theoretical debate of a different order.[5] The point that is being stressed here is that in complex sociocultural diversity, a multilayered and faceted nationhood, socioculturally speaking, seems the reality rather than the imaginary homogeneity much propagated in the discourses on nationalism and nationhood since the eighteenth century. Elsewhere I have analyzed in comparative terms the facets of this multilayered nationhood in India and Switzerland in the context of federalism and have shown how understanding nationhood in India has entailed taking a view of the near and the distant simultaneously (Bhattacharyya 2001a, 2007b).

Ronald Watts (Watts 2008) has discussed the various issues of decentralization, such as its measurement and its forms (legislative, financial and administrative), and has made a comparative assessment of decentralization.[6] (He used the terms 'non-centralization' and 'decentralization' interchangeably, however, because of the widespread use of the terms 'decentralization'.) He is also ready to concede that 'decentralization and devolution of powers may be desirable to accommodate linguistic, cultural, historical and economic diversity or to enhance administrative efficiency' (Watts 2008: 178). But the decentralization or non-centralization that Watts, like most authors on federalism, deals with is state- or provincial-level decentralization and not the level(s) below these, such as the districts. These are very important in their own right, because if the states or provinces are not adequately empowered and do not have the resources, the levels below them cannot function, because, in a federation, for any substate (or local)-level decentralization to be meaningful, it needs to be linked to and should flow through the state level. Any attempt to decentralize powers and resources directly to local bodies from the central authority will undercut the authority of the state government, thereby undercutting federalism itself. Such decentralization lacks the federal spirit.

For a variety of reasons, some kind of decentralization, as reported in some important research (Aziz and Arnold 1996), has been sweeping Asian countries such as China, Bangladesh, India, Nepal, Sri Lanka and the Philippines. The decentralizing experiments are varied, conditioned as they are by local political, cultural and economic factors. One of the major thrusts of these experiments, according to Aziz and Arnold, is the widespread consensus on decentralized decision making on the premise and political imperative that 'all those whose interests are affected by decisions ought to take part in the decision making process' (Aziz and Arnold 1996: 14). Local political pressures and factors apart, the process of globalization has also added a stimulus to decentralization (Bhattacharyya 2001a: 129–38).

While ever since the late 1950s India has been experimenting indigenously with forms of substate-level decentralization, a process which has gained added momentum since the early 1990s (more on this soon), Pakistan, which has been under a military dictatorship for much of the time since Independence, remains a late starter, where substate-level (its federal character, however, is questionable)

172 Federalism and forms of decentralization

decentralization was launched since 2000 under the overall military rule. Malaysia in this respect is a case apart, where, despite some constitutional provisions for local government and varieties of local government existing, as we will examine very shortly, democratically formed decentralized local bodies are yet to be established in the federation, which remains highly centralized.

Theoretically, it can be argued that decentralization assumes importance in federalism with respect to the following. First, the provisions for decentralization, whether identity-based or not (although identity-based decentralization is more federal in character than one based on population), are to be constitutionally guaranteed and not to be left to the goodwill of the central or state governments or to the power-seeking politicians. Second, the process of devolution of powers and resources is identity-based, as the process is linked to recognition of identity, defined as such in secular terms (e.g. language, region, tribal affiliations, or a combination thereof). Such identity may or may not be territory-based. But the satisfaction of identity in terms of power, autonomy and resources defines the required space of decentralization – a space that is marked by a congruence of culture and politics, cultural boundaries and political boundaries at the levels concerned. Third, decentralization is democratic. It could mean many things. The most important of course is that the decentralized bodies are democratically elected by the local citizens. The decentralized bodies are public service driven, that is, they deliver the required public goods to everyone, as well as some targeted groups in the case of specific-purpose-oriented grants without discrimination, since discriminatory service delivery cuts into the very legitimacy of the whole system. Democratic decentralization does not offer any ascribed status to the leaders or the local rulers, since such status is to be achieved democratically at some regular intervals in a process that also replaces the existing rulers. Even the ethnic leaders have to get elected or not by the citizens. Democracy does not recognize and accept any natural leaders as governors. That is, their claim to power is not ascriptive but achievement oriented. Finally, decentralization helps democratize the base of the polity by creating pressures from below as a check on concentration and centralization in the system as a whole, which is congenial for federalism.

Malaysia

The local governments in Malaysia, of various types, occupy a critical position between federal control and state autonomy in the constitutional system of the country. On the one hand, local government is a state subject falling within the competences of the states. This is stated under Clause 4 of the State List (Article 95 B (1) (a) (Ninth Schedule).

Local government outside the federal territories of Kuala Lumpur, Labuan and Putrajaya includes local administration; municipal corporations; local town and rural boards and other local authorities; local-government services; local rates; and local-government elections.[7]

Federalism and forms of decentralization **173**

On the other hand, the federal Constitution also provides for (under a separate chapter 7 titled 'National Council for Local Government') a National Council for Local Government (NCLG) (Article 95A) consisting of a chairman, one representative from each of the states and such a number of representatives from the federal government as the federal government may appoint (the number shall not exceed ten). The chairman, usually a federal cabinet minister, also has a casting vote.[8] Clause 5 of the article defines the job ('duty') of the NCLG as

> to formulate from time to time in consultation with the Federal Government and the State Government a national policy for the promotion, development and control of local government throughout the federation and for the administration of any law relating thereto; and the Federal and the State governments shall follow the policy so formulated.[9]

These constitutional provisions define a 'national' space within which the local governments will operate, and the NCLG, inserted into the Constitution by an amendment in 1960, is the instrument at the hands of the federal government to control the local governments, the laws governing them and their actual operation.[10] Thus, the local governments are designed to be integrated with the whole national system and hence to be subject to all the vicissitudes facing the country, and at the same time, they need local autonomy in order to respond to local needs and circumstances. One of the primary conditions for ensuring local autonomy is democracy, that is, democratically elected local-government bodies that are self-governing and autonomy-assuring. A brief critical account of the local-government bodies in Malaysia is given here to illustrate that there is much to be desired in this respect from the local-government bodies in Malaysia.

Historically, the local-government system in Malaysia is one of the legacies of the Raj, derived from and modelled on the English laws. With Independence (1957) and the passage of time, the local governments in the country have also evolved and adapted to changing times and contexts, to some extent. The Council of Assessors, introduced in Penang in 1801, is said to be the foundation of local government in Peninsular Malaysia. The main task of the council was planning and development of the municipality. The other states of the latter-day federation followed suit in introducing such local government. Until the country's independence, a series of laws and ordinances were passed by the colonial rulers to institutionalize local government – the Local Government Election Ordinance 1950, the Local Government Ordinance 1952 and so on. It is known from the official sources that until 1957 there were some 289 units of local council in Malaysia.[11] At Independence, in the federal Constitution, the local governments were placed under the direct control of the state governments.

From 1957 to 1973, there were six types of local government in Malaysia: Kuala Lumpur City Council, the municipal council, the town council, the town board, the rural district council and the local council. In 1973–76, as a result of a major restructuring undertaken (under the Local Government Act (Temporary Provision

174 Federalism and forms of decentralization

1973) and the Local Government Act 1976), the pattern was simplified by providing broadly for two types of local council – one each for the municipality and the rural areas. But following further modification by acts of central government and the state governments, the pattern that took shape comprised the following four types: the city hall or city council (12 in number); the municipality (municipal corporation) (36); the district council for the rural areas (96); and the special and notified local area authorities (7).[12] The most recent research on the subject shows that there are 144 local authorities, which can be grouped into three broad categories such as cities, municipalities and districts.[13]

Three distinctive features of local government in Malaysia stand out sharply for our consideration. First, the local bodies are not elected but nominated, and thus they lack democratic legitimacy. Ironically, the Local Government Act of 1976 (the Act of 171) made it clear that the local councilors were not to be elected but appointed by the state government. The local councilors are appointed by the state government for a three-year term, with the option for reappointment, and 'in most cases come from the ruling coalition' (Nooi 2008: 126). This is the result of the absence of political decentralization and the most important factor behind the failure of local government in the country to deliver efficient, transparent and effective services. Nooi (2008) reported that in 2007, after a week's survey on how to improve public-service delivery (conducted by the Malaysian Administrative Modernization and Management Planning Unit (MAMPU)), it was found that the organization had received nearly 700 emails of criticism and suggestions (Nooi 2008: 129). And yet the people are keen on taking part in decision making at the local level and are said to be hesitant to accept decisions that are imposed from above (Nooi 2008: 130). Quite predictably, there has been widespread public dissatisfaction with the quality of service delivery by the local government, and the Ministry of Finance itself (2006) admitted that the low-calibre leadership at the local level was responsible for the decline in the quality of service delivery (Nooi 2008: 130).

Second, the local-government bodies have also been made vulnerable to national exigencies, such that, in 1963, in the wake of the so-called Indonesian confrontation, the federal government suspended the local governments in the country, by the provisions of the Emergency (Suspension of Local Government Elections) of 1976, paving the way for centralization of the local-government system in the already highly centralized federation. True local government bodies, being under the state laws, constitutionally speaking, proliferated – numbering 374 until the 1970s in Peninsular Malaysia,[14] but then that was an indication of the local needs and circumstances that necessitated them. Third, the local government came to be centralized, that is, subject to implementing the national agenda or, to be more precise, the development agenda of successive national governments.[15] The institution of the National Council for Local Government in 1960 (by an amendment of the Constitution since it was not originally provided for in the Constitution) as a 'consultative committee' chaired by a federal minister with the provision for their casting vote (the members are one each from the states, plus no more than

Federalism and forms of decentralization **175**

10 members from the federal government) provided an early indication that the national issues were going to be of paramount consideration in the matters of the local government. For example, the Local Government Act of 1976 outlines 'the form, organizational structure, functions and responsibilities of a local authority'. The other successive legislation of the federal parliament ever since, in respect of town and rural planning, physical planning, land use in the local area, drains, roads and building, and so on, suggested that the federal government was increasingly playing a regulative role over the local government. Cheema, G. S. and Hussein (1978) saw this as 'local government reforms' pressed into the service of changing 'national development and political process':

> Rapid urbanization which is a by-product of the Malaysian government's strategy for inter-communal redistribution and restructuring society has substantially increased the demands for local services and an improved standard of living. This has made it imperative that powers and resources of local government be increased and their administrative capability be strengthened to enable them to perform new functions.[16]

Most recent well-informed research does suggest, however, that things have not improved for the better for the local government. As Nooi (2008) has argued, although the local government falls under the competences of the states, 'the federal government also exercises considerable power and influence over local government, especially in Peninsular Malaysia'.[17] Nooi further adds that the 'dynamics of the Malaysian federation is such that it has shifted the balance of power to the centre' (Nooi 2008: 126).

Finally, to view the issue from the perspective of Malaysian federalism, the Malaysian federation is heavily centralized, constitutionally as well as in practice, so that the federal laws always take precedence over state laws; the states are seldom in a position to offer financial assistance to the local government; and there has been, since Independence and more particularly since the 1970s, excessive centralization in the name of rapid development. For all these reasons, federal authority has triumphed, and the lower tiers of the government, such as the states and the local government, have been overshadowed. Its various ill-effects and somewhat self-defeating implications have been acknowledged by no less than the Ninth Malaysia Plan (2006–10) document, in which it is stated categorically that:

> The Government commits to improve the quality of public services as it is a fundamental prerequisite toward achieving the National Mission. Towards this end, the Government will continue to reduce bureaucratic red tape, especially at the local authority and district levels.
>
> *(Nooi 2008: 129)*

As already indicated, the local government operates in Malaysia within a framework of what is known as a top-down approach, with a high degree of federal

176 Federalism and forms of decentralization

centralization, and hence suffers from a host of structural limitations, such as lack of political decentralization, public participation and lack of transparency, and so on. Local-government bodies, to be truly meaningful as representative and participatory institutions for the people at the grassroots, require first of all a major overhaul of the federation itself. However, this is not on the agenda at the moment, despite the relative loss of strength of the UMNO-dominated BN in the last general elections held in 2008. A true federal framework for the local government, that is, a framework that recognizes and respects the states' rights as well as the autonomy and participatory nature of local governing bodies, is yet to evolve in Malaysia, although it could in fact add to the legitimacy of the regime as a whole from below. While there is a groundswell of discontent at the grassroots' level for democratic decentralization, these grassroots of the regime are not yet recognized politically.

Pakistan

The sub-provincial level devolutionary institutional arrangements introduced in Pakistan since 2002, under the yoke of military regime at the top and through the initiative of the same, gave birth to some 6,458 local-government bodies having 126,462 members, including more than 32,000 women members 'elected' on a non-party basis to such bodies. These changes aroused both optimism and cynicism: cynicism because they reminded people of the so-called basic democracies of former General Ayub Khan, who captured power in Pakistan through a coup and later also introduced 'basic democracies' as a means of acquiring popular legitimacy to military rule. Thus, there are genuine grounds to be suspicious of the introduction of local-level democratic institutions by military rulers who claim to love democracy but simultaneously hate the political parties and politicians and the existing institutional mechanisms of governance such as the states or the provinces. Nonetheless they inspire optimism, because such devolutionary measures allow some, albeit limited, popular involvement in governance at the grassroots and some scope for improvement in service delivery.

Two inherent limitations of such attempts, which, incidentally, are crippling for any successful devolution in Pakistan, merit attention to begin with. First, the devolution undercuts federalism in Pakistan because it simply bypasses the provinces, and funds are devolved directly from the centre to the local bodies. This is in sharp contrast to the rebellious minority provinces that have long demanded autonomy and rights. Second, any grassroots devolution of powers and the institution of local government cannot be considered in isolation from the rural power structure dominated by the landed gentry. In other words, bereft of any radical land reforms in favour of the poor and the landless, local government bodies are most likely to be vulnerable to powerful landed interests and social notables, as has happened to states in India – more particularly in West Bengal before 1978. The current understanding of the relationship between federalism and democracy, and that too with particular reference to Asia, as He (2007) has also argued (He 2007: 1–33), suggests that bringing government down to the people through devolution

Federalism and forms of decentralization **177**

and decentralization is also to be considered as part of federalization. The case of Pakistan does not seem to support this proposition, because the devolutionary measures in Pakistan were conceived not in federal terms but in military ones, as an instrument of serving the needs of the military regime for legitimacy. The so-called devolutionary measures in Pakistan were designed to strengthen the authoritarian centre at the expense of the provinces. Adeney (2007a) has argued that, on the one hand, while the devolutionary measures seek to give powers to the local government, they do not propose similar measures for the provinces (Adeney 2007a: 116). She even sees in such measures an attempt 'to encroach on the powers of a potential opposition to the centre' (Adeney 2007a: 116).

Data on the functioning of local-government bodies are scarce. The sample-based study undertaken by donor agencies such as the ADB, World Bank and DFID in 2003 on the working of them noted limited success in service delivery: 'but one that is already bringing change in some schools, courts and clinics and, most visibly, in the political life of the countryside and cities and town'.[18] The report also noted, rather predictably, 'the unaltered tendency of the provinces to interfere in policy-making and implementation by local governments'.[19] I call it predictable because the provinces feel jealous of powers and resources being devolved to the local governments below them while they themselves are starved of resources. Politically, too, these handouts undercut the power bases of the provincial/local politicians. The study report has recorded lots of problems and limitations: political, bureaucratic, financial and so on, but has broadly agreed, although cautiously, on the following:

> Overall, however, nazimeen are listening with new attention to citizens and to the councilors who speak for constituents and who elect the nazimeen. The study found out that the exercise of citizen power – on councilors as well as nazimeen – is manifesting itself in some significant achievements. For instances, it appears that doctors and teachers are now more likely to be at their posts. Drugs are more often available in clinics. Citizens undoubtedly appreciate the improved access they have to their political representatives. Councillors, both directly and through new dispute resolution arrangements at the local level, are now seen to be responding to people's needs and concerns. When access and response are improving in this manner, devolution would seem to be promoting the accountability that represents one of the basic political objectives. In that area, progress is encouraging.[20]

Thus, while the donor agencies see a lot of merits and achievements in the military-propelled process of decentralization in Pakistan ('uneven but encouraging progress on most fronts' (p. 14)) without serious concern for the overall context of federalism and provincial autonomy, the International Crisis Group (in 2004) in fact condemned the reform for its purported aim of 'strengthening military rule' in Pakistan (Adeney 2007a: 117). With comparative knowledge of experiments in democratic decentralization elsewhere in India,[21] there is reason to share the

178 Federalism and forms of decentralization

argument of Adeney in this context that decentralization without land reforms in Pakistan does not empower the people but the landed gentries (Adeney 2007a: 117). When there is so much regional discontent at provincial levels and below in Pakistan,[22] the decentralization measures should have considered devolving powers democratically down to those levels so that the regions do not remain discontented but contribute to the making of a nation of many communities and regions. But at the moment this is most unlikely to take place, because since 1971, if not before, the country's leaders have been centralizers, such as M. A. Jinnah, General Ayub, General Yahya Khan, and General Musharraf. Jinnah, the founder of the nation, is quoted to have said, irritatingly, to the Pakistanis immediately after the creation of Pakistan: 'Therefore, if you want to build yourself into a nation, for God's sake, give up this provincialism' (Cohen 2005: 205). Cohen argues that General Yahya Khan even went to the extent of destroying Pakistan 'by refusing to contemplate greater provincial autonomy' (Cohen 2005: 205) for the Bengalis, which resulted in the dismemberment of the state and the birth of Bangladesh in 1971. In short, since its formation Pakistan has witnessed 'national' leadership which has been more bent on weakening the cause of provincial autonomy. In this context, Cohen's comment on the implication of ex-General Musharraf's so-called decentralization during 2001–8 as another attempt 'to weaken provincial power and further centralize power' (Cohen 2005: 215). Cohen further wrote: 'He is gambling that the increase in direct control over the *Nazim* (also known as *Nazeem* district-level local-government officials) (via payments to the districts) will compensate for the decline in provincial responsibility'. However, the experience of India and other complex society-states indicates that the gains may be illusory, because of the difficulty of running a megastate from the center (Cohen 2005: 215). This is a further confirmation of the fact that decentralization in Pakistan during 2000–8 has undercut the authority of the already weakened provinces and thus has served to undermine federalism in Pakistan. That is a comparative lesson to learn from the 'pathology of federalism' in Pakistan.

The 18th Amendment and a paradigm shift in decentralization

However, Pakistan federalism has taken a new turn for the better since 2010. The 18th Amendment of the Constitution (1973) of Pakistan on 9 April 2010 was passed by the National Assembly of Pakistan by 292 out of 342 members as well as by the Senate remains the most radical reform in the history of federalism in Pakistan, which is rarely undertaken in any other federations in Asia, if not elsewhere. This radical institutional reform was propelled by international donors but not abrupt. A Charter of Democracy by late Prime Minister Benazir Bhutto and Nawaz Sharif (former prime minster) in London (14 May 2006), followed by popular pressures for democracy and federalism and the All Parties Conference in London resolved to restore parliamentary democracy and ensure provincial autonomy in Pakistan. To give constitutional shape to these objectives, a 24-member

Parliamentary Committee for Constitutional Reforms was formed in 2009 which held 77 meetings, each for many hours, and deliberated on the detailed issues to be considered for reforms. There were, however, dissenting notes, which were recorded too. One member raised a very pertinent point with regard to the rigidity of Article 239: Mr S M Jafar said that the

> procedure in the Constitution for creation of new provinces is cumbersome. The procedure should be much simpler which may allow the parliament to change the boundary of a province and the name in the more simpler and expeditious manner. I had suggested this as in future the redistribution of provinces into more provinces would be in the interest of Pakistan and the Federation but it was not agreed upon. For the purpose of record, I would like to place this reiteration as on record.
>
> *(www.na.gov.pk/uploads/documents/report_constitutional_18th_ amend_bill2010_020410_.pdf, accessed 26 July 2019)*

No devolution of powers can work in conditions of a semi-autocracy and undemocratic 'presidential' system of government. Any devolution is inherently democracy in character. This amendment basically took two revolutionary steps: restoration of parliamentary framework of governance from the semi-presidential (in the military sense of the term) and highly centralized one in favour of a decentralized federal state and provision for major devolution of powers and responsibilities to the provinces – both are mutually reinforcing – by amending about one-third of the original text of the Constitution (1973) and abolishing the Concurrent List of the distribution of powers between the federal and provincial governments. The first was done by making the president of Pakistan a titular head so that the president can no longer dismiss the governments – federal or provincial – unilaterally; she or he can no longer appoint the military chiefs and the election commissioner on her or his own; she or he cannot appoint the judges of the higher judiciary, a task now given to a judicial commission headed by the chief justice, and the president can no longer declare emergency unilaterally. The ban on the prime minister holding office for more than two terms was also lifted. To add further strength to a democratic and limited government to foster in Pakistan after several decades of dictatorship of one kind or the other, the name of the former President General Zia-ul-Haque was removed from the Constitution; also repealed was the 17th Constitutional Amendment (2003) and the Legal Framework Order (2002), and holding the Constitution in abeyance is now treated as high treason. These measures plus more restore the parliamentary form of government with executive powers vested in the elected prime minister and his council of ministers.

As far as provincial devolution was concerned, the centralist Concurrent List was abolished, and many items from the Federal List (part 1 and 2) were deleted. Politically, the political autonomy of the democratically elected provincial government was given more cover by limiting the president's power to dissolve the

180 Federalism and forms of decentralization

Provincial Assembly and the government, which now requires a resolution of the Provincial Assembly (Article 232 (2)). The Federal List (Part 1) contains 59 items, and Part 2 contains 18 items of national and international importance (with many items deleted from both), leaving them and the residual matters to the provinces. The Federal List Part 2 contains items which require joint supervision of federal and provincial governments such as railways, mineral oil and natural gas, major ports, interprovincial matters, the Council of Common Interests and consensus. Article 141 says 'a Provincial Assembly may make laws for the Province'. As many as 17 federal ministries were transferred to the province: education and professional training; Culture; National Health Regulation and Co-ordination; minority affairs (religious affairs); tourism development, women's development, youth affairs and so on. Article 160 (3A) further protects the provinces from the federal government in financial devolution by the National Finance Commission: the sum awarded to the provinces cannot be less than the previous year, and there will be no federal encroachment upon 57 per cent share of fiscal resources given to the provinces. Finally, as per Article 172 (3), mineral oil and natural gas within the provinces and in adjacent territorial waters shall be under the joint and equal jurisdiction of both the provinces and the federal government. Article 161 (1 and 2) provides that all royalty and excise duty collected by the federal government from mineral oil and natural gas located within the territory of the provinces shall be given to the provinces.

Beyond doubt, these changes empower the provinces, better protect their autonomy and meet much of their grievances in matters of royalty sharing and financial devolution by the NFC. The name change of the NWFP into Khyber Pakhtunkhwa symbolizes recognition of ethnic identity of the Pastos. This amendment act changes also the centre–provincial relations in Pakistan in a major way not seen since 1973. But the most vexing questions remain: are the provinces capable of handling that many affairs by way of transferring 15 federal ministries to them? How far has the 18th Constitutional Amendment Act 2010 been implemented? Were the massive devolution measures not rather too ambitious?

The amendment provoked since 2010 considerable debates among the donors, the media in Pakistan and the concerned scholars in Pakistan regarding its implementation after five years. Already in 2010, immediately after the Act was passed, *Dawn* (a newspaper in Pakistan) raised some pertinent questions that were thought to have been neglected: whether passing on the responsibilities to the provinces would in practice enhance provincial autonomy, result in better management of responsibilities at the provincial level and finally maintain consistency on policy issues that required a national direction (8 April 8 2010). Such questions are still to be effectively answered after five years. The UNDP's 2015 (https://www.pk.undp.org/content/pakistan/en/home/library/development_policy/development-advocate-pakistan—volume-2—issue-1.html, accessed on 23 May 2020) Pakistan survey of views and opinions of the stake holders suggests not too optimistic a picture that has come out in matters of implementation. The Editorial of *Development Advocate: Pakistan* (Vol. 2 (1) April 2015: www.undp.org/content/dam/pakistan/docs/DevelopmentPolicy/DAP%20April%202015%20ENGLISH.pdf, accessed 27 July 2019) expressed serious concern.

But significant federal institutions and implementation mechanism in charge of the devolution at all levels of governance are still little developed or even non-existent.

The Implementation Commission comprising members the of National Assembly representing all political parties in Pakistan formed on 2 May 2010 and complemented its designated task by 30 June 2010. It held 68 meetings and inter-governmental consultations and formed many subcommittees. It identified that 17 federal ministries were to be transferred; 61,231 federal staff needed to be repositioned; 48 federal laws needed to be amended and so on. The Council of Common Interests (CCI) identified 103 agenda items for discussion. But the implementation of the 18th Amendment Act is still locked in controversies, confusion and inter-governmental tussle, particularly over the provincial control over mineral oil and natural gas and a 50 per cent share in the provinces of Sindh and Baluchistan. In matters of higher education, too, there is conflict and lack of consensus. For example, Sindh and Punjab have formed, as per the 18th Amendment, their Higher Education Commissions, which the Federal Law Ministry has termed 'unconstitutional' (UNDP 2019). As a result, not only the donors but also civil society, media and scholars remain skeptical over the issue. The UNDP's analysis summed up the positions of the stakeholders as follows:

> The federal and devolutionary paradigms introduced by the 18th amendment has been swinging between charged narratives of "too-little-too-late" and "too-much-too-soon". The other more recent semi-government assessment on implementation raises questions about the validity of the many federal Regulatory Authorities on matters developed to the Provinces.
>
> *(http://library.fes.de/pdf-files/bueros/pakistan/14091.pdf, accessed 27 September 2019)*

The effective implementation of the near revolutionary devolution as per the 18th amendment requires the appropriate institutional and political cultural environment, drastic dismantling of many anti-provincial autonomy legislations and institutions and the leadership at both the federal and provincial levels which are not yet to be available in Pakistan today.

India

Compared with Malaysia and Pakistan, India's introduction of democratically elected decentralized bodies in both rural and urban areas of the whole country, particularly since 1992, nationally, is near-revolutionary and remarkably successful. (Bhattacharyya 2016: 125–38) Since the federation itself is based on the relative autonomy of the states (the process of state creation has remained somewhat of an ongoing process) in terms of the specified areas of their formal jurisdiction, decentralization has remained somewhat built in to the system. But that is not the specific meaning of decentralization that has acquired wide currency nowadays in

182 Federalism and forms of decentralization

the discourse on federalism. The reference today is made to substate-level decentralization. But, as we have already indicated in the introduction to this chapter, decentralization *per se* may not empower federalism, but democratic decentralization does. In fact, today, the relation between democracy and federalism is much more highlighted than ever before, for a number of reasons, all mutually reinforcing both democracy and federalism.[23] In the case of India, until the early 1990s, the decentralization experiments were state-specific, because as a state competence in the original Constitution (Article 40), the various states experimented with it variously, as it suited their political interests. However, the centre has since 1950 taken steps to integrate its various welfare measures into the rural decentralization process in order to activate it, partly from administrative political compulsion (since the centre does not have the administrative machinery to implement even its own welfare legislations and measures; it has to depend upon the states to do the job). India's experiments with various institutional arrangements for decentralization are of comparatively longer standing than many postcolonial states, including Pakistan and Malaysia. Both the ethnic-identity-based and the simple population-based decentralization provisions practiced at various levels of the Indian polity since the 1950s have served to enrich her federalism and democracy simultaneously.

India has had a favourable historical legacy of statehood, as has been examined by political theorists, historians and sociologists,[24] which has served to create the congenial environment for decentralization in subsequent times. As Sudipta Kaviraj (1991) has rightly pointed out, the modern Indian state was not and could not be built in an empty space: it has to rework the logic of existing structures, which in turn have their own, sometimes surprisingly resilient, justificatory structures (Kaviraj 1991: 73). The late Morris-Jones (1964/1987), the doyen of Indian politics, had noted earlier that the political system of modern states are usually developments from earlier, sometimes much earlier, times (Bhattacharyya, H. 2002: 43). It is now well-established that political centralization in India, historically, could make little headway because, in the political and cultural tradition and ways of life of the people, the state had always been marginal to society, and so society had remained self-governed. In other words, India rarely experienced a true centralized state *à la* the European absolutist states, as so brilliantly analyzed by Perry Anderson (Anderson 1979). Historically oriented scholars of state formation in India have found no conception of an absolute state in India, for 'there developed within India a concept and practice of sovereignty, which emphasized the multiple rights of different groups and sectors of society and not the existence – real or ideal – of a unitary, almost ontological existence of the state'.[25] Self-governance, respect for diversity and difference, and the condemnation of uniformity and over-centralization have been harped on by nationalist thinkers, social philosophers and nationalist leaders of India in different times.[26] While Mahatma Gandhi had had a somewhat sentimental attachment to India's time-honoured tradition of village self-governance (Swaraj/village republics) and wrote extensively on it, defending it as the foundation of the future polity in India, the subject received adequate importance in the political thought of Jawaharlal Nehru, India's top nationalist leader and thinker and architect of the modern Indian state, who pointed out that in ancient India, under the aegis of centralized monarchies:

> The village *panchayats* or the elected council has large powers both executive and judicial and its members were treated with greatest respect by the king's officers. Land was distributed by the *panchayats* which also collected taxes out of the produce and paid the government's share on behalf of the village. Over a number of these village councils there was a larger *panchayat* or council to supervise and interfere if necessary.
>
> *(Nehru 1980/1946: 249)*

During British colonial rule, under popular pressures and under compulsion to establish a more effective government at the village level, some attempts to institute local 'self-government', both rural and urban, had been made since the late 1880s.[27] This was not true self-government, as it acted under the control of the colonial government and was constituted of an undemocratic method of nomination and appointment rather than election. The late D. D. Basu (1997), the famous constitutional expert, said that many provincial legislatures, formed under the provisions of the Government of India Act 1935 and following the elections in 1937, enacted new acts vesting powers of administration, including criminal justice, in the hands of the *panchayats*, the rural local-government bodies named after the traditional system of the assembly of five. (The word 'panch' means five.) And yet, until Independence, such *panchayats* remained effectively *caste-panchayats*, reflecting the surrounding social order marked by the caste hierarchy. Morris-Jones (1964/1987) gave an indication of the type of governance that was the outcome of such caste-bound *panchayats*:

> Finally, the nature of political operation is clear. The work of the caste leaders is to ensure the conformity of members to the caste code, to maintain the position of the group in the village community to achieve appropriate readjustments in that position if the relative strength of the caste should for some reasons increase. The job of the village leader is two-fold: to produce a consensus – that is, to resolve and settle inter-caste disputes in such a way as if possible to maintain status quo or if necessary to secure a smooth readjustment of positions.
>
> *(Bhattacharyya, H. 2002: 50)*

The role of the village-based *panchayats* as self-governing bodies was taken up, in its deliberations, by the members of the Constituent Assembly (CA) of India (1946–49), although there was wide divergence of views about the role the *panchayats* would have in the emerging state structure of India. While Dr Rajendra Prasad (then Congress president) and a very influential member of the CA, was in favour of advocating the universal adult suffrage only for the village *panchayats* and for making the latter 'the electoral college for electing representatives to the

184 Federalism and forms of decentralization

provinces and the centre' (Bhattacharyya, H. 2002: 53), Dr B. R. Ambedkar, the Chairman of the Drafting Committee, held the opposite view. At any rate, the new state structure that was conceived was not based on the Gandhian idea of village *swaraj*, or *panchayats*, but a more top-heavy parliamentary federal democratic republic that, however, provided for accommodation of decentralization of varying forms and at various levels in order that ethno-local and ethno-regional interests, values and identity are recognized and accommodated with commensurate political institutions and autonomy.

We will take up first the simple population-based decentralization that was originally provided under Article 40 of the Indian Constitution and placed in Part IV of the Constitution (Directive Principles of State Policy, otherwise a nonjusticeable part of the Indian Constitution). It was also placed under the competence of the states in Indian federalism. Even after the famous 73rd Amendment Act, 1993, the *panchayats* remain a state subject, but with a difference. The difference lies precisely in the constitutional guarantee of the existence of the *panchayats* and the municipalities (under the 74th Amendment Act, 1993), something which was lacking in the pre-1993 period.

In the pre-1993 period, the central government had ever since 1957 made various institutional measures to operationalize the *panchayats* in order to utilize them for various developmental and social-welfare activities of the government, such as rural employment generation, rural housing, sanitation and so on. Various state governments have on their own have also experimented with various forms and degrees of local government, as their local circumstances dictated. In many, or rather, most cases, the state governments cared little for it, in case it grew into a threat to the state-level politicians. In other words, until the passage of the 73rd and 74th Constitutional Amendment Acts (1992/1993),[28] the local governments, both rural and urban, had little or no constitutional guarantee of their existence, let alone autonomy. This is precisely where the federal dimension of local government in India is to be searched for as far as the conventional kinds of local government system are concerned. The two aforementioned amendments have been path-breaking in state reforms in respect of institutionalization of substate-level self-governing bodies (to be democratically elected by the eligible voters of the locality at intervals of five years) as well as devolution of a very substantial amount of powers and resources at the disposal of the local governors for deliverance to the people and the locality. Backed by decades of trial and error, the institutions of local self-governance in India have thus been indigenously developed rather than as a prescription from some donor agencies. Quite predictably, the successful experiments in local governments in India, despite many flaws (the differential political impact of the locality; the lack of education among the masses as well as the elected representatives; a degree of corruption; and the nature of the state governments, etc.), have attracted quite considerable global and national academic attention.[29] Current research recognizes the value of local self-governing bodies in terms of empowerment of the disadvantaged groups, inclusion of the marginalized sections of society through reservation of seats (Scheduled Castes, SC; Scheduled Tribes,

Federalism and forms of decentralization **185**

ST; and women) at different tiers and positions of these bodies, enhancement of the social status and self-esteem of the poorer sections and better delivery of services (for this read rights) to the locality, to the disadvantaged and so on. All India-based surveys of trust in government have shown a greater degree of trust in local government. Popular participation in elections to form local-government bodies is also very high compared to the state and national-level elections. In some states, such as West Bengal, it is as high as 80 per cent, which compares quite favourably with the average turnout in subnational elections in some advanced countries in Europe.[30] Throughout rural India, *panchayats*, as grassroots democratic institutions, are dotted around the countryside. Despite variations in functioning, *panchayats*, mostly three-tier, are now very much accepted by the people as their own institutions that they can live with. Such grassroots governing institutions have offered scope and avenues for the downtrodden sections of society for political participation, contestation and bargaining as well as a platform for asserting their rights. Many state governments spend most of their development money through the *panchayats*. While the *panchayats* have added much-needed legitimacy to the democratic system in India, they have also performed federal tasks, not just by implementing federal welfare and developmental programmes (albeit through the state governments, not bypassing them!) but, more importantly, as the lowest democratic platform linking the local to the regional and then to the national. It is thanks to the relatively successful experiments with rural decentralization that Indian federalism is now based on a solid democratic footing, with much-needed legitimacy.

The following section will discuss the other types of decentralization in India, which have more direct federal implications and are identarian in content. I have in mind here the issues of state creation, sublevel regional and district councils for accommodation of distinct identity, which is territorially rooted. First, as we have already seen in Chapter 2 of this book, the creation of linguistic states in a federation after Independence was a nationalist pledge to those aggrieved groups which were demanding self-determination and recognition of identity. India's post-Independence federalization has entailed essentially a process of redrawing the internal political map of the country so that the constituent units of the federation (i.e. the states) correspond with the cultural identity of the people inhabiting the area(s) concerned. The Constitution of India gives the Parliament almost unilateral powers (Arts 2–3) to create new states, change the boundary of existing states and alter the name of any state, and so on. As I have discussed in detail elsewhere,[31] those provisions that are apparently most unfederal, if not anti-federal, have turned out to be most federal in the context of India, because they have allowed the required flexibility to accommodate the growing ethno-regional demands for recognition, power and autonomy. India's very complex ethno-regional and linguistic territory, with lots of mutual antagonism and inter-ethnic conflicts at the time of Independence, and that too comprising the directly governed former British provinces on the one hand and the 500-odd princely kingdoms of varying sizes and complexion on the other, could not simply be 'right-sized' at one go. Since Independence, the Indian federation has undergone several phases of state reorganization – in the

186 Federalism and forms of decentralization

late 1950s, in the late 1960s, in the 1970; and in 2000 – in order to accommodate various identities based on such markers as language, tribal ethnicity, a mix of language and religion; regional identity; ecology and so on.[32] The number of states, as a result, has gone up to 28 today. There are demands for more states in various parts of India, such as Gurkhaland in West Bengal, Vidharva in Maharashtra, Harit Pradesh in Uttar Pradesh and so on. The creation of more states out of the existing ones has meant more ethnically homogeneous political units and further decentralization of powers and resources within the federation.

The other types of identarian decentralization in India are special provisions for self-governance for the aboriginal peoples living in different parts of India, most notably in the NorthEast, today comprising seven states. First, the Constitution provides under the Fifth Schedule for self-governance for certain areas and communities, 'scheduled areas', however, falling under the jurisdiction of some states for the formation of tribal advisory councils in 'scheduled areas' in states other than Assam, Meghalaya, Mizoram and Tripura (all in the NorthEast) for giving advice on welfare and advancement of the scheduled tribes in the areas concerned. This schedule has been so designed in order to meet the requirement of the backward areas inhabited by the tribes in the states concerned. No less a person than the president of India has been empowered by the Constitution to declare a certain area as 'scheduled' for the said purpose, although subject to the law to be enacted by Parliament. The state governor has been empowered to direct that some laws of Parliament or of the state legislature shall not apply to the 'scheduled area'.

Second, unlike the Fifth Schedule, which makes the governor all-powerful, the Sixth Schedule of the Constitution (Arts 244 (2) and 275 (1)) provides for self-governance in the shape of an autonomous district or regional council for the tribal-inhabited areas in the NorthEast. The provisions in this schedule are at once decentralizing and democratic:

> There shall be a District Council for each autonomous district consisting of not more than thirty members, of whom not more than four persons shall be nominated by the Governor and the rest shall be elected on the basis of adult suffrage.[33]

After subsequent amendments to the Constitution, the tribal autonomous areas to be governed under the Sixth Schedule today are nine. Although the Autonomous district councils are outside the executive authority of the state(s), provision has been made for the formation of the district and regional councils as representative bodies with certain legislative and judicial powers regarding forest management, inheritance of property, marriage and social customs and other matters. The legislative autonomy of the councils has been protected by the Constitution, with the proviso that the acts of the state legislature shall not extend to such areas unless so desired by the council. The institution of such elected councils since the inauguration of the Constitution of India in the tribal areas has replaced the rule by the tribal chieftains. However, the chieftains were in part accommodated in the nominated category, although their powers are limited to giving advice. And yet this subordination of the traditional authority to the modern authority of the council did not mean the loss of tribal culture and customs. On the contrary, there are adequate constitutional guarantees. With regard to Naga customs and traditions, for instance, it is stated under Article 371 (A) that:

> Notwithstanding anything contained in the Constitution no act of Parliament in respect of religious or social practices of the Nagas, Naga customary laws and procedures, administration of civil and criminal justice involving decisions according to Naga customary laws, and the ownership and transfer of land and its resources, shall apply to the state of Nagaland unless the Legislative Assembly of Nagaland by a resolution so decides.[34]

The specific case studies[35] made of such autonomous district councils in the NorthEast of India have strongly suggested that self-governance for the aboriginal people in the shape of various operating district councils throughout India's NorthEast has led to better protection of their identity. The case of the Tripura Tribal Autonomous District Council (ADC) (instituted in 1983), governed by the Sixth Schedule of the Constitution, is a remarkable success – governing as it has been over two-thirds of the jurisdiction of the state (the eastern part along the hills, with about one-third of the population, mostly tribespeople), leaving one-third of the territory to the state government.[36] No wonder many subnational/ethnic rebels have demanded the introduction of the Sixth Schedule in their domain, as the provisions are more empowering and autonomy-ensuring than anything else. In some cases, some district councils created specially under the state laws (e.g. the Darjeeling Gurkha Hill Council in West Bengal formed in 1988 under a state law) first demanded that its status be upgraded to being brought under the Sixth Schedule, failing which the Gurkhas have begun a movement for statehood without West Bengal but within India.[37] It has also been a fact in India that ethnic political leaders gather enough experience in governance in such representative bodies before they spearhead movements for the creation of a larger political entity such as the state.

All in all, various forms of decentralization in India have ensured power-sharing among groups at different levels of the polity, as a result of which much of the ethnic and other social and cultural discontent is resolved without any major alterations in the dominant structures of authority. Since all forms of decentralization in India must be democratic, they have added to the legitimacy basis of the federal system as a whole. When conjoined to welfare measures of the governments of both the state and the centre, such decentralization has also served to function as a means of some degree of resource redistribution among the disadvantaged sections of society. The local, the regional and the national thus have been mutually reinforcing, ultimately strengthening the pluralist national identity in India's ongoing 'federal differentiation'.[38]

188 Federalism and forms of decentralization

Notes

1 See Bhattacharyya, H. (2001a), pp. 379–384, pp. 363–364. The current Swiss Constitution has recognized the institutional importance of the Communes at many places of importance (Articles 31, 41, 43, 44 and 74); in the 1874 Constitution they are recognized under Article 110. The structures, powers and functions of the Communes are governed by the Cantonal Constitutions, but the Communes are indispensable to the institutional structure of governance in the country. They are self-governing communities within the self-governing Cantons. One famous Swiss political scientist, Wolf Linder, argues that each Commune enjoys what may be called a 'core autonomy', which it enjoys as a right: 'A constitutional right to exist, including the freedom to merge with other communities or remain independent, which cannot be withdrawn by the cantons' (p. 379).

2 It is for this reason that Daniel Elazar has preferred to use the term 'non-centralization' to 'decentralization', because the latter term implies only a hierarchy with powers following from the top or the centre, while the term 'non-centralization' suggests a constitutionally guaranteed dispersal of powers and hence better represents the character of federations. For further details, see Watts (2008: 171).

3 See, for instance, Watts (1999, 2008); Bhattacharyya, H. (2001a); Jain (2005); Baviskar and Mathew (2009).

4 See Mitra and Singh (1999), chapter 5: 'The Dialectics of Nation and Region in Indian Politics', pp. 155–79, for a brilliant critical discussion based on empirical survey data on this subject. See also Bhattacharyya, H. (2005e).

5 See Burgess and Pinder (eds) (2007), especially chapter 10: 'Federations and Managing Nations' by John McGarry and Brendan O'Leary, pp. 180–212.

6 See Watts (2008: 171–8) (chapter 12); and Watts (1999), chapter 8, pp. 71–80.

7 Anon. (2002) *Federal Constitution (as at 10th April 2002)*, Kuala Lumpur: International Law Book Service, 2002, pp. 272–3.

8 Anon. (2002) *Federal Constitution*, pp. 112–13.

9 Anon. (2002) *Federal Constitution*, p. 113.

10 However, the states of Sarawak and Sabah are exempted from this federal control in respect of the organization of local governments in their domain (Articles 95 D and E of the *Federal Constitution*), p. 116.

11 Anon. (1972) *Report of the Royal Commission of Enquiry into the Working of Local Governments in West Malaysia*, Kuala Lumpur: Government of Malaysia. Paul Tennant reported that there were 48 'major local governments' in West Malaysia, which, with the sole exception of the one in Kuala Lumpur (the national capital) were run by elected local councils. But in 1972, following the so-called emergency situation in 1965, the local councils were abolished. Tennant argued: 'The abolition of elective councils in West Malaysia may be viewed essentially as a curtailment of local level political participation' (p 348). For further details on the circumstances leading to their curtailment, the real reasons for doing so and the politics behind such action, see P. Tennant (1973) 'The Decline of Elective Local Government in Malaysia', *Asian Survey*, Vol. 13, No. 4, April, 347–65.

12 These data are derived from Internet sources. (http://en.wikipedia.org/wiki/Local_Government_in_Malaysia).

13 P. S. Nooi (2008) 'Decentralisation and Recentralisation? Trends in Local Government in Malaysia', *Commonwealth Journal of Local Governance*, No. 1, May, 126 (Internet.

14 The States of Sabah and Sarawak have special autonomy in matters of local government by Article 95D of the federal Constitution, which debars the Parliament from intervening in matters of land and local government. However, both the states send representatives to the National Council for Local Government, a post-1976 institution which acts as a 'national' instrument in matters of local government and serves to take away the limited autonomy of the states in such cases.

Federalism and forms of decentralization **189**

15 Section 95A (added after the said amendment) of the federal Constitution provides that the NCLG can 'formulate policies for the promotion, development, control of local government throughout the federation and for the administration of any laws relating thereto' (quoted in Nooi 2008: 128).

16 G. S. Cheemaand A. A. Hussein (1978) 'Local Government Reform in Malaysia', *Asian Survey*, Vol. 18, No. 6, June, 577.

17 P. S. Nooi (2008) 'Decentralisation or Recentralisation? Trends in Local Government in Malaysia', *Commonwealth Journal of Local Governance*, No 1, May, 126; for details, see pp. 126–32.

18 Anon. (2004) *Devolution in Pakistan*, Washington, DC: Asian Development Bank, Department for International Development and World Bank), p. 1.

19 Anon. (2004) *Devolution in Pakistan*, op. cit., p. 4.

20 Anon. (2004) *Devolution in Pakistan*, op. cit., p. 5.

21 I have in mind in particular the cases in West Bengal, Kerala and Tripura in India.

22 See S. P. Cohen (2005), chapter 6, 'Regionalism and Separatism', pp. 201–26. Cohen has stated that:

> Ethnic and linguistic groups, identified by cultural markers, often claim they are a 'people' or a 'nation'. Some seek independence and want to form an ethnically or linguistically homogeneous state; some seek greater autonomy within a state or province, and others move back and forth between these two groups or remain ambiguous'.
>
> (p. 201)

But, sadly, all the fanfare of Pakistan's decentralization and power-sharing arrangements, that, too, donor-propelled, is far removed from any consideration of the ethno-regional dimensions of the issue.

23 Hardgrave and Kochanek (2000), p. 137. See B. He (2007) 'Democratization and Federalization in Asia', in He, B., Galligan, B. and Inoguchi, T. (eds) *Federalism in Asia*, Cheltenham: Edward Elgar, especially pp. 18–25 for the theoretically informed but Asia-specific analysis of the relation between the two.

24 I have discussed this aspect in greater detail in my (2001a) *India as a Multicultural Federation: Asian Values, Democracy and Decentralization (In Comparison with Swiss Federalism)*, Fribourg, Switzerland: Helbing and Lichtenhahn, pp. 138–40.

25 S. N. Eissentadtand H. Hartman (1997) 'Historical Experience, Cultural Tradition, State Formation and Political Dynamics in India and Europe', in Doornbos, M. and Kaviraj, S. (eds) *Dynamics of State Formation: India and Europe Compared*, New Delhi: Sage, p. 41.

26 For further details of the discussion on this aspect, see Bhattacharyya (2002) op. cit., pp. 43–53.

27 See H. Bhattacharyya (2002) op cit., pp. 49–52, for further details on the acts passed by the colonial authorities for the purpose.

28 A. Kashyap (1989) *Panchayati Ra: Views of the Founding Fathers and Recommendations of Different Committees*, New Delhi: Lancer's Books.

29 The Act of 1996 has been passed in Indian Parliament in order to operationalize *panchayats* in the 'scheduled areas' for extending the benefits of self-rule to the tribal people (aboriginal people) who constitute the majority of population in the scheduled areas. For further details, see S. K. Singh (1999) 'Self-Governance for the Scheduled Areas', in Jha, S. N. and Mathur, P. C. (eds) *Decentralization and Local Politics*, New Delhi: Sage, pp. 173–89.

30 See, for instance, Subrata K. Mitra (2001) 'Making Local Government Work: Panchayati Raj and Governance in India', in Kohli (ed) op. cit., pp. 103–27; C. Bates (2005) 'Development of Panchayati Raj in India', in Bates, C. and Basu, S. (eds) *Rethinking Indian Political Institutions*, London: Anthem Press, pp. 169–210; P. R. Desouza (2007) 'Decentralization: Explorations of Local Government in India and the United States', in

190 Federalism and forms of decentralization

Bajpai, K. S. (ed) *Democracy and Diversity*, New Delhi: Oxford University Press, pp. 262–98; L. C. Jain (ed) (2005) *Decentralization* and *Local Governance (Essays for George Matthew)*, New Delhi: Orient Longman; H. Bhattacharyya (2002) *Making Local Democracy Work in India: Social Capital, Politics and Governance in West Bengal*, New Delhi: Vedams; H. Bhattacharyya (2005d) 'Grassroots Democracy and Civic Participation in Rural West Bengal: The Case of Gram Sansad', in Sen Gupta, D. and Ganguly, S. (eds) *India (Essays in Memory of Late Prof. Prasanta Kr Ghosh)*, Kolkata: Arambarg Book House, pp. 63–76; H. Bhattacharyya (1998) 'Bengal Communism and Panchayats: Operation of Micro Democracy', in Bhattacharyya, H. (ed) *Micro Foundations of Bengal Communism*, New Delhi: Ajanta, pp. 102–41.

31 Mitra and Singh (1999), op. cit., p. 111.
32 Bhattacharyya (2002a), op. cit., p. 204.
33 Bhattacharyya (2001), op. cit., pp. 250–74.
34 I have discussed such experiments in various places. See for instance, H. Bhattacharyya (2001a, 2001b, 2003, 2005a, 2005b; H. Bhattacharyya (2007a) 'Federalism and Competing Nations in India', and H. Bhattacharyya 'India and Switzerland as Multinational Federations', both being chapters in Burgess, M. and Pinder, J. (eds) *Multinational Federations*, London: Routledge.
35 Quoted in Bhattacharyya (2002), op. cit., p. 262.
36 Quoted in Bhattacharyya (2002), op. cit., p. 263.
37 Apart from my own writings, as mentioned under Note 32, see Mukherjee, J. (2008) *Multicultural Decentralization in India*, Unpub. Ph.D. thesis, University of Burdwan, in which she has explored, with a wealth of evidence, various identity-based decentralizing experiments in India.
38 H. Bhattacharyya (2003) 'Federalism and Tribal Self-Rule', *Federations: What's New in Federalism Worldwide*, Vol. 3, No. 3, August; H. Bhattacharyya (2005c) 'Forms of Multiculturalism and Identity Issues in India', *Canadian Diversity (Ottawa)*, Vol. 4, No. 1, Winter; H. Bhattacharyya (2005b) 'India: Bodo People's Rights Take a Step Forward', *Federations (Ottawa)*, Vol. 4, No. 3, March.

8
FEDERALISM AND DEMOCRACY
New questions asked

Introduction

Democracy is the cutting edge of federalism, understood as an institutional space for political accommodation for diversity. Alfred Stepan, a leading scholar of the comparative politics of our times, believes that although the majority of people worldwide who live in democracies live in federal systems, the relation between democracy and federalism remains still largely neglected theoretically.[1] The very concept of federalism as a political principle that advocates a combination of shared- and self-rule implies that democracy better provides the basis for the legitimacy of such a combination. Watts (1999) has emphasized the 'representativeness' of federal institutions in order to 'minimize the 'democratic deficit' and technocracy' in the system.[2] Many years ago, K. C. Wheare (1953) wanted to see federalism as a way of reconciling the pressures for diversity and for unity, so that diversity is maintained as a value in itself (Wheare 1953: 245–6). At the same time, Wheare emphasized the (democratic) similarity of political institutions for the sake of federalism and hence for the sake of diversity. He cited the example of how the successful transformation of the Swiss Confederation (1291–1848) into a federal union in 1848 required that the 'great divergence of political institutions in the cantons' (oligarchies, a monarchy, aristocracies and democracies) was brought 'into line' (Wheare 1953: 46). The conclusion that he drew from the Swiss success is worth quoting here:

> A condition of the closer union which federation required was similarity of political institutions and after a hard struggle the democratic and republican cantons prevailed and all were brought into line. There seems little doubt that just as the desire to form a federal union is unlikely to arise among states which differed in regime, the capacity to form and work such a union can hardly exist without substantial similarity.
>
> *(Wheare 1953: 46–7)*

192 Federalism and democracy

What Wheare was basically arguing about here was whether or not the political institutions were based on democracy, that is, the principles of free election, free criticism and representative institutions.[3] Prior to Wheare, the federalist political thought in the West had for long also stressed the democratic dimension of political institutions in the federation.[4] The experiences also unmistakably suggest that all successful federations in the world are also successful democracies.

Wheare (1953) emphasized the necessary relationship between federalism and democracy as:

> Dictatorship, with its one-party government and its denial of free election, is incompatible with the working of the federal principle. Federalism demands forms of government which have the characteristics usually associated with democracy or free government.
>
> *(Wheare 1953: 48)*

Democracy is important for federalism in many respects which need to be highlighted before embarking upon a comparative study of our cases. First, apart from its strategic importance in running a union, as insisted by Wheare, democracy addresses the question of liberty in the polity, for, otherwise, citizen's rights, preferences and values could not be ensured and upheld. Second, linked to this, the democratic system alone is capable of maintaining effectively the values of diversity by reflecting the values of the society into the political systems and by translating them into appropriate policy. This adds, arguably, to the legitimacy of the polity. Third, since democracy also entails a process of democratization as a way of political life at both the general and constituent level, as a rule it prevents ethnicization of the political process. In other words, a distinction must be made between a democratic polity and an ethnic polity at various levels of the federation. Democracy prohibits the latter, so that even a successful ethnic political leader of a state or in a state has to be elected (or even rejected) by the people after some interval. Socioculturally speaking, democracy only advocates an achieved status and not an ascribed status, as far as the polity is concerned.

There is another very important aspect of democracy not addressed to in the existing literature on federal democracy. What does federalism do? Does it generate equality? This political aspect of democracy seemingly designed to extend political recognition to ethnic identity refers actually to what I have termed *diversity-claims*. The central question addressed there is political equality for ethnic groups. This is important for ensuring political order and stability. The other aspect of democracy is whether or not it meets the *equality-claims*. These claims are for producing more equality by way of redistribution and enablement of the vast majority of the people in matters of access to basic public goods and services. If a federation does not produce more equality, it will fail, ultimately. If the federal subunits do not pay attention to the *equality-claims*, it will falter. Federal discourse is yet to conjoin federalism to democracy in this sense.

Federalism and democracy **193**

On the negative side, there are risks and hence uncertainties involved in combining democracy with federalism. Since democracy allows for political mobilization of ethno-national identity groups, especially those that are territorially rooted, for rights and resources, there is always a potential risk of secessionism. Alfred Stepan forewarns us: '[T]his risk is especially grave when elections are introduced in the subunits of a formerly nondemocratic federal polity prior to democratic countrywide elections and in the absence of democratic countrywide parties'.[5] This is of course a special scenario that he referred to. But following William Riker's distinction between 'demos-constraining and 'demos-enabling', Stepan (2005) also argues that 'all democratic federations are "demos-constraining" in the sense that the agenda of the "demos" has to be restricted for the sake of protecting individual rights against encroachments by the federal government'.[6] This argument needs, I believe, to be stretched down to the subnational level because there, due to the specific patterns of distribution of powers between the federal and state governments, the latter are responsible for delivering a variety of services for the citizens and also for law and order, which inevitably relates to the protection of individual liberty, and a whole set of institutional guarantees are called for. In contemporary times, decentralized local democracy has therefore been attracting increasing attention from many quarters. This also seems to strengthen the case for taking a human-rights perspective in matters of decentralization.[7]

To argue a little further regarding the negative aspects of the democratic aspect of federalism, I would like to stress that due to the relative absence of appropriate guarantees against the 'demos' itself (implying of course majoritarian democracy), loss of rights may occur for groups of people on the other side of the fence. Second, democracy thus may result in the triumph of the dominant ethno-national group(s), who, considering themselves to be the *staatsvolk*, McGarry and O' LEary 2007 (180–212) may gain disproportionately and unjustly more from the system. Third, since democracy also implies power-sharing and accommodation of diversity (identity, values, interests, etc.), the absence of democracy where it is most needed may be the cause of the failure of the federation and may result in the disintegration of the system itself. Finally, democracy offers better scope for social integration at the base of the polity at both levels, which is necessary for holding the federation together.

Within this conceptual back-up, I will, in this chapter, centrally enquire into what has sustained democratic federations in India and Malaysia, and in what manner, and what has failed Pakistan, all three countries being multinational in character. Stepan would have us believe that this is the key question to answer in such a setting (Stepan 2001: 18).

Pakistan

Despite M. A. Jinnah's wish and solemn declaration (at the Constituent Assembly of Pakistan on 11 August 1947) that Pakistan would become a democratic republic

194 Federalism and democracy

with recognition of the rights of the individuals irrespective of colour or creed, Pakistan is considered to be a failed case of a democratic federation, proved, grotesquely, first by the secession of its eastern wing, East Pakistan, leading to the rise of Bangladesh in 1971 after a bloody nationalist upsurge by the Bengalis, and second, afterwards, in the dismembered nation-state, by successive bouts of military dictatorship alternating with short periods of so-called democratic regimes, including those under overall, but tight, military control (e.g. the 'Basic Democracy' of General Ayub Khan), that were very fledgling, unstable and unconsolidated. Like India and Malaysia, Pakistan also opted, after the Government of India Act, 1935 (itself modelled on the British North America Act, 1867), a parliamentary-cabinet system of government. Stepan has argued that a 'pure parliamentarianism' offers a series of incentives, such as 'coalition requiring', 'coalition sustaining', a multi-party system and more degrees of freedom to resolve a 'crisis of government', and hence is less prone to military coups (Stepan 2001: 15). While India and Malaysia have been cases in point, Pakistan has proved otherwise. While India maintained, more or less steadily (except for the period of the Emergency, 25 June 1975–23 March 1977), a pluralist and federalist democracy, Pakistan suffered, as Muhammad Waseem has pointed out, 'a lingering crisis of civil–military relations, which adversely affected the agenda for national integration'.[8] The federal implication of such a failure is that the military regimes have 'cultivated a spirit of intolerance for sub-national identities' (Waseem 2004: 85). A federal democracy ensconced in a multinational setting requires that subnational identities are tolerated in a spirit of accommodation. In the case of Pakistan, due to a series of factors which were path dependent – such as the enormous geographical distance between the two wings; the pronounced (dominated by the migrant Urdu-speaking élite) Muhajir character of the state at the formative stage; the numerical majority of the highly identity-conscious Bengalis inhabiting the eastern wing (the east of India, now Bangladesh); and in latter days, the Punjabization of the state (i.e. the post-Bangladesh phenomenon) – democratization of the state apparatus, while being intensely desired by many identity groups since the formation of the state in 1947, has had different significance for different groups in pre- and post-Bangladesh Pakistan.

Before we turn to reflect upon this issue, we need first to make ourselves familiar with the 'democratic history' of Pakistan, whose legacies, however, are doubted even by Pakistani scholars.[9] Any discussion of Pakistan's problems with democracy must refer to two primal factors; both are path dependent and institutional in implications. First, although M. A. Jinnah, the father of Pakistan, in public committed himself and the nascent state to a kind of 'constitutional social democracy' (Ali, T. 1983: 42), he himself set rather a contrary example. Until a new Constitution was drafted and adopted for Pakistan, the Government of India Act, 1935, with a lot of amendments, was taken to be the Interim Constitution of Pakistan. But the decision of Jinnah to retain the position of governor-general 'with broad powers concentrated in that office in the first Pakistan government' set, Rose argues, 'the basic trend toward an authoritarian system'[10] in the nascent state. Second, due to the failure of the Muslim League, the party of Pakistan's creation, to establish itself

Federalism and democracy **195**

as a national party across the ethnic groups and regions, the system of a 'separate electorate', reminiscent of the Raj, which divided the electorate between Muslims and non-Muslims, was retained in the matter of allocation of legislative seats (Rose 1989: 112). This, in effect, was continuing the two-nation theory, whose relevance was no longer credible after Pakistan was carved out. Rose (1989) argues that 'it was an antinational, anti-integrationist policy in the post-partition period when the Muslims constituted around 95 per cent of the population in West Pakistan and 80 per cent in East Pakistan' (Rose 1989: 112).

Pakistan has endured military rule (for 34 years) far longer than democratic rule (24 years), even if the latter is defined rather liberally. The country's Constitution-making took much longer (11 years!), the transition to democracy immediately after its birth (1947) with the new Constitution (1956) faced crisis,[11] and after 1958 the country began to witness bouts of military rule, which suspended the Constitution, banned political parties and cancelled the democratic political process. Up to now, of the democratic regimes, only the government led by J. A. Bhutto, of the Pakistan People's Party (PPP), the former prime minister of Pakistan (and father of the late Mrs Benazir Bhutto, former prime minister of the country, who was assassinated in 2008) completed a full five-year term (1972–77). Sadly, this was followed by a military coup led by General Zia-ul-Haq, who had Mr Bhutto executed! The democratic regimes during 1988–97, including the 'Caretaker' ones, were all short-lived and followed by frequent elections and dismissal of prime ministers. Cheema has shown that during 1988–96, the president dissolved the National Assembly and dismissed the elected prime ministers four times (Cheema, I. P. 2000: 25).

Pakistan's 'democratic history' will remain incomplete with some reference to what is known as 'Basic Democracy', which was introduced by General Ayub Khan (1958–69) in 1960 following the Basic Democracies Order promulgated on 27 October 1959, with elections being held on 26 December 1959. Deviating from the parliamentary tradition of governance as provided for in the 1956 Constitution (which he abrogated), and substituting for it a presidential system for Pakistan, he wanted his 'Basic Democracies' (i.e. local councils at three levels – the police station, district and division), numbering 8,261, with 79,846 'basic democrats', to be elected at levels from the division downwards and to work under the command of the corresponding civilian bureaucracies.[12] Formed in a crisis-torn and highly unfavourable environment (cancellation of political parties and activities and abrogation of a democratic Constitution under the heavy weight of the civil-military administration), the real intention of going for the so-called basic democracies was suspect from the very beginning, as nothing more than finding a basis for the legitimacy of the military regime. It was seen by an earlier generation of observers of Pakistan politics as an example of 'Ayub's Praetorian Rule in the Garb of a Guided Democracy'.[13] Ian Talbot (2005), an acute observer of Pakistan's modern history and politics, commented that Ayub was highly critical of the politicians and believed that democracy was unsuitable for Pakistan.[14] Given that context, 'basic democracies', Talbot argued, 'consolidated the power of feudal landowners, hardly the most democratic force in Pakistan' (Adeney 2007a: 112). While nobody would

196 Federalism and democracy

quarrel with any genuine attempts at decentralization further down the subnational level, undermining the subnational/provincial level through such processes is evidently anti-federal. As General Pervez Musharraf, the last military ruler of Pakistan (1997–2008), who also tried twice to experiment with party-less local decentralization in 2001 and 2005, found, such a strategy of reaching out directly to the people at the grassroots is designed basically to enhance the legitimacy of military rule. Introduced in a cancelled political process, and under military-civilian bureaucratic control, this policy is neither federalist nor democratic. The successive rulers of Pakistan, for a variety of reasons, have tended to avoid the logic and the requirements of a federal democracy, to which the state since its inception in 1947 has committed itself except during the military regimes.

Paradoxical though it may seem, a fear of democracy has haunted the rulers of Pakistan almost since its inception. In the pre-Bangladesh period, it was the fear on the part of the Muhajir–Punjabi (West Pakistan) rulers of being dominated by the Bengalis living in the eastern wing (which contained 56 per cent of the population, including 98 per cent Bengalis) in the event of a democratic verdict being honoured. Pakistan was created with what Waseem (2004) has called 'various demographic anomalies' (Waseem 2004: 190), the most important of which was the predominantly ethnically homogeneous (in religion, and more significantly, in language) East Pakistan (formerly East Bengal, i.e. the eastern wing) with the majority of the population (56 per cent) and the western wing (45 per cent), which, although it had the Punjabis as the single largest community, was ethnically very diverse. In terms of the control over the civil and military administration, particularly over the higher echelons,[15] and the economy, trade and commerce (Talbot 2002: 57–8), it was West Pakistan which predominated, so much so that very soon the eastern wing became virtually an internal colony of the western wing.[16] West Pakistan also became the seat of power in Pakistan, with its changing capitals, which, interestingly enough, coincided with the changes in the ethnic dominance over the state – from Karachi (Muhajir-dominated) to Islamabad (Punjabi-dominated). Painfully enough, with a rather weak Muslim League base in West Pakistan, the founder had to increasingly depend on the Pakistan civil service as the only 'political party' that he could rely on[17] at the formative stage of the republic. Khalid Bin Sayeed, the very perceptive observer of Pakistan politics, argued that Jinnah in his last days increased his dependence on the civil bureaucracy and tended to place the politicians 'under bureaucratic tutelage'.[18] This would subsequently be supplemented by the Punjabi-dominated military. This civil–military combine, backed socioeconomically by semi-feudal landlords, *comprador* bourgeoisie and metropolitan capitalists, to use the phraseology of Hamza Alavi,[19] would eventually try to keep the issue of democracy at bay. After the first military takeover of the country in 1958, democracy even in the most basic liberal sense would be the casualty, giving birth to stronger movements for federal democracy. As Waseem wrote:

> Over time, Bengalis, Sindhis, Pathans and the Baluch came to understand Pakistan as a Muhajirs-Punjabi state. Not surprisingly, East Bengal,

Sindh, NWFP and Baluchistan produced ethnic movements in pursuance of demands for provincial autonomy, effective representation in the federal government and an equitable share in government services.

(Waseem 2004: 189)

There are thus no grounds for holding a pessimistic view of the role of democracy[20] for strengthening federalism in Pakistan. In the post-Bangladesh period the ethnic minorities had grounds for fearing democracy, because, democracy or not, the Punjabi domination in Pakistan is inevitable. Democracy *per se* would always translate into Punjabi domination. Only federal democratic institutions could hold it in check: minority veto power; adequate protection of the rights of the units (states' rights); adequate diversity-accommodating measures including financial resources for the protection of minority identities (religious, linguistic, tribal, etc.) and so on. Beyond that, the introduction and maintenance of a multi-party political competition provides for the development of cross-cutting political institutions in response to basic socio-economic issues, which could undercut the élites' domination that derives from the ethno-national groups, more particularly the Punjabis (who are not homogeneous in any way). The political economy of federalism in Pakistan is such that without a thorough bourgeois socio-economic transformation, and with the heavy sway of the semifeudal landlords and other ruling cliques, the redistributive dimensions of the state had not been allowed to take shape. From the data given by Kukreja (2003), it is found that during the military regime of Ayub Khan, an attempt was made to introduce land reforms, which determined 500 acres (irrigated) and 1,000 (non-irrigated) acres to be the maximum permissible amount, as a result of which some 6,000 landlords were found to be possessing 1,236 acres of land each on average in the 1960s (Kukreja 2003: 89). The total amount possessed by them was about 15 per cent of the private land in the country, while some 2.2 million people owned less than five acres and some two and a half million were landless.[21] During the 'socialist' regime of J. A. Bhutto (1971–77), the land ceiling was lowered to 100 acres (irrigated) and 200 acres (non-irrigated). But even then, the measures did not really succeed, as only 1 per cent of the cultivable land could be distributed among 130,000 tenants (Kukreja 2003: 94). This was hardly surprising because Bhutto's 'socialist' Pakistan People's Party (PPP) had, out of the 50 top leaders, 27 landlords, six tribal chiefs, five businessmen and seven middle-class professionals, but only one trade-union leader (Kukreja 2003: 96). The situation has not changed much for the better in matters of land reform, and the Pakistan economy remains, despite some respite during General P. Musharraf's regime (1999–2008) with its pronounced focus on privatization, hugely crisis-torn.[22] This discussion suggests that federal democracy *per se* is not enough for a much-needed and long-awaited major redistributive phase in social policy in the political economy of Pakistan federalism for land reforms, for empowerment of the overwhelmingly majority of the people and for their rights. This calls for truly social democratic change, which will pave the way for mass integration into the system. As Jaffrelot has shown, some integration of the élites along ethno-national

198 Federalism and democracy

lines has taken place in Pakistan, for, in the early 1970s, J. A. Bhutto of Sindh rose to power in Pakistan and ruled as prime minister during 1972–77, and also a quota system for recruitment into various branches of general administration (excluding military administration) was introduced for various provinces and regions.[23] Such a mechanism of élite accommodation, and that too, only in civil administration, made some difference in defusing ethnic tensions, no doubt. But it could hardly undercut the Punjabi domination: the data provided by Jaffrelot are solid proof of that. Punjab has a share of 50 per cent, which has translated into a share of 53.5 per cent of senior civil servants in 1973 and 55.7 per cent in 1987 (Jaffrelot 2002a: 23). Such élite integration could hardly match the deep-rooted and large-scale mass discontent in almost all provinces of Pakistan, as ethno-nationalist upheavals in recent times testify (see Chapter 2 of this book). All available studies on Pakistan show that the masses, who have suffered greatly at the hands of the successive bureaucratic and military rulers, are very alienated from the political system. The observer of recent political developments in Pakistan reported that during the last eight years of military rule under General Musharraf (2000–08), the country had been further deeply divided, with the Baluch and the Sindhis based in Baluchistan and Sindh, two of the country's four provinces, rejecting the legitimacy of a Punjabi-dominated state.[24] In short, the rights of the provinces, ethnically so distinctive, have been denied by the military-bureaucratic state dominated by the Punjabis, further damaging the already fragile health of federal democracy in Pakistan. Needless to say, the consensus on power-sharing, an essential pillar of federal democracy, has remained severely strained (Ahmed, S. 2007: 8). It is suggested that only a true social democracy can link federalism to welfare[25] to deliver the distributive goods and values required to satisfy the requirements of identity in the long term. With the 18thAmendment to the Constitution in 2010 (discussed at length in Chapter 7), a new space has been created via major devolution of powers and responsibilities to the provinces, but it is yet to be implemented.

Malaysia

Paradoxical though it may seem, Malaysia's federal democracy has had a limited and negative audience. Except during the Emergency (1969–71), since 1957 the federation has maintained a democratic system by holding regular elections to form governing institutions at the national and state level. The country has changed its leaders, and also its governments – at least at the state level – following democratic means. The UMNO-led National Front (federal) government of Mr Abdullah Badawi, the prime minister, suffered significant losses in the national-level elections held on 9 March 2008, so much so that the opposition won in five out of 13 states, and the Front had to be content with 140 seats out of 220 in the National Parliament – which is short of the two-thirds majority required to amend the Constitution.[26] In 2018 a new coalition led by the Harapan Party under the leadership of Mahatir Mohammed ousted the BN government led by Sheik Najib Rajak (see Chapter 5). While this is to be seen as the proof of democracy itself, such that

Federalism and democracy **199**

it prepares further grounds for checking on undemocratic trends in the system, if there are any, the political observers of Malaysian politics have remained quite cynical about the nature and prospects for democracy in the federation. Several areas of concern have been identified by scholars in this respect: ethnic diversity and plurality; consociationalism of the Alliance (BN); parliamentary democracy vis-à-vis political compromise among the ethnic élites based communally; the uneasy relationship between democracy and authoritarianism; and so on.[27] Thus, democracy in Malaysia has hardly ever achieved full marks: such qualified terms as 'quasi democracy', 'semi-democracy' (Case 2007), 'modified democracy' and 'repressive responsive regime' are mostly used to describe the country's democracy.[28] Interestingly enough, in one way or the other, these qualifying terms may well be applied to most democracies of the world, because democracy nowhere is a perfect system. And yet the deep-rooted cynicism about democracy in Malaysia needs to be highlighted a little further. Due to historical reasons, the indigenous Malays were in a relatively disadvantageous position compared with the migrant Chinese, who were economically quite well off and in control of trade and commerce. The position of the Indians, formerly indentured labourers brought in by the colonial rulers, was, as expected, not good. Thus, the 1957 federal Constitution that promised a democratic state based on universal adult suffrage also did so with what Singh (2001) termed 'differential incorporation, whereby political rights [accrue] from citizenship based on group membership rather than on the individual'.[29] In short, for the Chinese and the Indians, the other two ethnic minorities, acquisition of citizenship rights was conditional on their acceptance of the special privileges of the indigenous Malays, who were to be specially protected and promoted. The successive political élites, to be exact the UMNO-led BN, extended extra support to the Malays in the name of state- (and nation-?) building in terms that smack of Malayanization. There is statistical proof that democracy has favoured the Malays: as a result of the pro-Malay NEP, Malay corporate ownership, which was negligible at the turn of Independence, was estimated to be around 24 per cent in 1988. And the incidence of poverty among the Malays declined from 64.8 per cent in 1970 to 23.8 per cent in 1988 (Singh 2001: 52). By comparison, the Chinese share of corporate wealth did not change much during 1970–88, remaining at 41 per cent (Singh 2001: 52). It is thus beyond doubt that in relative terms, and ethnically speaking, the Malays have benefited very favourably from the federal democratic system in Malaysia. But things have begun to take a better turn, mostly as a result of the economic successes. The country's politics has, since the 1990s, begun to be less ethnicized (the National Development Policy that replaced the NEP in 1990 does not make provisions for ethnic quota!); despite Islam being the official religion of the federation, inter-religious tolerance is said to be 'well entrenched'; varieties of multi-ethnic alliances among the business community and among workers are a growing reality in the country; and non-government organizations have proliferated, giving birth to a 'civil society' to stand face to face with the state (Singh 2001: 52–5). All of these seem to suggest that the federation has become more democratized than ever.

200 Federalism and democracy

And yet this is not enough evidence to prove the relationship between democracy and federalism in multi-ethnic Malaysia. Unlike Pakistan (with the secession of its eastern wing to form Bangladesh in 1971), Singapore's expulsion from the federation in 1965 could not simply be taken as an example of disintegration and hence of the failure of democracy in Malaysia. The 13 units of the federation are distinct territorial entities despite having a plural demographic composition, that is, two Borneo (island) states with a preponderance of aboriginal people and one, namely, Penang, with a Chinese majority in the population. Despite the centralist bias in the federal Constitution, the ethno-regional identity of the units has been maintained – democratically and in and through power-sharing. It can therefore be proposed that it is democracy that has sustained federalism in Malaysia and vice versa. The sustenance of diversity of institutions and identities would have been difficult, if not impossible, had there been no democratic space. Substantive, if limited, operational independence of state governments has been recognized in the critical accounts of Malaysian democracy/federalism (Case 2007: 129). Constitutionally, the state governments are allowed to raise some taxes and also retain important powers of dispensing their patronage among locally sensitive issues that are crucial for sustaining the basis of support for the governments. From the comparative statistics given by Watts (2008) on ten important federations, the Malaysian federal government tops the list in raising the most taxes, as much as 89.9 per cent as federal government revenues before intergovernmental transfers, as compared with Canada and Switzerland with 47.7 per cent and 44.7 per cent respectively (Watts 2008: 133). But when read in conjunction with the amount of intergovernmental transfers as a percentage of state revenues, the states in Malaysia are in a better position than these of Brazil, the United States, Mexico, Russia, Switzerland and Canada (Watts 2008: 105). Watts (2008) has argued that although Malaysia is a case of what he termed 'executive federalism' (which maintains the dominant role of the federal government), the representation of the states has been maintained in many areas of vital decision making (for example, the National Finance Council headed by the prime minister includes a representative of each state (Watts 2008: 113)). There is also no evidence to suggest that funds to the states were ever withheld and that the states were not allowed to function.[30]

The argument that is being made here is that the issue of democracy in Malaysia – or for that matter in any federation or even of multinational character – could not be raised in absolute terms. No federation of this type has ever set the goal of democracy alone without considering other factors. Whether formed from below or above, the maintenance and promotion of diversity – social, cultural and political – has remained the goal of federations in modern times. Democracy, meaning power-sharing, the rights of individuals and groups, contestation and bargaining in a competitive political environment, and so on, has been thought necessary in order to better serve federalism. Therefore, federalism proper is to be democratic in character. But since nowhere do the groups that imply diversity have equal standing in society, the federal system, however democratic, cannot deliver the goods equally, although, constitutionally, equality – the most fundamental tenet of democracy – remains the declared goal. In other words, like it or not, democracy has been co-existing with some degree and forms of discrimination. In Malaysia, the federal Constitution (Part II, Arts 5–13), as the supreme law of the land, has declared a few 'fundamental liberties' of both individuals and groups, such as liberty; equality; freedom of speech, assembly and association; freedom of religion (for both the individual and the group); the right to education; and so on. Reading these provisions of the federal Constitution and of the procedural and (limited) substantive aspects of democracy since Independence, it is beyond doubt that the federation has been founded on a liberal polity, despite many limitations such as the reservations for the Malays (see Chapter 4 of this book) and other restrictive practices[31] by the federal government that limit democracy. When judged in identity terms, that is, in respect of the success in promotion and maintenance of diversity, the record of the Malaysian federation with special reference to the Indians (who make up about 8 per cent of the population) is said to be far from satisfactory. Rather than being integrated with a 'united nation', they are said to be 'most marginalized', next only to the *orang asli*. The rate of suicides among the Indians is the highest; gangsterism and violent crimes are rampant among the Indians; and about 15 per cent of the Indians in the capital are squatters.[32] Under the successive pro-Malay regimes, particularly during the last 20 years or so under the former Prime Minister Dr M. Mahatir and his so-called New Economic Policy (NEP), the Malays have been uplifted; the Chinese had to agree to part with their 'disproportionate share in trade and commerce; and the Indians have been marginalized'. *Time* magazine estimated in 2000 that while the Malays shared some 19.4 per cent of the nation's wealth (they had started off from an almost zero position) and the Chinese had 38.5 per cent, the Indians' share was only 1.5 per cent.[33] The Malaysian Indians demonstrated twice against the federal government to try to gain better opportunities and against discrimination, twice in November (10 and 24) 2007, the first time in a decade. They demanded the end of 'Malay privilege', as well as asking for affirmative action for the poor Malays (but not for all Malays), the protection of the Indians, and even a Royal Commission to enquire into the violation of the federal Constitution, and so on.[34] When read in conjunction with the reduced electoral strength of the BN in the last general elections held in March 2008 and the rise in strength of the minorities, the Malaysian federation faces more powerful challenges from democracy than ever before. After all, democratically speaking, identity assertions of groups for their rights and opportunities are a sign of democracy itself. The federation needs to democratize itself by paving the ground for a multicultural nation. Added to this is the issue of the right balance between the centre and the states, which is yet to be achieved. It has been observed that the extent of autonomy or rights that a state enjoys is contingent upon the extent of compatibility of the state's policy with the National Front Policy (Randhawa 2008: 28). The protection of states' rights, beyond the rights of the communities, is strategically the most vital part of federal democracy. The federal reforms that are much needed in Malaysia must pay attention to this if political equilibrium is to be maintained. The federation is to pay critical attention why of late Sabah and

202 Federalism and democracy

Sarawalk demand independence from the federation on the basis of large-scale discrimination and deprivation.

India

The key to India's claim to be the largest democracy in the world lies in the country's relatively successful experiment with federalism since 1950. And conversely, the relative success of Indian federalism has much to do with democracy, that is, democratic accommodation of identity. India's records of democracy and federalism have thus remained intertwined. The issue has, however, suffered somewhat from a double neglect in the literature on federalism as well as on democracy in India.[35] In Kohli (2001), some attention has been paid to the issue of federalism in two of the chapters, one each by J. Das Gupta and J. Manor. A more comprehensive treatment is given in Das Gupta's chapter, in which the issue of the durability of India's federal institutions has been taken up for discussion on the basis of the

> assumption that India's bold experiment of combining democratic responsiveness to cultural differences with a federal conciliation of regional community, identity, and autonomy claims and a nationally concerted promotion of regional capability, has tended to ensure a novel mode of multicultural national development.
>
> *(Das Gupta 2001: 49)*

In my own comparative study of Indian and Swiss federalism (Bhattacharyya 2001a), democracy has been taken to be central to the success of federalism as the institutional space for the reflection and promotion of the values of diversity and identity and also as the bargaining chip for accession of autonomy to aggrieved ethno-national groups. I have shown further how democratization within the Indian political system at levels below the national one has entailed recognition of identity, values and interests for both individuals and groups, which has in turn served as a connecting thread that links the local, the regional, the individual and groups to the nation. Conversely, the 'creeping authoritarianism' in the system that developed from the early 1970s up until the mid-1970s was a bad omen for both democracy and federalism. The narrow partisan politics and refusal to accommodate identity, values and interests that is one offshoot of anti-democratic politics tends to lead to disunity and secessionism in the system, as the 'Punjab problem' during the 1980s and 1990s exemplified. Conversely, restoration of democracy within the Indian political system but under a different national leadership served to restore the federal balance for national unity and integrity.[36]

The 21-month-long Emergency rule (25 June 1975 to 23 March 1977) imposed by the late Mrs Indira Gandhi, then prime minister, which cancelled both democracy and federalism, was an exception to the rule that a vast country with complex diversity and backed by historical traditions of movements for rights and liberties and democracy (1952–75) could not be governed by anything apart from federalism

Federalism and democracy **203**

and democracy. India needed both. That India holds itself together as a state and a 'nation' despite many odds, with multiple loyalties (regions, religions, languages, tribal ethnicities, or a combination thereof) which are very challenging to the development of an overarching Indian identity, is not due to military-bureaucratic command of the system or to economic prosperity (which India lacks in any way!), but a specific combination, or perhaps more appropriately, a constellation, of federalism and democracy which seeks to respond to the needs of identity, values and interests of individuals and groups by providing for the open competitive political space determined by a democratic Constitution.

Three basic propositions can thus be advanced in this connection. First, pre-Independence identity movements (anti-colonial national liberation movements), albeit within the broad contours of the Indian National Congress and under the approval of the latter, were part of democratization with the INC and were themselves democratic in content for mobilizational purposes. The Indian anti-colonial nationalist movement, as we saw in Chapter 3 of this book, could not overcome India's deep ethno-linguistic diversity but gradually settled down to utilize it and to build on it in order to reach out to the common masses, a process which has gathered special momentum since the Bolshevik Revolution (1917) and the rise to leadership of the movement of Mahatma Gandhi since the 1920s. At the Nagpur Session of the INC in 1920, the INC formally pledged itself to linguistic statehood on which to base the Indian federation after Independence.[37] This helped consolidate the party's base among the various ethno-linguistic groups. Partha Chatterjee has drawn our attention to an interesting fact not usually considered in analyzing the INC's, or more generally, the nationalist movements' newfound love for the linguistic groups (Chatterjee 2000: 74). The move was connected with the INC's own transformation from an élite organization into a masses-based party/movement under the leadership of Mahatma Gandhi. But more importantly, the linguistic groups provided the most appropriate platform for the union of nationalism and democracy in the struggle against British colonialism (Chatterjee 2000: 74). Chatterjee argues that the organizational set-up of the INC, grown in the wake of national movement, eventually turned out to be the model of Indian federalism.[38] The fact that most of these region-based linguistic identity movements were articulated in terms of national self-determination further added to the democratic character and content of such movements.[39] Sumit Sarkar, one of India's leading historians, rightly argues that federalism in India, like democracy and secularism, involved important interconnected nationalist legacies in the positive sense of the term (Sarkar 2001: 23–47). At both national and regional/local levels, the collective rights of the communities (linguistic, tribal etc.) were encouraged and supported, which acquired legitimacy in the wake of the evolving nationalist movements in India. As we will explain in the next proposition, this created an immense stock of democracy through an accommodative approach to identity.

Second, all post-Independence attempts at federalization of the polity were accompanied by democratic processes. That is, the more federal India has become the more democratic it has become, and vice versa. India's increasing federal

204 Federalism and democracy

differentiation has meant more and more democratization. Achievement of statehood at many levels of the federal polity in India, with different degrees of powers and autonomy, as a political-institutional recognition of identity in the post-Independence period was preceded by mass movements under the leadership of civil-society associations and political parties. The often long-drawn-out campaign for the recognition of identity has worked. This has entailed mass demonstrations, submission of memoranda, fasts by leaders and other democratic means of attracting governmental attention, or hard political bargaining. In any case, popular involvement in the movement for statehood has demonstrated the democratic basis of such movements and their legitimacy. Consequently, several attempts at right-sizing the federal polity had to be made so that the cultural identity of the group at issue corresponded with the political identity as far as possible.[40] Although linguistically speaking, much success has been achieved in drawing and redrawing the federal political map of India, the process is not yet complete. Gurkhas, for instance, in northern West Bengal have been campaigning rather vigorously for a state of Gurkhaland to be carved out of West Bengal. The operation of the Darjeeling Gorkha Hill Council (DGHC), a substatestructure within West Bengal since 1988 (governed by state laws), has remained the basis on which the movements for a larger political unit, statehood within the Indian federation, have been gaining strength. Other movements exist in other parts of India, demanding statehood for Telengana in Andhra Pradesh, Vidharva in Maharashtra, Harit Pradesh in Uttar Pradesh and so on.

Third, democracy has been linked to political institutionalization at each level of the polity, starting from the village level. Political governship at each level of the polity (local, regional, state and central) is a matter of political achievement. Even an otherwise militant ethnic leader has to get him- or herself elected to the governorship of the realm at some regular intervals. It may also happen that the same ethnic leader is rejected by the electorate at the next available opportunity. If this has served to legitimize identity and the need for its political institutionalization at the level where it matters most to its adherents, for the sake of protection and promotion of diversity, then this has at the same time added strength to established democratic norms. Beyond leadership, the governing body at each level, according to the Indian Constitution, is to be elected after an interval of five years on the basis of universal adult suffrage. Even a tribal council is to be elected democratically following the same procedure, as indicated earlier. The impact of such democratization on identity issues is an interesting area of research, but what is beyond doubt is that the institutional arrangements serve to undercut any fundamentalist approach to identity. Additionally, this also provides for an open space for élite competition for power and position, and also avenues for alternative mobilization utilizing aspects of identity.

Unlike Malaysia, the extension of universal adult suffrage and citizenship to all Indians alike in India at Independence and in the Constitution (1950) was not conditional. The Constitution of India does discriminate, but that is positive discrimination in favour of the socially underprivileged and aboriginal people for the sake of social justice and equity. This has served to clear the space for integration of different people into a whole. The federal democratic experience in India's multinational setting suggests that parliamentary democracy based on universal adult suffrage may not augur badly for political stability; on the contrary, it may pave the way for better articulation and accommodation of identity, given the time and space. Thus, democracy has been integrative for India.

In India's federal democracy, like any federal democracy, two types of rights are critically important: the rights of individuals and groups (civil, political, social, economic and cultural) and the states' rights, that is, the rights of the federal units to exist, to protect their identity, to promote the interests of the states and to better secure the well-being of the citizens living within the jurisdiction of the states. In India, following a different approach to federation-building (from above and below, although mostly from above), the states have been the effects of federalization rather than the other way round. Therefore, on the face of it, the Union Parliament's almost unilateral powers (under Article 3 of the Constitution) to alter the names and the boundaries of the states or to split up the existing states etc. may sound very unfederal, if not anti-federal, because this power is incompatible with the territorial integrity of the states. But, as I have argued in different places,[41] this has served better to protect diversity by according political rights and autonomy to aggrieved ethno-linguistic groups and thus added to further integration of the federation. However, due to often partisan operation, the autonomy of the state governments has been adversely affected by the application of Article 356 (president's rule), which has meant sacking of the duly elected state government run by a different political party from that of the centre on the pretext of the breakdown of constitutional machinery, as received through the report of the state governor. Das Gupta (2001) argues that, since 1950, Article 356 has been used more than 100 times in cases which did not warrant major political breakdowns in the states (Das Gupta 2001: 64). Oddly enough, the Sarkaria Commission (1983–88), appointed by the government of India for the purpose of reviewing centre–state relations, admitted that of the 75 cases of the use of Article 356, only 26 cases were said to be 'inevitable'.[42] Nonetheless, the commission did not recommend the abolition of this constitutional provision but recommended its retention for the very purpose of the federal system, with the firm belief that 'the Article 356 should remain as the ultimate constitutional weapon to cope with "secessionist situations"'.[43] The political parties also were not unanimous about the abolition of the article, although in the past the same was a demand in the recommendations and memoranda submitted by anti-Congress opposition parties, most notably the Communist Party of India (Marxists), in favour of the major revisions of centre–state relations.[44] Needless to say, Article 356, its misuse in particular, has come in for much public criticism in recent times. No wonder the issue of president's rule became a subject of scholarly debate and research (Dua 1979). The Supreme Court of India has also stepped in, and through its famous judgement in *S. R. Bommai* v. *Union of India* (1994) has brought the use of this article under judicial scrutiny, paving the way for only the judicious use of the article (Das Gupta 2001: 65). Going

206 Federalism and democracy

by this verdict of the Supreme Court of India, the rationale of the use of Article 356 is now to be construed within the ambit of the so-called basic structure of the Indian Constitution, which very much includes Indian federalism. There are recent instances when, emboldened by these developments, the former president of India, Mr K. R. Narayanan, refused to give his assent to the decision to impose president's rule in Uttar Pradesh in 1997 and Bihar in 1998 (Das Gupta 2001: 66). Nowadays, much restraint is maintained on the part of the ruling political élites in New Delhi in resorting to the use of Article 356, a factor no less significant for the recovery of overall political stability in the political system in very recent times.

The issue of president's rule (Article 356) goes beyond the mere formal discussion of federalism in India. First, while it is beyond dispute that its injudicious and politically motivated use takes away state autonomy and the rights of the states as guaranteed in the Constitution, it is inevitably linked to democracy, the democratic and to rights of the citizens living within the states so affected, who have exercised their democratic rights to form the government. Second, it is linked to the identity of a people who inhabit the affected state, who feel injured and insulted in the event of such undue interference in self-governance. The observers of Indian politics will recall how, during the 1960s and 1980s, the heydays of the use and misuse of president's rule in the states in India, opposition parties who had borne the brunt of the interfering measures by the centre would engage in a warlike tirade against the centre for revision of centre–state relations in order to do away with Article 356[45] and, more importantly, to acquire more powers for the states. In more recent times, in the wake of India's globalization since the 1990s, the states have become strategically very important in implementing globalization programmes and hence have variously asserted their identity and autonomy. The post-globalization India is held to be synonymous with the era of the states in Indian politics. The Indian states are the true strategic players in respect of implementing the agenda of globalization (that is, constitutionally, most development programmes are to be implemented in the states and under the competence of the states); the importance of the states has assumed manifold significance; and hence today their autonomy can no longer be tampered with at leisure. However, since the states are unequally placed, socially and economically, in terms of development and opportunities, the newfound freedom of action following globalization has already produced very differential impacts on the states, creating further grounds for ethnic conflicts and disunity.[46]

Finally, it must be mentioned that democracy has not been destabilizing for Indian federalism and Indian unity; on the contrary, it has served to further cohesion in the system by providing for ventilation of pent-up feelings and grievances. Democracy has offered the various identity groups in India the relative bargaining power to negotiate for power, autonomy and resources. As we have already indicated, the process of decentralization in India, of various types and at various levels, has been accompanied by democracy, so much so that the identity, interests and values at stake become the subject matter of public debate and discussion. (The relatively free press provides a platform for this.) When aggrieved and rebellious identity groups demand, for example, the application of special Constitution provisions (such as the Fifth or the Sixth Schedule of the Indian Constitution) to the cases for self-governance, and when they are successful in achieving this, that is a double victory for democracy and federalism in India via the better protection of identity[47] and integration of many such identities in the making of what Amartya Sen would call a quintessentially plural Indian identity.[48] That regionalism, tribal ethnicity, and so on have mostly been accommodated within the system is largely due to the critical role that the federal democratic constellation has played in India. But as we have seen in Introduction, India's records in meeting the *diversity-claims* are laudable, but this is a poor match to her records in meeting the *equality-claims*.[49]

Notes

1 Stepan, A. (2001) *Arguing Comparative Politics,* Oxford, Oxford University Press, p. 14. He argues that even William Riker, a classic scholar of federalism, neglected to make a distinction between democratic and non-democratic federalism (p. 18).

2 Watts (1999), p. 83. For details, see pp. 83–97.

3 Wheare (1953), p. 47. Wheare, in fact, has found good grounds for the Indian nationalists' rejection of the British colonial authorities' offer of federalism by the Government of Indian Act, 1935, which envisages, as we have seen in Chapter 3 of this book, a union of autocracies (princely States) and democracy (provinces). He further appreciated the fact that Indian leaders who drafted their Constitution in 1950 took steps 'to promote homogeneity in the political institutions of the component states in the union' (p. 47).

4 See, for instance, Karmis, D. and Norman, W. (eds) (2005) op. cit.

5 Stepan, A. (2005) 'Federalism and Democracy: Beyond the US Model' in Karmis and Norman (eds), op. cit., p. 255. Stepan had in mind the states of the former USSR, Yugoslavia and Czechoslovakia, which have given birth, he argued, to most of Europe's ethnocracies and ethnic bloodbaths (p. 256).

6 Stepan (2005), op. cit., pp. 257–258. Various institutional devices are designed to do the above job in a federation: distribution of powers between the two levels of government; and bicameral legislature with the provision for a States' chamber to protect States' rights, a Federal Supreme Court and so on.

7 I have argued along that line in my (2007c) 'Approaches to Local Government: Arguing a Case for Human Rights', *The West Bengal Political Science Review,* Vol. 2, No. 2, July-December, pp. 1–14.

8 Waseem, M. (2004) 'Pluralism and Democracy in Pakistan' in Rex, J. and Singh, G. (eds) *Governance in Multicultural Societies,* Hants, UK: Ashgate Publishing, p. 185.

9 Cheema, Iqbal P. (2000) 'Pakistan: the Challenge of Democratization' in Basta Fleiner, L. R., Bhattacharyya, H., Fleiner, T. and Mitra, S. (eds) *Rule of Law and Organization of the State in Asia: the Multicultural Challenge,* Fribourg, Switzerland: Institute of Federalism, pp. 205–235. See also Waseem (2004), op. cit.

10 Rose, Leo E. (1989) 'Pakistan: Experiments with Democracy' in Diamond, L., Linz, J. and Lipset, S. M. (eds) *Democracy in Asia,* New Delhi: Vistar Publications, pp. 105–143: p. 111. There were at least three Provincial British Governors who worked under Jinnah, the Governor-General! The trend which was set, by contrast, in India was democratic, as Jawaharlal Nehru became the Prime Minister in a parliamentary system of government elected by the people on the basis of adult suffrage (p. 111).

11 A 'State of Emergency' was proclaimed all over Pakistan by M. A. Jinnah, the then Governor-General of Pakistan, followed by the death of Jinnah on 11 September 1948, and the assassination of Liaquat Ali Khan, the Prime Minister of Pakistan on 16 October 1951. Three years later, the Constituent Assembly of Pakistan, yet to deliver the

208 Federalism and democracy

Constitution, was dissolved by the then Governor-General of Pakistan, leading to the breakdown of constitutional machinery, and a 'State of Emergency' was proclaimed throughout Pakistan on 24 October 1954. A State of Emergency was proclaimed once again on 27 March 1955. Barely less than two years after the adoption of the new Constitution on 22 February 1956, the Constitution was abrogated by Major General Iskandar Mirza as the President of Pakistan and martial law was in the country. All these events were proofs that the country's early transition to democracy during the most crucial period (1947–58) was extremely difficult, if not impossible.

12 See, for details on the official version of 'basic democracies', the 1961 'Dawn of a New Era: Basic Democracies in Pakistan', Karachi: A Government of Pakistan Publication, reprinted in Grover, V. and Arora, A. (eds) (1995a) *Political System in Pakistan: Role of Military Dictatorship in Pakistan Politics,* Vol. 10, New Delhi: Deep & Deep, pp. 479–495. We will take up them for detailed discussion later in this book.

13 Prabhu, N. R. V. and Banumathy, K. (1995) 'The Fragility of Democracy in Pakistan: Military at the Root Cause' in Grover and Arora (1995), op. cit., p. 247.

14 Quoted in Adeney, K. (2007a) 'Democracy and Federalism in Pakistan' in He, Baogang, Galligan, B. and Inoguchi, T. (eds) *Federalism in Asia,* Cheltenham, UK: Edward Elgar, p. 112.

15 Talbot, I. (2002) 'The Punjabization of Pakistan: Myth or Reality' in Jaffrelot, C. (ed.) *Pakistan: Nationalism Without a Nation?,* New Delhi: Manohar, pp. 51–63, pp. 54–55.

16 This has been so forcefully pointed out with statistical evidences by various scholars. See, for instance, Ali, T. (1983) *Can Pakistan Survive? The Death of a State,* London: Penguin; Maniruzzaman, T. (1973) 'Radical Politics and the Emergence of Bangladesh' (pp. 223–281) in Brass, P. R. and Franda, M. (eds) *Radical Politics in South Asia,* Cambridge, MA: MIT Press; Wilson, J. and Dalton, D. (eds) *The States of South Asia: the Problems of National Integration (Essays in Honour of W. H. MorrisJones),* London: Hurst & Co., chaps 2, 6, and 7.

17 Ali, M. (1982), p. 42.

18 Quoted in Kukreja, V. (2003) *Contemporary Pakistan: Political Processes, Conflicts and Crises,* New Delhi: Sage, p. 10. For a good analytical discussion of the problems of democracy in Pakistan, see chapter 1 'Struggle for Democracy: 1947 and 1971–77'.

19 Alavi, H. (1979) 'The State in Post-Colonial Societies: Pakistan and Bangladesh' in Goulbourne, H. (ed.) *Politics and State in the Third World,* London: Macmillan, pp. 38–70; See also his (1988) 'Pakistan and Islam: Ethnicity and Ideology', pp. 64–112, in Halliday, F. and Alavi, H. (eds) *State and Ideology in the Middle East and Pakistan,* London: Macmillan.

20 Adeney (2007a) tends to take such a view when she says that 'democracy would not solve the problem of federalism in Pakistan, as Punjabis, although not a monolith, are dominant in a democratic system' (p. 119).

21 Kukreja (2003), p. 89. For further details, see p. 90.

22 For a summary of the many-sided crisis in the economy, see Kukreja (2003), chapter 3 'The Political Economy: Near Brink of Collapse', pp. 75–112.

23 Jaffrelot (2002a), pp. 22–23. The table (1.2) provided on page 23 contains statistical data.

24 Ahmed, S. (2007) 'Pakistan provinces uneasy as election looms', *Federations,* Vol. 6, No. 1, February-March, p. 5.

25 The relation between federalism and welfare is a neglected area of political scientific and comparative research. See Obinger, H., Castles, F. G. and Leibfried, S. (eds) (2005) *Federalism and the Welfare State: New World and European Experience,* Cambridge: Cambridge University Press, for a pioneering work.

26 For further details on the results of elections and the factors responsible for the same, see, Loh, Francis (2008) 'Malaysia: Governing Coalition Weakened by Losses in Regions', *Federations,* Vol. 7, No. 1. June-July, pp. 28, 32.

27 See, for details, Loh, F. and Boo, K. (eds) (2002) *Democracy in Malaysia: Discourses and Practices,* Surrey, UK: Curzon Press, p. 4.

28 For full references, see, Loh and Boo (2002), p. 4. For Case (2007), see He, Baogang (2007), pp. 124–143.

29 Singh, H. (2001) 'Ethnic Conflict in Malaysia Revisited', *Journal of Commonwealth and Comparative Politics,* Vol. 39, No. 1, March, p. 45.

30 Case (2007: 138).

31 Mention may be made of the government's powers to detain persons without trial for two years on suspicion of subversion; to deny newspapers a licence to print; and to ban demonstrations in the country. The Indians in Malaysia, comprising about 8 per cent of the population, have begun to protest against lack of access to housing, civil-service jobs and places at universities due to the policy of positive discrimination for the poor Malays. (For more details, see Randhawa, S. (2008) 'Malaysian PM faces pressures from ethnic and pro-democracy forces', *Federations,* Vol. 7, No. 2, February-March, pp. 26–8.

32 Internet sources (http://asiasentinel.com, accessed 9 January 2009).

33 Internet sources (http://asiasentinel.com, accessed 8 January 2009).

34 The joke shared among the Indians in Malaysia is in this connection very suggestive of the discriminatory system: 'When it is a Malay problem, it is a National Problem; when it is a Chinese problem, it is a Racial Problem; when it is an Indian Problem, it is Not a Problem.' (Internet sources accessed 8 January 2009).

35 See, for instance, Arora, B. and Verney, D. (eds) (1995) *Multiple Identities in a Single State: Indian Federalism in Comparative Perspective,* New Delhi: Konark Publishers Pvt. Ltd; Saez, L. (2002) *Federalism without a Centre: The Impact of Political and Economic Reform on India's Federal System,* New Delhi: Sage Publications; Jayal, N. G. (ed.) (2001) *Democracy in India,* Delhi: Oxford University Press; Kohli, A. (ed.) (1998) *India's Democracy,* Princeton, NJ: Princeton University Press; Bajpai, K. S. (ed.) (2007) *Democracy and Diversity: India and the American Experience,* Delhi: Oxford University Press; and Kohli, A. (ed.) (2001) *The Success of India's Democracy,* Cambridge: Cambridge University Press.

36 The so-called 'Punjab problem' is well studied. See, for instance, Singh, G. 'Ethnic Conflict in India: the Case Study of Punjab' in McGarr, J. and O'Leary, B. (eds) (1993) *The Politics of Ethnic Conflict Regulation,* London: Routledge, pp. 84–105; Singh, G. (1996) 'Re-Examining the Punjab Problem' in Singh G and Talbot, I. (eds) *Punjabi Identity,* New Delhi: Manohar, pp. 115–138; Singh, G. (1987) 'Understanding the Punjab Problem', *Asian Survey,* Vol. 27, No. 2, pp. 1268–1277; and Brass, Paul R. (1988) 'The Punjab Crisis and the Unity of India' in Kohli, A. (ed.) (1988), op. cit., pp. 169–214.

37 See Bhattacharyya, H. (2008) 'Ethnic and Civic Nationhood in India', etc. in Saha, Santosh, C. (ed.) *Ethnicity and Socio-Political Change in Africa and Developing Countries: a Constructive Discourse in State Building,* Lanham, Lexington Books, especially section titled 'Nationalist Movement and Ethnic Identity', pp. 180–183 for a neat summary of the connection between the INC and the ethno-linguistic identity in India. For fuller details, see Bhattacharyya, H. (2001a), chap. 2 'Federalism, Diversity and Multicultural Nation-building in India', pp. 91–129; and Mukarji, N, and Arora, B. (eds) (1992) *Federalism in India: Origin and Development,* New Delhi: Vikash Publishing House Pvt. Ltd., especially chapters, 1–3.

38 Chatterjee (2000), pp. 74–75. Interestingly enough, many even today castigate regional or ethno-linguistic movements as secessionist, and hence anti-national, rather easily forgetting the immensely democratic and anti-imperialist significance of such movements in the pre-Independence period. For further details, see Chatterjee (2000), chapter 5, 'Bandhan-chhedan', pp. 69–77.

39 A limited literature is available on the historical growth of such movements. See, for instance, Bhattacharyya, H. (1989) 'The Emergence of Tripuri Nationalism 1948–50', *South Asia Research,* Vol. 9, Nos 1 and 2, May, pp. 54–72; Desai, A. R. (1946) *Social Background of Indian Nationalism,* Bombay: Popular Prakashan, pp. 381–431; Vanaik, A. 'Is There a Nationality Question?', *Economics and Political Weekly,* Vol. 22–44, 29 October 1988; and Guha, A. 'Great Nationalism, Little Nationalism and the Problem of Integration: a Tentative View' *Economics and Political Weekly,* No. 15, 14–21 June, 1980. Interestingly, Indian Communist movements, as they developed in the regions, learnt a lesson or two from the INC's approach in this regard and cultivated such movements wherever they could do so. The regional concentration of Indian communism is a proof

210 Federalism and democracy

of such historical mobilization and nurturing of the bases of support, wherever possible. See Bhattacharyya, H. (2001c) 'Indian Federalism and Indian Communism: Conflict and Collaboration', *The Indian Journal of Political Science,* Vol. 62, No. 1, March, for an overall explanation and references.

40 I have discussed this subject in detail in several places. See, for instance, Bhattach-aryya, H. (2001a), chapter 6, 'Institutional Arrangements for Minorities and the Formation of Federal Units' (pp. 235–275); Bhattacharyya (2008), pp. 169–175; Bhattacharyya, H. (2007a) 'Federalism and Competing Nations in India' (pp. 50–68) in Burgess, M. and Pinder, J. (eds) *Multinational Federations,* London: Routledge; and Bhattacharyya, H. (2005) 'Federalism and Regionalism in India: Institutional Strategies and Political Accommodation of Identity', *Heidelberg Papers in South Asian and Comparative Politics,* Working Paper No. 27, May 2005 (ISSN 1617-5069) (Online Journal: http://www.hpsacp.uni-hd.de); for more recent cases, see, Bhattacharyya, H. (2001b) 'India Creates Three New States', *Federations: What's New in Federalism Worldwide,* Vol. 1, No. 3. (Ottawa, Canada); Bhattacharyya, H. (2005) 'Forms of Multiculturalism and Identity Issues in India', *Canadian Diversity (Ottawa),* Vol. 4, No. 1, Winter; Bhattacharyya, H. (2005) 'India: Bodo People's Rights Take a Step Forward', *Federations* (Ottawa), Vol. 4, No. 3, March; and Bhattacharyya, H. (2003) 'Indian Federalism and Tribal Self-Rule', *Federations: What's New in Federalism Worldwide,* Vol. 3, No. 3, August.

41 Bhattacharyya, H. (2001a); Mitra and Bhattacharyya (2000); Bhattacharyya, H. (2005e); and Bhattacharyya, H. (2007a).

42 Quoted in Das Gupta (2001) p. 65.

43 Das Gupta (2001), p. 65.

44 See Kurian, K. M. and Varughese, P. N. (eds) (1981) *Centre-State Relations,* Delhi: Macmillan, for further details.

45 Interestingly enough, only one State government in its memorandum to the Sarkaria Commission wanted Article 356 to be abolished (Das Gupta, 2001, p. 59).

46 I have discussed this aspect in my paper 'Globalization and Indian Federalism: Re-Assertions of States' Rights' in Lofgren, H. and Sarangi, P. (eds) (2009) *The Politics and Culture and Globalization: India and Australia,* New Delhi: Social Science Press; see also Saez (2002); Rudolph, L. and Rudolph, S. (2001) 'Redoing the Constitutional Design: From an Interventionist State to a Regulatory State' in Kohli, A. (ed.) (2001); Das Gupta, J. (2001) in Kohli, A. (ed.) (2001), op. cit., pp. 49–78; Guhan, S. (2005), 'Federalism and the New Political Economy in India' in Arora, B. and Verney, D. V. (eds) *Multiple Identities in a Single State: Federalism in Comparative Perspective,* New Delhi: Konark Publishers Pvt. Ltd; Saez, L. (2002) *Federalism Without a Centre: the Impact of Political and Economic Reform on India's Federal System,* New Delhi: Sage; Dua, B. D. and Singh, M. P. (eds) (2003), *Indian Federalism in the New Millennium,* New Delhi: Manohar; Rao, M. G. and Singh, N. (2005) *The Political Economy of Federalism in India,* New Delhi: Oxford University Press; Bhambri, C. P. (2003) 'Central Government in the Age of Globalization' in Dua and Singh, (eds) (2003) *Indian Federalism in the New Millennium,* New Delhi: Manohar; Tremblay, R. C. (2003) 'Globalization and Indian Federalism' in Dua and Singh (eds) op. cit.

47 I have argued, on the basis of empirical evidence, how the institution of democratically elected Tripura Tribal Autonomous District Council (TTADC) the (1983) under the Sixth Schedule of the Indian Constitution within Tripura, a State in India's North-East, governing over two-thirds of the territory of India and containing a little over a quarter of the people, has been effective in protecting the aboriginal people in the State from their further relative decline in relation to the majority Bengalis. For further details, see my (1999) *Communism in Tripura,* Delhi: Ajanta; my (2003) 'Indian Federalism and Tribal Self-Rule', *Federations: What's New in Federalism Worldwide* (Ottawa), Vol. 3, No. 3, August 2003; and my (2005b) 'India: Bodo People's Rights Take a Step Forward', *Federations: What's New in Federalism Worldwide* (Ottawa), Vol. 4, No. 3, March.

48 He has written on Indian identity in many places. See, for instance, his classic, Sen, A. (2005) *The Argumentative Indian: Writings on Indian Culture, History and Identity*, London: Penguin; and Sen, A. (2006) *Identity and Violence: the Illusion of Destiny*, London: Allen Lane.

49 Nepal and Myanmar are not taken up here for their role in democracy because it is too early to comment on them. These are what Breen called 'aspirational'. Despite the elections in Myanmar, the military still holds considerable clout in the state.

CONCLUSION

Beyond the diversity problematic

Introduction

From the foregoing it is seen that all five cases surveyed in this book have been marked by complex cultural diversity, based on community identity, language, religion, (aboriginal) tribal affiliations and region, or a combination of them. The issue of diversity has been of particular significance in Nepal because of two reasons. First, there were no pre-existing ethno-regional units to bank on. Second, culture and territory do not correspond, so subnational federal units are necessarily multi-ethnic, with no ethnic majority to dominate the others, which may turn out, if so willed, to be a desirable model of ethnic moderation and multicultural nationhood. In Myanmar, as Breen (http://50shadesoffederalism.com/case-studies/the-federalism-debates-in-nepal-and-myanmar-from-ethnic-conflict-to-secession-risk-management/, accessed 18 December 2019) has pointed out, most ethnic minorities are territorially rooted, and except a few, there are many relatively smaller ones within the large ethnic regions, and many such groups have been recognized at the level of the self-administered zones – which demand separate states of their own too. For instance, the Shan state is also inhabited by many non-Shan ethnic groups; in Kachin State, there are many small ethnic minorities too. There are arguments also in favour of merging the regions populated by the Bamars so that there is one large province for the Bamars. While the Bamars may not like such a proposal, other ethnic groups demand ethnic equality irrespective of their numbers. The founding father of modern Myanmar, also the father of Aung San Su Kyi, Aung San, stressed the point of ethnic equality way back in 1947 in the first Panglong conference. That was never implemented. In the federations studied here, this has obviated the need for meeting the *diversity-claims* for political order and stability – the central concern why federalism was considered as an important option. In the case of Malaysia, the communal diversity

Conclusion **213**

in population corresponds with racial divisions: the Malay, the Chinese and the Indians. Added to that is the *orang asli* (aboriginals) in Sabah and Sarawak whose racial stock is different from that of the rest. In the case of India, racial dimensions are pronounced in the case of its aboriginal people, particularly in the North East. In Nepal, the seven provinces mentioned in the Constitution (2015) had to be, for the reasons already indicated, numbered. The three provinces named since 2015 cannot be called ethnic provinces, for it was a combination of geography, language and resources that were taken into account. Nonetheless, varied, multi-layered arrangements were devised in Nepal's Constitution for meeting the *diversity-claims*. In Myanmar, the Bamars (68 per cent of the population) control the state and economy and inhabit the central and southern plains, while the ethnic minorities live mostly in the hills in the east, north and west. In all cases, there is a preponderance of regional rootedness for most types of diversity, except for religion. In Malaysia, the majority Malays (who again are mostly Muslims) live in Peninsular Malaysia; the Chinese are spread all over the country, but predominate in one state, namely, Penang (in Peninsular Malaysia); and the aboriginal people predominate in Sabah and Sarawak, two Borneo states. The Indians are the sole exception, as they do not have any regional concentrations but are widespread all over the country. In Pakistan, since the inception of the republic (1947), the ethno–linguistic communities have remained mostly regionally rooted. In Malaysia, Islam, the official religion of the federation, has remained a very important defining element of Malay identity. However, in Pakistan, which is also an Islamic republic with an overwhelmingly Muslim majority (although there are different, often conflicting, sects within this majority), the Islamic identity has been dwarfed by sharper ethnic differences based on secular markers. In India, religion has not been accepted as the legitimacy basis of claiming political identity, so that in the ongoing process of creation of federal units since Independence (in order to accommodate ethno-regional/national identity), religion has not been allowed to play any role (Punjab in 1966 being the sole exception, in which case a combination of language and religion was broadly considered). In both India and Pakistan, aboriginal tribes people are also regionally concentrated. Linguistic differences are also quite sharp in all federations except Myanmar; it is most anomalous in Pakistan, where Urdu, the official and national language of the state, is spoken by not more than 7 per cent of the population (2 per cent at the time of founding of the republic). For the people at large, or the children, Urdu is like a foreign language to be learnt. In India and Pakistan, ethno–national ('subnational') movements have remained strong, claiming recognition, autonomy and power. In India, their number has decreased as a result of continuous accommodation; in Pakistan, they remain rebellious. Malaysia does not seem to have any, since such forces were already accommodated in successive federalization since colonial times. In Malaysia, a federal coalition (BN) ruled over the federation for decades since 1957, but since 2008 its electoral position has been relatively weakened, and in 2018 elections it was ousted from power by the opposition, a coalition led by the Pakatan Harapan party under the leadership of the former Prime Minister Mahathir Mohamed, aged 92. But this does not

214 Conclusion

make much change insofar as the Malay hegemony over Malaysia is concerned. In post-split Pakistan (post-1971), the Punjabis have turned out to be predominant, whereas in India, the federal system is plural and does not provide for any ethnic suzerainty. The Hindi speakers in India are a divided lot in many different ways, and the Hindus in India do not speak the same language and do not have the same cultural practices throughout India. Various forms of cultural diversity in India, Pakistan, Malaysia, Nepal and Myanmar, as mentioned earlier, have been a menable to federal solutions, both territorial and consociational, although not in equal measure and to a level that will always maintain political equilibrium. Of the five, Nepal is clearly a transitional federation, but Myanmar is still a static and precarious one.

Although conceptually and institutionally derivative, federalism in the five countries (except Nepal) was familiar to the founding political élites by the time of independence and was quite a nationalist legacy too, at least for India and Malaysia, and for Myanmar to a limited extent. Various political movements, parties and alliances that developed in India and Malaysia during the colonial period variously represented strands for federal solutions to the problem of accommodation. The political leadership that headed those political formations was federalist and respectful of diversity and heterogeneity while emphasizing unity at the same time, reminiscent of the classical nationalist ideology of building nations by uniting disparate elements (Hobsbawm 1992). The limited political-institutional space being made increasingly available within the colonial state was utilized, which served to offer experiences in governance at the regional level. Pakistan in this respect was not as lucky, however. While its leadership, both at its foundations and, more recently, focused on federalism in order to unite its unavoidable diversity (ethno-regional/nationalist), its simultaneous and central emphasis on Islam (which, doctrinally does to seem to promote differences!) as the unifying force, undercuts the claims of ethno-regional/nationalist identity, which are many and very powerful. Jinnah's theory of building a strong state on the basis of the three-fold principle of 'one nation, one culture and one language' and his assumption of the position of governor-general of the Republic apparently did not bequeath a sound federal legacy for postcolonial Pakistan. For Nepal, federalism was foreign, as an idea and institution, and the public discourse on the subject was only about one decade and a half old beginning from the 1990s. However, the Maoists and various other Marxists parties which brought about the revolution in 2006 have finally settled down for federalism with a pronounced inclusive orientation. In Nepal, social discrimination and exploitation entailed social and cultural diversity issues, which the Maoists could not ignore.

Meeting the *diversity-claims* would not mean much without recognition, territory and powers. Federalism stands for power-sharing among different tiers of government and ethnic groups in cases. As regarding the institutions of power-sharing between the tiers of government, India and Malaysia defined the terms of power-sharing between the federal and constituent levels quite early on and adhered to it more or less successfully. However, Pakistan had experienced problems of doing so, having fallen victim to military dictatorship early on, which stood

Conclusion **215**

in the way of consolidation of the federation. The secession of its eastern wing, which culminated in the rise of Bangladesh in 1971, was the inevitable outcome. Both India and Malaysia were able to devise various institutional means of accommodation of diversity, territorial and non-territorial, and the attendant power-sharing at different levels of the polity, as well as adaptation of the federal idea to local traditions and conventions. As I have explained elsewhere, the Indian case of federalism represents a *hybrid solution* to the problem of order and political stability (Bhattacharyya 2016: 72–85). In Pakistan, some accommodation was made in the post-split period, when a four-unit federation was formed. But a major reform in federalism in Pakistan had to wait many decades: the 18th Amendment in 2010 provided for the restoration of democracy (parliamentary) and instituted radical devolution of powers to the province hitherto unheard of in any federation. However, the devolution has yet to be implemented (discussed in Chapter 8). Pakistan has also recognized for the first time the ethnic identity of the Pasto speaking people of the erstwhile North-West Frontier Province, now rechristened (since 2010) Khyber Pakhtunkhwa. In Nepal, the power-sharing arrangements are elaborate and the federation is made out to be inclusive and decentralized. The three tiers of government have been assigned powers and responsibilities by three lists. In Myanmar there are also constitutional distributions of powers between Union, state/region and local governments of many kinds, although the Union is heavily powerful, constitutionally speaking. It is designed as a parliamentary system with a very strong president, though.

In India, meeting the *diversity-claims* has been reflected even in the distribution of revenues among the tiers of government, so that the changing formula of distribution of finances between the federal and state governments reflects the concern for diversity of the regions. There are provisions for special grants and special-category states status (for economically backward states) which received a liberal unconditional central funding.

However, Malaysia remains highly centralized as compared to India, because the central government in the former not only collects most taxes but also spends most (84 per cent). In India, the Union government collects most taxes but spends 44.6 per cent, leaving the rest to the state governments. In India again, the states' revenue expenditure has always been higher than that of the Union, and the states' share of combined public expenditure also remains higher than that of the centre. Till 2014–17, while the Union's share was about 45 per cent, it was 55 per cent for the states (Reddy and Reddy 2019: 233). This added fiscal stability to the federation and made the federation more decentralized when coupled with the provision that the states implement their own laws as well as many central laws. In India, again, the quantum of devolution to the states from various sources has not been affected by the apparent political centralization of powers at the centre.[1] The Fourteenth Finance Commission (2014–19) doubled the states' share from 32 per cent to 42 per cent, which ensures better financial stability to the federation. However, there is doubt if the Finance Commissions can remain impartial and not politicized. (Reddy and Reddy 2019: 48) for long.

216 Conclusion

The introduction of GST in India in 2016 has been a major reform in Indian fiscal federalism in respect of indirect taxes. A GST council (a recommending body) has been formed with all chief ministers of the states as members under the chairmanship of the Union finance minister; so far the new system is said to have worked well, although there many challenges. (Reddy and Reddy 2019: 174–5) Reddy and Reddy argue that the GST council has strengthened Indian fiscal federalism by 'reducing the transaction cost of bargaining and conflict resolution' between the Union government and the states. (Reddy and Reddy 2019: 149)

The institutional arrangements of federalism in Pakistan and Malaysia show that they inequitably but definitely benefit the dominant ethno-national community – the Punjabis in Pakistan,[2] and the Malays in Malaysia. In Myanmar, it does so for the Bamars. This is somewhat inherent in meeting the *diversity-claims* in federation when not accompanied by the provision for meeting the *equality-claims*. In India, no such scenario is evinced at the national level, where the system is not biased towards any particular community. But India's federal success has not been without flaws (Bhattacharyya 2019b; Adeney and Bhattacharyya 2018) and not matched by its democratic success in meeting the *equality-claims*, to generate more equality, as I have been arguing. Its overall performance in the World Human Development Report (2019) places it with a rank of 129 (as medium human development), out of 183 countries, and Pakistan with 152, but Malaysia is ranked in the very high human development category, with a rank of 61. India's large population may be a factor, but then Brazil (another BRICS country like India), with a large population, is ranked 79, among the very high human development category, in which 116 countries figure. In India, at the state level, the scenario may be different, since the states, created as they were on the basis of some ethnic identity, are dominated by one or the other ethno-regional identity groups (dominant castes too). Most of the states, although ethnically heterogeneous in nature, are dominated by some ethno-regional/national groups. Be that as it may, this is still a little too far short of meeting the appropriate *equality-claims* –for redistribution of resources; generation of income for the underprivileged sections; gender equality; creation of work; and access to health care facilities, education, electricity, sanitation and so on.

The existing writings on federalism have not adequately highlighted the need for democracy for smooth federal functioning. Democracy is useful to federalism in many ways and most essential for adequately maintaining cultural diversity. As part of meeting the *diversity-claims*, identity recognition and accommodation is a democratic achievement connected as it is with the people's need for protection of identity and value of dignity. Democracy also prevents ethnicization (when a particular ethnic group becomes the *staatsvolk* (McGarry and O'Leary 2007: 180–212) (a dominant national group claiming to own the federation). Conversely, federalism also fosters democracy in a diverse country by providing for the political expression of dissent and difference. Comparatively speaking, it is democracy whose presence has ensured the success of federations in India and Malaysia (in terms of power-sharing and in other respects too), while in Pakistan, the federal failure was largely and very substantively a democratic failure in both senses of the term – meeting the *diversity-claims* and *equality-claims*. In Pakistan, even during the very short period of Jinnah's governor-generalship, the foundation of authoritarianism was laid. In India, by contrast, Nehru began experimenting with a parliamentary democratic and federal regime accompanied by state welfares in an economy dominated by the public sector. The Malaysian leadership also did not deviate from the federal democratic experiment begun in the colonial period and actually improved upon it in fact in the post-Independence period by extending political enfranchisement to all communities and by recognizing some fundamental rights of both the individuals and the groups, although not in equal measure for the smaller minorities such as the Indians and the *orang asli*. Pakistan also provided a major illustration of the fact that democracy (i.e. the majoritarian-parliamentary type) alone is not guarantee enough for the minorities, because in a country that is dominated by one community (the Punjabis after the split), democracy tends to translate into majority rule by that community. Democracy therefore needs to be conjoined to other safeguards such as minority veto-powers, special protection of the rights of the states through the upper chamber of Parliament and so on. But in Pakistan, under successive bouts of military dictatorship, even the minimum democratic space for the minorities could not be utilized by those minorities. Democratic regimes that alternated between the dictatorships had little effective space for redress. In India, except during the 21 months of Emergency rule (1975–77), a more or less liberal democratic regime has been the rule rather the exception, and the fundamental rights of individuals and groups (relating to identity, liberty, redistribution and equality, etc.) have been given constitutional protection and institutionalized in political practices at many levels of the polity. India's democratization has also done away with traditional sources of authority in favour of a modern secular authority based on achievement rather than ascription. Increasing differentiation in India's federal system since 1950s has been informed by identity recognition as well as by democracy. This has served, in effect, to produce more legitimacy for the system. However, in redistributive terms, democracy has not fared that well in either the Indian or the Malaysian federation, because federal democracy in both has not resulted in removing the large-scale social and economic exclusion (and political, to some extent, too) suffered by the smaller minorities and the downtrodden sections in all communities. Pakistan, in this regard, pales into insignificance. This points our attention to the question of meeting the *equality-claims*.

Constitutionally, as well as in practice, all five federations except Nepal are highly centralized. This has affected the mode of centre–state/provincial relations. In Pakistan, a centralized federal government, when dominated by the military-bureaucracy combine, has almost foreclosed any relation between the centre and the provinces, for a long time pushing the minority-inhabited provinces onto the path of insurgency and rebellion. The situation has been abated to some extent, of late, by devolution of resources to the provinces and co-optation of minority ethnic elements into the state's strategic organs (Adeney 2007b), strengthened further by the 18th Amendment Act (2010). But, again, due to ethno-national considerations, the smaller ethno-national communities have found no reasons to consider

218 Conclusion

the centre as an honest broker, because behind the central powers lurk the dominant Punjabi interests. The military-bureaucratic-led centre thus remained insensitive to the other ethno-national concerns and freely encroached upon provincial rights. In terms of finances, population size remained for a long time the sole criterion of the quantum of devolution to the provinces, which inevitably favoured Punjab. It was only very recently, in 2006–7, that backwardness as a criterion was also taken into consideration.

Of the five federations, Malaysia remains the most centralized constitutionally as well as in practice. The federation collects most of the taxes and also spends most of them, unlike in India and Pakistan. The centre's list of constitutionally allotted powers is also quite lengthy. The UMNO-led BN as a federal coalition (or a 'grand coalition') of ethnic communities-based parties/associations (though not of the states) had until 2008 enjoyed a more than two-thirds majority in Parliament and freely amended the Constitution in matters adversely affecting the federal principle (e.g. the composition of the second chamber of Parliament). The centre's partisan action towards the states run by non-BN governments and other instances of encroachment into the states' rights have meant that the states have been vocal of late for their rights, cutting across ethnic and ideological lines; regionalism has grown in some peninsular states too. While the old multi-ethnic compromise (BN) has ensured Malayan domination in the federation, the federation pact has not considered non-Malay, non-Muslim and non-Chinese ethnic groups who have also become assertive (Shafruddin 1988). In May 2018, the UMNO-led BN was ousted from power by the opposition. This very effective challenge to the UMNO-dominated BN by the opposition signals among others that there is a need for repairing and improving upon the federal design and principle adopted in the country.

Unlike Malaysia and Pakistan, India's originally highly centralized federation has been in practice, and administratively, decentralized, given the growing ethno-national pressures from below for recognition of identity, autonomy and power and hence for further federalization. Unlike the other two federations, no single dominant ethno-national group has been able to dominate the federation, although, as in the other two cases, ethno-national concerns have remained at the heart of centre–state relations and conflicts in India too. This picture has changed rather dramatically with the rise of the centre-right Hindutva party (*Bharatiya Janata* Party or BJP); the BJP ran a coalition at the centre between 2014–19 and was returned with a much larger majority in 2019. This has raised genuine concerns about the fate of the federation, for this party believes in a unitary state, one nation, one state and one culture, and is ideologically committed to a Hindu *rashtra* – an oxymoron of sorts! In India, the states have significant powers on their own (via the State List), and enjoy powers while implementing many federal legislations apart from their own. The states have since long have joined hands to fight against the centre for revision of centre–state relations and for a more federal India. As regards the distribution of financial powers, India has followed an evolving set of criteria that have taken into consideration the true diversity of the country. The federal government has taken institutional measures for reviewing centre–state relations (in 1983, then again in 2007). Thus, in practice, the states have real, significant powers. Since 1991, when India adopted neoliberal reforms, the states have been given more freedom of action and autonomy, not legislatively but by the fiat of executive federalism. It was realized since the mid-1990s that the states had to be taken on board, because it was in the states and through the states that a globalization-propelled development agenda was to be implemented (Bhattacharyya 2009: 99–112). Many states in India have made good use of this new-found power and autonomy and developed themselves, although there are many laggards for a variety of reasons.

In both India and Malaysia, 'integrated political parties' have been instrumental in working out the federations, while the sudden absence of the same in Pakistan immediately after the rise of the state has to a large extent served to explain why the federation failed to put down roots in Pakistan. 'Integrated parties' nation-wise have been conducive to federal stability in India and Malaysia, but in Pakistan a true federal party system with 'integrated parties' is yet to take shape. In the last general election held in 2017, the PTI got the majority at the centre and Punjab; PPP controlled Sindh; KPK in Khyber Pakhtunkhwa; and the Baluch regional parties controlled Baluchistan. This is a major structural limitation to the further development of federalism in Pakistan. In India, the once highly integrated Congress Party, which since pre-Independence days had served as a kind of federal political platform for the evolving federation for future India, disintegrated since the late 1960s, paving the way for the rise to prominence of regional/state parties, which have been playing an important role in the national policy formation by being part of the national-level coalition governments since the late 1980s. This has not been a problem for Indian federalism. On the contrary, it has created better prospects for Indian federalism by offering the states the scope for negotiation for participation, autonomy and power. Also, since the INC was historically a 'party of parties' or a 'coalition of state parties', many state parties (e.g. the Trina Mul Congress, TMC) are breakaway groups from the INC. In Malaysia, the BN at both the federal and state levels acts as the federal political coalition of communal interests and as a major factor of integration in the federation. In Pakistan, by contrast, the Muslim League, which had defended the case for a federal Pakistan, had almost disappeared after 1947, and, in any case, has few or no bases in the provinces in today's Pakistan. Therefore, unlike the two success stories, the Pakistan federation here suffers from a congenital defect in not having a truly national/federal political party(ies). As the latest electoral data (Table 5.1) show, political parties in Pakistan are all province- and ethno-regionally/nationally based. In Nepal the Nepali Congress and the Maoists and other Marxist parties represent two truly national level parties situated ideologically at two opposed ends, and the Constitution of Nepal has provide for a multi-party democratic federal system. A multi-party electoral competition is also allowed by the Constitution of Myanmar (2008). As of now, the only national-level party is the NLD, led by Aung San Suu Kyi; however, the party has yet to develop its roots and branches all over the country.

In respect of decentralization, and that too being federal and democratic, India stands head and shoulders above the other cases surveyed with regard to achieving

220 Conclusion

successes in institutionalizing grassroots democratic bodies, constitutionally guaranteed, particularly since 1993, and entrusted with delivering a number of services (e.g. social well-being and empowerment) to the citizens at the locality, and also as the means of fulfilling demands for identity. In all the federations, decentralization has been provided in the constitutions as state competence. In Pakistan, the first non-party 'elections' to such bodies, under a military regime and by bypassing the provincial autonomy, were held in 2000, and then again in 2005. If and when the mandate in the 18th Amendment (2010) is realized to its full potential, the prospects for sub-province level decentralization will be better. However, local government elections have taken place in Khyber Pakhtunkhwa on 30 May 2015; in Baluchistan on 7 December 2013; Punjab on October–December 2015; and Sindh on 5 December 2015. So a modest beginning has been made to introduce directly elected local governments, urban and rural, in Pakistan post-2010. Their success would obviously depend on the sustenance of the democratic process in the provinces and Pakistan generally.

In Malaysia, nominated (by the ruling BN coalitions) local bodies have been functioning since 1976. And yet the new expanding role of such bodies is recognized in the country in the wake of globalization and rapid urbanization. Also, the poor-quality service delivery and leadership at the local level in Malaysia and the widespread public criticisms of the same indicates the relative lack of local-level mass support for the system. In India, decentralization of many kinds has offered the spaces for articulation of local and regional interests at the base of the system, and the relatively successful functioning of such bodies, despite many limitations, has contributed to the constellation of a multilayered federalism and nationhood. The federally sponsored social and economic empowerment programmes in India, for instance, to be implemented by the state governments and the decentralized democratic bodies, at once link the national, state and local in mutual interdependence and reciprocity and serve to dissipate centrifugal political tendencies.

In a very small but perceptive essay titled 'Federalism in Asia: the Potential and the Limits', Ronald Watts (2000) emphasizes that 'federal systems can take different forms' and also that 'the applicability of federalism to a specific situation may depend upon the particular form of federalism as upon federalization in general' (Watts 2000: 1). In drawing some lessons out of the comparative study of federalism in Asia, Watts's suggestion about the variety of forms of federalism and the specific application of the same to specific situations is of seminal importance. Before proceeding any further, we will remind ourselves of the basic impulse that had driven the political élite in these countries towards federalism: the imperative need for uniting disparate elements within a single polity, essentially the task of nation-state-building in the countries under conditions of very complex diversity in the postcolonial period after the Second World War. In this respect, India and Malaysia represent the success stories of federalism (India being more successful than Malaysia), while post-split Pakistan is a case of relative failure. However, post-split Pakistan has not experienced any further territorial disintegration so far, although the potentialities are there. As Adeney (2007a) has shown, some devolution to the

Conclusion **221**

provinces and limited co-optation of the minorities into the state structure have served to pave the way towards some co-existence, which can be broadened by sustained democratization and the willingness on the part of the powers-that-be, and more particularly the majority community, to mutually recognize each other. Pakistani scholars have pointed out the persistent failure of Pakistan to accommodate diversity, which is emblematic:

> Yet as an independent nation, Pakistan largely ignored the social diversity of its people, and the economic disparity of its regions. It constructed a national ideology based on a mechanical nation of unity and simplistic ideas of cultural homogeneity. This neglect of social diversity and disregard of ethnic and regional interests have exacted a heavy cost from Pakistan.
>
> *(Ahmed, F. 1998)*

F. Ahmed's (1998) further poignant remark in this connection is worth quoting:

> The state and its ideologues have steadfastly refused to recognize the fact that these regions are not mere chunks of territory with different names but areas which were historically inhabited by people who had different languages and culture, and even states of their own.
>
> *(Ahmed, F. 1998)*

The message contained in these passages is indicative of the strategic failure in federation-building under conditions of sociocultural diversity (particularly that which is regionally rooted) in a mode reminiscent of the state-building efforts of the classical variety in such countries as France, Italy and the United Kingdom. Historically speaking, homogenizing nation-states were built in the West in predominantly unitary modes of state-building that largely disregarded diversity – in fact an attempt was made to submerge diversity (Anderson 1979; Giddens 1985; Oommen 2004). By contrast, the federal method was adopted in the Asian countries such as India and Pakistan in order to serve, so as to speak, an opposite purpose. The federal solution typically entails, as Watts has cautioned us, the 'accommodation of multicultural groups within a polity', 'the rule of law, acceptance of multiple loyalties on the part of citizens, and the view that unity and diversity are not mutually contradictory' (Watts 2000: 4). It can thus be seen that the federal solution is not a particularly easy one; on the contrary, it is a difficult solution. But then it was unavoidable in nation- and state-building efforts in these countries, given the particular contexts. To extend the lesson for other Asian countries, the federal solution remains unavoidable because, first, homogenizing nation- and state-building are no longer acceptable and in fact much condemned; and second, in the rights-sensitive age we are living in, the massive violation of human rights that such homogenizing efforts would involve is also not acceptable legally, morally and politically.

It is to be recognized that federation-building in diverse societies inevitably involves power-sharing with territorially rooted communities as well as various

222 Conclusion

consociational arrangements of power-sharing. It also involves a politics of difference/recognition, not only territorially but also non-territorially and symbolically. In India, for instance, the provisions for officially recognizing languages and placing them under the Eighth Schedule of the Indian Constitution as 'official languages' of the Union have served to contain much of the ethno-linguistic tensions. Ethnonational chauvinism of the majority community, if there is any, is most likely to harm federalism; an ethnic majority must learn to mutually recognize identities and to co-exist with the smaller minorities within a single polity. (Bhattacharyya 2019b) This is particularly relevant for the transitional, or what is termed the second and third generation federations. (Breen 2017)). Nepal has made a robust beginning to an inclusive federalism; Myanmar's federalism has yet to be sustained in practice, because ethnic minorities' 'union' with the Union remains largely unresolved.

Our study shows that in Pakistan and Malaysia, for different reasons, federations have favoured the dominant ethno-national community, which is unhealthy for the further development of the federation because the smaller communities feel marginalized. If this sharpens, then the loyalty to the federation weakens at the cost of the regional, local identities. As I have argued elsewhere (Bhattacharyya 2007a, 2007b), in complex sociocultural diversity, federation-building and nation-building may not be contradictory to each other provided that both the civic (federalism) and ethnic elements are appropriately combined to clear the space for a nationhood which is an 'ethno-civic space' (Bhattacharyya 2008).

Finally, in the theoretical discourse on federalism, the very important question that has remained unaddressed concerns *what federalism does*. To be more specific, does it produce enough democracy? What does it do for meeting what I have termed the *equality-claims*: social and economic redistribution; income equalization; access to health, education, sanitation and electricity, employment and so on for the socially and economically underprivileged? Meeting *diversity-claims*, as we have pointed out earlier, is necessary in a multicultural social context but not enough to sustain a federation for long, for while that resolves the categorical conflicts, the distributional conflicts may remain as the potent source of further conflicts. In a recent research article (Bhattacharyya 2015, 2019a), I have shown how the otherwise 'successful' federations (including those in the West) have performed very poorly on meeting the *equality-claims* in federalism in Asia. The empirical researches have shown that although the Malays are over-represented in the governing system, most of the poor and insecure in the country are the Malays. (Zawawi 1989) Fenton has found areas of deprivation in and around Kuala Lumpur (Fenton 2004: 148). There is a strong undercurrent among the so-called *orang asli* in Sabah and Sarawak in Malaysia about whether to stay with the federation or demand independence, given the unfair deal they receive from Kuala Lumpur (Bhattacharyya 2019a). The Indian communities have remained mostly marginalized. In Pakistan, the majority of people are very poor. The majority of the Punjabis also remain poor and do not benefit particularly from federalism, i.e. the Punjabi domination over the federation. Anwar Shah (1997) argued that Pakistan ranked among the worst performers among a sample of some 80 countries in terms (among others) of distributive justice. In India, despite decades of democracy and federalism, poverty, malnutrition, illiteracy and lack of access to opportunities are abysmally high among the overwhelming majority of people. In other words, the majority suffer from manifold social and economic exclusion in India (Bhattacharyya *et al.* 2010; Oxfam 2019). The point that is being made here is the delivery aspects and social-welfarist content of federalism. Federalism may be unavoidable in countries marked by sociocultural diversity. However, federalism is not the panacea for all ills. For instance, ethno-linguistic/regional boundaries of the newly created federal units in India since the 1950s resolved, by and large, ethno-linguistic conflicts, but they have served to intensify caste (and also class) conflicts within the new boundaries, because the newly created federal units have mostly benefited the dominant castes to the exclusion of the downtrodden within the castes and beyond. Thus, federal solutions, typically, attend to categorical conflicts but not distributional conflicts. The problem has been hinted at in the new research on federalism (Obinger *et al.* 2005) published in *Federalism and the Welfare State*, in which various dimensions of the relation between social policy and federalism, paying particular attention to the impact of globalization, have been analyzed. The editors have rightly argued that 'in multiethnic federations, social policy may serve as the cement for reducing the depths of political cleavages' (Obinger *et al.* 2005: 6). In this context, the role of the welfare state assumes added importance. It may help generate mass loyalty to the polity by contributing to the containment or reduction of centrifugal forces that seek to endanger social and political cohesion (Obinger *et al.* 2005: 6). The success of federalism in India has to answer the question as to why there is abysmal inequality and discrimination in the country. Why is it that the top 1 per cent of the people now control over 51 per cent the nation's wealth in India? Why is that the bottom 60 per cent of the population own only about 5 per cent of the nation's wealth? The Oxfam Inequality Report concluded:

> Similarly, in India, wealth inequality is on the rise. The Gini wealth co-efficient in India has gone up from 81.2% in 2008 to 85.4% in 2018, which shows inequality has risen. Rising inequality threatens the social fabric of the nation. Inequitable growth provides fuel for social unrest and rising crime. In the last 12 months, the total wealth of India has increased by US$151 billion (INR 10591 billion). Wealth of the top 1% increased by 39% whereas wealth of bottom 50% increased by a dismal 3%.
>
> *(Oxfam 2019)*

The macro level inequality and socio-economic discrimination in India is variously experienced in the states where the existing caste discriminations have been further reinforced by the sharp inequalities following India's neoliberal reforms since the early 1990s. Most of India's so-called forward states in terms of attracting investment, indigenous and foreign, have made remarkable progress in infrastructural development but could not avoid the experiences of growing inequality. The available recent researches strongly suggest that the socially underprivileged

224 Conclusion

sections (*dalits*; tribes; some OBCs) have been the worst victims. To cite an odd example, Kerala in India's south, globally known for its good social development indicators but without much growth and its left politics, today has shown higher growth records but also a high degree of inequality (HDI) (Sreraj and Vamsi 2016). Other researchers have shown that since the 1990s, Kerala has experienced a sharp rise in wealth inequality (Yadu 2017). However, Kerala's record should not be blown out of proportion because the state's ranking in HDI and IHDI (UNDP 2011) was number 1. However, Kerala was in the same league as other advanced states of India such as Maharashtra, Andhra Pradesh and Gujarat, where growth has taken place, but their records in respect of the rule of law index are appalling. Andhra Pradesh shows a decline from an index value (in respect of Rule of Law) of 0.124 in 1981 to 0.084 in 2011; Maharashtra 0.80 in 1981 to 0.100 in 2011 and Gujarat 0.119 to 0.081 in 2011 (Mitra and Bhattacharyya 2018: 241. In Kerala from 1991, the records of the rule of law index showed decline: 0.163 (1991); 0.102 (2001) and 0.067 in 2011 (Malhotra 2014: 149–50). Such apparently unpalatable data suggest the democratic deficit, the relative failures in meeting the *equality-claims* of the citizenry.

In Pakistan, the picture is abysmal. H A Pasha pinpointed that there top 1 per cent of the people own 20 per cent of the farmland (in this predominantly agricultural country); the top 20 per cent own 69 per cent of the farm land; and 40 per cent people live in poverty in a society where feudalism still exists, and where no land reforms have taken place since (www.fes-connect.org/people/growth-and-inequality-in-pakistan/, accessed 17 December 2019). The *Express Tribune* noted editorially with indignation:

> Income and wealth inequality in Pakistan is from top to bottom. Only 22 persons in the country have billions of wealth and reserves. The rest spend their life in hunger and poverty. Education and health infrastructures are on the verge of collapse. Institutions are rotten. Moral and ethical values are decaying.
>
> (*The* Express Tribune, *September 19, 2017 Editorial; https://tribune.com.pk/story/1509963/rising-inequality-pakistan/, accessed 15 December 2019*).

This is the logical fall out in a federation based on feudalism, where federal design problems, i.e., the *diversity-claims*, are not a major issues because the four provinces were pre-existing, although without autonomy, and the remaining issues of diversity accommodation are resolvable. It is the democratic aspect, or the grotesque failure of it, that produces so much inequality.

Now that parliamentary democracy has been 'restored' in Pakistan, the major test for federalism in Pakistan would be to generate more equality in the social and economic realms and alleviate poverty for the vast majority of the poor sections of society among all regionally rooted ethnic groups via the successful implementation of the major devolution provided for in the 18th Amendment to the

Constitution Act (2010). The said devolution so far has remained mired in institutional quagmires.

Intriguingly, but happily, the Malaysian federation is Malay dominated and very centralized, but it has alleviated poverty to a major extent. The official data suggest that poverty has almost been eradicated from around 50 per cent people under poverty line income in 1970 to 3.6 per cent in 2014. (Nair and Sugarnan 2015) Officially, it is claimed that there has been a 33 times increase in income of the households since 1970 (Nair and Sugarnan 2015). There is, however, scholarly dispute about the base line of poverty as determined by the government. But on the whole poverty performance in Malaysia is very satisfactory. This holds an important lesson for other federations like India, Pakistan, Nepal and Myanmar, which are still struggling to find ways of removing poverty for decades. At the same time, it raises the question of effectiveness of federalism and democracy in India and reinforces my argument about the need for meeting the *equality-claims*, for, if the diversity accommodation is not accompanied by adequate provisions for meeting the *equality-claims*, the political equilibrium that federalism is supposed to bring about and maintain will falter. The issue is more poignant in the days of neoliberal reforms, and a market-driven growth model, which are less likely to generate more equality.

Notes

1 This Special Category States Status is said to have since 2014 been withdrawn by the Central government headed by PM N Modi along with the abolition of the Planning Commission, and the National Development Council. The Structure has been replaced by the NITI Aayog. But scholars are not sure about this (Raddy and Reddy 2019).
2 With the introduction of GST in 2016 the picture has changed for the better for the States too.

BIBLIOGRAPHY

Adeney, K. (2007a) 'Democracy and Federalism in Pakistan', in He, Baogang, Galligan, B. and Inoguchi, T. (eds) *Federalism in Asia*, Cheltenham: Edward Elgar, pp. 101–23.

Adeney, K. (2007b) *Federalism and Ethnic Conflict Regulation in India and Pakistan*, New York: Macmillan.

Adeney, K. and Bhattacharyya, H. (2018) 'Current Challenges to Multinational Federalism in India', *Regional and Federal Studies*, Vol 28, No. 4 (Online).

Ahmar, M. (2019) 'Conflict Prevention and the New Provincial Map of Pakistan: A Case Study of Hazara Province', *Journal of Political Studies*, Vol. 20, No. 2, 1–19.

Ahmed, F. (1998) *Ethnicity and Politics in Pakistan*, Karachi: Oxford University Press.

Ahmed, H. Z. (1989) 'Malaysia: Quasi Democracy in a Divided Society', in Diamond, L., Linz, J. and Lipset, S. M. (eds) *Democracy in Asia*, New Delhi: Vistar Publications, pp. 347–83.

Ahmed, I. (1995) *State, Nation, and Ethnicity in South Asia*, London and New York: Pinter.

Ahmed, S. (2007) 'Pakistan Provinces Uneasy as Election Looms', *Federations*, Vol. 6, No. 1, February–March, 5–7.

Ahmed, S. J. (1990) *Federalism in Pakistan: A Constitutional Study*, Karachi: Pakistan Study Centre (University of Karachi).

Alavi, H. (1979) 'The State in Post-Colonial Societies: Pakistan and Bangladesh', in Goulbourne, H. (ed) *Politics and State in the Third World*, London: Macmillan, pp. 38–70.

Alavi, H. (1988) 'Pakistan and Islam: Ethnicity and Ideology', in Halliday, F. and Alavi, H. (eds) *State and Ideology in the Middle East and Pakistan*, London: Macmillan, pp. 64–112.

Alavi, H. (1989) 'Politics of Ethnicity in India and Pakistan', in Alavi, H. and Harriss, J. (eds) *South Asia: Sociology of Developing Societies*, London: Macmillan, pp. 5–19.

Alavi, H. and Harriss, J. (eds) (1989) *South Asia: Sociology of Developing Societies*, London: Macmillan.

Ali, M. (1995) 'Federalism and Regionalism in Pakistan', reprinted in Grover, V. and Arora, R. (eds) *Political System in Pakistan, Vol. 2, Constitutional Developments in Pakistan*, New Delhi: Deep & Deep, pp. 447–501.

Ali, T. (1983) *Can Pakistan Survive: The Death of a State*, London: Penguin.

All India Congress Committee (1985) *A Centenary History of the Indian National Congress*, five vols., New Delhi: Vikas.

Bibliography   227

Amnesty International (1997) *Ethnicity and Nationality: Refugees in Asia*, London: Amnesty International.

Andaya, B. W. and Andaya, L. Y. (2001) *A History of Malaysia*, second edition, Hampshire: Macmillan.

Anderson, G. and Chaudhry, S. (eds) (2019) *Territory and Power in Constitutional Transitions*. Oxford: Oxford University Press.

Anderson, P. (1979) *Lineages of the Absolutist States*, London: Verso.

Anon. (2001) *The Constitution of India*, New Delhi: Delhi Law House, 2001.

Anon. (2002) *Federal Constitution (of Malaysia) as at 10th April 2002*, Kuala Lumpur: International Law Book Services.

Anon. (2003) 'Malaysia Bans Hindu Rights Action Force', *The Statesman*, Kolkata, 17 October, p. 5.

Anon. (2004) *Devolution in Pakistan*, Washington, DC: Asian Development Bank, Department for International Development and World Bank.

Appleby, P. (1953) *Public Administration in India: Report of a Survey*, New Delhi: Government of India.

Aron, R. (1965) *Main Currents in Sociological Thought*, Vol. 1, London: Penguin.

Arora, B. (2004) 'Political Parties and the Party System: The Emergence of New Coalitions', in Hasan, Z. (ed) *Parties and Party Politics in India*, New Delhi: Oxford University Press, pp. 404–53.

Arora, B. and Verney, D. (eds) (1995) *Multiple Identities in a Single State: Indian Federalism in Comparative Perspective*, New Delhi: Konark Publishers Pvt. Ltd.

Asghar, M. U. (2002) 'Demands for New Provinces in Pakistan' (ISSRA) Institute for Strategic Studies and Research Analysis, National Defence University, Pakistan (Online) Paper 2012, 59–78.

AsiaSentinel.com.(Online: http://asiasentinel.com, accessed 9 January 2009).

Ataur, Rahman (1989) 'Pakistan: Unity or Further Divisions', in Wilson, A. J. and Dalton, D. (eds) *The States of South Asia: Problems of National Integration (Essays in Honour of W. H. Morris-Jones)*, London: Hurst & Co., pp. 197–221.

Austin, G. (1966) *The Indian Constitution: The Cornerstone of a Nation*, New Delhi: Oxford University Press.

Austin, G. (1999) *Working a Democratic Constitution: The Indian Experience*, New Delhi: Oxford University Press.

Aziz, D. D. and Arnold, D. (eds) (1996) *Decentralized Governance in Asian Countries*, New Delhi: Sage.

Baechler, G. (ed) (1997) *Federalism Against Ethnicity? Institutional, Legal, and Democratic Instruments to Prevent Violent Minority Conflicts*, Zurich: Verlag Ruegger.

Bahadur, K. (1994) 'Ethnic Problems in Pakistan', *World Focus*, Vol. XV, No.4–5, April–May [page numbers not available].

Bajpai, K. S. (ed) (2007) *Democracy and Diversity India and the American Experience*, New Delhi: Oxford University Press.

Bakar, I. (2007) 'Multinational Federations: The Case of Malaysia', in Burgess, M. and Pinder, J. (eds) *Multinational Federations*, London: Routledge, pp. 68–85.

Banerjee, A. C. (1961) *Indian Constitutional Documents 1757–1947*, Calcutta: A. Mukherjee & Co.

Banerjee, A. C. (1978) *The Constitutional History of India*, Vol. 3, 1919–1977, Meerut: Macmillan.

Barua, B. P. (1995) 'Constitution-Making in Pakistan, 1947–56', in Grover, V. and Arora, R. (eds) *Political System in Pakistan: Role of Military Dictatorship in Pakistan Politics*, Vol. 10, New Delhi: Deep & Deep, pp. 137–75.

228 Bibliography

Basam, A. L. (1982) *The Wonder That Was India*, New Delhi: Rupa.

Basta Fleiner, L. R., Bhattacharyya, H., Fleiner, T. and Mitra, S. (eds) (2000) *Rule of Law and Organization of the State in Asia: The Multicultural Challenge*, Fribourg, Switzerland: Institute of Federation.

Basu, D. D. (1997) *Introduction to the Constitution of India*, New Delhi: Prentice Hall of India.

Bates, C. (1988) 'Congress and the Tribals', in Shepperdson, M. and Simmons, C. (eds) *The Indian National Congress and the Political Economy of India 1885–1985*, Aldershot: Avebury, pp. 231–52.

Bates, C. (2005) 'Development of Panchayati Raj in India', in Bates, C. and Basu, S. (eds) *Rethinking Indian Political Institutions*, London: Anthem Press, pp. 169–84.

Bates, C. and Basu, S. (eds) (2005) *Rethinking Indian Political Institutions*, London: Anthem Press.

Baviskar, B. S. and Mathew, G. (eds) (2009) *Inclusion and Exclusion in Local Government*, New Delhi: Orient Longman.

Bereciartu, G. L. (1994) *Decline of the Nation-State*, Reno: The University of Nevada Press.

Bertrand, R. (2019) 'Indonesia: Special Autonomy for Aech and Papua', in Anderson, G. and Choudhry, S. (eds) *Territory and Power in Constitutional Transitions*, Oxford: Oxford University Press, 119–40.

Bhambri, C. P. (2003) 'Central Government in the Age of Globalization', in Dua, B. D. and Singh. M. P. (eds) *Indian Federalism in the New Millennium*, New Delhi: Manohar, pp. 319–34.

Bhargava, P. K. (1984) 'Transfers from the Center to the States in India', *Asian Survey*, Vol. XXIV, No. 6, June, 665–88.

Bhargava, R. (ed) (1999) *Secularism and Its Critics*, New Delhi: Oxford University Press, pp. 177–234.

Bhattacharyya, H. (1989) 'The Emergence of Tripuri Nationalism 1948–50', *South Asia Research*, Vol. 9, No. 1–2, May, 54–71.

Bhattacharyya, H. (1992) 'Deinstitutionalization of Indian Politics: A Micro Critique', *Journal of Socio-Political Studies, (Burdwan University)*, Vol. 1, No. 1, 64–85.

Bhattacharyya, H. (1998a) *Micro-Foundations of Bengal Communism*, New Delhi: Ajanta.

Bhattacharyya, H. (1998b) 'Bengal Communism and Panchayats: Operation of Micro Democracy', in Bhattacharyya, H. (ed) *Micro Foundations of Bengal Communism*, New Delhi: Ajanta, pp. 102–41.

Bhattacharyya, H. (1999) *Communism in Tripura*, New Delhi: Ajanta.

Bhattacharyya, H. (2000) 'Federalism, Decentralization and State-Building in India: Aspects of Centre-State Fiscal Relations', in Bird, R. and Stauffer, T. (eds) *Intergovernmental Fiscal Relations in Fragmented Societies*, Fribourg, Switzerland: Helbing & Lichtenhahn, pp. 247–305.

Bhattacharyya, H. (2001a) *India as a Multicultural Federation: Asian Values, Democracy and Decentralization (In Comparison with Swiss Federalism)*, Fribourg, Switzerland: Institute of Federalism.

Bhattacharyya, H. (2001b) 'India Creates Three New States', *Federations: What's New in Federalism Worldwide, (Ottawa)*, Vol. 1, No. 1–3.

Bhattacharyya, H. (2001c) 'Indian Federalism and Indian Communism: Conflict and Collaboration', *Indian Journal of Political Science*, Vol. 62, No. 1, March, 41–61.

Bhattacharyya, H. (2002) *Making Local Democracy Work in India: Social Capital, Politics and Governance in West Bengal*, New Delhi: Vedams.

Bhattacharyya, H. (2003) 'Indian Federalism and Tribal Self-Rule', *Federations: What's New in Federalism Worldwide*, Vol. 3, No. 3, August, 11–12.

Bhattacharyya, H. (2004a) 'Internal Threats to Security: Federalism and Ethno-Regional Accommodation of Identity in India', in Bhattacharyya, P., Banerjee, S. and Chakrabarty, T. (eds) *Anatomy of Fear: Essays on India's Internal Security*, New Delhi: Lancer's Books, chap. 5, pp. 74–101.

Bhattacharyya, H. (2004b) 'The CPI-M: From Rebellion to Governance', in Mitra, S. K., Enskat, M. and Spiess, C. (eds) *Political Parties in South Asia*, Westport, CT: Praeger Publications, pp. 76–103.

Bhattacharyya, H. (2005a) 'Changing Contours of India's Federal Debates', *West Bengal Political Science Review*, Vol. 3, No. 1–2, January–December, 59–86.

Bhattacharyya, H. (2005b) 'India: Bodo People's Rights Take a Step Forward', *Federations (Ottawa)*, Vol. 4, No. 3, March, 17–18.

Bhattacharyya, H. (2005c) 'Forms of Multiculturalism and Identity Issues in India', *Canadian Diversity (Ottawa)*, Vol. 4, No. 1, Winter, 46–9.

Bhattacharyya, H. (2005d) 'Grassroots Democracy and Civic Participation in Rural West Bengal: The Case of Gram Sansad', in Sen Gupta, D. and Ganguly, S. (eds) *India (Essays in Memory of Late Prof. Prasanta Kr Ghosh)*, Kolkata: Arambag Book House, pp. 63–76.

Bhattacharyya, H. (2005e) 'Federalism and Regionalism in India: Institutional Strategies and Political Accommodation of Identity', *Heidelberg Papers in South Asian and Comparative Politics*, Working Paper No. 27, May (ISSN:1617-5069) (Online: www.hpsacp.uni-hd.de).

Bhattacharyya, H. (2007a) 'Federalism and Competing Nations in India', chap. 4 in Burgess, M. and Pinder, J. (eds) *Multinational Federations*, London: Routledge, pp. 50–68.

Bhattacharyya, H. (2007b) 'India and Switzerland as Multinational Federations', in Burgess, M. and Pinder, J. (eds) *Multinational Federations*, London: Routledge, pp. 50–68, chap. 11, pp. 212–25.

Bhattacharyya, H. (2007c) 'Approaches to Local Government: Arguing a Case for Human Rights', *The West Bengal Political Science Review*, Vol. 2, No. 2, July–December, 1–14.

Bhattacharyya, H. (2008) 'Ethnic and Civic Nationhood in India: Concept, History, Institutional Innovations and Contemporary Challenges', in Saha, S. C. (ed) *Ethnicity and Socio-Political Change in Africa and Other Developing Countries: A Constructive Discourse in State Building*, Lanham: Lexington Books, chap. 8, pp. 169–95.

Bhattacharyya, H. (2009) 'Globalization and Indian Federalism: Re-Assertions of States' Rights', in Lofgren, H. and Sarangi, P. (eds) *The Politics and Culture of Globalization: India and Australia*, New Delhi: Social Science Press, chap. 6, 99–119.

Bhattacharyya, H. (2010) *Federalism in Asia: India, Pakistan and Malaysia*, London and New York: Routledge.

Bhattacharyya, H. (2011) 'Sensing and Acknowledging India's Cultural Diversity for Nationhood: Budeb Mukhopadhyay, Rabindranath Tagore and Jawaharlal Nehru', *The Calcutta Review*, Vol. Xlll, No. 1–2, 102–19.

Bhattacharyya, H. (2012) 'UPA-2004- and Indian Federalism: A Paradigm Shift?' in Saez, L. and Singh, G. (eds) *New Dimensions of Politics in India: The United Progressive Alliance in Power*, Abingdon: Routledge.

Bhattacharyya, H. (2015) 'Indian Federalism and Democracy: The Growing Salience of Diversity-Claims Over Equality-Claims in Comparative and Indian Perspectives', *Regional and Federal Studies*, Vol. 25, No. 3, 211–27.

Bhattacharyya, H. (2016a) 'Indian Federalism: A Hybrid Solution to the Problem of Diversity and Political Order', in Koenig, L. and Chaudhuri, B. (eds) *Politics of the Other in India and China: Western Concepts in Non-Western Contexts*, Abingdon: Routledge.

230 Bibliography

Bhattacharyya, H. (2016b) 'Governing India's Localities: Limits of Structural and Governance Reforms', in Bhattacharyya, H. and Koenig, L. (eds) *Globalization and Governance in India: Fresh Challenges to Society and Institutions*, Abingdon: Routledge, pp. 125–38.

Bhattacharyya, H. (2017) 'Federalism over Democracy in India: Dialectics of Diversity-claims and Equality-claims', *US-China Law Review*, Vol. 14, No. 8, August, 531–49.

Bhattacharyya, H. (2019a) 'States Reorganization and Accommodation of Ethno-Territorial Cleavages in India', in Anderson, G. and Chaudhry, S. (eds) *Territory and Power in Constitutional Transitions*. Oxford: Oxford University Press, 81–99.

Bhattacharyya, H. (2019b) 'Pitfalls of India's Pitfalls of India's Ethno-Federal Model of Ethnic Conflict Management: Tension Between Tribal Ethnicity and Territory in India's North East', *Ethnopoliticist*, 4 July (Online).

Bhattacharyya, H. and Hausing, K. K. S. and Mukherjee, J. (2017) 'Indian Federalism at the Crossroad: Limits of the Territorial Management of Ethnic Conflict', *India Review*, Vol. 16, No. 1, 149–78.

Bhattacharyya, H. and Mukherjee, J. (2018) 'Bodo Ethnic Self-Rule and Persistence Violence in Assam: A Failed Case of Multinational Federalism in India', *Regional and Federal Studies*, 31 May (Online).

Bhattacharyya, H. and Nossiter, T. J. (1988) 'Communism in a Micro-State: Tripura and the Nationalities Question', in Nossiter, T. J. (ed) *Marxist State Governments in India*, London and New York: Pinter, pp. 144–69.

Bhattacharyya, H., Sarkar, P. and Kar, A. (eds) (2010) *The Politics of Social Exclusion in India: Democracy at the Crossroads*, London and New York: Routledge.

Bhattacharyya, M. (1992) 'The Mind of the Founding Fathers', in Mukerji, N. and Arora, B. (eds) *Federalism in India: Origin and Development*, New Delhi: Vikash Publishing House Pvt. Ltd, pp. 87–103.

Bhattacharyya, P., Chatterjee, S. and Chakrabarty, T. (eds) (2004) *Anatomy of Fear: Essays on India's Internal Security*, New Delhi: Lancer's Books.

Bird, R. (1986) *Federal Finance in Comparative Perspective*, Toronto: Toronto Tax Foundation.

Bird, R. and Stauffer, T. (eds) (2000) *Intergovernmental Fiscal Relations on Fragmented Societies*, Fribourg, Switzerland: Helbing and Lichtenhahn.

Brass, P. R. (1966) *Factional Politics in an Indian State: The Congress Party in Uttar Pradesh*, Berkeley: University of California Press.

Brass, P. R. (1988) 'The Punjab Crisis and the Unity of India', in Kohli, A. (ed) *India's Democracy*, Princeton, NJ: Princeton University Press, pp. 169–214.

Brass, P. R. (1989) 'Pluralism, Regionalism and Decentralizing Tendencies in Contemporary Indian Politics', in Wilson, A. J. and Dalton, D. (eds) *The States of South Asia: Problems of National Integration* (Essays in Honour of W. H. Morris-Jones), London: Hurst & Co., pp. 223–64.

Brass, P. R. (1994) *The Politics of India Since Independence*, second edition, New Delhi: Foundation Books, pp. 65–6.

Brass, P. R. and Fronda, M. F. (1973) *Radical Politics in South Asia*, Cambridge, MA: MIT Press.

Brass, P. R. and Robinson, F. (eds) (1987) *The Indian National Congress and Indian Society, 1885–1985: Ideology, Social Structure, and Political Dominance*, New Delhi: Chanakya.

Breen, M. G. (2017) 'The Origins of Holding-Together Federalism: Nepal, Myanmar, and Sri Lanka', *The Publius: The Journal of Federalism*, 1–25. (doi:10.1093/publius/pjx027)

Breen, M. G. (2018) *The Road to Federalism in Nepal, Myanmar and Sri Lanka*, Abingdon: Routledge.

Breton, J. L. R. (1997) *Atlas of Languages and Ethnic Composition of South Asia*, New Delhi: Sage.

Bibliography 231

Burgess, M. (1995) *The British Tradition of Federalism*, Leicester: Leicester University Press.

Burgess, M. and Pinder, J. (eds) (2007) *Multinational Federations*, London: Routledge.

Case, W. (2007) 'Semi-Democracy and Minimalist Federalism in Malaysia', in He, Baogang, Galligan, B. and Inoguchi, T. (eds) *Federalism in Asia*, Cheltenham: Edward Elgar, pp. 124–44.

Census Reports of India (2001) *Central Report of India*, New Delhi: Government of India.

Char, S. V. Desika (1983) *Readings in the Constitutional History of India 1757–1947*, New Delhi: Oxford University Press.

Chatterjee, P. (1986) *Nationalist Thought and the Colonial World: A Derivative Discourse*, London: Zed Books.

Chatterjee, P. (1993) *The Nation and Its Fragments*, New Delhi: Oxford University Press.

Chatterjee, P. (2000) *Inheritances of History* (in Bengali), Kolkata: Ananda Publishers.

Cheema, G. S. and Hussein, A. A. (1978) 'Local Government Reform in Malaysia', *Asian Survey*, Vol. 18, No. 6, June, 572–91.

Cheema, I. P. (2000) 'Pakistan: The Challenge of Democratization', in Basta Fleiner, L. R., Bhattacharyya, H., Fleiner, T. and Mitra, S. (eds) *Rule of Law and Organization of the State in Asia: The Multicultural Challenge*, Fribourg, Switzerland: Institute of Federalism, pp. 205–35.

Chhiber, P. K. (1999) *Democracy Without Associations: Transformation of the Party System and Social Cleavage Theory*, New Delhi: Vistar Publications.

Chhiber, P. K. and Petrocik, J. R. (1989) 'The Puzzle of Indian Politics: Social Cleavages and the Indian Party System', *British Journal of Political Science*, Vol. 19, April, 191–210.

Choudhury, Nirod C. (1996/1979) *Hinduism: A Religion to Live by*, New Delhi: Oxford University Press, 1996/orig. 1979.

Cohen, S. P. (2005) *The Idea of Pakistan*, New Delhi: Oxford University Press.

Das Gupta, J. (2001) 'India's Federal Design and Multicultural National Construction', in Kohli, A. (ed) *The Success of India's Democracy*, Cambridge: Cambridge University Press, pp. 49–78.

Desai, A. R. (1946) *Social Background of Indian Nationalism*, Bombay: Popular Prakashan.

De Silva, K. M. (1989) 'The Model Colony: Reflections on the Transfer of Power in Sri Lanka', in Wilson, A. J. and Dalton, D. (eds) *The States of South Asia: Problems of National Integration* (Essays in Honour of W. H. Morris-Jones), London: Hurst & Co., pp. 77–88.

Desouza, P. R. (2007) 'Decentralization: Explorations of Local government in India and the United States', in Bajpai, K. S. (ed) *Democracy and Diversity: India and the American Experience*, New Delhi: Oxford University Press, pp. 262–98.

Diamond, L., Linz, J. and Lipset, S. M. (eds) (1989) *Democracy in Asia*, New Delhi: Vistar Publishers.

Doornbos, M. and Kaviraj, S. (eds) (1997) *Dynamics of State Formation: India and Europe Compared*, New Delhi: Sage.

Dua, B. D. (1979) 'Presidential Rule in India: A Study in Crisis Politics', *Asian Survey*, Vol. 19, No. 6, 611–26.

Dua, B. D. and Singh, M. P. (eds) (2003) *Indian Federalism in the New Millennium*, New Delhi: Munohar.

Dyck, R. (1991) 'Link Between Federal and Provincial Parties and Party Systems', in Bakvis, H. (ed) *Representation, Integration and Political Parties in Canada*, Toronto: Dundurn Press, pp. 129–77.

Edrisinha, R. and Welikala, A. (eds) (2008) *Essays on Federalism in Sri Lanka*, Colombo: Centre for Policy Alternatives.

Eisenstadt, S. N. and Hartman, H. (1997) 'Historical Experience, Cultural Traditions, State Formation and Political Dynamics in India and Europe', in Doornbos, M. and

232 Bibliography

Kaviraj, S. (eds) *Dynamics of State Formation: India and Europe Compared*, New Delhi: Sage, pp. 195–214.

Elazar, D. (1987) *Exploring Federalism*, Alabama: The University of Alabama.

Elazar, D. (ed) (1991) *Federal Systems of the World: A Handbook of Federal, Confederal and Autonomy Arrangements*, Harlow, Essex: Longman.

Elazar, D. (ed) (1994) *Federal Systems of the World*, second edition, Harlow, Essex: Orient Longman.

Evans, P., Rueschemeyer, D. and Skocpol, T. (eds) (1985) *Bringing the State Back In*, Cambridge: Cambridge University Press, pp. 169–92.

Fenton, S. (2004) 'Malaysia and Capitalist Modernization: Plural and Multicultural Models', in Rex, J. and Singh, G. (eds) *Governance in Multicultural Societies*, Hants: Ashgate Publishing Company, pp. 49–56.

Filippov, M., Ordeshook, P. C. and Shvetsova, O. (2004) *Designing Federalism: A Theory of Self-Sustaining Federal Institutions*, Cambridge: Cambridge University Press.

Fisher, C. A. (1961) *South-East Asia: A Social, Economic and Political Geography*, London: Methuen & Co.

Fisher, C. A. (1964) *South-East Asia: A Social, Economic and Political Geography*, London: Methuen & Co.

Franda, M. F. (1971) *Radical Politics in West Bengal*, Cambridge, MA: MIT Press.

Galligan, B. (2007) 'Federalism in Asia', in He, Baogang, Galligan, B. and Inoguchi, T. (eds) *Federalism in Asia*, Cheltenham: Edward Elgar, pp. 290–315.

Ghaus-Pasha, A. and Bengali, K. (2002) 'Pakistan', in Griffith, A. and Nerenberg, K. (eds) *A Handbook of Federal Countries*, Montreal and Kingston: McGill Queen's University Press, pp. 177–86.

Giddens, A. (1985) *Nation-State and Violence*, Cambridge: Polity Press.

Goulbourne, H. (ed) (1979) *Politics and State in the Third World*, London: Macmillan.

Griffith, A. and Nerenberg, K. (eds) (2002) *A Handbook of Federal Countries*, Montreal and Kingston: McGill Queen's University Press.

Grover, V. and Arora, A. (eds) (1995a) *Political System in Pakistan: Role of Military Dictatorship in Pakistan Politics*, Vol. 10, New Delhi: Deep & Deep.

Grover, V. and Arora, R. (eds) (1995b) *Political System in Pakistan, Constitutional Developments in Pakistan*, Vol. 2, New Delhi: Deep & Deep.

Guha, A. (1980) 'Great Nationalism, Little Nationalism and the Problem of Integration: A Tentative View', *Economic and Political Weekly*, 15, 14–21 June, 455–8.

Guhan, S. (1995) 'Federalism and the New Political Economy in India', in Arora, B. and Verney, D. V. (eds) *Multiple Identities in a Single State: Indian Federalism in Comparative Perspective*, New Delhi: Konark Publishers Pvt. Ltd, pp. 237–72.

Guibernau, M. and Hutchinson, J. (eds) (2001) *Understanding Nationalism*, Cambridge: Polity Press.

Gunasinghe, N. (1989) 'Ethnic Conflict in Sri Lanka: Perceptions and Solutions', in Alavi, H. and Harriss, J. (eds) *South Asia: Sociology of Developing Countries*, London: Macmillan, pp. 247–55.

Gupta, S. (1995a) 'The Political Crisis in Pakistan', in Grover, V. and Arora, R. (eds) *Political System in Pakistan*, Vol. 2, New Delhi: Deep & Deep Publishers, pp. 17–38.

Gupta, S. (1995b) 'Constitution-Making in Pakistan', in Grover, V. and Arora, R. (eds) *Political System in Pakistan*, Vol. 2, New Delhi: Deep & Deep Publishers, pp. 97–121.

Halliday, F. and Alavi, H. (eds) (1988) *State and Ideology in the Middle East and Pakistan*, London: Macmillan.

Hardgrave, R. L. Jr. and Kochanek, S. A. (2000) *India Government and Politics in a Developing Nation*, sixth edition, Orlando, FL: Harcourt College Publishers.

Hasan, Z. (ed) (2004) *Parties and Party Politics in India*, New Delhi: Oxford University Press.

He, B. (2007) 'Democratization and Federalization in Asia', in He, Baogang, Galligan, B. and Inoguchi, T. (eds) *Federalism in Asia*, Cheltenham: Edward Elgar, pp. 1–33.

He, B., Allison-Reumann, L. and Breen, M. (2018) 'The Covenant Connection Re-Examined: The Nexus Between Religions and Federalism in Asia', *Political Studies*, Vol. 66, No. 3, 752–70.

Held, D. (1989) *Political Theory and the Modern State*, Cambridge: Polity Press.

Hemming, R. (1997) 'India', in Ter-Minassian, T. (ed) *Fiscal Federalism in Theory and Practice*, Washington, DC: IMF, pp. 527–39.

Hettige, S. (2000) 'Politics, Social Order, and Conflict in Sri Lanka', in Basta-Fleiner, L., Bhattacharyya, H., Fleiner, T. and Mitra, S. K. (eds) *Rule of Law and Organization of the State in Asia: The Multicultural Challenge*, Fribourg, Switzerland: Institute of Federalism, pp. 187–205.

Hettige, S. (2012) 'Building Citizenship in Sri Lanka Dynamics of State Action and Conflict', in Bhattacharyya, H., Kluge, A. and Koenigh, L (eds) *Politics of Citizenship, Identity and the State in South Asia*, New Delhi: Samskriti, pp. 203–25.

Hewitt, V. (1998) 'Ethnic Construction, Provincial Identity and Nationalism in Pakistan: The Case of Baluchistan', in Mitra, S. K. and Lewis, R. A. (eds) *Subnational Movements in South Asia*, New Delhi: Segment Books, pp. 43–67.

Hing, Lee Kam (1981) 'Malaya: New State and Old Elites', in Jeffrey, R. (ed) *Asia: The Winning of Independence*, London and Basingstoke: Macmillan, pp. 213–25.

Hobsbawm, E. (1992) *Nations and Nationalism Since 1780*, Cambridge: Cambridge University Press.

Horowitz, D. (1985) *Ethnic Groups in Conflict*. Los Angeles: University of California Press.

Huntington, S. P. (2004) *Who Are We? America's Great Debate*, New Delhi: Penguin.

Iftikhar, H. Malik (1998) 'The Politics of Ethnic Conflict in Sindh: Nation, Region and Community in Pakistan', in Mitra, S. K. and Lewis, R. A. (eds) *Subnational Movements in South Asia*, New Delhi: Segment Books, pp. 68–104.

Jaffrelot, C. (ed) (2002a) *Pakistan: Nationalism Without a Nation?* New Delhi: Manohar.

Jaffrelot, C. (2002b) 'Introduction: Nationalism Without a Nation Pakistan Searching for Its Identity', in Jaffrelot, C. (ed) *Pakistan: Nationalism Without a Nation*, New Delhi: Manohar, pp. 7–51.

Jain, J. C. (ed) (2005) *Decentralization and Local Governance (Essays for George Mathew)*, New Delhi: Orient Longman.

Jalal, A. (1994/1985) *The Sole Spokesman: Jinnah, the Muslim League and the Demand for Pakistan*, Cambridge: Cambridge University Press.

Javaid, U. (2018) 'Federation of Pakistan and Creation of New Provinces: A Case Study of Bahawalpur Province', *Pakistan Journal of History and Culture*, Vol XXXIX, No. 1, 15–36.

Jayal, N. G. (ed) (2001) *Democracy in India*, New Delhi: Oxford University Press.

Jeans, J., Wright, H. and Wright, V. (eds) (1996) *Federalising Europe: The Costs, Benefits, and the Preconditions of Federal Political Systems*, Oxford: Oxford University Press.

Jeffrey, R. (ed) (1978) *People, Princes and Paramount Power: Society and Politics in the Indian Princely States*, New Delhi: Oxford University Press.

Jeffrey, R. (ed) (1981) *Asia: The Winning of Independence*, London and Basingstoke: Macmillan.

Jha, S. N. and Mathur, P. C. (eds) (1999) *Decentralization and Local Politics*, New Delhi: Sage.

Karmis, D. and Norman, W. (eds) (2005) *Theories of Federalism: A Reader*, New York: Palgrave.

Kashyap, A. (1989) *Panchayati Ra: Views of the Founding Fathers and Recommendations of Different Committees*, New Delhi: Lancer's Books.

Kaviraj, S. (1991) 'On State, Society and Discourse in India', in Manor, J. (ed) *Rethinking Third World Politics*, London: Longman, pp. 72–99.

234 Bibliography

Key, V. O. (1964) *Politics, Parties, and Pressure Groups*, fifth edition, New York: Crowell.

Khan, A. (2005) *Politics of Identity Ethnic Nationalism and the State in Pakistan*, New Delhi: Sage.

Khan, H. (2001) *Constitutional and Political History of Pakistan*, Karachi: Oxford University Press.

Khan, W. (1998) *Pakistan: A Modern History*, London: Hurst & Co.

Kincaid, J. (ed) (2019) *A Research Agenda for Federalism Studies*, Cheltenham: Edward Elgar.

Kochanek, S. A. (1968) *The Congress Party of India*, Princeton, NJ: Princeton University Press.

Kohli, A. (ed) (1988) *India's Democracy*, Princeton, NJ: Princeton University Press.

Kohli, A. (ed) (2001) *The Success of India's Democracy*, Cambridge: Cambridge University Press.

Kothari, R. (1961) 'Party System', *Economic Weekly*, 3 June, 1–18.

Kothari, R. (1967) 'The Congress System in India', *Party System and Election Studies*, Occasional Papers of the Centre for Developing Societies, No. 1, Bombay: Allied Publishers.

Kukreja, V. (2003) *Contemporary Pakistan: Political Process, Conflicts and Crises*, New Delhi: Sage.

Kumar, D. and Santasilan, K. K. (eds) (1989) *Ethnicity and Conflict Crisis*, Hong Kong: Arena Press.

Kurian, K. M. and Varughese, P. N. (eds) (1981) *Centre-State Relations*, New Delhi: Macmillan.

Lakhi, M. V. (1995) 'Constitutional Developments in Pakistan: The First Phase, 1947–56', in Grover, V. and Arora, R. (eds) *Political System in Pakistan*, New Delhi: Deep & Deep, pp. 122–36.

Lau, B.(2019) 'The Philippines: Peace Talks and Autonomy in Mindanao', in Anderson G. and Choudhry, S. (eds) *Territory and Power in Constitutional Transitions*, Oxford: Oxford University Press, pp. 202–19.

Lawoti, M. (2012) 'Ethnic Politics and the Building of an Inclusive State', in Einsiedel, S., von. Malone, D. and Pradhan, S. (eds.) *Nepal in Transition: From People's War to Fragile Peace*, Cambridge: Cambridge University Press, pp. 129–55.

Livingstone, W. S. (1956) *Federalism and Constitutional Change*, Oxford: Clarendon Press.

Lofgren, H. and Sarangi, P. (eds) (2009) *The Politics and Culture of Globalization: India and Australia*, New Delhi: Social Science Press.

Loh, F. (2008) 'Malaysia: Governing Coalition Weakened by Losses in Regions', *Federations*, June–July, 28–32.

Loh, F. and Boo, K. (eds) (2002) *Democracy in Malaysia: Discourses and Practices*, Surrey: Curzon Press, p. 4.

Macmahon, A. (ed) (1955) *Federalism: Mature and Emergent*, New York: Doubleday.

Majumdar, B. B. and Majumdar, B. P. (1965) *Congress and Congressmen in the Pre-Gandhian Era, 1885–1917*, Calcutta: Firma KLM Pvt. Ltd.

Malagodi, M. (2019) ' "Godot has arrived": Federal Restructuring in Nepal', in Anderson, G. and Choudhry, S. (eds) *Territory and Power in Constitutional Transitions*, Oxford: Oxford University Press, pp. 161–81.

Malhotra, R. (2014) *India's Public Policy Report 2014 Tackling Poverty, Hunger and Malnutrition*, New Delhi: Oxford University Press.

Mallikarjun, B. (2004) 'Indian Multilingualism, Language Policy and the State', *Language in India*, Vol. 4, 4 April (Online: http://edla.org/en/proj/scalla/SCALLA/2004/mallikarjun3.pdf).

Maniruzzaman, T. (1973) 'Radical Politics and the Emergence of Bangladesh', in Brass, P. R. and Franda, M. F. (eds) *Radical Politics in South Asia*, Cambridge, MA: MIT Press, pp. 223–81.

Bibliography   235

Manor, J. (1988) 'Parties and the Party System', in Kohli, A. (ed) *India's Democracy*, Princeton, NJ: Princeton University Press, pp. 78–103.

Manor, J. (1991) *Rethinking Third World Politics*, London: Longman.

Manor, J. (1995) 'Regional Parties in Federal Systems', in Arora, B. and Verney, D. V. (eds) *Multiple Identities in a Single State: Indian Federalism in Comparative Perspective*, New Delhi: Konark Publishing Pvt. Ltd, pp. 105–36.

Manor, J. (2001) 'Center-State Relations', in Kohli, A. (ed) *The Success of India's Democracy*, Cambridge: Cambridge University Press, pp. 193–225.

Mathew, G. (2002) 'India (Republic of India)', in Griffiths, Ann, L. and Nerenberg, K. (eds) *A Handbook of Federal Countries*, Montreal and Kingston: McGill Queen's University Press, pp. 161–77.

Mathew, G. (ed) (2009) *Inclusion and Exclusion in Local Governance*, New Delhi: Sage.

McGarry, J. and O'Leary, B. (eds) (1993) *The Politics of Ethnic Conflict Regulation*, London: Routledge.

McGarry, J. and O'Leary, B. (2007) 'Federalism and Managing Nations', in Burgess, M. and Pinder, J. (eds) *Multinational Federations*, London: Routledge, pp. 180–212.

McLane, J. R. (1977) *Indian Nationalism and the Early Congress*, Princeton, NJ: Princeton University Press.

Means, G. P. (1976) *Malaysian Politics*, London: Hodder & Stoughton.

Menon, V. P. (1956) *The Story of the Integration of the Indian States*, New York: Macmillan.

Milne, R. S. and Mauzy, D. K. (1989) *Malaysian Politics Under Mahathir*, London: Routledge.

Mitra, S. K. (2001) 'Making Local Government Work: Panchayati Raj and Governance in India', in Kohli, A. (ed) *The Success of India's Democracy*, Cambridge: Cambridge University Press, pp. 103–27.

Mitra, S. K. and Bhattacharyya, H. (2000) 'The Multicultural Challenge: The Post-Colonial State and Sub-National Movements in India's North-East', in Basta-Fleiner, L., Bhattacharyya, H., Fleiner, T. and Mitra, S. K. (eds) *Rule of Law and Organization of the State in Asia: The Multicultural Challenge*, Fribourg, Switzerland: Institute of Federalism, chap. 6, pp. 91–135.

Mitra, S. K. and Bhattacharyya, H.(2018) *Politics and Governance in Indian States: Bihar, West Bengal and Tripura*, Singapore: World Scientific Publishers.

Mitra, S. K. and Lewis, R. A. (eds) (1998) *Subnational Movements in South Asia*, New Delhi: Segment Books.

Mitra, S. K. and Singh, V. B. (1999) *Democracy and Social Change in India: A Cross-Sectional Analysis of the National Electorate*, New Delhi: Sage.

Mitra, S. K., Spiece, C. and Enskat, M. (eds) (1997) *Political Parties in South Asia*, Westport, CT: Praeger Publications.

Morris-Jones, W. H. (1957) *Parliament in India*, London: Longman.

Morris-Jones, W. H. (1964/1987) *The Government and Politics of India*, Cambridgeshire: The Eothen Press.

Mukarji, N. and Arora, B. (eds) (1992) *Federalism in India: Origins and Development*, New Delhi: Vikash Publishing House Pvt. Ltd.

Mukherjee, J. (2008) *Multicultural Decentralization in India*, University of Burdwan, Unpubl. Ph.D. Thesis.

Mukhopadhyay, Bhudev (1892) *Samajik Prabandha* (Essays on Society) (in Bengali), Chinsura: West Bengal Book Board.

Mustaq, M. (2016) 'Regional Identities in Quest for Separate Provinces: A New Challenge for the Pakistan Federation', *Journal of Political Studies*, Vol. 23, No. 1, 289–307.

Mutalib, H. (2000) 'Malaysia's 1999 General Elections: Signposts to Future Politics', *Asian Journal of Political Science*, Vol. 8, No. 1, June, 65–87.

Nagarkar, V. V. (1975) *The Genesis of Pakistan*, New Delhi: Allied Publishers Pvt. Ltd.

236 Bibliography

Nahappan, A. (1972) *Report of the Royal Commission of Enquiry into the Working of Local Governments in West Malaysia*, Kuala Lumpur: Government of Malaysia.

Nair, S. and Sugarnan, S.(2015) 'Poverty in Malaysia: Need for a Paradigm Shift', *Institution and Economics*, Vol. 7, No. 3, 99–123.

Narayanan, K. R. (1998) 'Foreword', in Vijapur, A. P. (ed) *Dimensions of Federal Nation-Building*, New Delhi: Manak Publications [page numbers not available].

Nehru, J. (1980/1946) *The Discovery of India*, New Delhi: Oxford University Press; Calcutta: The Signet Press (orig).

Nehru, J. (1985) *Letters to Chief Ministers*, Vol. 1, New Delhi: Oxford University Press.

Nehru, J. (1986) *Letters to Chief Ministers*, Vol. 2, New Delhi: Oxford University Press.

Nooi, P. S. (2008) 'Decentralisation or Recentralisation? Trends in Local Government in Malaysia', *Commonwealth Journal of Local Governance*, No. 1, May, 126, Internet journal (Online:http://epress.lib.nts.edu.au/ojs/index.ph.p/cjlg/article/vie-wARTICLE/1269, accessed 30 October 2009).

Nossiter, T. J. (1982) *Communism in Kerala: A Study in Political Adaptation*, New Delhi: Oxford University Press.

Nossiter, T. J. (1988) *Marxist State Governments in India*, London and New York: Pinter.

Oberst, R. C. (1998) 'Youth Militancy and the Rise of Sri Lanka: Tamil Nationalism', in Mitra, S. K. and Lewis, A. (eds) *Sub-National Movements in South Asia*, New Delhi: Segment Books, pp. 140–70.

Obinger, H., Castles, F. G. and Leibfried, S. (eds) (2005) *Federalism and the Welfare State: New World and European Experience*, Cambridge: Cambridge University Press.

O'Neill, M. and Austin, D. (eds) (2000) *Democracy and Cultural Diversity*, Oxford: Oxford University Press.

Oommen, T. K. (2004) *Nation, Civil Society and Social Movements*, New Delhi: Sage Publications.

Oxfam Inequality Report. (2019) (Online: https://www.oxfamindia.org/sites/default/files/Davos-India_Supplement.pdf, accessed 29 April 2020).

Pal, B. C. (1950) 'Composite Nationalism: A Nationalist View', *New India*, 27 May [page numbers not available].

Pant, H. (ed) (2017) *A Handbook of South Asia: Political Development*, Abingdon: Routledge.

Parekh, B. (2000) *Rethinking Multiculturalism*, New York: Macmillan.

Phadnis, U. and Ganguly, R. (2001) *Ethnicity and Nation-building in South Asia*. New Delhi: Sage.

Philips, C. H. (ed) (1963) *Politics and Society in India and Pakistan*, London: Allen & Unwin.

Pinder, J. (2007) 'Introduction to Multinational Federations', in Burgess, M. and Pinder, J. (eds) *Multinational Federations: Concept, Theory and Case Studies*, London: Routledge, pp. 1–13.

Prabhu, N. R. V. and Banumathy, K. (1995) 'The Fragility of Democracy in Pakistan: Military at the Root Cause', reprinted in Grover, V. and Arora, R. (eds) *Political System in Pakistan, Vol. 2, Constitutional Developments in Pakistan*, New Delhi: Deep & Deep, pp. 240–67.

Przeworski, A. (2010) *Democracy and the Limits of Self-government*, Cambridge: Cambridge University Press.

Putnam, R., Leonardi, R. and Nanetti, R. (1993) *Making Democracy Work: Civic Traditions in Modern Italy*, Princeton, NJ: Princeton University Press.

Qader, M. A. (1998) 'Foreword', in Ahmed, F. (ed) *Ethnicity and Politics in Pakistan*, Karachi: Oxford University Press, pp. 1–3.

Ramasubramanium, K. A. (1992) 'Historical Development and Essential Features of the Federal System', in Mukarji, N. and Arora, B. (eds) *Federalism in India: Origins and Development*, New Delhi: Vikash Publishing House Pvt. Ltd, pp. 105–23.

Bibliography 237

Randhawa, S. (2008) 'Malaysian PM Faces Pressure from Ethnic and Pro-Democracy Forces', *Federations*, February–March, 26–8.

Rao, M. G. and Singh, N. (2005) *The Political Economy of Federalism in India*, New Delhi: Oxford University Press.

Rao, M. G. and Vaillancourt, F. (1994) 'Interstate Tax Harmony in India: A Comparative Perspective', *Publius: The Journal of Federalism*, Vol. 24, Fall, 99–114.

Reddy, Y.V. and Reddy, G.R. (2019) *Indian Fiscal Federalism*, New Delhi: Oxford University Press.

Reilly, B. (2001) *Democracy in Divided Societies*, Cambridge: Cambridge University Press.

Rex, J. and Singh, G. (eds) (2004) *Governance in Multicultural Societies*, Hants: Ashgate Publishing Company.

Riker, W. (1964) *Federalism: Origin, Operation, Significance*, Boston: Little, Brown.

Riker, W. (1996) 'European Federalism: The Lessons of Past Experience', in Jeans, J., Wright, H. and Wright, V. (eds) *Federalising Europe: The Costs, Benefits, and the Preconditions of Federal Political Systems*, Oxford: Oxford University Press.

Robinson, F. (1974) *Separatism Among Indian Muslims: The Politics of the United Provinces' Muslims (1860–1923)*, Cambridge: Cambridge University Press.

Rose, Leo E. (1989) 'Pakistan: Experiments with Democracy', in Diamond, L., Linz, J. and Lipset, S. M. (eds) *Democracy in Asia*, New Delhi: Vistar Publications, pp. 105–43.

Rudolph, L. and Rudolph, S. (1987) *In Pursuit of Lakshmi: The Political Economy of the Indian State*, Chicago: University of Chicago Press.

Rudolph, L. and Rudolph, S. (2001) 'Redoing the Constitutional Design: From an Interventionist State to a Regulatory State', in Kohli, A. (ed) *The Success of India's Democracy*, Cambridge: Cambridge University Press, pp. 127–63.

Saez, L. (2002) *Federalism Without a Centre: The Impact of Political Economic Reform on India's Federal System*, New Delhi: Sage.

Saha, S. C. (ed) (2007) *Ethnicity and Socio-Political Change in Africa and Other Developing Countries: A Constructive Discourse in State Building*, Lanham: Lexington Books.

Samudavanija, Chain-Anan (1991) 'The Three-Dimensional State', in Manor, J. (ed) *Rethinking Third World Politics*, Essex: Longman, pp. 15–23.

Sarkar, S. (2001) 'Indian Democracy: The Historical Inheritance', in Kohli, A. (ed) *The Success of India's Democracy*, Cambridge: Cambridge University Press, pp. 23–47.

Sen, A. (2005) *The Argumentative Indian: Writings on Indian Culture, History and Identity*, London: Penguin.

Sen, A. (2006) *Identity and Violence: The Illusion of Destiny*, London: Allen Lane.

Sen, Kshiti Mohan (1961) *Hinduism*, Harmondsworth: Penguin Books.

Sen Gupta, D. and Ganguly, S. (eds) (2005) *India (Essays in Memory of Late Prof. Pras-anta Kr Ghosh)*, Kolkata: Arambarg Book House.

Shafruddin, B. H. (1988) 'Malaysian Centre-State Relations by Design and Process', in Sha-fruddin, B. H. and Iftikhar, A. M. Z. (eds) *Between Centre and States: Federalism in Perspective*, Kuala Lumpur: Institute for Strategic and International Studies, pp. 3–29.

Shafruddin, B. H. and Iftikhar, A. M. Z. (eds) (1988) *Between Centre and States: Federalism in Perspective*, Kuala Lumpur: Institute for Strategic and International Studies.

Shah, A. (1997) 'Federalism Reform Imperatives, Restructuring Principles and Lessons for Pakistan', *The Pakistan Development Review*, Vol. 36, No. 4, Winter, 499–536.

Shapiro, I. and Hacker-Gordon, C. (eds) (1990) *Democracy's Value*, Cambridge: Cambridge University Press.

Shepperdson, M. and Simmons, C. (eds) (1988) *The Indian National Congress and the Political Economy of India 1885–1985*, Aldershot: Avebury.

Singh, G. (1987) 'Understanding the Punjab Problem', *Asian Survey*, Vol. 27, No. 2, 1268–77.

238 Bibliography

Singh, G. (1993) 'Ethnic Conflict in India: The Case Study of Punjab', in McGarry, J. and O'Leary, B. (eds) *The Politics of Ethnic Conflict Regulation*, London: Routledge, pp. 84–105.

Singh, G. (1994) *Communism in Punjab*, New Delhi: Ajanta.

Singh, G. (1996) 'Re-Examining the Punjab Problem', in Singh, G. and Talbot, I. (eds) *Punjabi Identity*, New Delhi: Manohar, pp. 115–38.

Singh, G. and Talbot, I. (eds) (1996) *Punjabi Identity*, New Delhi: Manohar.

Singh, H. (2001) 'Ethnic Conflict in Malaysia Revisited', *Journal of Commonwealth and Comparative Politics*, Vol. 39, No. 1, March, 42–65.

Singh, M. P. and Kukreja, V. (2014) *Federalism in South Asia*, New Delhi: Routledge.

Singh, S. K. (1999) 'Self Governance for the Scheduled Areas', in Jha, S. N. and Mathur, P. C. (eds) *Decentralization and Local Politics*, New Delhi: Sage, pp. 173–89.

Sisson, R. (1970) *The Congress Party in Rajasthan*, Berkeley: University of California Press.

Sisson, R. and Wolpert, S. (eds) (1988) *Congress and Indian Nationalism: The Pre-Independence Phase*, Berkeley: University of California Press.

Smith, A. (1991) 'Myanmar', in Elazar, Daniel J. (ed) *Federal Systems of the World: A Handbook of Federal, Confederal and Autonomy Arrangements*, Essex: Longman, pp. 168–71.

Smith, A. (1997) 'Ethnic Conflict and Federalism: The Case of Buram', in Baechler, G. (ed) *Federalism Against Ethnicity? Institutional, Legal, and Democratic Instruments to Prevent Violent Minority Conflicts*, Zurich: Verlag Ruegger, pp. 231–59.

Smith, A. (2007) 'Ethnicity and Federal Prospects in Myanmar', in He, Baogang, Galligan, B. and Inoguchi, T. (eds) *Federalism in Asia*, Cheltenham: Edward Elgar, 188–201.

Smith, D. E. (1963) *India as a Secular State*, Princeton, NJ: Princeton University Press, pp. 177–234.

Smith, D. E. (1999) 'India as a Secular State', in Bhargava, R. (ed) *Secularism and Its Critics*, New Delhi: Oxford University Press.

Smith, G. W. (ed) (1995) *Federalism: The Multiethnic Challenge*, Essex: Longman.

Smith, G. W. (ed) (2002) *Liberalism*, 4 vols., London: Routledge.

Sreraj, A. P. and Vamsi, V. (2016) 'High Growth and Rising Inequality in Kerala Since the 1980s', *Oxford Development Studies*, Vol. 44, No. 4.

Sridharan, E. (2004) 'The Fragmentation of the Indian Party System, 1952–99', in Hasan, Z. (ed) *Parties and Party Politics in India*, New Delhi: Oxford University Press, pp. 475–504.

Stepan, A. (1999) 'Federalism and Democracy: Beyond the U.S. Model', *Journal of Democracy*, Vol. 10, No. 4, October, 19–34.

Stepan, A. (2001) *Arguing Comparative Politics*, Oxford: Oxford University Press.

Stepan, A. (2005) 'Federalism and Democracy: Beyond the US Model', in Karmis, D. and Norman, W. (eds) *Theories of Federalism: A Reader*, New York: Macmillan.

Talbot, I. (1998) *Pakistan: A Modern History*, London: Hurst & Co.

Talbot, I. (2002) 'The Punjabization of Pakistan: Myth or Reality?' in Jaffrelot, C. (ed) *Pakistan Nationalism Without a Nation?* New Delhi: Manohar, pp. 51–63.

Talbot, I. P. (2005) *Pakistan: A Modern History*, London: Hurst & Co.

Taylor, Robert H. (1987) *The State in Burma*. London: C. Hurst & Company.

Tennant, P. (1973) 'The Decline of Elective Local Government in Malaysia', *Asian Survey*, Vol. 13, No. 4, 1973, 347–65.

Ter-Minassian, T. (ed) (1997) *Fiscal Federalism in Theory and Practice*, Washington, DC: IMF.

Tilly, C. (ed) (1975) *The Formation of National States in Western Europe*, Princeton, NJ: Princeton University Press.

Tilly, C. (1985) 'War-Making and State-Making as Organized Crime', in Evans, P., Rueschemeyer, D. and Skocpol, T. (eds) *Bringing the State Back In*, Cambridge: Cambridge University Press, pp. 169–92.

Tremblay, R. C. (2003) 'Globalization and Indian Federalism', in Dua, B. D. and Singh, M. P. (eds) *Indian Federalism in the New Millennium*, New Delhi: Manohar, pp. 335–51.

'Troubled History of Federal-Provincial Relations'. (Online: http://alaiwah.wordpress.com/2008/09/24Pakistan-constitution-national finance commission, accessed 24 September 2008).

Truman, D. (1955) 'Federalism and the Party System', in Macmahon, A. (ed) *Federalism: Mature and Emergent*, New York: Doubleday.

Tun, Sai Aung. (2009) *History of the Shan State (From Its Origins to 1962)*. Chia Mai: Silworm Books.

UNDP Human Development Report (2011) Online: http://hdr.undp.org/sites/default/files/reports/271/hdr_2011_en_complete.pdf, accessed 29 April 2020.

Vanaik, A. (1988) 'Is There a Nationality Question?', *Economic and Political Weekly*, No. 22–44, 29 October, 22–44. (Online: https://www.pk.undp.org/content/pakistan/en/home/library/development_policy/development-advocate-pakistan—volume-2—issue-1.html, accessed on 23 May 2020).

Veritatem, Q. (n.d.) *Justice Shall Prevail: The Struggle for Samjukta Maharashtra*, Poona: Kesari Printing Press.

Vijapur, A. P. (ed) (1998) *Dimensions of Federal Nation-Building*, New Delhi: Manak Publications.

Waseem, M. (2004) 'Pluralism and Democracy in Pakistan', in Rex, J. and Singh, H. (eds) *Governance in Multicultural Societies*, Hants: Ashgate Publishing, pp. 185–98.

Watts, R. L. (1966) *New Federations: Experiments in the Commonwealth*, Oxford: Clarendon Press.

Watts, R. L. (1967) *New Federations: Experiments in the Commonwealth*, Oxford: Clarendon Press (reprint of 1966 edition).

Watts, R. L. (1996) *Comparing Federal Systems in the 1990s*, first edition, Kingston: Queen's McGill University Press.

Watts, R. L. (1998) 'Federalism, Federal Political Systems, and Federations', *Annual Review of Political Science*, Vol. 1, 117–37.

Watts, R. L. (1999) *Comparing Federal Systems*, second edition, Kingston: Queen's McGill University Press.

Watts, R. L. (2000) 'Federalism in Asia: The Potential and the Limits', in Basta-Fleiner, L., Bhattacharyya, H., Fleiner, T. and Mitra, S. K. (eds) *Rule of Law and Organization of the State in Asia: The Multicultural Challenge*, Fribourg, Switzerland: Institute of Federalism, pp. 1–4.

Watts, R. L. (2008) *Comparing Federal Systems*, third edition, Montreal: McGill Queen's University Press.

Wechsler, H. (1954) 'The Political Safeguards of Federalism: The Role of the State in the Selection and Composition of National Government', *Columbia Law Review*, Vol. 54, 543–60.

Weiner, M. (1967) *Party Building in a New Nation*, Chicago: University of Chicago Press.

Wellikala, A. (2019) 'Sri Lanka's Failed Peace Process and the Continuing Challenge of Ethno-Territorial Cleavages', in Anderson, G. and Choudhry, S. (eds) *Territory and Power in Constitutional Transitions*, Oxford: Oxford University Press, pp. 249–74.

Wheare, K. C. (1953) *Federal Government*, third edition, New York: Oxford University Press.

Wikipedia. (Online: http://en.wikipedia.org/wiki/Local_Government_in_Malaysia, accessed 20 May 2009).

Wilson, J. A. (1989) 'Sri Lanka and Its Future: Sinhala Versus Tamils', in Wilson, A. J. and Dalton, D. (eds) *The States of South Asia: The Problems of National Integration (Essays in Honour of W. H. Morris-Jones)*, London: Hurst & Co., pp. 295–312.

Wong, Chin Huat. 'Weakened Federalism in the New Federation' (Online: http://malaysianbar.org.my/echoes_of_the_past/weakened_federation_in_the_new_federation, accessed 23 October 2009).

240 Bibliography

World Human Development Report (2019) (Online: http://hdr.undp.org/sites/default/files/hdr2019.pdf, accessed 1 January 2020).

Yadu, C. R. (2017) 'Evolving Wealth Inequality in Kerala: Mapping the Winners and the Losers Since the 1990s', Research Gate (Online).

Zaidi, AL-Ali. (2019) 'Dealing with Territorial Cleavages in Constitutional Transitions in Iraq', in Anderson, G. and Choudhry, S. (eds) *Territory and Power in Constitutional Transitions*, Oxford: Oxford University Press, pp. 99–119.

Zawawi, I. (1989) 'Ethnicity in Malaysia', in Kumar, D. and Santasilan, K. K. (eds) *Ethnicity, Identity and Conflict Crisis*, Hong Kong: Arena Press.

INDEX

5th and 6th Schedule (India) 186–7, 207
8th Schedule (India) 7
17th Constl. Amendment 179
18th Constl. Amendment (Pakistan) (2010)
  23, 34–5, 95, 148, 178, 197–8, 217,
  220; failure to implement 220–1
73rd and 74th Constl. Amends (India) 186

Adeney, K. 145, 177
Africa 4, 16, 20
Agong 99
'agreed political relationship' (Pakistan) 149
Ahmed, F. 221
Ahmed, I. 37, 40, 87
Ahmed, S. I. 87
Ahmed, S. J. 87, 147, 198
Ahmedis 35
AIDMK 134
Akali Dal 134
All Parties Conference 87
alliance (Malay) 59–60, 136–7; Alliance of
  BN 199
'All Staff, no line' (Appleby) 154
American Revolution 15
Ambedkar, Dr B R 108, 183
Anderson, B. 221
Andaya, B. W. 44, 151
Andaya. L. Y. 44, 151
Anderso, G. 1, 6
Anglo-Saxon 101, 114, 153
Appleby, P. 115, 154, 166, 227
Arnold, D. 171
Arora, B. 20, 83, 167

Article 239 (4) (Pakistan Const.) 36
Article 3 (Indian Const.) 107
Article 356 (India) 167, 205–6, 210
Article 370 (J & K) (abolished) 30
Article 371 (A) (Indian Const.) 110
Article 40 (Indian Const.) 181
Asghar, M. U. 36
Asian Development Bank 177
Aung San 212
Aung San Su Kyi 50, 80–1, 84, 123, 212,
  213, 219; as *State Counselor* 81, 119
Australian Const 107, 195
Autonomous District Council 187, 210
autonomy 1, 2, 6, 8, 16, 18, 23, 38–40,
  49, 51, 54, 84, 176, 205–6, 224, 232,
  234, 238; absence of 171; action (of)
  15, 27, 57, 65; autonomy (Malay
  states)100; autonomy in Indian States
  63; core 188; ethnic 77; extent of
  201; financial 60; of the frontiers 78;
  greater 189; legislative 186; limited
  188; local 170–2; participation, and
  219; political 7, 27, 31, 37, 78, 163,
  177, 181; power and 218; provincial 65,
  66, 67, 68, 177–8, 180–1, 220; as self-
  determination 81; special 228; of the
  States 61, 67, 181; territorial/regional,
  50, 51, 76, 165
autonomy-assuring provisions 173
Awami League 128
Ayub Khan, Muhammad 93–4, 176,
  194–5, 197
Aziz, D. D. 171

242 Index

Badwai, A. 102
Bakar, I. 46, 58, 60
Baluch insurgency 47–8
Baluch nationality 39–40
Banerje, A. C. 69
Bangladesh 129, 214
Barisan Nasional 96–7, 149, 176, 213, 218
'Basic Democracies' 177, 193
Basic Principle Ctte 92–3
Basic Structure Doctrine 122
Basu, D. D. 107
Bengali, K. 34
Bengali ethnicity 170
Bengal-Punjab crisis 92
Bertrand, J. 27
Besant, Anne 74
Bhambri, C. P. 162
Bharat 109
Bhargava, R. 19
Bhasa Malaysia 48
Bhattacharyya, H. 3, 5, 6, 7, 12, 26, 37, 49,
    53, 82, 107, 110, 130, 131, 132, 134,
    142, 165, 166, 167, 182, 183, 184, 188,
    190, 207, 309, 210, 228, 229
Bhumiputera 42, 96–7, 100–1, 103–4, 139,
    151–2
Bhutta, Z. A. 94, 129, 146, 197
Bhutto, B. 129
BJP 135, 218
Breen, M. 1, 2, 3, 5, 6, 23, 49, 54, 78, 222
British North America Act (1867) 105
British Protection 57–8
Buddhism 106
Burgess, M. 2, 33
Burman nationality 79–80

CA (11) (Pak) 93–4; composition of 136–7
CA (1) (Pak) 89–91
Cabinet Mission 1, 69–71, 83, 141
CA debates (India) 67–8
Canada 143
Canadian Provinces 20
Case, W. 96, 200
Caste panchayats 183
Census of Nepal (2011) 48
Char, D. 69–71, 75, 82, 231
'Charter of Democracy' 178
Chatterjee, P. 74, 203
Cheema, I. P. 195, 207, 231
Cheema, G. S. 175
Chhiber, P. K. 132
Chief Comm. Province 90
China 2, 3, 6, 28, 171
Choudhry, S. 1, 6
citizenship 47, 57, 58, 76; acquisition
    of 195; building 233; Equal 47; full

citizenship 101; as group membership
    199; infamous Citizenship Law in
    Myanmar 79; in Malaysia 101; no State
    citizenship 122; politics of 233; (for
    Rohingya) 79, 118; Single 122; universal
    in India 113
'Civil Society' (Malaysia) 200
Cohen, S. 129, 178
colonial federalism (India) 64–5
colonial federation 57–9
colonialism (South-East Asia) 42
colonialism and decolonization 9
colonial legacy 55
Commission on Decentralization (1909) 65–8
Communal Award 67
communal-racial division 213
communist insurgency (Malaya) 58–9
comprador bourgeoisie 197
Conference of Rulers (Sultans) 98, 99
'Congress System' 133
consociational power sharing 137, 234,
    214, 222
Constituent Assembly (India) 31–2
Constitutional Tribunal 119
Council of Common Interests 179
CPI-M 131, 205
'creeping authoritarianism' 202 (Morris-Jones)
culture and territory 213

Dalits 117–18
DAP 139
Dar Commission 31–2
Das Gupta, J. 73, 205
Dawn, The (Editorial) 180
decentralization and non-centralization 188
decentralization and tribal self-rule 190
decolonization 4
demand for 118
democracy and culture 202
democratic and ethnic polity 191
democratic deficit 190
democratic effects 3
demos-constraining and demos-enabling 193
DFID 177
DGHC 187, 202
dictatorship 191
'diminished state sovereignty' 12
Directive Principles (India) 183–4
Disintegration 1, 3, 4, 14, 83, 84, 85, 108,
    144n 209, 220; Nepal 77; of Pakistan 34,
    89, 144, 170; of the USSR 16, 20
Diversity-claims & Equality-claims 7, 8, 9, 27,
    49–50, 116, 191, 214, 216, 217, 222
Divide and Rule 85
divisible pool (Pak) 148
DMK 134, 135

Index

dominant nationality 22–3
DPD 26
Dua, B. 205

East Bengal Muslim League 129
Eastern Europe 17
Elazar, D. 4, 5, 15, 17, 21, 64
emergency (India) 202, 207–8, 217
emergency (Malaysia) 199
ethnic cleavages 21
ethnic diversity in Malaysia 43
ethnic equality 6, 118, 212
ethnic heterogeneity 23
ethnic minorities 213
ethnic minority (Myanmar) 51
ethnic resentment in Nepal 77–8
ethnic self-rule 18–19
Ethnic States in Myanmar 79–80
ethnic/racial identity 51
Ethno-civic space 223–4
European Enlightenment 20
European Union 16
executive federalism 200

FATA 38, 94
fear of disunity 89
federalism: federal diversity 23; federal
    loyalty 148; federal principle (Wheare)
    20; federalism and democracy 20–1;
    'good party system' (Wheare) 125;
    normative dimension of 22; 'operative
    reality' 125; 'Second generation'2, 6;
    'Third generation' 2, 6
federalism in India 2, 64, 70, 72–3, 106,
    130, 133, 223
federal template 18
federation building 221–2
Fenton S. 222, 223, 237
Finance Commission 155–7
Fillipov, M. 125
Finance Commission 134
Finance Commission (India) 14th 215
Fiscal federalism in India 154–6
Fisher, C A. 42
Forward States 163
France 221
French Revolution 16

Galligan, B. 6
Gandhi, Indira 115, 131, 133, 141, 158,
    159, 202
Gandhi, M. K. 74, 182, 203
Gandhi, Rajiv 141
Gandhi, Sonia 133, 141
Gandhi 'Frontier' 127
Ganguly, R. 26

Gen Musarraf, P. 196
Gen. Musharraf 147, 178
Gen Yahya Khan 88
Gen. Zia-ul-Haque 179
Ghaus-Pasha, A. 34
Giddens, A. 221
globalization 9, 10, 13, 220, 230, 234, 238;
    federalism and 13–14, 15; impact of 102,
    104, 154; impact on States in India 158,
    161, 162; impact on Welfare state 223;
    propelled development in India 206, 210,
    219, 220; rapid urbanization and 220
Government of India Act 1935 66, 82
grants-in-aid 156–7
greater autonomy (India) 130
GST 2, 216
GST Council 2
Guibernau, M. 14, 15
Gujarat 224
Gupta, S. 91
Gurkhaland 186

Hargrave, R. 133, 153
HDI & IHDI 224
He, B. 5, 6, 7, 177
Held, D. 14
Hettige, S. 233
Hewit, V. 40
Hindi Speaking States (India) 32
Hinduism 106
Hindu majority 8
Hindu Rashtra 106
Hing, K. L. 46, 58, 60
Hobsbawm, E. 12
Horowitz, D. 80, 233
Huntington, S. P. 13
Hussein, A. 175
Hutchinso, J. 14, 15
Hybrid solution (Indian federalism) 215

identity-based decentralization (Pak) 171
Implementation Comm 180
INC 1, 37, 80, 41, 54, 68, 70, 72, 73–4,
    105, 130, 135, 141, 142, 203, 209, 219;
    federal turn in 74–5; Nehru Report
    74–7; Working Committee of 133–4
individual & groups rights 204
Indonesia 6, 26; special autonomy in 228
inequalities in India 223, 224
'Integrated Political parties' 219
integration: concept of 126; Elite 198;
    federal 178; of the Frontiers (Myanmar)
    78; further integration in federalism 205;
    of identities 219; Indian 246; national 1,
    122, 194; social 139, 193; in South Asia
    142; Space of 205; special problems of

244 Index

(Princely States)165; of the tribes 73–4;
  Watt's views on 9, 14, 107
inter-communal accommodation 138
Iraq 4, 240; ethnic diversity in 27;
  federalism in 27; Kurds in 27
Interim Constitution (Iraq) 27, 76
Islamic dominance (Pakistan and Malaysia) 213
Italy 221

J & K 105, 106
Jacobins 13
Jaffrelot, C. 37, 86, 127, 198
Janajati 50
Japanese colonialism 56
Jatiyobha 82
Javaid, U. 36
Jinnah, M. A. 39, 56, 68, 70–1, 73, 83,
  86, 87, 88, 119, 126, 127, 128, 129,
  130, 141, 128, 178, 193, 193, 130, 141,
  178, 193, 194, 196, 207, 214, 217, 233;
  Address to the CA 140

Karmis, D. 15, 86
Kaviraj, S. 182
Kelantan State Constitution 150
Kerala 134, 163
Key, V. O. 125
Khan, A. 37
Kincaid J. 1, 234
Kochanek, S. 133, 153
Kothari, R. 133
KPK 35, 127, 219
Kukreja, V. 5, 37, 39
Kurian, K. M. 160

Lahore Resolution 141
language and racism 103
Larkana riots (Sindh) 54
Latin America 16
Lau, B. 27
Lawoti, M. 78
Legal Framework Order 179
Letters to Chief Ministers 32
Liaqat Ali Khan 120; limits of 7
linguistic minorities (India) 7
Livingstone, W. S. 64
local government 154, 172–6
Local Government Act 174
local political pressures 171
Loh, F. 103
Lok Sabha 111
LTTE 26

Madhesi 50
Madhesi politics 77–8
Maharaja of Bikaner 68

Maharashtra 224
Mahatir, Dr. M. 201, 213
Majumdar, B. B. 73
Majumdar, B. P. 73
Malay Union 42
Malhotra, R. 234
Mallikarjun, B. 32
Maniurzzaman 128
Manor, J. 135
Mauzy, D. K. 160
Maya 56
MCA 137
McGarry, J. 193, 235
Means, G. 44, 45
Milne, R. S. 160
Mitra, S. K. 54, 110, 142, 165, 132, 210,
  228, 229, 235
Moros (The Phillippines) 27
Morris-Jones, W. H. 64, 134, 183
Mother tongues (Pakistan) 34
Muhajirs 129, 130, 197
Mukherjee, J. 7
Muslim ethnic self-rule (Philippines) 27
Muslim League 37–9, 68–9, 70–1, 90–1,
  98, 126–7, 194–5, 219; Bengal Muslim
  League 128, 141; Lahore Session 72;
  position on federalism 70–2; Sindh
  Muslim League 41; weak position of, in
  West Pakistan 195
Muslim majority (State) 29
Mustaq, M. 38

Nagpur Session (INC) 74
Nair, S. 225
Narayanan K. R. 205
National Assembly 129
National Ceasefire Agreement (Myanmar)
  80–1, 131–4
National Council for Local Government
  172
National Finance Commission 200
National Front 131, 99
National integration 2
National language of Pakistan 35
National Petroleum Act 1974 151
National Planning Commission 148
nationalist legacy (of federalism) 55
Nazim/Nazimeen 177–8
NDA 132, 135; electoral losses of 51
Nehru, J. 62, 63–4, 67, 71, 83, 121, 131,
  134, 135, 158, 182, 183, 207, 217, 229,
  238; *Letters to Chief Minister* 82; Nehru
  (Motital) Report (1928) 75, 86
Nehru-Gandhi dynasty 133
Nehru Report 74–7; *see* also INC
neo-liberal reforms 206, 219

NEP 105, 135–6
Nepali Congress 219
Nepali language 31, 47, 48–9, 50, 77, 84; as official language 116
NFC 148, 179
Ninth Sch (Pak) 150
NITI Aayog 163
NLD 8, 50–1, 81, 119, 136
NOC 136
Non-Malay Ethnic groups 154
Nooi, P. S. 172
Norman, W. 15, 86
North East of India 7, 105
NWFP 127, 145, 147

Oberst, R. C. 26, 53, 223
Obinger, H. 208, 223, 236
official language (Myanmar) 52
official language (Pakistan) 34
official languages (India)30
O' Leary, B. 193, 235
Oommen, T. K. 221
Orang Asli 98, 201, 217
over-dominance 119
Oxfam Inequality Report (2019) 223

Pakhtun nationalism 38
Pakistan 144; meaning of 71–2
Pakistan as Homeland 86–7
Pal, B. C. 236; 'composite nationalism' 82; defence of federalism 62
Panglong Conference (1) 1
Panglong (1st) Conference 1, 78, 79, 231
Panglong (21st century) Conference 2 (21st century) (2016) 84
Pant, H. 36
Parekh, B. 19
parliamentary democracy 2, 79, 199, 205, 217, 224
party position in 129
PAS 139
PBS 137
Petrocit, J. R. 132
Phadnis, U. 26
Philadelphia Convention 19–20
Philippines, The 6, 23, 171
Pinder, J. 12, 19, 21
PKR 139
Planning Commission of India 134, 157
political community 3
political identity 25
post-classical nation-state 14
Post-Revolution 56
PPP 129, 195
pre-requisites of federalism 25
provinces in Nepal 117

provincial autonomy 197
Przeworski, A. 5, 8
public discourse on federalism in Nepal 76–8
Punjab 88
Punjabi domination 214
Punjabi in Pakistan 126
Punjabisation 193
'Punjab problem' 209
Putnam, R. 86

Rajak, Tun Abdul 105
Rajamannar Ctte 167
Rajya Sabha 111
Rakhaine state 52
Ramasubrahmanyam 65
Rao, G. 160
re-centralization 188
Reddy, G. R. 133, 163, 216
Reddy, Y. V. 133, 163, 216
regionalism in Malaysia 151
regionalism in Pakistan 170
Reid Commission 149
Reilly, B. 21
representation (Montesquieu) 20
restored in (Pakistan) 224
Riker, W. 17, 125
Rohingya 52, 79
Roman Republic 15
Round Table (London) 68
Rudolph, L. 131, 161
Rudolph, S. 131, 161

Sabah 42, 98, 137
Saraiki nationality 37
Sarawalk 42, 98, 137
Sardar Patel 131
Sarkar, S. 72
Sarkaria Commission 204–5
Scheduled Tribes (ST) 33
Second World War 16
Self-Administered Zones 213
self-determination 203
Semi-Democracy 199
service delivery 172
Shafruddin, B. H. 149
Shah, A. 222
shared-rule and self-rule 22
Sharif, N. 146–7
Sikhism 106
Sindh Circular 74
Sindhi Muslim League 442
Sindhi nationality 40
Singapore 2, 144, 149
Singh, G. 237, 238
Singh, M. P. 5

246 Index

Singh, N. 160
Sinhalese 26
Smith, G. 14, 19, 80
socialist federation 13
socialist regime of 197
Soviet Union 17
Special Category States 225
Sri Lanka 1, 6, 14, 26, 171, 239, 383; bleak federal prospects in 26; failed federalism 87; federalism in 235; ethnic conflict in 231, 235; minority problems 28; Sinhala dominance 53; transfer of power to 235
Staasvolk 193, 216
state counselor 81, 119
States, A, B, C 108–9
States in India 28–9, 154, 219
state-society interface 5
States Reorganization 28–9
States' Rights 68, 201, 210
Struggle for Democracy 208
subnational culture 13
substatehood 109
Suganan, S. 225
Supreme Court (India) 204
Swaraj 182
Swiss Cantons 20, 188
Swiss Communes 169
Swiss confederation 15
Swiss federalism 202
Switzerland 143, 169

Talbot, I. 37, 89, 195
Tamil 26
Tatmadaw 80–1
Tax devolution (formula) 157
Taylor, R. 2
Telangana 32
Tilak's, B G.: defence of federalism 73
tolerance 64
top down approach (local govt.) 174
traditional approach 125
Tremblay, R. 163
Tribes in North east 213
Tripura 132
Tun, Sai, Aung 78

UAE 23
UK 221
UMNO 57–8, 102, 137, 151, 176, 199, 216
UNDP (2019) 180–1
Union 2
Unionist Party 140
Unitary state 4, 11, 27, 88, 106, 149, 161, 169, 218
United Front 131
unity: absence of in Pakistan 67; and diversity 96, 100; federal 28; of the Federation (Myanmar) 151; and integration 25; moments of in Pakistan 73; national 1950 89; national (Myanmar) 50; and nation-building 28; Nehru on 63–5; political 1–2, 5, 16, 18, 19, 23, 25; purpose of 22; racial 58; symbol of 89; unity-in-diversity 19, 20, 22
unity and diversity 19–20
UPA 135
Urdu 86, 88, 120, 213; as associate official language (Telangana) 32; as national language (Pakistan) 144–5
US 3, 19, 20, 21, 27, 40, 169, 170
US Confederation 20
Uttar Pradesh 157

Vargughee, P. N. 160
veto powers 217
Village Panchayats 183

Watts, R. L. 3, 5, 6, 7, 16, 22, 24, 56, 64, 78, 85, 88. 95, 153, 145, 151, 171, 200, 220
Wellikala, A. 26, 239
West Bengal 163, 187
West Pakistan 88, 129
Wheare, K. C. 20, 25, 64, 125, 191
World Bank 177
World Human Development Report (2019) 216

Yudi,C. R. 224

Zaid, A. 27
Zawawi, I. 222